AMERICA
AND THE
GREAT WAR

A LIBRARY OF CONGRESS ILLUSTRATED HISTORY

AMERICA AND THE GREAT WAR

INTRODUCTION BY DAVID M. KENNEDY

MARGARET E. WAGNER

ATHENA ANGELOS, PICTURE EDITOR

BLOOMSBURY PRESS

NEW YORK · LONDON · OXFORD · NEW DELHI · SYDNEY

Bloomsbury Press
An imprint of Bloomsbury Publishing Plc

1385 Broadway   50 Bedford Square
New York   London
NY 10018   WC1B 3DP
USA   UK

www.bloomsbury.com

BLOOMSBURY and the Diana logo are trademarks of Bloomsbury Publishing Plc

First published 2017

© Library of Congress, 2017

Introduction © David M. Kennedy

ISBN: HB: 978-1-62040-982-4
        ebook: 978-1-62040-983-1

LIBRARY OF CONGRESS CATALOGING-IN-PUBLICATION DATA IS AVAILABLE.

2 4 6 8 10 9 7 5 3 1

Designed and typeset by Elizabeth Van Itallie
Printed and bound in China

To find out more about our authors and books visit www.bloomsbury.com. Here you will find extracts, author interviews, details of forthcoming events, and the option to sign up for our newsletters.

Bloomsbury books may be purchased for business or promotional use. For information on bulk purchases please contact Macmillan Corporate and Premium Sales Department at specialmarkets@macmillan.com.

For my treasured siblings, John, Janet, and Bobbie
and for those Americans of the WWI era who kept struggling to build
a more just and democratic country in a time
of unprecedented military conflict and radical social change

CONTENTS

INTRODUCTION

A century ago, on the evening of April 2, 1917, a solemn and subdued President Woodrow Wilson stood before a hushed joint session of Congress and asked that the United States declare war against the German Empire. "It is a fearful thing to lead this great peaceful people into war," he said. But he believed that Germany's recent declaration of unrestricted submarine warfare grossly violated international law and intolerably insulted national honor. America must now "abandon the peace which she has treasured," he concluded. "God helping her," he declared, "she can do no other." Over the protests of fifty-six dissenting voices, four days later—for only the fourth time in the history of the Republic—Congress issued a declaration of war.

Fear has ever been war's dread comrade, but what was then called the Great War had already unleashed unimaginably monstrous havoc across Europe and beyond. Since the fighting had erupted in the summer of 1914, the great slaughter-engines of modern industrial warfare had felled millions and maimed millions more. The machine gun in particular—"concentrated essence of infantry"—had conferred spectacularly lethal advantages on defensive positions, congealing the fighting fronts into static killing grounds that consumed men like chaff in a bonfire. Millions more would fall before an exhausted Germany and its no-less-enfeebled Austro-Hungarian ally surrendered in November 1918.

Small wonder, then, that Wilson had urged the European combatants to embrace a "peace without victory" and struggled for more than two years to maintain American neutrality. But it was in vain. Forsaking the isolationist principles that had guided American statecraft for more than a century, the United States now plunged headlong into the Great War.

Few aspects of that plunge were more surprising, and few have more persistently fascinated historians, than the frenzied alacrity with which countless Americans swiftly jettisoned the venerable wisdom of their Founders as they girded for combat in the Old World that their Revolution had repudiated and from which so many of their forebears had fled.

To be sure, not all hearkened readily to the bugler's call. After two decades of massive immigration, one in every three Americans in 1917 had either been born abroad or had at least one foreign-born parent. Some four million had roots in Ireland, where rage against British rule had exploded into open rebellion in 1916; another ten million of them traced their ancestry to either Germany or Austria-Hungary. The enthusiasm of the Irish for a war alongside Britain or of the others for taking up arms against the lands of their fathers could scarcely be taken for granted. Understandably unsure of their loyalties, Wilson's government proved regrettably ruthless in compelling their compliance with the war effort.

And yet legions of Americans worked themselves into near-manias of martial exuberance. They cheered lustily when the Committee on Public Information's "Four-Minute Men" preached the war's merits from stage and street-corner. They flocked to films like *The Kaiser, the Beast of Berlin*. They booed the music of German composers like Beethoven and Wagner, renamed sauerkraut "liberty cabbage" and hamburger "liberty steak." They shamed their neighbors into buying war bonds, and clucked approvingly when antiwar protestors like Eugene Victor Debs were imprisoned under the Espionage Act of 1917. An Illinois jury in 1918 took less than an hour to acquit eleven defendants accused of brutally lynching a supposed German sympathizer. The *Washington Post* hailed the whole sorry episode as "a healthful and wholesome awakening in the interior of the country."

Amidst the hysteria, the nation proceeded methodically to mobilize for war. The freewheeling, laissez-faire economy that had chafed under the modest attempts of progressive reformers to tame it in the pre-war years now felt the much heavier hand of wartime government controls.

The War Production Board sought to orchestrate myriad sectors of the sprawling industrial apparatus necessary for the prosecution of modern warfare. The fledgling Federal Reserve System, born in 1913, spread its wings over the entire nation's credit system. Women served in countless new capacities, facilitating the passage of the Nineteenth Amendment in 1920, granting women at long last the right to vote.

The Selective Service System, called into being in the month following Wilson's War Address, eventually pressed about four million men into uniform (another 337,000, or one in 12 inductees, unlawfully evaded service). Half of them made it to France, and about half that number saw combat, mostly in the war's closing days in the battles of St. Mihiel and the Meuse-Argonne. Segregation kept all black soldiers in separate units. Two black divisions (under white officers) saw action in France, but most black troops were relegated to service tasks like stevedoring. Some 53,000 troops in the American Expeditionary Force perished on the battlefield, and a somewhat larger number died from accidents and disease, notably the worldwide influenza epidemic that scourged the globe in 1918.

His own countrymen rejected the peace treaty that Wilson valiantly championed until crippled by a stroke in 1919. But his vision of a world bound together by bonds of mutual interest and shared membership in an array of multilateral institutions helped mightily to inspire the revolution in international affairs to which the United States helped give birth at the end of the next world war, in 1945.

America and the Great War draws on the incomparably rich holdings of the Library of Congress to offer a uniquely colorful chronicle of this dramatic and convulsive chapter in American—and world—history. It's an epic tale, and here it is wondrously well told.

—David M. Kennedy
Stanford University

1912 – JULY 1914

A NEW AGE AND A NEW PRESIDENT

We must . . . satisfy the thought and conscience of a people deeply stirred
by the conviction that they have come to a critical turning point in their moral
and political development . . . Plainly, it is a new age.
—Woodrow Wilson, August 7, 1912

We've got to start to make this world over. —Thomas Edison, 1912

One hundred and thirty-six years old in the summer of 1912, the proud, bustling, and resource-rich United States of America was an increasingly bold and influential presence on the world stage, though it had not yet joined the ranks of major world powers. While it had triumphed over a declining Spain in the 1898 Spanish-American War, its military forces remained comparatively small, reflecting the country's inherent distrust of standing armies. Large professional armed forces, most Americans believed, were a principal cause of the bloody wars that had stained centuries of European history. Commerce, industry, agriculture, and representative democracy: These were the chief sources of American strength and the proper conduits for extending American influence abroad.

As the United States looked toward the fall 1912 presidential election, confidence in the country's future was strong. Yet that confidence was tempered by widespread concern over a host of societal problems—and by questions arising from one of the great turning points in the development of the American nation. In January and February 1912, New Mexico and Arizona had been admitted to the Union, completing the "lower forty-eight" states and bringing to a formal close some three hundred years of Euro-American expansion across the continent. "The frontier has gone," historian Frederick Jackson Turner had proclaimed at Chicago's 1893 Columbian Exposition, "and with its going has closed the first period in American history."[1]

The new period that was commencing as the frontier formally closed found

1

the country of nearly 100 million people continuing an unprecedented surge in industrial and financial might. Beginning after the American Civil War—and tempered periodically by rending financial panics—decades of growth had brought vast improvements to American society, tremendously increased the flow of U.S. goods to countries around the world, and attracted millions more hopeful immigrants to American shores (6.3 million between 1901 and 1910 alone).[2] Unlike earlier immigrant waves, this new influx included millions of people from eastern and southern Europe and the Middle East,[3] a significant percentage of whom could not speak or read English.[4] Many of these new arrivals settled in already crowded urban areas in the East; others headed west to work in silver and coal mines, the nation's booming oil fields, or the burgeoning automobile industry.

Strangers in a land more comfortable with the accents and cultures of northern and western Europe, they were often regarded with wariness—at times with bitter prejudice—by Americans of longer standing. Yet the United States had always been a nation of immigrants, and this most recent chapter in the history of U.S. immigration was only one of the great and rapid-fire changes to which Americans were adapting in 1912, changes that were for the most part enthusiastically embraced. Twelve years into a new century brimming with technological and artistic innovations, most Americans looked forward to a brighter tomorrow.

Optimism soared aloft with the motorized flying machines that had become a reality with the Wright brothers' historic 1903 flight and were steadily improving. In 1912, Wilbur Wright died and his brother Orville sold his interest in their

WAITING FOR THEIR STARS.

Columbia *(to the three territories)*.— Your stars shall be given just as soon as these politicians in Congress will let me.

This illustration by Udo J. Keppler in the July 23, 1902, edition of *Puck* depicts the territories of New Mexico, Arizona, and Oklahoma waiting for Columbia to award them their official state stars. By 1912, all three states were in the Union, and the lower forty-eight states were complete.

Above: Spectators watch an Aero Club of America show at Belmont Park, New York, on October 30, 1910. The new world of motorized flight entranced many Americans, but before the Great War, government investment in military aviation was extremely limited.

Right: By the 1910s, Americans had firmly embraced the automobile. Ford's Model T was the most popular and affordable, but electric cars were also gaining ground, as shown by this ad from the October 1912 edition of the original *Life* magazine.

aircraft-manufacturing company. But the Wright Company continued to develop and make planes, as did U.S. companies founded by other upward-looking entrepreneurs, including Glenn H. Curtiss and Glenn L. Martin. The U.S. armed forces had already acquired their first fragile motorized aircraft, and in 1912, a U.S. Navy captain, Washington Irving Chambers, suggested new aeronautical terms that would also take off: "airplane" instead of "aeroplane"; "landing gear" instead of "chassis."[5] Powered flight was attracting U.S. civilians, too, adventurous women and men such as Katherine Stinson and Tony Jannus, who wanted to touch the clouds and observe the new century's promising world from above.[6]

Still, airplanes were relatively rare sights in the American skies. Other young technologies were much more common. Those who could afford the latest in domestic conveniences were enjoying better telephone service, longer-lasting light-bulbs, and the enticing adventure of darting among the horse-drawn vehicles on the nation's generally appalling roads in a variety of motorized vehicles. The wealthy could travel in upscale automobiles such as General Motors' Cadillac, which sold for a hefty $1,890—at a time when the median U.S. annual income was $750.[7] Americans with less disposable income turned to humbler cars, particularly Henry Ford's classic Model T, introduced in 1908 at a cost of $825 but available in 1912 for a mere $525. Here was a true bargain, for, when properly equipped with available attachments or converted with the use of a kit, the tough and versatile "tin Lizzie" could pump or bail water, function as a tractor, saw wood, thresh wheat, and in myriad other ways be a helpmate as well as a traveling companion.[8]

Ford's innovations were in a class of their own, but all earthbound modes of transportation were being improved and becoming more affordable. Better railroads and riverboats were boosting domestic trade and travel, while larger and faster naval and merchant vessels were writing a new chapter in the continuing saga of

globalization. Recognizing the importance of sea transport to its own prosperity and security, the United States was building a canal across the Isthmus of Panama, employing not only Americans for that epic undertaking but also hosts of workers from Panama, the Caribbean islands, Europe, and Asia. Well on the way to completion by 1912,[9] the canal, once finished, would drastically shorten the time it took for ships to move between the Atlantic and Pacific Oceans, a great boon in a world that was so heavily reliant on maritime traffic not only for military purposes and transportation of goods but increasingly also for business travel and tourism.

"The world is now covered with playgrounds," British economist Francis Wrigley Hirst wrote as the Panama Canal neared completion. "The commercial traveler is ubiquitous."[10] To accommodate international travelers, fleets of modern ocean liners, their passengers strictly segregated by economic class, were plying the seas

in 1912. Practical in purpose, these great passenger ships were also symbols of the inevitable march of progress, an idea that permeated European and American thinking during the first fourteen years of the twentieth century. No ship expressed that idea more than the White Star Line's RMS *Titanic*, the world's largest and most luxuriously appointed vessel, which, despite its British registry, was owned by a shipping trust headed by American banking magnate J. P. Morgan.[11] The loss of more than fifteen hundred passengers and crew when this supposedly unsinkable vessel encountered an iceberg and rapidly sank on the night of April 14–15, only four days into its maiden voyage, was a rending shock to people on both sides of the Atlantic.

In the United States, official reaction was unusually swift, the U.S. Senate Commerce Committee launching an investigation into the cause of the sinking even before the British government began its own inquiry. Preparing its eleven-hundred-page report, the committee interviewed dozens of witnesses, including Bruce Ismay, the White Star Line's managing

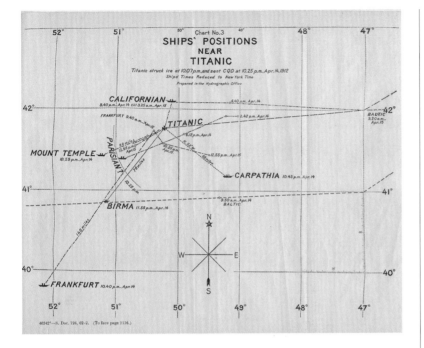

Above: The published report, *"Titanic" Disaster: Hearings before a Subcommittee of the Committee on Commerce, United States Senate,* 1912, included this chart showing the positions of *Titanic* and other vessels steaming through the same region of ocean when the era's most rending maritime tragedy occurred.

Above right: In late May, 1912, the Bain News Service published this picture of America's "Unsinkable Molly Brown" presenting an award to Arthur Henry Rostron, captain of the *Carpathia*, the Cunard Line passenger ship that rescued *Titanic* survivors.

director and a *Titanic* survivor.[12] Mrs. J. J. (Margaret Tobin) Brown—known after the Titanic voyage as "Unsinkable Molly," though Molly was not her nickname—was to become perhaps the most celebrated U.S. survivor. Though not among the six women asked to provide testimony, she was able to make at least one brief public statement, telling a reporter shortly after her rescue that "hundreds of lives were needlessly sacrificed in this great disaster, and I, for one, am eager to see justice done."[13]

On May 29, 1912, the day after the U.S. hearings ended,[14] another devastating maritime tragedy occupied the nation's front pages, this one geographically closer to home. After colliding with another ship in the fog-shrouded St. Lawrence River on its way out to sea, the Canadian Pacific passenger liner RMS *Empress of Ireland* sank in just fourteen minutes, killing 1,012 of the 1,477 people aboard.[15] Yet it was the dark fate of *Titanic*, a sparkling symbol of privilege and technological progress, that

Americans embraced as the greater disaster. *Titanic* became a touchstone in a number of ongoing national debates, including those surrounding women's rights (the number of female *Titanic* survivors, some declared, proved that "women and children first" had long been an accepted tenet and women should therefore be satisfied with their status); and the rights of the less affluent (why, some asked, were a majority of the passengers who lost their lives, including the vast majority of children, housed in steerage?).[16] Even investigations not remotely related to maritime affairs were laced with *Titanic* references. In a May 11, 1912, story headed "Lax Inspection of Meat Worse Than Loss of a Titanic," the *Washington (D.C.) Times* reported the assertion of a sanitary expert, Caroline Bartlett Crane, that flabby enforcement of U.S. meat inspection laws caused "thousands of Americans [to] go down, not under two miles of water, but under six feet of earth."[17]

Other stories soon occupied America's front pages, including strikes by baseball players and newsboys, state presidential primary elections, and the increasing role of women in political campaigns.

(In 1912, Arizona, Kansas, and Oregon joined the limited roster of states that allowed woman suffrage, while the struggle for a constitutional amendment continued.) In late April, African American papers gave extensive coverage to the April 28–30 annual meeting of the four-year-old National Association for the Advancement of Colored People (NAACP). The first session, chaired by a white social worker, Jane Addams, was devoted to "Our Common Humanity," a theme largely alien to the thinking of most white Americans in this time of bitter race prejudice.[18] Yet there were some hopeful signs. On May 2, a gathering of New Yorkers briefly looked past that prejudice when composer-conductor James Reese "Jim" Europe shattered precedent by taking the stage at New York City's Carnegie Hall with his all-black 125-piece Clef Club Orchestra, a chorus, and soloists to present a "Concert of Negro Music." Featuring the works of African American composers, the program presented by this vibrant ensemble of "every kind of instruments [sic] you ever heard of" moved the equally precedent-shattering mixed-race audience to waves of applause with a program that interlaced classical tempos with the distinctive, syncopated rhythms of ragtime.[19]

Composer-conductor-arranger James Reese Europe (1880–1919) briefly broke through racial barriers with his May 1912 Carnegie Hall concert. The June 1912 issue of the NAACP magazine *The Crisis* published his picture in its feature on "Men of the Month." That issue also reported on the April 1912 NAACP annual meeting and included the photo, below, of "Some of the Delegates."

Rooted in African American culture, ragtime was all the rage in mainstream America by 1912, and it was a musical form that almost *demanded* movement. The ragtime beats of such popular tunes as young composer Irving Berlin's "Alexander's Ragtime Band" and Lewis F. Muir and Maurice Abrahams's "Ragtime Cowboy Joe" helped birth a host of so-called "animal dances" that by 1912 had couples turkey trotting, chicken scratching, and kangaroo dipping across the land.[20] And here, too, Jim Europe played a leading role—especially after joining with the popular white dance team of Vernon and Irene Castle late in 1913. As that trendsetting trio were creating the fox trot, Europe and his new group, the Society Orchestra, became the first African American ensemble to win a contract with a major recording label,[21] the Victor Talking Machine Company.[22]

Broadcast radio had not yet become a reality, and live vaudeville and musical theater performances were rare treats to most Americans. But those who could afford the machines to play Victor's disk recordings or the wax cylinders sold by Victor's main rival, Thomas Edison, Inc., could listen to a variety of artists in their own living rooms. Meanwhile, a new entertainment medium that still lacked sound but had plenty of motion had begun to fascinate the populace. In 1912, with the Biograph, Vitagraph, and Edison studios cranking out twelve-minute one-reel "flickers" for customers of the nation's ten thousand "nickelodeons" (admission one nickel),[23] Congress recognized the new film industry as "a business of vast proportions" and amended the U.S. copyright law to include dramatic motion pictures and newsreels.[24] That year, the American premiere of French actress Sarah Bernhardt's forty-four-minute starring vehicle, *Queen Elizabeth*, proved a portent of greater artistry and sophistication in films to come.[25] By 1914, longer films were the norm and the first of the great movie palaces, the three-thousand-seat Strand Theatre, was open for business and pleasure in New York City. A rise in prices (the Strand

Above: In 1911, four years after publishing his first song, twenty-three-year-old composer-lyricist Irving Berlin had his first big hit, "Alexander's Ragtime Band." The Ted Snyder Company in New York published this colorful sheet music the year the song was released.

Right: To prevent contemporary fashions in millinery from causing anguish in nickelodeons and movie palaces, the New York firm of Scott and Van Altena published this lantern slide in June 1912 to run among the pre-feature announcements.

charged from 10 to 50 cents) did not deter Americans from flocking to their local cinemas to revel in productions ranging from high drama to low comedy.[26]

That same range of highbrow to lowbrow could be found in America's expanding book-publishing industry[27] and in the growing number of U.S. magazines and newspapers. Under the guiding hand of editor-publisher S. S. McClure, *McClure's Magazine* had gained fame for the muckraking articles it published on corporate corruption and the social problems that accompanied the U.S. industrial revolution. By 1912 the magazine's influence was waning, but the reform movements its articles had encouraged remained a hallmark of American life. *McClure's* shared crowded newsstand shelves with somber and respected periodicals such as *Harper's Weekly* and the *Nation*; such increasingly sophisticated topical magazines as *Scientific American*; popular weeklies such as *Ladies*

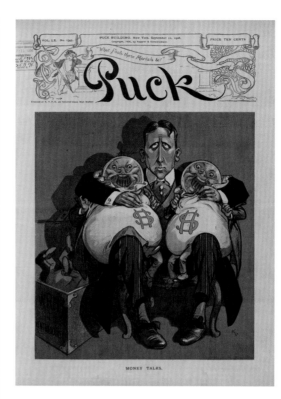

MONEY TALKS.

Home Journal and the *Saturday Evening Post*; and humor magazines, including the original *Life* magazine, which often featured illustrations by Charles Dana Gibson, creator of that paragon of American femininity, the "Gibson Girl." At opposite ends of the spectrum of newspaper publishers, William Randolph Hearst, not renowned for scruples or accuracy, was adding both newspapers and magazines to his publishing empire, while a titan of precision and objective reporting, Adolph Ochs, continued to burnish the reputation and increase the circulation of the *New York Times*.[28] Out in the hinterland, meanwhile, highbrow and lowbrow were also part of a unique phenomenon known as the Circuit Chautauqua.[29] Created to accommodate Americans' thirst for both entertainment and knowledge, traveling Chautauqua presentations brought to eagerly receptive rural communities everything from

In advertisements for its March 1912 issue, *McClure's Magazine* characterized Burton J. Hendrick's lead article on the Gould railroad dynasty as "a startling narrative of misfortune, mismanagement and almost inconceivable incompetence." The editors of *Puck* seemed to be implying corruption rather than incompetence in their September 1906 cover illustration of media magnate William Randolph Hearst.

band music and bell ringers to educational lectures and the histrionic sermons of the most popular evangelist of the day, the aptly named Billy Sunday.

Dubbed "the most American thing in America" by no less a figure than the much-admired former president Theodore Roosevelt,[30] Circuit Chautauquas often featured social commentators and political theorists of a variety of persuasions. William Jennings Bryan, a three-time Democratic presidential candidate, dealt with the privileges and obligations of American citizenship in "The Value of an Ideal," his hallmark lecture.[31] "What we need today is an ideal of life that will make people as anxious to render full service as they are to draw full pay," Bryan asserted midway through his oration, "an ideal that will make them measure life by what they bestow upon their fellows and not by what they receive."[32] His only true rival for most popular Chautauqua lecturer, the Baptist minister and founder of Temple University, Dr. Russell Conwell, expressed a profoundly different idea of Americans' obligations in "Acres of Diamonds," a speech he delivered to rapt audiences some six thousand times. "You ought to be rich; you have no right to be poor," Conwell declared. "You and I know there are some things more valuable than money; of course, we do . . . Nevertheless, the man of common sense also knows that there is not any one of those things that is not greatly enhanced by the use of money. Money is power."[33]

Both Bryan and Conwell were considered "progressives," an extremely elastic designation that covered a multitude of sometimes conflicting politicians, theorists, social welfare workers, and others dedicated to greater justice and the general betterment of American life. Most Americans, progressive or otherwise, might have agreed with Conwell's declaration about the power of money, yet many progressives joined Bryan in questioning the wisdom of placing the pursuit of wealth in such an exalted position. In this period, when the richest 10 percent of Americans owned 90 percent of the country's wealth,[34] two of the central problems on which progressives focused were the harms wrought by pervasive income inequality and the control of huge portions of the nation's commercial infrastructure by a few industrialists via business combinations known as trusts. These problems, many progressives believed, struck at the very fundamentals of American life. "We must make our choice," the progressive attorney

Politician, publisher, and in 1912, still a figure of great influence in the Democratic Party, William Jennings Bryan (1860–1925) was one of the most popular and powerful speakers on the Circuit Chautauqua. This photo was taken in 1908, the year of Bryan's third and last unsuccessful campaign for the U.S. presidency.

and future Supreme Court justice Louis Brandeis is said to have told a protégé at about this time. "We may have democracy or we may have great wealth concentrated in the hands of a few, but we can't have both."[35]

Progressives favoring the triumph of democracy recommended increasing government regulation of business and instituting an income tax to help ameliorate income disparity. To be effective, however, both measures would require honest government, and since the turn of the century progressives had won a number of battles in the war against government corruption at the local and state levels. At the same time, they worked to expand American democracy by placing more power in the hands of ordinary citizens, scoring a major victory with congressional passage of the Seventeenth Amendment to the U.S. Constitution in 1912 and its ratification by the states in 1913. As a result, the 1914 elections would be the first time in the nation's

Left: In his popular speech "Acres of Diamonds" minister and educator Russell H. Conwell (1843–1925) saluted the power of money in an era of troubling disparity between the very wealthy few and the general U.S. population. Photograph, 1922, by the Kúbey-Rembrandt Studios, Philadelphia.

Below: Premier American architect Richard Morris Hunt (1827–1895) made this watercolor rendering of the house he designed in Newport, RI, for merchant and railroad magnate John N. A. Griswold. Grand homes like these were a marked contrast to the crowded tenements that housed increasing millions of the urban poor in the 1910s.

-SOUTH EAST VIEW-history that voters in the forty-eight states, rather than state legislatures, would directly elect their U.S. senators.[36]

Other prime progressive causes included conservation of natural resources, improving education, helping the urban poor through the settlement house movement, and, perhaps the most vexing problem of all, eliminating child labor and improving conditions for the tens of millions of workers who labored long hours for subsistence pay in the nation's factories and mines, often under dangerous conditions. Tragically underscored by the Triangle Shirtwaist Factory fire of 1911, which killed 146 workers who were locked in their New York City sweatshop,[37] the plight of the nation's vulnerable workers

was the source of many turbulent strikes from 1912 through 1914 and beyond. Often aided by sympathetic progressives from many strata of society, such as the young journalists John Reed and Walter Lippmann and the socialite Mabel Dodge, as well as diehard union organizers from the conservative Samuel Gompers to the more radical William (Big Bill) Haywood of the International Workers of the World (IWW), strikers sometimes gained life-improving concessions from their employers. "We hold that as useful members of society, and as producers we have the right to lead decent and honorable lives; that we ought to have homes and not shacks; that we ought to have clean food and not adulterated food at high prices; that we ought to have clothes suited to the weather," the textile workers of Lawrence,

Immigrants from many lands were among those who crowded into the poorer sections of the nation's cities. Reform-minded sociologist and photographer Lewis W. Hine (1874–1940) titled this photo "Housing conditions, Rear of Republican St., Providence [RI], Nov. 23, 1912."

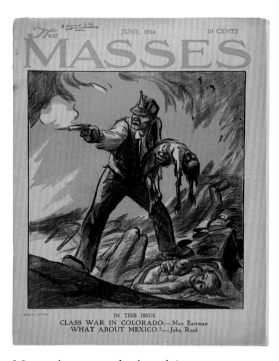

Founded in 1911 and devoted to "the interests of the working people," *The Masses* magazine vividly depicted the April 1914 violence at Ludlow, Colorado, on its June 1914 cover, which also announced the feature story by editor Max Eastman, "Class War in Colorado."

Massachusetts, declared in a statement during a 1912 strike.[38] After two turbulent months, they won some major concessions. More often, however, strikers were defeated by time, hunger, and dwindling resources. The silk workers of Paterson, New Jersey, ended their 1913 strike with little to show for five months of struggle. Even a massive pageant John Reed produced in Madison Square Garden in June to provide both moral and financial support could not bring the exhausted strikers victory.[39] Violence became a feature of many strikes, flaring from both sides of the picket line, although strikers generally suffered the most. On April 20, 1914, company police and state militia opened fire with small arms and machine guns on a tent city housing the families of mineworkers on strike from John D. Rockefeller's Colorado Fuel and Iron Company at Ludlow, setting fire to the settlement and killing nearly two dozen women, children, and men. Among the bloodiest labor-related clashes

of the period, the Ludlow massacre sparked months of investigations and both violent and peaceful protests.[40]

With labor and capital increasingly at odds, in August 1912 Congress passed legislation establishing the U.S. Commission on Industrial Relations, its nine members evenly divided between representatives of employers, employees, and the public, to "inquire into the general condition of labor in the principal industries of the United States . . . especially in those which are carried on in corporate forms." From mid-1913 until late summer of 1915, when the commission issued its report, commission members and a staff of twenty-one investigators visited work sites, interrogated workers and employers, and studied labor-management relations in other countries. This tremendous undertaking marked a new chapter in U.S. industrial relations—and in the life of one commission member, a wealthy activist who had previously regarded the problems of labor from afar. "I felt now that it was tremendously important for me to thoroughly understand the industrial war because I was a public servant," Florence (Mrs. J. Borden) Harriman later reported. "I also felt that I was on my honor as a woman, the only one on the Commission, to make as few mistakes as possible. There were too many critics of women in public life."[41]

An activist in politics as well as social causes, Harriman had by 1912 become intrigued by the achievements of a new figure on the country's political stage. That January, she co-hosted what she called "a dinner for the next President of the United States."[42] The guest of honor was New

Jersey's Democratic governor, Woodrow Wilson. Then serving his first term in any political office, the well-known scholar, orator, author, and former president of Princeton University had wooed and, after his election, defied the state's old-line political bosses. He then proceeded rapidly and skillfully to push through a progressive program, including campaign finance reform and primary-election legislation that allowed voters, rather than the state's political machine, to nominate candidates. In the process Wilson gained the enmity of New Jersey's political old guard, the approval of progressives in both major parties, and the national spotlight.[43]

In remarkably short order, he also embraced larger ambitions. In March 1911, Wilson met with three principal supporters—magazine editor Walter Hines Page, businessman Walter L. McCorkle,

and William F. McCombs, an attorney—and privately agreed to their plans for a campaign to secure the 1912 Democratic presidential nomination. That same month, through the canny offices of his wife, Ellen, Wilson entertained William Jennings Bryan at a family dinner in New Jersey. Beaten three times in his own runs for the presidency and out of the running for 1912, Bryan still wielded huge influence in the party. Both progressives, but

NATIONAL PROGRESSIVE CONVENTION
CHICAGO AUGUST 6 - 1912

so different in their approach to reform that they had never before been friendly, the old pol and the new pol managed to charm each other to such a degree that Ellen Wilson confided to a friend sometime later, "That dinner put Mr. Wilson in the White House."[44]

Things were far from that simple. As Wilson's backers mounted a skillful publicity campaign and the governor traveled around the country giving well-received speeches, several other prominent Democrats, running the gamut from political-machine-affiliated conservatives to moderate progressives, were also aiming for their party's nomination. Only one Democrat had been elected to the

presidency since the Civil War, but with each passing month, 1912 seemed filled with the promise of a Democratic victory. In the long-dominant Republican Party a bitter rift had developed between the conservative old guard and a growing number of Republican progressives, who believed, despite some evidence to the contrary, that President William Howard Taft was too beholden to special interests. In June 1911, Senator Robert La Follette of Wisconsin, the leader of a small group of especially fervent progressive Republican "insurgents," announced that he was a candidate for president. His candidacy was eclipsed the following February, however, when the effervescent Teddy Roosevelt, urged on by many moderate progressive Republicans, disregarded a pledge he had made in 1904 not to seek a third presidential term and entered the race. Most Republican progressives promptly turned toward Roosevelt as the candidate most likely to wrest the nomination from Taft.

The national political party conventions began in May 1912, when delegates of the Socialist Party, then at its peak membership and influence, met in Indianapolis. After an internecine tussle that saw the more conservative wing of the party expel the IWW and similar radical elements, for the fourth time the Socialists chose Eugene V. Debs as their presidential candidate. Though sometimes radical in rhetoric, Debs was moderate in approach, firmly convinced that American workers were law-abiding and that "direct [i.e., radical] action will never appeal to any

considerable number of them while they have the ballot and the right of industrial and political organization."[45]

On June 18, the Republican National Convention opened in Chicago. Flouting the tradition that candidates should remain remote and above the fray, Teddy Roosevelt was in the city. "Our opponents, the men of reaction ask us to stand still," he told a crowd of some six thousand supporters before the convention began. But Americans could not stand still, he said, in this fight against "the powers that prey . . . against bossism, against privilege social and industrial . . . [and] for the elemental virtues of honesty and decency"—a battle waged by Americans for all mankind. "We stand at Armageddon," he roared in conclusion, "and we battle for the Lord."[46]

The battle was all uphill. Although Roosevelt had piled up 1,157,397 votes over Taft's 761,716 in state primary elections,[47] most states still chose national delegates

by convention, and most state conventions were controlled by the Republican old guard. In Chicago, Roosevelt challenged the right of more than two hundred questionably chosen Taft delegates to be seated, and time after time Roosevelt's challenges were denied, his loyalists hurling accusations of "steamroller" tactics at Taft supporters as emotions boiled. "Coats off and flashing

OFFICIAL PROGRAM AND SOUVENIR OF THE NATIONAL DEMOCRATIC CONVENTION

CONVENTION HALL

THE SKY LINE OF BALTIMORE

BALTIMORE, MARYLAND. WEEK OF JUNE 24, 1912.

THIS COVER DESIGNED AND PRINTED BY THE AMERICAN LABEL MANUFACTURING COMPANY BALTIMORE, MARYLAND

CASSEDY & KLOSTERMAN, PUBLISHERS.

fists—delegates pummeling each other," Florence Harriman, a Democrat who was there as an observer, later reported. "Rumors flashed like lightning . . . Everybody jostled, pushed, whispered . . . Sand-paper rubbed together and a shrill toot-toot kept the steam-roller image vivid . . . A delegate rose to a point of order. 'The steam-roller is exceeding the speed limit,' he said."[48]

Revved to maximum, the steamroller flattened Roosevelt's bid, and TR's supporters streamed out of the hall and into what many hoped would be a new chapter in American political history. With the financial backing of a few wealthy supporters and emotional backing from hosts of less well-to-do progressives, Roosevelt agreed to abandon the Republicans and lead a new organization. On August 4, fifteen thousand delegates of the new Progressive Party returned to Chicago for their

own national convention. Again, Roosevelt was there—giving the new party a nickname when he declared, on arrival, that he was as "strong as a bull moose."

Overwhelmingly middle class, the assembled thousands included many women and both white and black people. Yet because Roosevelt was seeking to pry the southern states from the strong grip of the Democratic Party, he refused to seat any African American delegates from the Deep South. Moreover, the convention platform, a compendium of progressive demands from woman suffrage to legislation for safer workplaces and unemployment insurance, said nothing about African American civil rights.

"We stand for a nobler America," the convention chairman and keynote speaker, Albert Beveridge, declared. "We stand for . . . a broader liberty, a fuller justice . . . We stand for a representative Government that represents the people." The delegates stood to sing "Onward Christian Soldiers" and "The Battle Hymn of the Republic." They stood to give Roosevelt a fifty-five-minute ovation before he gave a second keynote address, titled "A Confession of Faith," in which he again evoked the battle of Armageddon. And after Jane Addams became the second woman in U.S. history to second a nomination at a political convention and delegates officially chose Roosevelt as their presidential candidate, everyone stood to sing the doxology, "Praise God from Whom All Blessings Flow." "It was not a convention at all," wrote a *New York Times* reporter. "It was an assemblage of religious enthusiasts."[49]

Remarkably, for a national political convention, "the tough type was not there," the same reporter noted. The tough type, the seasoned machine politicians, had been well in evidence at the Democratic Convention. Held in steamy Baltimore from June 25 to July 2, that gathering became

a grueling ordeal that featured public and private maneuvering, long speeches, short tempers, and a seemingly endless series of votes as delegates tried to achieve the required two-thirds majority for one of the presidential aspirants. Speaker of the House of Representatives James "Champ" Clark was the early leader; but after the New York political machine, Tammany Hall, threw its support behind Clark, William Jennings Bryan led others in turning away from the Speaker because he was backed by what Bryan called the "reactionary element of the party."[50] "There's one thing I know," Oklahoma delegate "Alfalfa Bill" Murray drawled as Clark lost votes and the tally for Woodrow Wilson began to climb, "Oklahoma ain't going to follow Tammany Hall."[51] On the forty-sixth ballot, with Bryan now firmly on his side, Wilson won.

Following tradition, the New Jersey governor was not at the convention. Formally notified of his nomination on August 7 at his summer retreat in Sea Girt, New Jersey, Wilson delivered his somber acceptance speech to an enthusiastic crowd while standing on the front porch. "The nation has awakened to a consciousness that the rank and file of her people find life very hard to sustain . . . because of circumstances of privilege and private advantage which have interlaced their subtle threads through almost every part of the framework of our present law," he said. "The nation has been unnecessarily, unreasonably, at war within itself."[52]

He made one brief mention of foreign policy in the speech, a passing reference to the Philippines. Acquired from Spain after the 1898 Spanish-American War, it had been the site of a brutal three-year war with Filipino guerrillas (1899–1902) and a continuing source of distress to Americans uncomfortable with U.S. territorial expansion. On the same day that Wilson spoke, Roosevelt accepted the Progressive Party nomination in Chicago, with startlingly short remarks that included no mention of foreign relations at all. Even in his much longer "Confession of Faith" keynote address, the former president had given foreign affairs short shrift. After stating that the United States "should behave toward other nations exactly as an honorable citizen behaves toward other private citizens," he stressed the need for preparedness—a subject that, within two years, would become the focus of heated domestic debate. "Our small army should be kept at a high pitch of perfection," he declared, and "the navy should be steadily built up."[53]

At that time, the U.S. Navy had slipped from third to fourth place in the world in terms of size.[54] Yet it was still an impressive force, especially when compared with the regular U.S. Army, which at some 75,000 men was well under the 100,000-man strength that had been authorized by Congress in 1902. Divided into small units stationed at some forty-nine posts in twenty-four states and territories, ill equipped and poorly led, the army fell far short of perfection, something that kept its chief of staff, General Leonard Wood, at a high pitch of dissatisfaction. Well aware of the much greater size and more polished capabilities of the armies of the great European powers and the Japanese army in the east,[55] Wood was also concerned by dangers close to home. The revolution that

WHY WE HAVE NO ARMY
An Interview With
GENERAL LEONARD WOOD
Chief of Staff of the United   *States Military Establishment*

THE United States has now, practically speaking, no army at all. It spends $100,000,000 a year for one — two thirds as much as France pays for her immense army.

General Leonard Wood, Chief of Staff of the United States military forces, in the following interview given to George Kibbe Turner of Mc-CLURE'S, tells why we have no army now; and how we can have one, provided Congress will receive and act upon the plans for reorganization which the experts of the War Department are working out.

There is, as usual, great political pressure being exerted in Congress to continue the present ridiculous waste of money in the War Department, and prevent its use for preparation for war.—EDITOR.

THE United States spends over $100,000,000 a year on our military establishment [said General Wood]. It is the natural popular belief that we have an army —

As a matter of practical fact, we have no such army.

Our officers and soldiers are as good as any on earth. We have an excellent coast artillery — I believe the best in the world — defending our main harbors; we have, or shall have a few months from now, small but efficient garrisons in our foreign possessions; and we have — in place of a mobile army — another series of garrisons in about fifty military posts scattered across this continent. That is all. The War Department is now seeking from Congress permission to give the people of the United States what they should have — a modern army.

The growth of the present extraordinary military situation in the United States has been a very simple one. At the close of the Civil War the American people saw no need for a standing army. They had no fear of invasion of their own soil and no intention of invading others'. They retained a

GENERAL LEONARD WOOD

a mobile army, properly trained and organized, few regiments, serving largely as Indian constabulary, and scattered these in companies and, though small, always available for use.

677

had erupted in Mexico in 1910 was still unfolding south of the haphazardly patrolled U.S. border, imperiling some forty thousand Americans living and working in Mexico, as well as those living in the U.S. Southwest. It also put at risk the massive U.S. financial interests and property holdings in Mexico. Wood was keenly aware that European military observers had been in Texas during a border crisis in 1911. At that time it had taken the U.S. Army three full months to assemble one understrength and ill-trained division and get it to the area, where the Europeans had no trouble discerning the unit's weaknesses. It was thus no secret how hard-pressed the U.S. Army might be to enforce the ninety-year-old Monroe Doctrine and prevent major foreign intrusions into America's troubled southern neighbor—a prospect that was not all that remote.[56]

Great Britain, which was converting its navy, the greatest in the world, from coal power to oil, had deep interests in oil-rich Mexico. The German government, which was building up its own navy, resented Britain's vast empire. Harboring imperial ambitions of its own, it was strengthening its ties with Mexico, where it had already made one attempt to purchase land for a base in Baja California. Japan, a country bristling with resentments over U.S. domestic policies that discriminated against Japanese immigrants, had also considered establishing a base in Baja, and its navy was no stranger to Mexican ports. Americans, meanwhile, were concerned not only by what they considered Japan's intrusions in Mexico, where the Japanese were exploiting Mexican resentment of the United States, but also by Japanese ambitions in China, where the United States had interests significant enough to be protected with military outposts. Tensions between the United States and Japan had brought the two countries close to war in 1906–1907, and the specter of armed conflict with Japan continued to haunt American thinking.[57]

Wood's efforts to revitalize the U.S. Army, inhibited by lack of both civilian and congressional support, repeatedly hit snags, then came to a near halt in the uncertain months of the 1912 presidential campaign. With the Socialists unlikely to make significant inroads among voters and Taft mounting a tepid campaign, the two prime contenders were General Wood's friend and fellow preparedness advocate Theodore Roosevelt and Woodrow Wilson, who had no military experience and who believed that soldiers "should be seldom seen and never heard."[58]

Through August and September and into October, the two rival progressives traveled the country on separate trajectories, giving speech after speech on domestic policy, the similarities in Roosevelt's "New Nationalism" and Wilson's "New Freedom" tending to obscure the divergent attitudes and approaches of these two very dissimilar men. On the question of big businesses and trusts, for example, Roosevelt leaned toward more effective regulation, contending that large business enterprises promoted

efficiency and were now a fact of life. Wilson believed that enterprises large and aggressive enough to stifle competition and free enterprise should be broken up. Regulation would not suffice—in fact, it could lead to unfortunate consequences. "Once the government regulates the monopoly," he declared at a rally in Buffalo, New York, "then monopoly will see to it that it regulates the government."[59]

On October 14, a mentally disturbed New Yorker named John Schrank, obsessed with preventing Roosevelt from winning a third term, caused a near-tragic lull in the frantic campaigning when he fired a bullet into Roosevelt's chest as the candidate was preparing to speak in Milwaukee. Stunned, Roosevelt still had presence of mind enough to shout, "Stand back, don't hurt him," to the crowd that was surging toward Schrank with cries of "Lynch him, lynch him."[60] Roosevelt also insisted on delivering his speech, though the bullet, slowed somewhat by the contents of his breast pocket, had done significant damage. Only after speaking did he go to a hospital for treatment. Taft, Debs, and Wilson all declared that they would curtail their campaigning until Roosevelt had recovered.[61]

During the period of relative quiet between October 14 and October 30, when the still-recovering Roosevelt reentered the political jousts with a major speech at Madison Square Garden, U.S. papers and magazines carried news and commentary on the outbreak of war in southeastern Europe.[62] This conflict, between the recently formed Balkan League (Montenegro, Serbia, Bulgaria, and Greece) and the once-mighty Ottoman Empire (Turkey),

Left: Greek immigrants sail from New York City to fight for their homeland in October 1912 during the first Balkan War, one distant indication of building unrest in Europe.

Opposite: After Victoriano Huerta started a new chapter in the Mexican Civil war by deposing Francisco Madero and assuming the presidency, he sat (center chair) for this formal portrait with his cabinet. Both photographs are by the Bain News Service.

threatened to reverberate throughout greater Europe, where countries of the Triple Entente (France, Russia, Britain) and the Triple Alliance (Germany, Austria-Hungary, Italy), each with interests in the area of contention, maintained an ever-more-delicate balance of power. Before the end of the year, the European powers would convince the two warring sides to sign an armistice. Yet the region remained a powder keg.[63]

To most Americans not of Turkish or southeastern European descent, however, the war was no more than a distant rumble, receding to less than that after the November 5 election. On November 6, Eugene Debs learned that his Socialist ticket had gained over 900,000 votes, more than twice the number he had received in 1908. Taft was next, with nearly 3.5 million, followed by a bitterly disappointed

Roosevelt, whose 4.1 million votes earned him a mere eighty-eight votes in the Electoral College—and the enmity of many of his former Republican supporters, who viewed him as a power-hungry spoiler.[64]

The champion of the hour, Woodrow Wilson, received nearly 6.3 million popular votes and 435 votes in the Electoral College. The voters had also given his Democratic Party a majority in both houses of Congress, providing Wilson with the legislative support he would need to realize his New Freedom. Just three months later, in February 1913, the House Committee on Banking and Currency released a report that highlighted, for progressives, the need for Wilsonian reforms. The product of a year-long investigation, the report confirmed that "a vast and growing concentration of control of money and credit in the hands of a comparatively few men" did exist in the United States, "a condition which if permitted to continue, will render impossible all attempts to restore normal competitive conditions in the industrial world."[65] Furthermore, testimony before the committee indicated such a close relationship between banks and the stock exchange that, as the *Philadelphia North American* editorialized, "the Stock Exchange is the machinery through which the Money Trust operates." In the midst of shocked reactions to the report, progressivism moved another step forward with ratification of the Sixteenth Amendment to the U.S. Constitution, which made possible the levying of an income tax. (Unlike the Seventeenth Amendment, which was ratified only a year after it passed Congress, ratification of the Sixteenth Amendment, passed in 1909, had taken four years.)[66]

February also saw a new wave of violence in Mexico, when General Victoriano Huerta deposed and then engineered the assassination of the duly elected president, Francisco Madero, whom Huerta had been serving as chief of staff. Though relative calm prevailed for a period, it was unlikely to last. Emiliano Zapata, Francisco "Pancho" Villa, Álvaro Obregón, and Venustiano Carranza were each gathering forces to defy Huerta.[67] Yet foreign affairs still seemed safely distant when, on March 3, 1913, Wilson, his wife, and their three grown daughters traveled by special train to Washington, D.C., their route lined with flag-waving supporters. No crowds lined their way from Washington's Union Station to the Shoreham Hotel, however, prompting the puzzled president-elect to ask, "Where are all the people?"[68]

Many of the people were attending a huge pro-woman-suffrage parade, the first ever held in the nation's capital. Led by attorney Inez Milholland, who was mounted on a white horse, a grand procession comprising nine bands, four mounted brigades, three heralds, more than twenty floats, and an estimated eight thousand marchers moved down Pennsylvania Avenue, intent on launching the administration of a new progressive president with a forceful "protest against the present political organization of society, from which women are excluded."[69] Orderly at first, the procession was soon assailed by crowds of men who surged into the street, tripping, grabbing, shoving, and insulting women marchers in full view of police, who were demonstrably unsympathetic to the suffragists' cause. Finally rescued by a cavalry troop, the marchers moved on to the Treasury Building, where a cast of one hundred women and children presented an allegorical tableau to demonstrate "those ideals toward which both men and women have been struggling through the ages."[70]

On March 4,[71] Wilson accompanied President Taft to the Capitol in a horse-drawn carriage along a much-calmer Pennsylvania Avenue, witnessed the swearing in of his vice president, Thomas Marshall, in the Senate Chamber, and then went out to the East Portico, where he was sworn in as the twenty-eighth president of the United States. His 1,699-word inaugural address praised the nation's accomplishments and the U.S. system of government—a model for the world. Yet, "the great government we loved has too often been made use of for private and selfish purposes," Wilson declared, "and those who used it had forgotten the people . . . There can be no

equality or opportunity, the first essential of justice in the body politic, if men and women and children be not shielded in their lives, their very vitality, from the consequences of great industrial and social processes which they cannot alter, control, or singly cope with."[72]

Over the ensuing seventeen months, Wilson wasted little time as he guided the Democratic Congress toward passage of the chief items on his domestic progressive agenda. Shocking tradition-steeped members by becoming the first president since John Adams to travel to the Capitol and speak to Congress personally, he addressed a joint session on April 8 regarding the need to lower the nation's protective tariff. Wilson's first great legislative triumph, the Underwood-Simmons Tariff, which became law in October 1913, lowered tariffs enough, progressives believed, to "introduce real competition into American markets and thus to help beat the power of the trusts."[73] On June 23, the president again addressed a joint session of Congress on the need to assist the nation's businessmen by reforming the banking and currency system—a need underscored by the House committee report that had been released in February. On December 23, Wilson signed what many have deemed the most important piece of domestic legislation of his presidency: the Federal Reserve Act. Aimed at stabilizing the economy and making it difficult for speculators to wreak havoc, the act created the Federal Reserve System that remains in place today.

Wilson opened the new year of 1914 with another presidential address to a joint session of Congress on January 20, this time regarding "the very difficult and intricate matter of trusts and monopolies." "We are all agreed that 'private monopoly is indefensible and intolerable,'" the president said, initiating what would prove to be many months of complex maneuvering to achieve effective antitrust legislation. He noted that the antitrust measures he was proposing would be "a comprehensive but not a radical or unacceptable program,"[74] but that did little to mollify those seated on the Republican side of the aisle. With one eye on the approaching midterm elections, Republicans were already blaming Wilson's policies for a deepening recession that was sending stock prices down and unemployment skyrocketing, especially in the Republican strongholds of the Northeast and Midwest. "I feel greatly alarmed about the outlook, for I fear we are on the edge of a condition which will cause great suffering in all directions," Massachusetts' Republican senator Henry Cabot Lodge wrote to Theodore Roosevelt, who was returning from a harrowing post-election trip to South America. "It is not," Lodge added, "the fault of business.[75]

Republican legislators were not the president's only critics. As a presidential candidate in this time of segregation and disfranchisement of African Americans, Wilson had assured black Americans that as president he would be fair and do what he could to advance their interests.[76] Yet almost as soon as his administration began, members of the Wilson cabinet, a majority of whom had been raised in the South (as had Wilson himself), began segregating the federal workforce, in which black and white people had worked side by side for

RAISING U.S. FLAG, VERA CRUZ

more than fifty years. Alarm spread through the black press to African Americans across the country. "Segregation untenable, morally, politically . . . Indignation [among] colored rising," African American editor and activist William Monroe Trotter cabled to Wilson's secretary, Joseph Tumulty, in August 1913. On November 12 Trotter headed a delegation that met with Wilson in the White House to convey to the president an anti-segregation petition signed by twenty thousand people in thirty-eight states. Somewhat defensive, the president at least listened to the delegation's arguments, and Trotter left the meeting with some hope for future improvement. Yet after listening to Trotter describe the meeting, an African American federal worker, Swan Kendrick, said resignedly, "Whether anything will come of it or not no one knows, except, perhaps, the president." (Kendrick proved prescient. A year later, when Trotter and others met again with the president and Trotter closely questioned the chief executive about the continuing federal segregation, Wilson's response was to declare Trotter persona non grata.)[77]

In other areas, the country did seem to be moving forward in the spirit of the Progressive Era. In 1913, the Woolworth Building, then the world's tallest, opened in New York City, and the Keokuk, Iowa, Dam and Keokuk Power Plant, the largest privately funded enterprise of its kind in the world, opened along the Mississippi River. A few months after John D. Rockefeller Sr., got the Rockefeller Foundation off

to a running start with gifts totaling $100 million, Henry Ford inaugurated a new assembly line system—and distressed other employers by raising the salaries of some of his auto workers to an unprecedented five dollars a day. (Elsewhere, labor unrest continued to undermine domestic tranquility.) In July 1913, Americans gained greater hope that they would someday have more extensive and less bone-rattling highways when the Lincoln Highway Association came into being to support the creation of good roads, including a highway spanning the continent. That same month, as plans moved forward to begin construction of the Lincoln Memorial in Washington, the nation commemorated the American Civil War with a gathering of both Union and Confederate veterans at Gettysburg, Pennsylvania, on the fiftieth anniversary of the epic battle there.[78]

Immediately after the Civil War veterans vacated their Gettysburg encampment, college students moved in, instituting a new chapter in General Leonard Wood's preparedness campaign. In May Wood had sent a circular to college and university presidents announcing "two experimental military camps of instruction for students . . . to increase the present inadequate personnel of the trained military reserve of the United States." The brainchild of Lieutenant Henry T. Bull, with planning assistance from Captain Douglas MacArthur, the summer camps at Gettysburg and Monterey, California, trained a total of 223 young men from eighty-nine schools in basic military skills.[79] The program proved so popular with students and college administrations alike that more than six hundred students registered in 1914, and that summer, as Wood completed his tenure as chief of staff and assumed command of the army's Eastern Department, the number of camps increased to four.[80]

Few American civilians outside the educational community paid attention to these camps or supported the expansion and strengthening of U.S armed forces. There were brief flutters of anxiety about a war with Japan after California passed the Webb Alien Land-Holding Bill in May 1913, forbidding Japanese immigrants from owning land in that state; but Wilson administration diplomacy and Japanese reluctance to start an armed conflict over the issue combined to bring relative calm to those troubled waters.[81] For all other contingencies, existing American arms seemed adequate for what was required—as evidenced by U.S. response to the latest trouble with Mexico.

Despite pressure from foreign governments and American investors who believed General Victoriano Huerta's regime would protect their interests in that country, President Wilson had adamantly refused to recognize the Mexican strongman who had achieved power through brute force; he stated privately that he would not "recognize a government of butchers."[82] For a while, Wilson held the United States to a neutral policy as fighting raged in Mexico, a U.S. arms embargo applying to both Huerta's government and the loosely affiliated Constitutionalist forces, nominally headed by Venustiano Carranza, that were opposing the Huerta regime. In February 1914, however, with Huerta still in power, Wilson provided some marginal support to Carranza's forces by lifting the embargo on the Constitutionalists. Yet by then two rival Constitutionalist leaders, Carranza and Pancho Villa, seemed more interested in displacing each other than in removing Huerta.[83] In April, therefore, Wilson chose to respond militarily after Mexican authorities arrested and briefly detained eight American sailors who had attempted to go ashore in Tampico for supplies. The U.S. troops that landed in Veracruz on April

21, one day after Congress authorized the action, rapidly gained control of the city, where they would remain through November. The U.S. intervention in Mexico sparked protest demonstrations throughout Latin America, contributed to Huerta's resignation in July—and helped open a new chapter in the Mexican Revolution, as Villa and Emiliano Zapata began actively opposing Carranza.[84]

Like U.S. interventions in Cuba, Haiti, and Nicaragua during the Taft administration, the Mexican incursion was generally regarded, in the United States, as necessary to maintaining proper order in the Western Hemisphere. These U.S. military operations bore no relationship whatsoever, in American minds, to the large international conflicts of the past. Along with many Europeans, most Americans believed that great wars of conquest between the armed forces of individual nations, or coalitions of nations, had become obsolete. As a British pacifist, Norman Angell, asserted in his 1910 international bestselling book, *The Great Illusion*, what today would be termed the developed countries of the world had reached such a high degree of interdependence in trade and finance that the type of wars waged in the past would, in this new twentieth century, harm the conqueror as much as the conquered. War had become an enemy of progress.[85] Arbitration of international disputes, rather than armed conflict, was the wave of the future, a belief embraced with such fervor by Wilson's secretary of state, William Jennings Bryan, that he would conclude so-called "cooling-off" treaties with thirty countries during his term of office.[86] Outside government

circles, between 1889 and 1914 Americans established some forty-five societies devoted to securing permanent world peace,[87] and one of America's wealthiest citizens, the millionaire industrialist Andrew Carnegie, both established the Carnegie Endowment for International Peace in 1910 and underwrote construction of the Peace Palace in The Hague. That grand, optimistic edifice, built to house the Permanent Court of Arbitration, a major instrument for avoiding future wars, opened in August 1913.[88]

In such a hopeful atmosphere, intermittent rumbles of trouble in faraway Europe made no great impression. A second war that flared in the Balkans in late June 1913, a costly squabble over territory won by the Balkan League during the first conflict there, concluded by mid-August without any apparent adverse consequences except to defeated Bulgaria. Yet Serbia, a country supported by that bulwark of the Triple Entente, czarist Russia, had gained territory and confidence through both Balkan wars and intended to continue expanding its influence. Serbia's growing strength and ambition in turn alarmed the government of neighboring Austria-Hungary, a member of the Triple Alliance and Germany's closest ally. Tensions were increasing between the two rival European alliances, while nationalism and military budgets were also on the rise. At the same time domestic troubles— labor unrest, demands for broader suffrage, gains by leftist parties, and, in Britain, the real possibility of a revolution over the fate of Ireland—were leading some to suggest that war against external forces would be an effective remedy for internal divisions,

Artist Udo J. Keppler depicts members of the two great European alliances as birds of prey looking over battlefields in the Balkans in this illustration from the November 13, 1912, edition of *Puck*. The second Balkan War (June–August, 1913), though short, helped set the stage for a greater European conflict.

uniting each country, each alliance, in a patriotic quest.[89] The increasing danger of war was not lost on Woodrow Wilson's close friend and adviser Colonel Edward House, an advocate of American diplomatic intervention in European affairs, who began a semi-official tour of European capitals in May 1914. "The situation is extraordinary. It is militarism run stark mad," he wrote to the president on May 29, before leaving Berlin for London. "Unless someone acting for you can bring about a different understanding, there is some day to be an awful cataclysm."[90]

One month later, a young Serbian nationalist, Gavrilo Princip, assassinated Archduke Franz Ferdinand, the heir to the throne of Austria-Hungary, and his wife, Sophie, while they were on a state visit to Sarajevo, Bosnia. Tragic and jarring,

the murders did not at first seem likely to result in a major European crisis; none had resulted from other assassinations that had occurred on the Continent since the turn of the century. Few among the estimated 130,000 U.S. citizens then traveling in Europe on business or pleasure paid more than passing attention to the news. "I imagine that Austria will not grieve much—though she may be mad—over the loss of a none too popular crown prince," American writer Mildred Aldrich, a longtime resident in France, declared in a letter to a friend. "If a man will be a crown prince in these times," she added, "he must take the consequences."[91] Visiting London on her way to the Continent, Florence Harriman noted in her diary after a dinner party the evening of June 28 that "Colonel House was the only one who seemed gravely concerned about the assassination of the Austro-Hungarian heir-presumptive, in some little Bosnian town." Calm still prevailed, at least among most civilians, when, two weeks later, the U.S. vice-consul in Budapest, F. E. Mallett, reported that within diplomatic circles in that city the general impression was "that a war between Austria-Hungary and Servia [*sic*] is unavoidable and that hostilities will begin soon after crops are harvested." But his report, sent by regular mail, would become a mere footnote to the rush of events.[92]

On July 23 the Austro-Hungarian government delivered an ultimatum to Serbia filled with such stringent conditions that the Serbs rejected it two days later—their rejection generating shockwaves across the Continent. In St. Petersburg, Russian men swarmed around the Serbian legation, offering their services should Austria-Hungary attack their Balkan ally. Still hoping for peace, Europeans began to acknowledge the possibility of war. July 24 marked the beginning of a heavy sell-off of American stocks, European investors demanding payment in gold and selling stocks in such escalating amounts that U.S. officials began to grow restive at the depletion of America's gold reserves.[93] On July 27, with French citizens demonstrating before the Austro-Hungarian embassy in Paris, Austrians surging toward the Russian embassy in Vienna, and German students marching the length of Berlin's Unter den Linden singing patriotic songs, reporters in the White House asked President Wilson if he intended to

intercede and try to ease the growing crisis. Perhaps distracted by the rapidly deteriorating health of his wife, Wilson replied almost curtly that it was not U.S. policy to "take part" in political affairs outside the Western Hemisphere.[94] As U.S. papers carried his reply the next day—the *New York Times* asserted, "A general European war is unthinkable"—Austria-Hungary declared war on Serbia.[95]

July 29: The British cabinet, shaken out of its preoccupation with internal troubles by events on the Continent, placed ground forces on "precautionary" alert, directed First Lord of the Admiralty Winston Churchill to cable naval units about the possibility of war, and discussed what Britain should do if war enveloped the Continent and Germany invaded Belgium, whose neutrality Britain was pledged to protect. "The papers have telegrams from all over Europe," Florence Harriman, then in Germany, wrote in her diary as she and her family mobilized to leave the Continent and return to the relative safety of Britain. "Everybody is doing something; preparations, precautions. We can't tell whether everybody is going to war or is trying not to." Alarm, uncertainty, rumors of mobilizations and counter-mobilizations moved many Americans visiting Europe to push through patriotic crowds and panicked civilians, through throngs of young men anticipating a call to their colors, trying to find transportation away from a Continent that seemed suddenly seized by madness.[96]

July 31: Russia and Austria-Hungary ordered full mobilization. In Germany Kaiser Wilhelm proclaimed "a state of imminent threat of war," and increased that threat by sending ultimatums almost sure of rejection to Russia and France. Across the English Channel, the British government struggled to resist the strengthening tide toward war, while soaring demands by frightened civilians to exchange paper money for gold caused the London Stock Exchange to shut down. Hours later, U.S. stock markets followed suit, and soon all the other leading stock exchanges had closed as well.[97]

In Paris, Harriman reported, "Tears were in the air." Looking through the window of her train on her way to the City of Light, she had glimpsed a future that most people would have thought impossible just days before: "interminable lines of troops marching, gray uniforms winding like a great writhing serpent over the white roads between the yellow wheat and rye. Like ants swarming out of anthills—those gray moving things might have come up out of the earth, mobilized from nowhere."[98]

CHAPTER 1

AUGUST 1914 – DECEMBER 1915

AMERICA, EXEMPLAR OF PEACE

We shall not turn America into a military camp. We will not ask our young men to spend the best years of their lives making soldiers of themselves.
—Woodrow Wilson, December 8, 1914

I am out for national preparedness, and I am going to get it.
—General Leonard Wood, U.S. Army, Letter to Theodore Roosevelt, September 17, 1915

And the war came.[1] In country after European country people disregarded their political and social differences in favor of patriotic fervor. Overcome by the excitement of a major conflict on continental, rather than faraway colonial, soil, most citizens of the combatant nations assumed the war would be short, glorious, and triumphant. ("You will be home before the leaves have fallen from the trees," Kaiser Wilhelm II of Germany told his departing soldiers.)[2] On August 1, a crowd in the streets of Berlin began singing, "Nun danket alle Gott" ["Now Thank We All Our God"] upon hearing that Germany had announced general mobilization and declared war on Russia.[3] That same day people throughout France gathered around freshly posted mobilization notices, few

Frenchmen believing President Raymond Poincaré's assertion that mobilization did not mean war. In her small community near the Marne River, Mildred Aldrich joined the Frenchwomen who had rushed out to read the proclamation. "It was [my] first experience . . . of a thing like that," Aldrich wrote a friend. "I had a cold chill down my spine as I realized that it was not so easy as I had thought to separate myself from Life."[4] Another American writer living in France, Edith Wharton, wrote of the "sense of exaltation [that] seemed to penetrate the throngs who streamed up and down the Boulevards [of Paris] till late into the night" as France prepared for war.[5]

On Sunday, August 2, while visiting France, U.S. diplomat and philanthropist Oscar Straus wrote to the American ambassador to Great Britain, Walter Hines Page:

"The Powers have gone crazy—unless some great wise leader arises the booted and spurred generals will have their inning. Fortunately, we are out of it."[6] That same day the Ottoman Empire drew closer to Germany when, in Constantinople, the two countries signed a secret military alliance.[7] In St. Petersburg, Russia, meanwhile, a mob entered and sacked the German embassy, while crowds outside the British embassy sang "God Save the King," anticipating help from Britain, though that country had not yet declared war. In London, the British cabinet broke precedent by meeting on the Sabbath, the prevailing sentiment still being to avoid involvement in a continental war. Yet Chancellor of the Exchequer David Lloyd George, heretofore opposed to armed conflict, wrote to his wife, "If the small nationality of Belgium is attacked by Germany all my traditions & even prejudices will be engaged on the side of war."[8] That same evening, in Brussels, the German ambassador presented an ultimatum to the Belgian government.

Both Great Britain and Prussia, the dominant German state,[9] had been among the guarantors of Belgian neutrality in the 1839 Treaty of London. Yet the August 2 German ultimatum warned the Belgians against resisting a gross violation of that neutrality: the movement of the bulk of the kaiser's troops into France through Belgian territory, a vital component of Germany's secret Schlieffen Plan. After those troops defeated France, which the Germans expected to occur within six weeks, the German high command would transfer thousands of troops from the Western

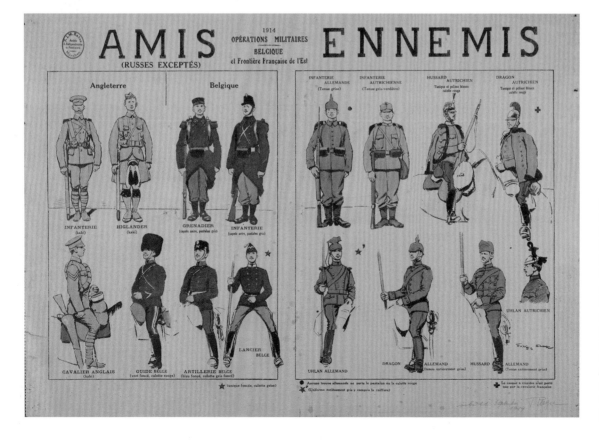

In August 1914, a crowd gathered before the Evangelical Supreme Parish and Collegiate Church in Berlin to cheer the onset of war. The following month, an unknown European publisher released a color print showing uniforms worn by Allied units ("*Amis*," or friends) and units of the Central Powers ("*Ennemis*").

BERLIN — CHEERING DECLARATION OF WAR   3189-15

Front to the East to reinforce the German and Austro-Hungarian forces that were expected to hold the more slowly mobilizing Russian army. The combined forces would then defeat Russia. Impressive on paper and when tested in war games, the plan failed to solve various logistical problems and badly miscalculated probable Belgian and British reactions to Germany's violation of its 1839 pledge to guarantee Belgium's neutrality.[10]

On August 3, as Italy quietly withdrew from the Triple Alliance with Germany and Austria-Hungary—the remaining two members of that alliance becoming the core of the wartime Central Powers—newspapers worldwide reported both Germany's declaration of war against France and Belgium's defiance of the German ultimatum. Behind the scenes, King Albert I of Belgium telegraphed Britain's King George V, appealing for Britain's "diplomatic intervention . . . to safeguard

the integrity of Belgium."[11] As Kaiser Wilhelm's troops entered Belgium and the smaller neutral state of Luxembourg, the British cabinet ordered the country's land forces to mobilize. By then, among both officials and civilians, British sentiment was beginning to turn. Late in the day, members of Parliament cheered Foreign Secretary Edward Grey when he reiterated the government's position that Britain "could not bargain away whatever interests or obligations we had in Belgian neutrality."[12] Privately, Grey expressed his anguish at the seemingly unstoppable forces of war: "The lamps are going out all over Europe," he said as he watched lamplighters igniting the gas streetlights outside. "We shall not see them lit again in our lifetime."[13]

The spreading conflict intensified the alarm of the more than 130,000 Americans then traveling in Europe, many of whom were trying to reach London to find

ENVER · PASCHA
GENERALISSIMUS DER TÜRKISCHEN ARMEE.

transport back to the United States. "We have been kept busy every minute by the Americans, of all sorts and conditions, who are pouring into Brussels from all over the Continent, in panic, demanding to know how they are to get home," the U.S. ambassador to Belgium, Brand Whitlock, wrote in his diary on August 2. "It has been a strain, listening to so many tales of hardship—their money suddenly useless, and no one knows about the ships—but I have tried . . . to reassure them all." Those Whitlock managed to help cross the English Channel joined thousands of other American travelers who had, by August 3, made it to the British capital, weary and rattled by their pell-mell retreat from the Continent. They found little in the way of immediate financial succor in the tense city, for British banks and the American

Express Company were closed. Thousands of "crazy men and weeping women" besieged the U.S. embassy, "imploring and cursing and demanding," Ambassador Walter Hines Page wrote to President Wilson. "It was bedlam turned loose."[14]

More than two thousand crowded into the Waldorf hotel on August 3 to attend a mass meeting, chaired by stranded American bankers Fred I. Kent and Theodore Hetzler and diplomat Oscar Straus, that saw the formation of the American Citizens' Committee, which liaised with U.S. embassy staff and assisted the stranded with such things as finding lost luggage and arranging temporary housing and transport home. The following day, August 4, the American Express office reopened, helping thousands of Americans by cashing some $200,000 in traveler's checks that day alone. Wealthy American mining engineer Herbert Hoover, then living in London, also offered his organizational skills to U.S. Consul General Robert Skinner. "Altogether, Mr. Hoover provided assistance to three hundred Americans who were absolutely without cash," the *New York Evening Telegram* reported the next day, "and announced that he would aid them as long as his currency lasts." Recognizing this could not be a one-person effort, within days Hoover had organized and was directing the Committee of American Residents in London for Assistance of American Travelers. His wife also joined the relief effort. "A Mrs. Hoover is doing most wonderful work in caring for the refugees," Florence Harriman, herself a

refugee, wrote approvingly in her diary in mid-August.[15]

Another stranded American, corporation lawyer Solomon Stanwood Menken had recently arrived in London after witnessing the beginnings of French mobilization.

On August 4, he temporarily suspended his own efforts to aid fellow travelers to spend time in the visitors' gallery of the House of Commons—where he glimpsed a shadowed future for the United States. Listening to British parliamentarians' increasingly belligerent speeches he suddenly realized, he later reported, "America's condition of unpreparedness and the possibility of America getting into this war."[16] His concern was reinforced when, late that night, after the German government failed to guarantee Belgian neutrality by the eleven P.M. deadline the British government had set, Britain declared war on Germany. Big Ben tolled to mark the moment, and crowds filling London's streets burst into patriotic songs as First Lord of the Admiralty Winston Churchill directed the British fleet to COMMENCE HOSTILITIES AGAINST GERMANY.[17]

Crowds filled U.S. streets that night as well, straining to read the bulletins from Europe that were posted outside newspaper offices. In New York City, an estimated

300,000 to 400,000 people milled around the *New York Times* offices in Times Square, cheers arising for both Germany and England as the two countries declared war.[18] Despite the crowd's divided loyalties, the general mood among New Yorkers that night was upbeat, unlike that of at least one official in Washington who had previously viewed the growing European crisis without much emotion. "I had a feeling that the end of things had come," U.S. Secretary of Agriculture David Franklin Houston later wrote about Britain's tumble into the abyss. "I stopped in my tracks, dazed and horror-stricken."[19]

In Europe and the United States governments, businesses, philanthropic and reform organizations, and individuals tried to adjust to a rapidly unraveling world order. On the morning of August 5, social worker and activist Jane Addams, a dedicated pacifist, looked out from her summer home near Bar Harbor, Maine, and was stunned to see a massive German passenger liner, the *Kronprinzessin Cecilie*, moored in Frenchman's Bay—not normally an anchorage for great ships. The liner was among many ships of belligerent nations that had retreated to, or elected to remain in, the relative safety of a U.S. port after the week's rapid-fire declarations of war. Unlike the ships of most other belligerent nations, the *Kronprinzessin*

One Who Does Not View With Alarm. —By Webster.

"GEE! T' HEAR EVER BODY TALK YUH'D THINK THIS HERE WAR WAS A BAD THING!"

EXTRA DAILY PAPER EXTRA
MANY TEACHERS STRANDED IN EUROPE; OPENING OF SCHOOLS MAY BE POSTPONED

Cecilie, the even grander *Vaterland*, and many more German vessels that were in or near U.S. ports as the war began would remain in America for years, their route back to Germany effectively blocked by Great Britain's powerful Royal Navy. "The huge boat in her incongruous setting," Addams later wrote of her *Kronprinzessin Cecilie* sighting, "was the first fantastic impression of that fantastic summer when we were so incredibly required to adjust our minds to a changed world."[20]

The personal world of Woodrow Wilson changed tragically on August 6, when his beloved wife, Ellen, his partner and close adviser for more than thirty years, died after a brief battle with Bright's disease.[21] In Belgium, grief and destruction descended upon the people of Liège, where German army commanders, frustrated by resistance from Belgian forces manning the city's imposing forts, sent zeppelin *L-Z* lumbering into the air to bomb the city, a modest first salvo in what would become the world's first air war.[22] With ground combat increasing and bombs beginning to drop, the Americans stranded in Europe grew even more desperate to leave. Happily for them, August 6 marked a positive turning point. That day the armored cruiser USS *Tennessee* left New York on a voyage that was to be a central feature of the multifaceted mission to bring those travelers home.

The *Tennessee* carried $3 million in gold from private American banks and $1.5 million in gold coin appropriated by the U.S. Congress, funds that were to be—and in the event, largely were—repaid to the banks and the government once the stranded Americans were safely home. Among those squeezed into the ship's crew quarters were Assistant Secretary of War Henry Breckinridge, twenty-four military and naval officers in addition to the *Tennessee*'s crew, five representatives of the Treasury Department, a diplomatic adviser from the State Department, eight War Department clerks, five U.S. bankers, the national director of the American Red Cross and his secretary, and a messenger. During the Relief Commission's nine-day voyage to England, the bankers provided a crash course in international exchange, the diplomatic adviser gave tutorials on the organization of the diplomatic and consular services, the chief clerk of the Treasury Department taught a simple system of accounting, and the voyagers established a set of mission-specific regulations.[23]

From mid-August to the first week in October, members of the commission traveled through Europe, coordinating with U.S. diplomats, their host governments, and small armies of volunteers; arranging for special trains and other modes of transportation; and doling out financial resources—assisting stranded South Americans as well as U.S. citizens. In Holland, they discovered some two thousand Americans awaiting rescue. In Berlin, they calmed their anxious countrymen who were besieging the U.S. embassy by arranging with the kaiser's government for one special train each day until all who wished to leave had departed. Switzerland, Sweden, Norway, Russia, Italy, Austria-Hungary, and France were all on the commission's agenda. Like the Hoover and Kent committees assisting stranded Americans in London, members of the commission dealt with complaints as well as unalloyed gratitude—one prominent complaint being that the rescue effort was too slow. Yet within nine weeks of England's declaration of war, as passenger liners registered to Allied and neutral countries cautiously reestablished their transatlantic schedules, the complex government-and-private-sector relief operation saw most of the American travelers safely back on U.S. soil or on their way home.[24] "Except that the ship was overcrowded and that we showed no lights at night," Florence Harriman wrote of her own return to America, "the trip was not exceptional."[25]

The war was sending exceptional tremors through the U.S. economy, however. Already in the throes of a deep recession and heavily dependent on revenue from international trade—particularly with its two greatest trading partners, Britain and Germany—the nation now reeled from the near total suspension of transatlantic commerce.[26] Diversion of European merchantmen to war-related duty or, in the case of German vessels, to the safety of neutral ports was one problem. Another was the naval blockade that the British navy was establishing to prevent

Germany from receiving any supplies that could further the military aims of the Central Powers. On August 6, the U.S. Department of State received the first list of goods that Great Britain deemed either "absolute" or "conditional" contraband because those materials would inevitably or under certain conditions be used to support the enemy's war effort. Under the prevailing rules of warfare, material listed as contraband could be intercepted and seized on its way to enemy territory—and Britannia ruled the waves between the United States and Europe. The first British contraband list was modest, but if the war lengthened and the list grew, this could only add to America's trade problems.[27]

Loss of vital imports was an immediate concern. Herman A. Metz, a Democratic congressman from New York and formerly a manufacturer and importer affiliated with the American office of Germany's Hoechst company, wrote the State Department in mid-August that if the United States stopped receiving the dyestuffs usually imported from Germany, within two months "at least half the mills in the United States manufacturing cotton and woolen goods will have to shut down . . . and all industries requiring colors will be similarly affected." He added later that it would take the United States years to establish its own dyestuff industry. In the following months, other U.S. businessmen would voice similar concerns, among them the president of Goodyear Tire, Paul W. Litchfield, who complained to Secretary of Commerce William C. Redfield about British restrictions on the sale of rubber, a commodity produced largely in the British empire and vital to the Allied war effort but also required to make Goodyear's product.[28]

As the U.S. government began engaging in an extended campaign of diplomatic

maneuvers surrounding wartime commerce, a specially formed committee of the Rubber Association of America, a private trade association, embarked on direct negotiations with the British government, a step inspired by similar negotiations being conducted by trade associations of other neutral countries. The result was an agreement that allowed U.S. businesses requiring rubber to import the material if they subscribed to a system of tight controls geared to assure that no rubber imported by American firms, or products made with that rubber, found their way to the supply depots of the Central Powers. The success of this agreement inspired other American trade associations to negotiate similar arrangements during the years of U.S. neutrality, including ones governing the export of U.S. copper and wheat and the import of British wools and jute. (Jute was used to make the millions of burlap sandbags that shored up battlefield trenches, as well as the sacks in which American businesses transported coffee, sugar, and other domestic staples.)[29]

The first private-sector trade agreement with the Allies was not concluded until January 1915. In the late summer and fall of 1914, meanwhile, American goods were piling up on U.S. docks awaiting export, including grain and a bumper crop of cotton, which southern growers badly needed to export to European markets to maintain their solvency. Yet the United States had precious few vessels that could convey the goods to market. Since the Civil War, the U.S. merchant fleet had dwindled to almost nothing as Americans increasingly relied on European-owned vessels to carry their goods abroad. "For the fiscal year 1913, foreign ships carried 91 percent of the water-borne foreign commerce of the United States outbound, and 88.6 percent of that inbound," financial editor Samuel H. Barker reported unhappily in the August 7, 1914, *Philadelphia North American*. "The figures would look even worse were it not that American vessels on the Great Lakes handle the lion's share of the traffic between American and Canadian ports." With most European merchantmen currently diverted, THE FIRST PROBLEM, the editors of the *New York American* thundered in capital letters on August 5, IS TO GET THE SHIPS.[30]

The United States needed more merchant vessels not only to address the current economic crisis, but also to take advantage of wartime opportunities. "Two thousand millions in trade is the prize which world conditions have set before the American people," the *New York American* exulted. "The whole rapidly developing trade of South America—to say nothing of other parts of the globe—heretofore almost solely in European and especially in German hands, is invitingly open to the United States through the annihilation of Europe's foreign trade!"[31]

A special committee of the National Foreign Trade Council called on the Wilson administration to provide "an adequate merchant marine." J. P. Morgan, Jr., transportation magnate James J. Hill, and other influential members of the New York Chamber of Commerce urged government action, looking to Secretary of the Treasury William Gibbs McAdoo, who had done much to steady the nation's economy after the world's stock markets closed, to take the lead. Married in May to Woodrow Wilson's daughter Eleanor, McAdoo was becoming, according to banking magnate Frank A. Vanderlip, "the strong man of the administration" during this period when the president was coping with the loss of his wife as well as both foreign and domestic crises.[32]

On August 14, McAdoo convened what he later called "the first publicly conducted conference of businessmen that government had ever held in Washington." Bringing together administration officials, congressmen, and more than sixty representatives of American banking, shipping, foreign trade, and maritime insurance interests, the Conference on Foreign Exchange and Shipping urged government passage of a means to provide special wartime insurance for American ships that were available for international trade.

A potent force in the Wilson administration, Secretary of the Treasury William Gibbs McAdoo (1863–1941) married President Wilson's daughter, Eleanor, in May 1914. Photograph by Harris & Ewing, 1914.

The British government had debarred the world's leading maritime insurer, Lloyds of London, from paying for cargoes seized by the British navy, and few other private insurers were eager to take the risk.[33] Thus on September 2, Congress passed legislation establishing a Bureau of War Risk Insurance within the Treasury Department, granting the secretary of the treasury authority to issue, through the new bureau, insurance on U.S. vessels and their cargoes and appropriating the necessary funds to do so. This supposedly temporary measure would be expanded and modified many times throughout what Americans in 1914 were calling "the European war."[34]

The Washington conference also supported passage of a liberalized ship registry bill that would expand the conditions under which foreign-built ships would be allowed to sail under the U.S. flag. Already before Congress, this measure became law on August 18, and by the end of the year about one hundred vessels that had been flying foreign flags were sailing under the Stars and Stripes. Many, however, were vessels that had long been owned by such internationally operating American companies as Standard Oil of New Jersey, United Fruit, and U.S. Steel. To augment this core of available ships, Philip A. S. Franklin, vice president of J. P Morgan's International Mercantile Marine Co., suggested to McAdoo that the United States buy fifteen of the fifty-four German-owned and -operated vessels that the war had stranded in U.S. ports. This suggestion became the seed of a plan McAdoo suggested to the president on August 16: the formation of a government corporation, run by

a shipping board comprising cabinet officials, which would both purchase ships and regulate the trade conducted with them. This emergency measure would, McAdoo believed, facilitate the fast and efficient development of an American merchant marine, freeing the country from dependence on foreign vessels and allowing the United States to exploit, among other opportunities, those presented by the Panama Canal, which opened to commercial traffic on August 15, with subdued fanfare because of the war.[35]

President Wilson put his own considerable political muscle behind the plan. Yet the proposed shipping bill immediately encountered stormy waters. Domestic foes called it socialistic and likely to impede the progress of private business. Allied nations criticized the measure as a way around international conventions that prohibited the transfer of belligerent vessels to neutral

flags to avoid capture. France, particularly, assailed the plan to pay Germany for its ships as violating the spirit of America's much-proclaimed neutrality. "The President of the United States . . . cannot possibly . . . allow his country thus to take sides against us in this solemn hour when the fate of France and also the fate of the ideas that France personifies are at stake," the French ambassador to the United States, Jules Jusserand, wrote to Secretary of State Bryan on September 3. Such statements fed domestic fears of one possible consequence of passing the bill. "A fleet of government owned merchant ships on the high seas," the *Chicago Evening Post* opined, "means a daily and deadly tinder box for war."[36]

As the shipping bill went into legislative stasis, U.S. trade revenues continued to plummet. On September 4, Wilson reported to Congress the loss of more than $10 million in customs revenue in August alone, a fiscal emergency in this era when the national budget was relatively small and the federal income tax was still in its infancy. "We ought not to borrow," the president told Congress. "We ought to resort to taxation, however we may regret the necessity of putting additional temporary burdens on our people." Within seven weeks, Congress passed an emergency revenue act, initially to last only through 1915 but later extended, that increased or imposed taxes on such things as beer and wine, toilet articles and chewing gum, telegraph and telephone messages, and various forms of public entertainment.[37]

Everyone, it seemed, was scrambling for funds. In mid-August the French government approached J. P. Morgan and

Before succeeding his father as head of J. P. Morgan and Company in 1913, J. P. Morgan Jr. (1867–1943) worked eight years in the firm's London branch and developed an affection for Britain. His sister, Anne, would play an important role in French relief. An employee of the Harris & Ewing photography studio captured Morgan departing the White House after one of his wartime visits.

Company with a request for a $100 million loan, monies that undoubtedly would be used to support the Allied war effort. Morgan contacted the Wilson administration, which determined that such loans were allowable under both international and U.S. law. Yet simple legality was not the greatest consideration. The United States had to maintain peace within its own borders, which embraced citizens and aspiring citizens from all the warring nations—including some 9 million German Americans and more than 4.5 million Irish Americans, some of whom favored the Central Powers because of Britain's troubled history in Ireland. Moreover, both President Wilson and Secretary of State Bryan believed that America, the most powerful of the neutral countries, could someday find a way to guide the warring nations back to peace. Thus the country should do nothing that would seem to favor one side in the conflict over the other. It was with Wilson's full backing that Bryan declared on August 15, 1914, "In the judgment of this Government loans by American bankers to any foreign nation which is at war are inconsistent with the true spirit of neutrality." Morgan denied the French request—though the French did not give up. In September they opened negotiations with another New York bank.[38]

French persistence coupled with practical domestic considerations led the Wilson administration to retreat, quietly, from its no-loans policy, insofar as loans floated by private American banks were concerned. It quickly became evident that without loans, belligerent nations would not be able to purchase U.S. manufactures.

Without orders from belligerent nations, State Department counselor Robert Lansing predicted, the United States would suffer "industrial depression . . . financial demoralization, and general unrest and suffering among the laboring classes." Starting in late October 1914, with the government's tacit approval, private American banks began providing banking credits to belligerents—principally Britain and France, though some went to Germany. Most of that money, amounting eventually to hundreds of millions of dollars, did flow back into the U.S. economy through the purchase of American goods. In January 1915, as war orders came in and the nation began pulling out of recession, the house of Morgan signed the British Commercial Agency Agreement and became Britain's official purchasing agent in the United States, a role it later assumed for France as well.[39]

Courtesy of the British navy, which kept most of Germany's powerful surface fleet bottled up in its home ports and intercepted merchant vessels suspected of carrying contraband goods intended for enemy nations, the Central Powers remained largely cut off from the copious outflow of American agriculture and industry. In the meantime, the war was unfolding in a manner few had anticipated. German and Austro-Hungarian forces were having mixed success in the east against the large but poorly led and equipped Russian army—which faced a new threat when the Ottoman Empire entered the war on the side of the Central Powers at the end of October. In the west, however, Germany's planned quick conquest of France had been thwarted. The kaiser's army lost its forward momentum just short of Paris, where it was halted by a combination of logistical problems and stiff Allied resistance at the First Battle of the Marne (September 5–12, 1914). By October, far from returning home victorious as Kaiser Wilhelm had promised in August, German forces were entrenching opposite Allied armies along a 450-mile front stretching from the English Channel to Switzerland. The Schlieffen Plan had gone bust, the projected short war was lengthening—and during their march into Western-Front stalemate, the Germans had ignited a firestorm of indignation over their treatment of civilians in Belgium and northern France.

Complaints from Berlin in mid-August about the unconscionable behavior of Belgian civilians were actually the first indications the U.S. State Department received that accepted rules of war were being bent to the breaking point. The Germans charged that Belgian and French civilians, incited by their governments, were taking up arms and waging a war of terror on German troops. It was only in response to the behavior of the Belgians, the Germans asserted, that German soldiers were forced to execute civilians and wreak destruction, including burning much of the ancient city of Louvain and the irreplaceable contents of its university library. Not so, Allied authorities cried; civilians were *not* engaging in guerrilla warfare. The Germans were destroying cultural

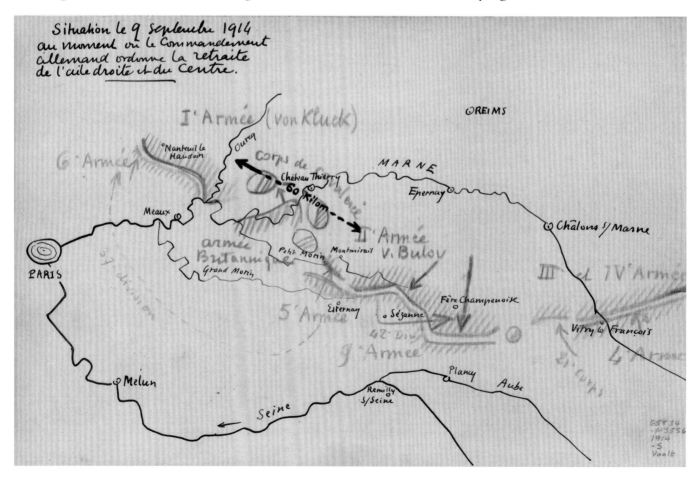

treasures, murdering and terrorizing civilians without provocation.

Experienced American news correspondents in Europe seemed as divided on this issue as the contending belligerents. A Massachusetts-born journalist, Mary Boyle O'Reilly, bluffed her way into Louvain in late August and reported seeing bodies of civilian men, women, and children "all . . . shot or bayoneted," one body chained to a pillar and burned, as squads of German soldiers passed through the city's streets, setting buildings ablaze. "Thus proceeded . . . this great war crime," she reported."[40] Before famed U.S. war correspondent Richard Harding Davis went to Louvain, German general Walther von Lüttwitz told both him and Ambassador Brand Whitlock that the city was to be destroyed because civilian snipers had murdered German soldiers. Arriving in Louvain by train the evening of August 27 with fellow U.S. correspondents Will Irwin and Gerald Morgan, Davis found the city in flames. "The sparks rose in steady, leisurely pillars, falling back into the furnace from which they sprang," Davis reported. "In their work the soldiers were moving from the heart of the city to the outskirts, street by street, from house to house . . . In the two hours during which the train circled the burning city war was before us in its most hateful aspect . . . it was war against the defenseless." Davis did not agree with General von Lüttwitz's excuse for this action. "No one defends the sniper," he declared. "But because . . . Mexicans, when their city was invaded [by U.S. troops in April 1914], fired upon our sailors, we did not destroy Vera Cruz."[41]

Le Coup de Massue de l'un.

Other U.S. correspondents in Europe denied the stories of German atrocities. Irvin S. Cobb of the *Saturday Evening Post*, James O'Donnell Bennett and cartoonist John McCutcheon of the *Chicago Daily Tribune*, Harry Hansen of the *Chicago Daily News*, and Roger Lewis of the Associated Press, all of whom had been traveling with the German army, even signed a declaration defending the Germans. Transmitted from Berlin to the German-owned wireless station at Sayville, Long Island, the dispatch appeared in U.S. papers on September 7: "In spirit we unite in rendering the German atrocities groundless, as far as we are able to," these reporters declared. "After spending two weeks with and accompanying the troops upward of 100 miles we are unable to report a single instance unprovoked. We are also unable to confirm rumors of mistreatment of prisoners or of non-combatants with the German columns."[42]

Allied armies halted the German push toward Paris at the First Battle of the Marne (September 5–12, 1914). The manuscript map at left shows the situation on September 9, when the German command ordered a retreat. Artist Felix Lacaille (1856–1923) deemed this Allied victory a *"coup de massue"* or crushing blow, in the hand-colored lithograph, ca. 1914–1918, at right. In fact, it was the beginning of nearly four years of brutal trench warfare.

FIRST BATTLE OF THE MARNE

Location: Along the Marne River, between Paris and Verdun, France

Date: September 5–12, 1914

Objectives: As part of the Schlieffen Plan, invading German armies pushed toward Paris to capture the capital and knock France out of the war.[1] The battle began when Allied forces attacked in an effort to drive the Germans back.

Synopsis: French field armies and the British Expeditionary Force held off the German offensive as the Allies, in the first use of aerial reconnaissance and intercepted radio transmissions in a major battle,[2] located and exploited a gap in enemy lines (although they failed to take full advantage of it). More than 2 million soldiers took part in the battle,[3] with some five thousand French troops famously arriving by taxi.[4] During the German retreat, a news reporter observed, "It is no single battlefield—rather a continuous line of battles . . . Peasants today were shoveling into long trenches the terrible harvest of death. All around was the litter of battle—smashed rifles, smashed helmets and broken life. I could follow the fighting foot by foot."[5]

Casualties: French: 250,000. German: 250,000. British: 12,800.[6]

Outcome: The battle marked the closest (30 miles) the Germans came to reaching Paris and ending the war quickly.[7] The Allies successfully turned them back. But the combatants dug in when the battle ended, establishing extensive fortified lines from the French coast to the Swiss border,[8] the start of four years of deadlocked trench warfare that would characterize the Western Front. After the failure of the Marne initiative, the Germans, situated between the western Allies and the Russians in the east, were burdened with a two-front war in Europe, as well as military responsibilities in the Middle and Near East.

Commentary: "It would be fair to say that Pickett's charge at Gettysburg decided the Civil War. The advance of the Old Guard crushed Napoleon and altered the map of Europe. But fiercer and bigger battles than Waterloo and Gettysburg have been fought during the last month without any result whatever."[9] —Harry Carr, *Los Angeles Times* war correspondent, September 13, 1914.

"The great battle in France is going down as the battle of the Marne, and fortunately for all of us, as well as for the students of future generations, Marne is easy to pronounce."[10] —Editorial, *Boston Daily Globe*, September 15, 1914.

As that dispatch appeared, both the Central Powers and the Allied nations were becoming deeply engaged in a propaganda war in which the United States government and the American people were principal targets. In August, the German Foreign Office established the German Information Service in New York. Headed by Bernhard Dernburg, it became the motivating force behind a veritable whirlwind of pro-German articles, bulletins, speeches, pamphlets, and posters. The following month, the British established an organization to "inform and influence public opinion abroad and to confute German misstatements and sophistries." Headquartered at London's Wellington House, the organization included a "most important special branch" devoted to influencing the United States.[43] That same month a

Belgian delegation arrived in America to deliver the results of Belgium's own investigation into German behavior within its borders. "This army not only seized a great portion of our territory," Belgian Minister of Justice Henri Carton de Wiart told President Wilson at the White House on September 16, "it committed incredible acts of violence . . . contrary to the law of Nations." The delegation had come to the United States, Carton de Wiart said, because "the American people has always displayed its respect for Justice, its search for progress and an instinctive attachment for the laws of humanity."[44]

Faced with complaints from each warring alliance that the other was violating the rules of war, Wilson was also leader of a nation that, while overwhelmingly sympathetic to the Belgians, was divided

on the questions of whether atrocities had occurred and, if they had, who was to blame. Even former president Theodore Roosevelt, usually a man of firm opinions, said in an article published in a September 1914 edition of the *Outlook*, "It is possible sincerely to take and defend either of the opposite views . . . The rights and wrongs of these cases where nations violate the rules of abstract morality in order to meet their own vital needs can be precisely determined only when all the facts are known and when men's blood is cool." In that he echoed the judgment of President Wilson, who told both the Belgian delegation and the Germans, "It would be premature . . . to express a final judgment" on the questions of civilian guerrilla warfare and German atrocities before the charges could be properly investigated.[45]

Some facts about Belgium's unhappy plight *were* becoming clear: battle damage, lack of manpower to bring in undamaged crops, requisitioning of foodstuffs by the military, and the British blockade were conspiring to create dangerous shortages in this small nation that yearly imported fully three fourths of its staple food. Two American businessmen living in Brussels, William Hulse and Daniel Heineman, along with Ambassador Brand Whitlock and his fellow neutral, the Spanish ambassador, the Marquis of Villalobar, began working with a Belgian committee to provide short-term assistance to those most in need and to establish a longer-term strategy before winter set in and Belgians began to starve. In some areas the situation was already dire.

"A man came from Dinant and laid on my desk a loaf of moldy black bread," Whitlock reported, "all that the people of the stricken town had to eat." It soon became evident that the only solution was to get help from abroad. At the end of September, the committee sent Millard Shaler, another U.S. businessman living in Brussels, to London to seek assistance.[46]

Shaler's odyssey initiated a wholly unprecedented relief effort, one that both warring sides agreed—after a tense month of meetings, negotiations, and frantic telegraphic pleas between capital cities—could go forward under the patronage of individuals representing the neutral United States. Even though the U.S. government did not officially sanction the effort, lest that be viewed as a violation of America's neutrality, both belligerent alliances agreed that they would not confiscate food and clothing sent to Belgian civilians under this nascent program whose honorary chairmen were the U.S. ambassadors to Britain, Holland, and Belgium, joined by neutral Spain's ambassadors to Belgium and Britain. Although many individuals were involved in the effort's conception,

In its September 23, 1914, edition, *The Outlook* magazine published this photo of the Belgian delegation as it arrived in the United States to report on German atrocities. Minister of Justice Henry Carton de Wiart is second from right.

Right: Mrs. Herbert (Lou Henry) Hoover (1874–1944), who helped create the American Women's War Relief Fund in London and was active in Belgian relief and other wartime causes. Photograph by Harris & Ewing, 1928.

one American soon emerged as the central figure in what would become the Commission for Relief in Belgium (CRB). Herbert Hoover, so recently commended for his short-term emergency aid to thousands of stranded American tourists in London, once again turned away from his own business interests to organize a lifeline for some 8 million Belgians living under German occupation—a lifeline that would have to last much longer than anyone anticipated and would shortly expand to include the people of northern France.[47]

One of Hoover's first initiatives was to promote as much press coverage for Belgium's plight as possible. CRB press releases sent almost daily from London were joined by those prepared by Hoover's friend, the veteran newsman Will Irwin, who volunteered to be the CRB's "publicity manager in America." Personal appeals augmented the press campaign, including statements from the king and queen of Belgium and pleas by Mrs. Hoover to prominent businessmen in California, to which she and Hoover's sons had returned in October. Members of the Belgian delegation that had arrived earlier to present Belgium's case against Germany toured the United States after their meeting with President Wilson, and the wife of one commission member made a particular impression. Speaking in several American cities, Madame Lalia Vandervelde pledged not to return to Belgium before she had acquired at least a million dollars for the relief of her country. All this activity inspired many Americans to organize their own ad hoc relief efforts, some of which would later be subsumed under the CRB umbrella.[48]

A Belgian Relief Fund established in New York City soon had branches across the country, raising money for food and clothing. American flour millers from several states, organized by William C. Edgar, editor of *Northwestern Miller* magazine, contributed 14 million pounds of specially milled and packaged flour. Railroad companies carried these special flour shipments to Philadelphia ports free of charge, and Edgar managed to secure the ship *South Point* at a charitable charge to carry the flour—along with condensed milk, blankets, children's underwear, and woolen jackets—to Rotterdam for distribution by the CRB. John Wanamaker, a Philadelphia merchant and civic leader, hired the merchant ship *Thelma* and asked Philadelphians to help him fill it with food and supplies. "It was on Saturday morning . . . that the first announcement was made," the *Philadelphia North American*

MR. HERBERT CLARK HOOVER
Chairman Commission for Relief in Belgium

reported on November 17. "Inside of forty-eight hours the cargo had been provided for, in cash or consignments of food . . . and on Thursday the *Thelma* sailed, loaded to the hatches." Between the first of November and the end of the year, the ships *Massapequa*, *Agamemnon*, and *Neches* departed New York, chartered by the Rockefeller Foundation and filled with goods provided by the CRB's U.S. committee. The foundation also procured more than 303,000 bushels of wheat and sent them to Europe aboard two ships chartered by the CRB. The number of these initiatives inevitably led to confusion and misunderstandings. Yet by the end of the year, Hoover's CRB office in London, staffed by some forty volunteers, was effectively coordinating a massive relief effort, with U.S. contributions augmented by those from Spain, the British Empire, and the Belgian government-in-exile.[49]

The Belgian relief effort aimed solely at civilians. American volunteers in Europe, supported by individuals and organizations in the United States, were also assisting wounded and ill soldiers of the belligerent nations and their dependents. As soon as Britain declared war, U.S. citizens living in that country began organizing the American Women's War Relief Fund. Before the end of the year, this group had established the state-of-the-art 230-bed American Women's War Relief Hospital in a donated mansion in South Devon; set up work programs for women deprived of jobs or their principal breadwinner by the war; and raised enough money to buy seven motorized ambulances. As the women were forming their organization, a well-connected Harvard graduate, Richard Norton, having heard too many tales of the suffering of wounded soldiers, began pounding the pavement in London, visiting friends and government officials until

William C. Edgar's 1915 report on *The Miller's Belgian Relief Movement* (cover below) included the portrait at left of Herbert Hoover (1874–1964), then heading the Commission for Relief in Belgium.

The photograph at right of a former music hall transformed into the great central clothing supply station in Brussels was reproduced in a 1918 book by Edward Wilson Morse, *Vanguard of American Volunteers in the Fighting Lines and in Humanitarian Service*.

he had everything required to establish the American Volunteer Motor-Ambulance Corps, sponsored by the British Red Cross. Norton's organization, comprising U.S. volunteers and fifteen cars, sailed to France at the end of October and was soon transporting wounded. As the war intensified, Norton's organization grew.[50]

In France, Americans were mobilizing in similar fashion. On August 9, prominent U.S. citizens living in Paris established the American Hospital in the suburb of Neuilly. After transforming ten chassis donated by the Ford Motor Company's French assembly plant into extremely crude ambulances, the hospital also ran its own ambulance service, the seed of what would eventually become the American Field Service. In October, H. Herman Harjes, senior partner in the J. P. Morgan bank in Paris, established another field hospital with its own small fleet of Packard ambulances. Throughout 1915, the fleet expanded to forty cars, augmented, in the Vosges Mountains, by a number of "ski-sleighs" under the command of Chicagoan Herman Webster. Meanwhile, donations of food and clothing were pouring into France from both established and ad hoc relief organizations in the United States. To create order out of chaos Americans in Paris established the American Distributing Service, which organized and allocated these materials to the French hospitals most in need, an effort joined in November by the American Relief Clearing House. In

Paris, too, American writer Edith Wharton helped establish the American Hostels for Refugees to house and feed displaced persons and provide them with some work.[51]

Most U.S. relief went to Allied nations, but Americans did try to assist all the belligerents. In September 1914, the American Red Cross (ARC) dispatched its first relief vessel, dubbed the "Mercy Ship," from New York, carrying nearly two hundred doctors and nurses and a cargo of medicines and hospital equipment. In the first year of the war ARC personnel operated sixteen hospital units in a variety of challenging locations, including a Russian school, a German theater, and a French casino. Serbia was the scene of an especially concentrated effort. In March 1915, in cooperation with the Rockefeller Foundation and private contributors, the ARC dispatched a fifty-person team led by Dr. Richard P. Strong, professor of tropical medicine at Harvard, to reinforce ARC staff already in Serbia in their intense battle against a typhus epidemic that was threatening to spread beyond Serbia's borders. Dr. Strong estimated that more than 130,000 people died before American and Allied efforts ended the epidemic. At about the time Dr. Strong returned to the United States in fall 1915, the ARC stopped staffing their overseas hospitals because the tightening Allied blockade made it difficult to administer and send relief staff to units assisting the Central Powers, and the ARC could not serve one side only. Other American hospitals continued to operate, however, and the ARC continued sending supplies to both sides until Allied strictures made that, too, impossible.[52]

Not all Americans were content to volunteer in noncombatant roles. Despite President Wilson's August 20, 1914, plea that Americans be "impartial in thought as well as in action," a few decided to enlist in belligerent forces. Most served with the Allies, though there were exceptions. Anton Dilger, born in Virginia but raised and trained as a physician in Germany as well as the United States, joined the German army's medical corps, then transferred to an intelligence group that assigned him to biological warfare. By the end of 1915 he had returned to the United States to engage in subversive activities.

Karl N. Llewellyn, who had also lived several years in Germany, was studying at the Sorbonne in August 1914. "The German Nation, all that is German, is in . . . fearful danger, and without guilt. This summons me, who owe Germany so much, to do what I can to help," he wrote explaining his decision to join the German army. Denied formal status as a soldier when he would not renounce his U.S. citizenship and swear allegiance to the kaiser, he nevertheless was allowed to fight in the ranks of the Seventy-eighth Prussian infantry. Wounded in November 1914, he was awarded the Iron Cross, Second Class, before returning to the United States in 1915 to enter Yale Law School.[53]

Harvard man Dillwyn P. Starr began his volunteer service as a driver in Richard Norton's ambulance corps, where he developed such a low opinion of German soldiers' behavior that he felt he must "get at them with cold steel." He fulfilled that desire by transferring to a British armored car division. Other Americans were attracted by the "romance" of the French Foreign Legion. "I am to take a part, however small, in the greatest and probably last, war in history, which has apparently developed into a fight of civilization against barbarism," Pittsburgh's William Thaw wrote to his family in late August, after enlisting in the Foreign Legion. Among his fellow recruits was "a Columbia Professor (called 'Shorty') . . . a preacher from Georgia, a pro gambler from Missouri . . . [and] a couple of hard guys from the Gopher Gang of lower N.Y." An African American in Paris, Eugene Bullard, joined the legion on October 9, his nineteenth birthday, to defend

DOCTORS & FAMILIES GOING TO WAR ZONE 10|17|14   3267-E

X DR. MARY CRAWFORD

the country in which he had found such happy relief from the racial prejudice then rampant in the United States. After five weeks of tough training, he and his polyglot regiment were thrust into an active sector of the battle line. Another American legionnaire, the budding poet Alan Seeger, described trench life in winter to his fellow Americans via a letter to the *New York Sun* in December 1914. While artillerymen behind the lines kept relatively warm continuously lobbing shells, the ordinary soldier's role "is simply to dig himself a hole in the ground and to keep hidden in it as tightly as possible . . . continually under the fire of the opposing batteries . . . His feet are numb, his canteen frozen, but he is not allowed to make a fire." At night, on edge in the cold and dark in case he is called to action, he must "lie down cramped in the dirty straw to sleep as best he may."[54]

Christmas Day 1914 ("one of the most beautiful of cold winter days," Seeger wrote) brought a brief unofficial ceasefire to parts of the Western Front, as a few daring trench dwellers in scattered sections of the front ventured out into the normally lethal No Man's Land between the opposing trench lines. When those first few survived, others followed. Enemies collected and buried the dead, shook hands, sang carols, and swapped cigarettes for food. The pope had tried to arrange a Christmas truce, one U.S. publication reported, but "what His Holiness failed to achieve through an appeal to emperors and kings and war-captains . . . the Almighty brought about through the hearts of men . . . For one day the angel of peace descended upon the field of battle."[55]

But what of Christmas on the European home front? Months before the unauthorized Christmas truce (which commanders on both sides made clear to their men must never happen again), some Americans had begun to wonder how to help St. Nicholas

Citizens of a neutral country, Americans provided aid to both sides. *At left, below:* A poster by Winold Reiss advertises a March 1916 "Charity Bazar [*sic*]" for the relief of Central Powers war victims. After Karl Llewellyn returned from brief service in the German army, he gave several talks about his experiences. The July 19, 1915 *Oklahoma City Times* advertised his appearance there.

Opposite: Four Americans are included in this picture of French Foreign Legionnaires on leave in Paris published in Edward Morse's *Vanguard of American Volunteers . . . .*, 1918. Seated in the center is Edmond Genet, with William Dugan, from Rochester, N.Y., on his left. Standing, third from the left, is Joseph Lydon, from Boston, with Victor Chapman on his left.

make it through checkpoints and artillery barrages to leave gifts for the children of war-torn Europe. Because Santa's usual mode of transportation would undoubtedly be challenged by the military aircraft patrolling skies over the Continent, James Keeley, owner of the *Chicago Herald*, and John Callan O'Laughlin, one of the paper's chief correspondents, floated the idea of a shipload of Christmas presents. "More than ninety of the big daily newspapers . . . have joined in the movement," O'Laughlin wrote to Congressman Lemuel P. Padgett in early October. "It has been endorsed by the International Sunday Schools Association, which represents 179,000 Sunday Schools in the United States and involved the interest of some 18 million Sunday School pupils. The Women's Christian Temperance Union and many other prominent organizations and societies . . . are doing everything they can for its success." The toy drive being a huge success and Mr. Claus being of no specific nationality, Uncle Sam determined that it would not be a violation of American neutrality for the U.S. Navy to contribute the collier USS *Jason* as transportation. The governments of belligerent nations vowed not to hinder the vessel and to work with civilian organizations to properly distribute the gifts.[56]

The toy-laden *Jason* sailed from New York in mid-November with O'Laughlin aboard. He later reported in a lengthy letter to President Wilson that he had visited England, France, Italy, Austria, Hungary, Germany, and Holland on this gift-giving mission, stressing that he and Commander Courtney, captain of the *Jason*, "were particularly careful not only in speeches but in private conversations, to say nothing which possibly could be interpreted as sympathy for one side or the other." A good friend and former aide to Teddy Roosevelt and a seasoned observer, O'Laughlin did not publicly discuss or publish any articles about the political or military conditions he had observed on that trip, lest that cast a shadow over the Christmas ship's mission. But he included some pithy observations in his private report to the president.[57]

In England, he was astonished to find "a growing feeling against the United States . . . among the middle class. 'We are fighting for your ideals and your institutions, and you are chasing the dollar' was the usual view expressed," he reported. "It was felt that we ought to join the allies, that we should not object to the seizure of contraband or even permit it to leave our shores with Germany and Austro-Hungary as the destination . . . I did not find much enthusiasm for the war in England," he declared, "but an obstinate, determined purpose to win."[58]

O'Laughlin found Germans "patriotic, united and confident." Even in these early days of the British blockade, the kaiser's government "was taking measures . . . to conserve the food supply" but O'Laughlin was assured "that the people could be fed." In talking with Gottlieb von Jagow, Germany's minister of foreign affairs, O'Laughlin learned that if Germany made

Opposite: A group of American volunteers pack crates of toys that the "Christmas ship" USS *Jason* will deliver to European children on both sides of the conflict.

Above: John Callan O'Laughlin (hatless, in suit at center) and the *Jason*'s captain, Lieutenant Commander C. E. Courtney (in uniform, third from right) with a group of well-wishers before the *Jason* leaves New York, November 14, 1914. Bain News Service photographs.

peace, it would do so directly, "not through the mediation of the United States." Von Jagow also asserted, "If it had not been for the military supplies received by the Allies from the United States Germany at the moment would be the recognized victor." He and other German officials with whom O'Laughlin spoke "referred constantly to the hostile sentiment in the United States against Germany. They said they could not understand it."[59]

"Each side is seeking earnestly to involve the United States against the other," O'Laughlin wrote in his conclusion. The only way to ensure that America did not get drawn into the war, he told the president, was to become strong enough to confound such efforts. Thus, "the development of our navy and the strengthening of our army" were of paramount importance. "The former is not regarded abroad as especially efficient," O'Laughlin wrote, "and our army is laughed at."[60]

Few people in America were laughing. The European war had reinvigorated the ongoing tug of war between those favoring reorganization and expansion of U.S.

armed forces and those defending the status quo. Many of those opposed to expansion pointed to the war as proof of the folly of large standing armies. "A final end has now been put to the contention, always stupid and often insincere, that huge armaments are an insurance policy against war and an aid in maintaining peace," the president of Columbia University, Nicholas Murray Butler, asserted in September. Americans who had embraced the belief that war among the economically entwined Western nations had become outmoded viewed the European conflict as a heartrending throwback to more primitive times—anguish at this lapse dramatically expressed at the end of August when some two thousand women dressed in mourning clothes marched silently down New York City's Fifth Avenue to the beat of muffled drums. Citizens of this persuasion embraced President Wilson's determination to maintain peace at home while inspiring a return to it abroad. They looked askance at plans to expand the nation's own military and turned for inspiration to American democratic traditions, the country's longtime policy of staying out of European quarrels, and the small but determined European peace movements that had arisen to protest the descent into war.[61]

Two European peace activists, Rosika Schwimmer and Emmeline Pethick-Lawrence, toured the United States in the fall of 1914. On September 6, Schwimmer, accompanied by American suffragist Carrie Chapman Catt, presented to President Wilson a petition signed by women of belligerent and neutral European nations urging him to coordinate an appeal for an armistice from all neutral countries.

Several weeks later, Pethick-Lawrence inaugurated her tour of the country with an address to a mass meeting of the Women's Political Union of New York, during which she suggested that American suffragists adopt peace as an additional cause. Suffrage advocates were the vast majority of the three thousand women who crowded into the Grand Ballroom of the new Willard Hotel in Washington, D.C., on January 10, 1915, to begin a three-day meeting that resulted in the formation of the Women's Peace Party, chaired by Jane Addams. "Equally with men pacifists," the preamble to the party's platform declared, "we understand that planned-for legalized, wholesale human slaughter is today the sum of all villainies." Among the party's eleven specific goals: "limitation of armaments and the nationalization of their manufacture" (thereby presumably removing the profit motive) and "opposition to militarism in our own country."[62]

Security, rather than militarism, was the watchword for those who advocated preparedness. Republican representative Augustus Peabody Gardner of Massachusetts witnessed Britain's scramble to mobilize when he was among the Americans stranded in England—and gave his first speech on preparedness the day he returned to the United States. His initial concern

Spectators line New York City's Fifth Avenue on August 29, 1914, as two thousand women dressed in mourning march for peace. Bain News Service photograph.

PEACE PARADE 8/29/14   3207-10

was for the navy as the nation's first line of defense. "The wisest thing the United States can do," he declared, "is to build a Chinese wall of dreadnaughts and battleships around this country and do it now!" Assistant Secretary of the Navy Franklin Delano Roosevelt helped Gardner prepare a resolution calling for an investigation of the state of the nation's defenses, which the congressman introduced on the House floor in early December 1914. Gardner's father-in-law, the powerful Republican Henry Cabot Lodge, introduced it in the Senate.[63]

Coastal security was a particular concern. Whoever prevailed in the European conflict might be tempted to turn next to vulnerable America. Teddy Roosevelt claimed to have seen, on prewar visits to two of the current belligerents, plans for seizing and holding East Coast cities for ransom.[64] Many on the West Coast saw a threat looming in Asia, where in October 1914 Japan, an Allied combatant since late August, occupied Pacific island chains previously claimed by Germany, depriving the few German warships and armed merchantmen then ranging the oceans of coaling and resupply bases in the Marshall, Caroline, Mariana and Palau islands. In November, the Japanese fulfilled a treaty obligation to the British when, with some British assistance, they seized the German concession in Shandong, China, including the harbor of Tsingtao.

Then, in January 1915, the Japanese flexed their strengthening muscles in the fledgling republic of China, a neutral nation still feeling the aftershocks of the revolution in 1911–1912 that had toppled the Qing (Manchu) dynasty. Several of the "Twenty-one Demands" Japan presented to the Chinese government that month threatened the considerable business and philanthropic interests Americans had developed in China after the great powers acceded to the U.S. government's "Open Door" policy at the turn of the century. "If Japan's demands on China are really such as the cablegrams just published show," Chicago's *Day Book* opined at the end of February, "Japan is going to close that 'open door' with a bang." And where might Japanese ambitions then lead? The Japanese navy had already made clear its interest in Mexico, and now the United States also had to worry about the security of the Panama Canal. Even as the Wilson administration successfully used diplomatic channels to address the Japanese demands that troubled American interests, Admiral Bradley A. Fiske proposed preparing contingency plans for the U.S. military: "Black" in case of war with Germany and "Orange" in case of war with Japan.[65]

Despite these possible threats, the Gardner-Lodge resolution went nowhere, roughly the same destination achieved by Secretary of War Lindley M. Garrison's strenuous efforts to increase and improve military forces. For reasons of both principle and practicality, few members of Congress were willing to push for military expansion. As Alabama congressman Oscar Underwood noted, the 1914 war-related crimp in U.S trade revenue made economizing imperative. Representative James Mann of Illinois even cut a small fund that would have allowed the War Department to send experienced military observers to Europe, thereby depriving military planners of

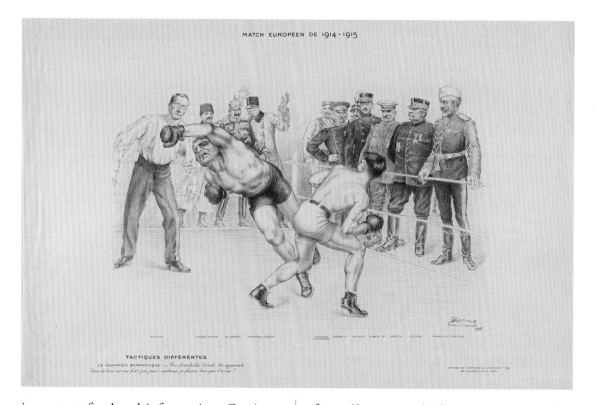

MATCH EUROPÉEN DE 1914-1915

TACTIQUES DIFFÉRENTES

important firsthand information. Garrison excepted, most Wilson cabinet members, and the president himself, saw little reason to augment current forces. To expand the armed forces, institute universal military training (UMT), or engage in other steps proposed by ardent preparedness advocates would mean, Wilson declared in his Second Annual Message to Congress in December 1914, "that we had lost our self-possession, that we had been thrown off our balance by a war with which we have nothing to do, whose causes cannot touch us, whose very existence affords us opportunities of friendship and disinterested service which should make us ashamed of any thought of hostility or fearful preparation for trouble."[66]

Preparedness advocates continued their campaigns. General Leonard Wood, whose summer military training camps

for college men had proved so popular, worked preparedness speeches to civilian audiences into his wide-ranging military inspection tours, quietly advised individuals who wished to write on the subject, and got into some hot water with the president and Secretary of War Garrison when he publicly supported a new, short-lived preparedness group, the American Legion (not to be confused with the veterans organization founded after the war, whose founding members included Wood's friend and former comrade-in-arms Teddy Roosevelt and Roosevelt's four sons).[67] In December 1914, S. Stanwood Menken, whose first thoughts of preparedness had come as he watched British parliamentary debates on the eve of war, called a meeting of like-minded and similarly well-connected men at New York's Hotel Belmont, where the publisher George H. Putnam addressed the assembly on Germany's secret plan to conquer the United States. Not all in the room might have subscribed to Putnam's belief in German perfidy, but all were sufficiently concerned about the country's preparedness to establish the National Security League (NSL), formally incorporated in January with Menken as president. Devoted to investigating the state of the nation's defenses and to ensuring "the preservation of our nationality," the NSL was soon engaged in a full-scale pro-preparedness propaganda campaign and establishing branch offices around the country.[68]

Yet as the Allied and Central Powers entered their seventh month of war in January 1915, most Americans still sided with the president on national defense, while arguing about Wilson's ongoing quest for domestic reforms, particularly in the realm of business. Both the Federal Trade Act, signed on September 26, 1914, and the Clayton Antitrust Act, signed on October 14, aimed "to make men in a small way of business as free to succeed as men in a big way," Wilson wrote to Congressman Oscar Underwood, "and to kill monopoly in the seed."[69] Killing monopoly required increased federal regulation, and Wilsonian legislation introduced restraints that elicited outraged roars from many lions of American industry, J. P. Morgan

THE ILLUSTRATION OF THE GRAET EUROPEAN WAR. NO. 39.   BANZAI, BANZAI THE FALL OF TSINGTAU.

growling, "The situation here is perfectly unspeakable."[70] Some hard-core "insurgent" progressives, on the other hand, felt the new reform legislation did not go far enough. The Federal Trade Act itself drew less criticism than did the Federal Trade commissioners Wilson appointed, a roster that led the Republican insurgent leader Robert La Follette to charge Wilson with creating a commission that, instead of regulating business, would be "a counsellor and a friend to the business world."[71] The Clayton Antitrust Act drew even stronger fire. When first written, "It was a raging lion with a mouth full of teeth," Missouri's Democratic senator James A. Reed declared, but "It has degenerated to a tabby cat with soft gums, a plaintive mew and an anemic appearance."[72]

Provisions in the act favoring workers—including legalization of the rights to strike and to picket and boycott employers—made it less disappointing to Samuel Gompers, head of the American Federation of Labor, who called it labor's Magna Carta. Yet those provisions did little to better the lives of the majority of wage workers. So many were unemployed at the end of 1914 that delegates to the second National Conference on Unemployment, held in Philadelphia that December, called for action from the federal government to augment private and municipal programs that were proving insufficient.[73] The rising tide of war orders that carried the unemployed back to work as the new year unfolded made such emergency action unnecessary. But the return to work did not end the country's strike- and violence-pocked "industrial war," which the recently widowed

Florence Harriman continued to investigate as a member of the Commission on Industrial Relations. Before her December 1914 inspection of the site where some two dozen people had been killed at Ludlow, Colorado, she had listened to testimony in New York from miners and family members who had survived that bloody encounter. With each witness's story, "it sank deeper home," Harriman said, "that something must be done to make such conflicts impossible."[74]

In some areas of the country problems in agriculture echoed those in the "industrial war." In March 1915, Harriman participated in commission hearings in Texas, where she learned that, unlike forty years before, when almost all Texas farmers owned their own land, now "more than half were 'renters,' and there was growing up the same bitter antagonism between landowner and tenant farmer as we had seen between capital and labor in industry." Texas was not the only state in which there was tenant-farmer unrest, but for some suffering tenant farmers in the South and Southwest, and for other low-wage workers seeking a better life, 1915 was the beginning of an era of opportunity. At the same time that war orders to U.S. industries were on the rise the war was causing a sharp decline in European immigration. Hence the businesses that were beginning to boom sought human resources already within U.S. borders. Advertisements for work at decent wages began luring white southern workers north. As news spread that jobs in northern industries were also open to African Americans, more and more black southerners followed, initiating the first major wave in what would become known as the Great Migration.[75]

As this population shift began, D. W. Griffith premiered his groundbreaking silent film, *Birth of a Nation*. America's first cinema extravaganza was based on two novels, *The Clansman* and *The Leopard's Spots: A Romance of the White Man's Burden*, by Thomas A. Dixon, a man who declared that he aimed to "teach the North . . . the awful suffering of the white man during the dreadful Reconstruction period" and to "demonstrate to the world that the white man must and shall be supreme." Filled with scenes that glorified the post–Civil War terrorism of the Ku Klux Klan and denigrated the African Americans who endured it, the film was advertised as the "Eighth Wonder of the World" and drew both high praise and pointed criticism. The most pointed came from the National Association for the Advancement of Colored People (NAACP) in a nationwide campaign launched to expose the film's distorted history. "The harm it is doing the colored people cannot be estimated," NAACP secretary Mary Childs Nerney wrote in April 1915. In some locations, some of the film's objectionable scenes were exorcized; a few places banned it entirely. But white Americans continued to flock to this cinema spectacle, which fed the country's appetite for innovation and entertainment. It also fed the fires of racial prejudice. In December 1915, Georgia granted a new charter to the Klan, which had been dormant for decades.[76]

Other dangerous fires were burning, not *in* the United States but very close to it. Depressed by the Industrial Relations Commission hearings in Dallas, where she became convinced that "the social scheme of things had gone wrong at the root," Florence Harriman took time off at the end of March 1915 to visit friends living near the Mexican border—and rode right into an episode in the Mexican Revolution. At the town of McAllen, Texas, she saw thousands of soldiers loyal to Pancho Villa camped with their families on the Mexican side of the Rio Grande. President Wilson's neutrality policies made it impossible for her military escort to cross the river or talk with the "Villistas," but Harriman did both, finding most of the soldiers "nothing but boys" but the army well equipped. Traveling on, she arrived in Brownsville, Texas, in time to witness, from a rooftop perch, the Battle of Matamoros, a Mexican town which Villa's men were attempting to take from troops loyal

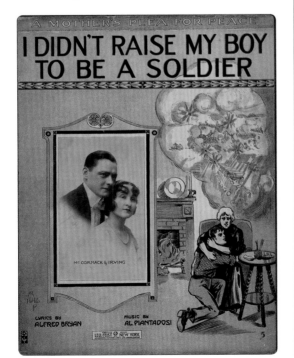

General Leonard Wood's continuing quest for greater U.S. military preparedness faced stiff resistance, with arguments against militarism surfacing even in popular music. In 1915, composer Al Piantadosi and lyricist Alfred Bryan published "I Didn't Raise My Boy to Be a Soldier," billed as "a mother's plea for peace."

to Venustiano Carranza, formerly Villa's comrade-in-arms. Stray bullets pinged all around the International Bridge between the two countries, guarded by U.S. cavalrymen and used by a single ambulance to bring Mexican wounded into Brownsville. After helping out in a makeshift hospital, where she admired the young fighters' stoicism, she managed to get permission to visit Matamoros, although Villa's men were expected to attack it again at any moment. The town was almost deserted, its women and children now "refugees seeking a haven on American soil" and most men in the trenches. But Harriman talked with Carranza's local commander, Emiliano Nafarrate, who assured her that his two thousand well-dug-in men could hold the town against Villa's nine thousand. As proof, he produced Villa battle standards his troops had already captured—banners like those she had seen in the Villa camps near McAllen. The ones Nafarrate held, however, were "shot into ribbons; some were stiff with blood. My sense of adventure vanished," she wrote. "Here by the Rio Grande and over there in Europe war is all the same piteous game."[77]

Europe's piteous game was spreading geographically and gaining in brutality. With the Ottoman Empire now one of the Central Powers, in February 1915 the Allies began naval operations in the narrow waters east of the Gallipoli Peninsula separating the Ottomans' small European territory from the bulk of its empire in Asia. An attempt to take pressure off the Russians, increase pressure on the Ottomans' German ally, and perhaps help break the stalemate on the Western Front, this effort to sweep the Dardanelles clear of mines and destroy the enemy's landward artillery by naval bombardment alone ended in failure on March 22. A month later, Allied ground troops landed at Gallipoli, beginning a long and costly land campaign that would also end in defeat.[78] Five days after that landing, on April 30, 1915, the U.S. ambassador to the Ottoman Empire, Henry Morgenthau, sent an urgent dispatch to the State Department, the first official notice of a campaign the Ottomans were waging that had little to do with the war: "Continued reports of persecutions, plunder and massacres of Armenians in certain parts of empire had been received." By September Morgenthau was stating, "Destruction of Armenian race in Turkey is progressing rapidly."[79]

Confirmation of the Muslim Ottoman government's persecution of the Christian Armenian minority—who, the Ottomans insisted, had subversive ties to the Ottomans' Russian enemy—came from the large community of American missionaries operating schools and hospitals in Turkey and the Middle East. In September 1914, before the Ottomans entered the war, a German officer had warned evangelist Mary L. Graffam that "a certain fate was in store for all Armenians, but if the Germans were in the country, there would be no massacres." His warning came true; his assurance did not. Missionary Theodore Elmer carried back to America with him memories of "tens of thousands of innocent women and little children . . . packed in cattle trucks, or languishing in the open fields . . . waiting . . . for transportation to unknown places of death by starvation

A U.S. military survey crew from Fort Brown in Brownsville, Texas, set their sights on Matamoros, Mexico, the scene of a bloody encounter on March 29, 1915, between the forces of Pancho Villa and Venustiano Carranza. A single ambulance made many harrowing trips across the International Bridge to get wounded to safety in Brownsville. Bain News Service photograph.

FINDING RANGE OF MATAMOROS FROM INT. BRIDGE

GALLIPOLI CAMPAIGN

Location: Dardanelles Straits and Gallipoli Peninsula, Turkey

Date: April 25, 1915–January 9, 1916

Objectives: Allied strategists sought to open a new front in the east as a potentially faster path to victory than was available on the stalemated Western Front. At Gallipoli, Britain, with French assistance, planned to take the Dardanelles and thus obtain a convenient and vital supply route to Russia, force the Ottoman Empire out of the war, and lure German forces eastward, out of France.[1]

Synopsis: After failing to open the Dardanelles with naval power, Allied ground troops from Britain, Australia, New Zealand, and France landed at multiple sites on the European peninsula of Gallipoli and one on the Asiatic side of mainland Turkey. They were met by scattered Turkish troops and German officers who in some areas were entrenched in the steep, rocky cliffs and hillsides.[2] The Allies clung to coastal toeholds, unable to break out, and were soon wracked by disease and extreme summer heat. Winter blizzards, flooding, and tenacious Turkish troops ended the costly and disastrous campaign. The only major Allied success was its virtually flawless evacuation from Gallipoli.[3]

Casualties: Allied: 265,000 (48,000 killed, including Australian, British, Canadian, French, Indian, and New Zealand troops); Turkish: 300,000 (65,000 killed).[4]

Outcome: Poorly prepared and badly managed, the Allies failed to achieve any of their objectives. The failure to establish a supply line to Russia exacerbated its collapsing military and political fortunes.[5] The Allied defeat helped prompt neutral Bulgaria to join the Central Powers and subsequently destroy Serbia in October 1915.[6] In the British dominions of Australia and New Zealand, the heroics and devastation of their first military campaign made Gallipoli a potent and unifying symbol of nationhood for both countries.[7] The Turks remained in the war, finding a hero and, later, a national leader in the campaign veteran Mustafa Kemal Atatürk. First Lord of the Admiralty Winston Churchill, a Gallipoli enthusiast, resigned from the cabinet because of the Gallipoli debacle and took command of a battalion on the Western Front.

Commentary: "Everyone who has inquired, even casually, into the matter knows that the United States forces, as now constituted and organized, could not have made as good a showing as was made by Britain in the Dardanelles fiasco."[8] —Editorial, *Washington Post*, January 8, 1916.

"It does seem strange, though, that navies and armies, fights, sieges, war before the living eye, don't interest them . . . The ingenuous youth of the colleges need to read the newspapers and not confine their attention to the 'sporting pages' thereof."[9]—Editorial, *New York Times*, January 12, 1916, lamenting reports that the majority of American college men who had taken recent current events exams could not locate Gallipoli or correctly answer other widely discussed war-related questions.

or violence and outrage." American missionaries Tacy and Henry Atkinson started what Tacy described as "sort of an underground railway" which, over the year and a half of its operation, helped spirit hundreds of Armenians out of harm's way. All over Turkey and the Middle East, American missionaries and consular officials sought to protect as many Armenians as they could. The diplomats initially achieved success primarily with those few who were officially employed by the U.S. government, but soon they were also providing assistance to refugees who managed to escape the Ottoman net and find havens in Syria, the Russian Caucasus, Palestine, and Egypt.[80]

Despite pleas from Ambassador Morgenthau, the Wilson administration refused to endanger American neutrality either by lodging an official protest with the Ottomans or supplying government funds for relief. Secretary of State Bryan did pass Morgenthau's plea to James L. Barton of the American Board of Commissioners for Foreign Missions, however, and Morgenthau, too, appealed to his influential friends at home. This sparked a relief effort that drew resources from American churches, wealthy philanthropists, the Rockefeller Foundation, and individuals moved by a nationwide press campaign. Organized in 1915 as the American Committee for Armenian and Syrian Relief, and later known as Near East Relief, the program began modestly but gradually built into a huge operation, the Near Eastern counterpart to the Commission for Relief in Belgium.[81]

At the end of April 1915, meanwhile, The Hague in neutral Holland became the point of convergence for more than twelve hundred women from both neutral and belligerent countries seeking to find some relief for the entire war-plagued world. Forty-seven prominent American activists—among them Jane Addams, sociologist Emily G. Balch, and physician and educator Alice Hamilton—sailed across the troubled Atlantic to attend the International Congress of Women. Both ridiculed and vilified in the press, with little support from any government and none at all from belligerent leaders, the women at The Hague chose Addams as conference president and organized the Women's International Committee for Permanent Peace (later renamed the Women's International League for Peace and Freedom). The Hague conference also

After news of the Ottoman government's persecution of Armenians reached the United States, Americans gave generously to an evolving relief effort that soon rivaled the size and effectiveness of the Committee for Relief in Belgium. Polish-American artist Wladyslaw Benda (1873–1948) created this affecting poster, published ca. 1916.

GIVE OR WE PERISH
AMERICAN COMMITTEE
FOR RELIEF IN THE NEAR EAST
ARMENIA - GREECE - SYRIA - PERSIA
CAMPAIGN for $30,000,000

established a framework for achieving peace that both reflected earlier pacifist proposals and presaged elements of the Fourteen-Point program that President Wilson would unveil nearly three years later—including the creation of a society (or league) of nations, freedom of the seas, and an end to secret treaties.[82]

After the conference, special delegates spent many weeks traveling across Europe to discuss the peace plan with representatives of fourteen neutral and belligerent countries, the number of belligerents increasing during their journey when Italy—lured by guarantees given it in the secret April 26, 1915, Treaty of London—entered the war as an Ally. "We were impressed with the fact that in all countries the enthusiasm for continuing the war was largely fed on a fund of animosity growing out of the conduct of the war," Addams later reported, "England on fire over the atrocities in Belgium, Germany indignant over England's blockade to starve her women and children." The growing enthusiasm for pressing on to victory was in turn inspiring technological advancements in the dark art of destruction that either ignored or were not adequately covered by the prevailing rules of war.[83]

On April 22–24, as the women were converging on The Hague, German forces launched the Second Battle of Ypres, Belgium, by sending clouds of chlorine gas across the muddy expanse of shell-pocked No Man's Land and into the lungs of French Algerian (Zouave), Canadian, and English soldiers in the Allied trenches. Men who had found ways to endure bone-rattling artillery barrages, airborne

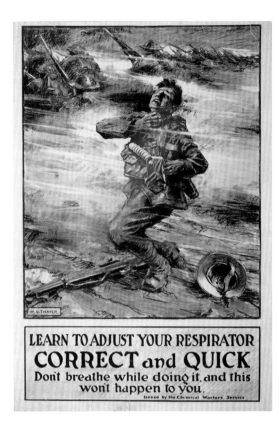

LEARN TO ADJUST YOUR RESPIRATOR
CORRECT and QUICK
Don't breathe while doing it, and this won't happen to you.
Issued by the Chemical Warfare Service

In April 1915, the Germans sent clouds of chlorine gas across No Man's Land, the first successful use of lethal gas in war. The Allies quickly developed defenses and gas weapons of their own. This poster, issued by the British Chemical Warfare Service in 1915, emphasizes the importance of respirators in preserving soldiers' lives.

assaults, snipers' bullets, and futile attacks on enemy lines protected by barbed-wire and machine-gun batteries were wholly unprepared for this first successful use of lethal gas in battle. Those who could not escape by retreating or rigging makeshift protection quickly fell, their lungs filling with fluid, their airways contracting, their bodies twisting as they asphyxiated. The Germans gained ground, then lost it again as the Allies regrouped, devised rudimentary respirators, and pushed back. Having flouted the 1899 and 1907 Hague Conventions' prohibition of poison or poisonous weapons, the Germans nevertheless failed in their bid to achieve a war-shortening breakthrough. They did succeed in adding a new horror to war. Over the next three and a half years, both sides would produce more than 124,000 tons of poisonous gases, each advance in gas technology matched by an advance in countermeasures.[84]

At sea as on land, new technologies and the thirst for victory led each side to defy existing rules of war. As soon as war was declared, both sides began laying mines in the North Atlantic, their minefields almost immediately straying far past the territorial waters of belligerent nations and into international sea lanes. As each side scrambled to improve its mine-sweeping practices, American newspapers on November 3 trumpeted Britain's declaration that the entire North Sea, except for the territorial waters of neutral nations, was henceforth to be considered a military area, ostensibly because of the danger from mines laid not by German warships but by enemy-controlled merchant vessels "flying a neutral flag." All neutral merchantmen sailing past Britain for ports in northern Europe were ordered to sail through the English Channel on a route specified by the British Admiralty or risk being damaged or destroyed by mines or by British vessels mistaking them for clandestine mine layers.[85]

Controlling the route of merchant vessels made boarding and inspecting them that much easier as the British continued to tighten their blockade, using methods that were out of sync with rules of blockading written before the age of the submarine and the dreadnaught.[86] Nearly nonstop negotiations with the Wilson administration on matters related to commerce did not prevent Britain from adding more goods to the contraband lists. Each new addition, each new seizure of American shipments, provoked complaints from businessmen to their government and

from Washington to London. "The present policy of His majesty's Government toward neutral ships and cargoes . . . constitutes restrictions upon the right of American citizens on the high seas which are not justified by the rules of international law or required under the principle of self-preservation," Secretary of State Bryan declared on December 26, 1914. "Producers and exporters, steamship and insurance companies are pressing . . . for relief from the menace to transatlantic trade which is gradually but surely destroying their business and threatening them with financial disaster." Such protests continued, though American complaints over British seizure of foodstuffs directed to Germany through neutral ports were blunted in January 1915, when the German government announced it was assuming control of all major food staples on February 1. A sign of the increasing strain caused by Britain's blockade, the announcement meant, according to British Foreign Secretary Edward Grey, that "all food in effect belongs to the army." Thus, all food destined for Germany was considered contraband.[87]

America's commercial rights were not the only focus of Wilson's behind-the-scenes negotiations with representatives of the belligerent governments. For months he had been quietly exploring formal and informal avenues through which the United States might help end the war. While these efforts had done little to advance the cause of peace, they had lowered the president's assessment of his secretary of state's aptitude for such delicate negotiations. By the end of 1914, Wilson

SECOND BATTLE OF YPRES

Location: Ypres, Belgium

Date: April 22–May 25, 1915

Objectives: At the First Battle of Ypres (October 22–November 22, 1914), on the route to Belgium's English Channel ports, the Allies regained the German-occupied city and fighting ended with the onset of winter.[1] The second battle saw the Germans renew attacks against Allied lines in order to reach the coast.

Synopsis: The second battle is infamous as the first significant and successful use of poison gas in the war.[2] The Germans launched several chlorine gas attacks as they gained high ground above the town and forced an Allied retreat. Even so, the "Ypres Salient," the Allied-occupied territory surrounding the city, though reduced, remained intact, and the Germans did not reach the ports.

Casualties: Allied: 69,000 (including British, Canadian, French, and French colonial Algerian and Senegalese troops). German: 35,000.[3]

Outcome: The Germans gained some ground, but the Allies won a propaganda victory, promoting the gas attacks as cowardly and inhumane, and Germany's standing in American public opinion further deteriorated.[4]

Commentary: "And as the evidence came in, I, for one, could not avoid one conclusion: the German had 'lifted the lid' in that battle. He had abrogated every rule of civilized warfare—if warfare is ever civilized . . . And he made of himself for those few days a barbaric, slaughtering beast."[5] —American war correspondent Will Irwin, *New York Tribune*, June 9, 1915.

"The submarine is a new condition, just as the dirigible and aeroplane, and, therefore, cannot be governed by antiquated international law. They will have to be recognized in the future along with gas bombs as a weapon of a newer time. The human aspect of using such weapons on an enemy is entirely a matter of how you look upon such warfare. The Indian, with his inferior arrow, might have considered the rifle and gun a very inhuman instrument of warfare, but to no avail, the gun and rifle remained and the Indian was conquered."[6]
—Letter to the editor signed "German-American," *Baltimore Sun*, May 17, 1915.

UN SOLDAT ALLEMAND EN FEU
L'Eclaireur

Germany introduced another new weapon to warfare in 1915, using flamethrowers against the French near Verdun in February and the British in June. This lithograph with hand coloring published in 1915 is an unknown French artist's depiction of the horror of a fiery death, in this case of a German soldier who may have been one of the first to carry a flamethrower into battle. Those terrible weapons could be as dangerous to the user as to the target.

had come to rely more on his own friend and confidant, Colonel Edward House, as counselor and spokesperson, while also relying on the legal advice and strategic suggestions of State Department Counselor Robert Lansing. It was House rather than Bryan whom Wilson dispatched to Europe at the end of January 1915 to reenergize the quest for peace by meeting directly with Allied and German leaders. The colonel's passage to England aboard RMS *Lusitania* was quiet—except for a storm that tossed the great liner around "like a cork in the rapids" and a minor event at the end of the voyage. "This afternoon, as we approached the Irish coast," House wrote on February 5, "the American flag was raised." Widely reported in the press, the substitution of the Stars and Stripes for the Union Jack had occurred, House later discovered, because *Lusitania*'s captain, Daniel

Dow, had "expected to be torpedoed," the assumption being that no U-boat would torpedo a ship flying a neutral flag. "I can see many complications," House added, "arising from this incident."[88]

House debarked from *Lusitania* just as the Germans were embarking on a new naval campaign, a counter-blockade of Great Britain to be enforced by the vessels most likely to elude the British fleet in this time before radar and sonar: the kaiser's slowly expanding fleet of submarines, called U-boats (*Unterseeboote*, or "undersea boats"). "The waters around Great Britain, including the whole of the English Channel, are . . . hereby to be included within the zone of war," the German government declared on February 4. Neutral as well as Allied merchant vessels were at risk in the war zone, the declaration continued, because of "the misuse of the neutral flags ordered by the Government of Great Britain . . . and of the hazards of naval warfare." This elicited a forceful protest from the U.S. government, which stated that the United States would "hold the Imperial German Government to a strict accountability" should German vessels, acting on "the presumption that the flag of the United States was not being used in good faith," destroy "an American vessel or American lives." At the same time, a note went out to the British, protesting their use of the American flag as "a serious and constant menace to the lives and vessels of American citizens."[89]

With protests from the United States and still-neutral Italy in mind, on February 18, 1915, the Germans began the U-boat-enforced counter-blockade with caution, ordering their submarine commanders to do everything possible to avoid sinking Italian and American ships "by mistake." Concern about Italy evaporated with the Italian declaration of war against Austria-Hungary in May. German-American relations, meanwhile, were rapidly deteriorating. When, in mid-March, the British reacted to the German U-boat blockade by declaring that henceforth the Royal navy would "prevent commodities of any kind from reaching or leaving Germany"—not just materials listed as contraband—the Wilson administration protested, but in a manner that seemed to Germans so tepid as to signal virtual acquiescence in Britain's tightening stranglehold on the German Empire. Even more damning was news of the increasing shipments of arms and ammunition from the United States to the Allies, munitions that would surely be used against the

kaiser's soldiers. This caused an upsurge in what one American reporter termed "the hatred against everything and everybody American" that he was encountering in Germany. A German friend of Christmas ship organizer John Callan O'Laughlin confirmed this anti-American feeling in a letter he wrote at the end of March: "Some of the Christmas presents you brought over cannot be disposed of . . . Some of the poorest villages . . . refused to accept them when the population heard they were American."[90]

For their part, Americans were none too pleased when, in mid-April, Germany's ambassador to the United States, Johann von Bernstorff, published in U.S. newspapers a memorandum bitterly condemning America's failure to protest effectively against "the violations of international law by Great Britain" and accusing the United

ZEICHNET
KRIEGS-ANLEIHE
FÜR U-BOOTE GEGEN
ENGLAND

Opposite: The German vision of a successful U-boat blockade of the British Isles is effectively represented in this poster published by Mainzer Verlagsanstalt in 1914.

On Abraham Lincoln's 106th birthday, February 12, 1915, as fighting raged in Europe and Germany prepared to begin its U-boat counter-blockade, workers in Washington, D.C., laid a cornerstone of the Lincoln Memorial. Fifty thousand people would attend the completed memorial's dedication on May 30, 1922.

States of violating the spirit of neutrality by sending munitions to only one side in the conflict. Von Bernstorff, who supported an effort by some Americans to embargo arms shipments to all combatants, told his superiors that his memorandum would "serve as a banner around which the advocates of an embargo will gather." It actually served as a target for American critics of von Bernstorff's "offensive and arrogant" behavior. "If the allies were directing the affairs of the German Embassy in Washington," the *New York World* opined the day after the memorandum appeared, "they could hardly have hit upon anything more shrewdly calculated to prejudice American opinion against the German cause than the von Bernstorff note."[91]

Out of range of these home-front controversies, U-boats continued to hunt in the waters around the British Isles, but without sufficient reward. In the six weeks between February 18 and April 1, 1915, the German counter-blockade had sent only 132,000 tons of shipping to the bottom, losses that Britain and its large merchant fleet easily absorbed. A quest for greater success, coupled with the proven impracticality of conducting U-boat warfare according to rules of naval warfare that were written with only surface ships in mind, led the Germans gradually to relax the constraints that had initially been placed on the U-boat fleet. An increasing number of "accidents" occurred, destroying or damaging neutral vessels.[92]

Mines, rather than U-boats, claimed the American cargo ship *Carib* in late February, killing three crewmen, an incident that underlined the danger of sending

American ships into areas designated as war zones.[93] *U-28* highlighted the risks Americans took by traveling on Allied-flagged passenger ships when it sank the British liner *Falaba* on March 28, 1915, killing more than one hundred passengers, including Leon C. Thrasher, a mining engineer from Massachusetts. American editorials expressed horror at the "barbarism" of the *Falaba* sinking and the entire U-boat campaign, while the incident confronted the Wilson administration with the question of how, exactly, it could hold Germany to "a strict accountability" for Thrasher's death. "In its note to the German government upon submarine warfare on merchant vessels the United States plainly intimated that it would regard the loss of American

lives through such attacks as an unfriendly act," the *Journal of Education* noted on April 8. "It remains to be seen whether any pressure can be brought to bear to check this horrible warfare upon noncombatants and neutrals."[94]

Many in Germany thought it was up to noncombatants and neutrals to stay out of the U-boats' way. "If Americans, as well as other neutrals in spite of the given warning are still careless enough to travel on English ships," John Callan O'Laughlin's German friend wrote to him three days before the *Falaba* sinking, "they have only themselves to blame if they come to grief. If one of our submarines should get the Lusitania, either under English or American flag, she would sink her, if she could, without a moment's hesitation. The British have loudly proclaimed their intention to starve our peaceful people, women and children, so we need not bother about their being drowned incidentally."[95]

Incidents continued as Wilson, Bryan, and Lansing took time to frame a firm protest to Germany that would not provoke a break in relations but would include "the whole question of the use of submarines against merchant vessels." On April 29, a German airplane attack damaged the U.S. freighter *Cushing* with no loss of life. On May 1, a torpedo fired by *U-30* damaged the American tanker *Gulflight*, provoking a heart attack that killed its captain and causing two crewmen to drown. That same day, the *New York Times* reprinted a warning to transatlantic travelers from the German Embassy dated April 22: "Vessels flying the flag of Great Britain, or any of her allies are liable to destruction in those waters [adjacent to Great Britain] and . . . travelers sailing in the war zone

on ships of Great Britain or her allies do so at their own risk." The accompanying article included a statement from Charles P. Sumner, New York agent of Britain's Cunard Line, that he had "absolutely no fear with regard" to Cunard vessels, which could travel at speeds unattainable by any U-boat. This applied especially to the grand and ultra-swift RMS *Lusitania*, which left New York on the morning of May 1 carrying 1,959 passengers and crew, including 189 Americans. Many of its passengers had become aware of the German warning. "Lots of talk about submarines, torpedoes and sudden death," wealthy sportsman Alfred Vanderbilt said to newsman Jack Lawrence. "I don't take much stock in it myself. What would they gain by sinking the *Lusitania?*" Steaming past the British squadron that was stationed off New York to prevent any sequestered German vessels from escaping, the imposing liner headed across the Atlantic, bound for Liverpool at a speed and on a course that six days later brought it into range of Kapitänleutnant Walther Schwieger's *U-20*.[96]

Hit by a single torpedo the morning of May 7, 1915, *Lusitania* sank in just eighteen minutes, killing 1,198 people, including three German stowaways and 123 Americans, Alfred Vanderbilt among them.[97] First news reports were sketchy, but when the extent of the catastrophe became apparent, Americans were outraged. The perpetrators of the tragedy were "wild beasts," the *Nation* declared, "against whom society has to defend itself at all hazards. Teddy Roosevelt called *U-20*'s action "not merely piracy, but

piracy on a vaster scale of murder than any old-time pirate ever practiced . . . It seems inconceivable that we can refrain from taking action in the matter," he declared, "for we owe it not only to humanity but to our own national self-respect."[98]

Attempts by German spokesmen and German-American organizations in the United States to justify the sinking only exacerbated this bitter feeling, especially a May 10 note from the Foreign Office in Berlin that expressed sorrow for civilian losses while blaming the British government for the sinking because "its plan of starving the civilian population of Germany, has forced Germany to resort to retaliatory measures." Similar statements made by Germany's chief propagandist in the United States, Bernhard Dernburg, provoked so much ire that Dernburg returned to Germany. "We might as well

admit openly that our propaganda here has *collapsed completely* under the impact of the Lusitania incident," Ambassador von Bernstorff wrote Berlin, adding that it could not begin again "until this storm has abated."[99]

"We can no longer remain neutral spectators," Colonel House cabled President Wilson from London on May 9. "Our action in this crisis will determine the part we will play when peace is made and how far we may influence a settlement for the lasting good of humanity . . . Our position amongst nations is being assessed by mankind." Outwardly calm but inwardly tense, the president was all too mindful that America's position among nations was being assessed—in many arenas. As he began drafting a protest to the German government, his administration was also dealing with Ambassador Morgenthau's pleas on behalf of Armenians, protesting Japanese encroachment on U.S. interests in China, and contending with a stream of alarming reports about the deepening chaos in Mexico, where Americans trapped in beleaguered Mexico City were now in particular danger. "If I could but have you at my side to pour my thoughts out to," he wrote to a recent acquaintance and growing love interest, Edith Bolling Galt, "I would thank God and take courage."[100]

America's position among nations was much on Wilson's mind when he spoke to four thousand newly naturalized citizens in Philadelphia the evening of May 10. "This is the only country in the world which experiences this constant and repeated rebirth," he told the new Americans. "It is as if humanity had determined to see to

NORMAN LINDSAY in *Sydney Bulletin*

Can He Remain on the Tight-Rope?
A cartoon published when the submarine crisis became acute last June.

it that this great Nation, founded for the benefit of humanity, should not lack for the allegiance of the people of the world." Cautioning his audience against separating themselves into national groups rather than dedicating themselves to their new country, Wilson obliquely addressed the current world crises. "The example of America must be the example not merely of peace because it will not fight, but of peace because peace is the healing and elevating influence of the world and strife is not. There is such a thing as a man being too proud to fight. There is such a thing as a nation being so right that it does not need to convince others by force that it is right."[101]

This "first intimation" of the course the U.S. government would follow in response to the *Lusitania*'s destruction seemed to indicate, the *New York Times* reported, that "while the United States would remain at peace it would seek to convince Germany of the injustices to all mankind of the tragedy of last Friday." The stock market soared and the majority of Americans, appalled by the sinking but still unwilling to go to war, sighed in relief. The relative few whom the *Lusitania* sinking had converted to advocates of preparedness and of U.S. intervention on the Allied side could only vent their frustration. "Wilson and Bryan are cordially supported by all the hyphenated Americans, by the solid flubdub and pacifist vote . . . [by] every man whose god is money, or pleasure, or ease," Teddy Roosevelt fulminated in a letter to his son Archie. "They are both of them abject creatures, and they won't go to war unless they are kicked into it." Though a critic

of Britain's blockade, Roosevelt had decided that autocratic Germany was a much greater menace—an opinion that could only have been reinforced when American papers published summaries of a British report on German atrocities in Belgium.[102]

Named for James Bryce, head of the investigating commission and a popular former ambassador to the United States, the Bryce Report would prove in later decades to contain exaggerations and fantasy as well as facts (for there were atrocities). But Americans in 1915 believed it was authoritative, and the details circulating in the newspapers did nothing to lighten their darkening view of Germany.[103] In some papers, the Bryce revelations appeared near reports of President Wilson's first "*Lusitania* note" to the Imperial German Government. Formally delivered on

Two Americans devoted to peace, William Jennings Bryan, left, and Henry Ford (1863–1947) meet at the Biltmore Hotel in New York City to discuss a peace initiative Ford will launch in December 1915.

Opposite: Germany's submarine warfare gave a boost to the U.S. preparedness movement. Men who have signed up for the civilian military training program march in a Washington, D.C. preparedness parade. Photograph by Harris & Ewing, 1916.

May 13, the protest cited the attacks on *Falaba*, *Cushing*, *Gulflight*, and *Lusitania* and called on the Germans to disavow those acts and Germany's recent methods of submarine warfare, to "make reparation so far as reparation is possible," and to avoid any similar acts in the future. The note was widely praised in the United States as both diplomatic and forceful. Germany's reply at the end of May, conciliatory about *Cushing* and *Gulflight* but defensive about *Falaba* and *Lusitania*, was widely condemned as "the answer of an outlaw who assumes no obligation toward society."[104]

Cabinet debate on a second *Lusitania* note resulted in a permanent rift between Wilson and his secretary of state over two major issues. Bryan believed that to maintain true neutrality the United States should couple a firm response to Germany regarding its unsatisfactory reply to the first *Lusitania* note with an equally strong protest to Britain regarding its continuing disruption of America's overseas trade. Wilson preferred to deal with Germany first. To avoid further crises caused by American deaths, Bryan pushed for a public government caution against U.S. citizens traveling through the war zones in Allied vessels. The president rejected the measure as "weak and futile." Believing that the administration was placing the country on a trajectory toward war, Bryan resigned on June 8. Robert Lansing, who within two weeks would be named Bryan's successor, sent the second *Lusitania* note to Berlin the following day.[105]

Meanwhile, the *Lusitania* tragedy—coupled with turmoil in the Western Hemisphere, where unrest plagued the Dominican Republic and Haiti as well as Mexico—was giving a boost to the preparedness movement. Immediately after the sinking, a group of young East Coast businessmen petitioned General Leonard Wood to allow them and others to join the summer military training camps he had organized for college students. Within three months, Wood provided the men with their own training camp, at the same site as the recently vacated student camp at Plattsburg, New York, kicking off a nationwide effort that would become known as the Plattsburg Movement. President Wilson and former president Taft both declined Wood's invitation to speak to

the assembled trainees. Former president Roosevelt accepted, getting both himself and Wood into greater hot water with the president when he lambasted the Wilson administration: "To treat elocution as a substitute for action, to rely upon high sounding words unbacked by deeds is proof of a mind that dwells only in the realm of shadow and shame."[106]

Long-established preparedness boosters, such as the Navy League, strengthened their fundraising and lobbying efforts, and the sinking caused a split in the ranks of the National Security League; members favoring harsher criticism of the Wilson administration formed the American Defense Society. Rising concern for preparedness also inspired a major motion picture. Released in September 1915, *The Battle Cry of Peace* depicted unprepared East Coast cities overwhelmed by unnamed but obviously German invaders, an unhappy fate that could have been prevented had Americans been prepared to resist. Even President Wilson took some tentative steps toward preparedness, calling for a strengthened navy in May, praising the student military training camps in June, and in July asking Secretary of the Navy Josephus Daniels and Secretary of War Lindley Garrison to have their staffs develop a plan for an "adequate national defense."[107]

———

Yet peace activists were also on the march. On June 17, some three hundred prominent citizens from across the country who still believed arbitration was a better answer to world crises than military strength met in Philadelphia and formally

A recruitment poster published by the Military Training Camps Association, established in February 1916, likens civilian military trainees to Revolutionary War–era minutemen.

———

Opposite: Washington, D.C., is one of the East Coast cities ravaged by invaders in the 1915 film *The Battle Cry of Peace*, a dramatic argument for preparedness as the best way to preserve peace. The film's co-author and director, J. Stuart Blackton, simultaneously published the story as a book, which includes this illustration.

inaugurated the League to Enforce Peace. Chaired by William Howard Taft, the new organization was devoted to creating "an effective League of Nations designed to establish and to maintain peace." Later in the year, pacifists in New York formed the Anti-Militarism Committee, which in January 1916 changed its name to the Anti-Preparedness Committee and established a lobbying arm in Washington.[108]

Throughout the summer of 1915, tension between the United States and Germany overshadowed Americans' irritation with British blockade policies. Erich Muenter, a German instructor at Cornell University, did little to relieve the situation when he set off a bomb in a U.S. Senate reception room on July 2. There were no casualties from the late-night explosion, but the following day on Long Island, Muenter did manage to shoot J. P. Morgan, wounding him slightly—both acts, Muenter declared before taking his own life, being part of his personal crusade for peace. *U-24*'s June 28 warning to, and subsequent sinking of, the British ship *Armenian* carrying mules destined for service in France, which took the lives of some twenty African American muleteers,

did not cause nearly as much anger as did Germany's unsatisfactory July 8 reply to Wilson's second *Lusitania* note. The tone of Wilson's third *Lusitania* note, with its concluding statement that the United States would regard further action by the German navy that violated neutral rights and affected Americans as "deliberately unfriendly," caused a similar uproar in Germany.[109]

Then, on August 19, *U-24* created a new crisis by sinking the 16,000-ton British liner SS *Arabic* without warning not far from where *U-20* had destroyed the 31,000-ton *Lusitania* three months before. Of the 443 passengers and crew, 44 were killed, including 2 Americans. The incident sparked consternation in both Berlin and Washington. In Germany, where Chancellor Theobold von Bethmann Hollweg had been arguing for months with the navy hierarchy over a submarine-warfare policy he considered too dangerous, a flurry of meetings resulted in the determination that Germany did not yet have enough U-boats to take Britain out of the war before U.S. presence as a combatant could be felt. So the German government gave the United States the "*Arabic* pledge," in which it disavowed the sinking and vowed not to attack liners without warning and without seeing to the safety of their passengers and crew ("provided that the liners do not try to escape or offer resistance"). This apparent abandonment of Germany's unrestricted submarine warfare eased political tensions, inspired celebratory headlines in American papers, and boosted Wilson's stock with the American people.[110]

At the same time, there was a surge of resentment over German subversion within U.S. borders, revealed in newspaper articles that started to appear in mid-August. Early stories were based on papers that a German consular official, Heinrich Albert, had absentmindedly abandoned on a New York City elevated train (and that were quickly snapped up by U.S. agents who had been trailing him). These revealed that Germany was subsidizing American publications and organizations friendly to the Central Powers, German agents had purchased a large munitions plant in Connecticut to prevent its output from going to the Allies, and Germans were fomenting resentment toward the British for their U.S. trade-inhibiting activities. Papers seized by British authorities in London

from James F. Archibald, an American correspondent in German employ, outlined plans for stimulating strikes and labor unrest in munitions and steel factories across the United States. "I am under the impression that we could, if not entirely prevent the production of war materials in Bethlehem [PA] and the Middle West, at any rate strongly disorganize it and hold it up for months," Austria-Hungary's ambassador to the United States, Konstantin Dumba, wrote in one of the more damning documents. (Dumba was subsequently recalled to Vienna, at U.S. insistence.)[111]

The Wilson administration was also aware of the activities of Franz von Rintelen, a German naval officer and secret agent whose April-to-August undercover stay in the United States constituted a

In 1915, as Herbert Hoover's Commission for Relief in Belgium continued to funnel food and clothing into their occupied country, thousands of Belgian schoolchildren and many of their teachers wrote thank-you notes to President Wilson and the American people. Many children expressed their gratitude in art; some letters included photographs. All these letters are preserved in the Library of Congress Manuscript Division.

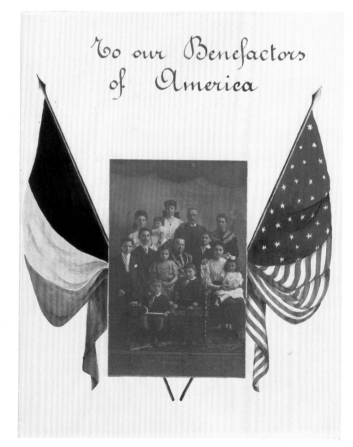

Long a resident in Belgium, British nurse Edith Cavell treated military casualties from both sides in her Brussels hospital after the German occupation—and sometimes helped Allied soldiers escape to neutral Holland. Cavell's execution by a German firing squad on October 12, 1915, incited outrage in Allied and neutral nations and inspired American artist George Bellows (1882–1925) to include *Murder of Edith Cavell* in a series of Great-War-themed lithographs he created in 1918.

veritable symphony of espionage and subversion, including fomenting strikes, developing various types of time bombs to damage docks and ships used to supply war goods to the Allies, and establishing an espionage cell in Baltimore that remained undetected until after the war. Von Rintelen's most elaborate plan, to use the deposed Mexican dictator, Victoriano Huerta, to add to the chaos in Mexico, thereby diverting American attention and resources from Europe, came to nothing. After Huerta rendezvoused with von Rintelen in New York, the two men discussed their plot in a hotel room virtually surrounded by U.S. and Allied agents equipped with listening devices. Closely monitored thereafter, Huerta and a cohort, General Pascual Orozco, were arrested at Newman, New Mexico, before they could cross the Mexican border. Jailed in Texas for actions that violated U.S. neutrality, they became a new source of tension with Mexico—especially after Orozco escaped and was killed by an American posse, which had apparently mistaken him for a bandit.[112]

"Germany desires to keep up the turmoil in Mexico until the United States is forced to intervene; *therefore we must not intervene*," Robert Lansing wrote in his diary as this episode was unfolding. "Germany does not wish to have any one faction dominant in Mexico; *therefore, we must recognize one faction as dominant in Mexico*." As much to bring some order out of chaos as to defeat German plans, in October Wilson turned away from the failing Pancho Villa, whom he had once favored, and extended formal U.S. recognition to Venustiano Carranza, who seemed to be in the strongest position to bring order to the troubled country.[113]

In October, too, the Wilson administration balanced U.S. protests to Germany by sending a forceful note to the British government protesting blockade methods that the message termed "ineffective, illegal, and indefensible." The United States, which could not "submit to the curtailment of its neutral rights by these measures," would thenceforth champion "the integrity of neutral rights" not just for itself but for all neutral nations. "The American note causes us little concern," London's *Spectator* responded editorially in mid-November. "Its harsh and unsympathetic tone will not make us relax in the slightest degree the grip on the throat of Germany which sea power gives us." In his diary, the British ambassador in Paris was less diplomatic, dubbing the note the product of "a rotten lot of psalm-singing, profit-mongering humbugs."[114]

In December, the SS *Oscar II*, a liner hired by one of America's most prominent capitalists, Henry Ford, departed from New York City for Europe. Carrying peace activists possessing varying degrees of common sense, plagued by disorganization, and surrounded by ridicule, the ship proceeded through U-boat-infested waters on an admirable, if futile, mission: to get the boys out of the trenches by Christmas. "We come in this time of trouble not to add to your burdens but to help lift them," Ford wired the rulers of the belligerent nations as *Oscar* neared its destination, "not to consider which nations are most to blame for the disaster that has befallen Europe, but to end the strife . . . Has not war been tried long enough?"[115]

While *Oscar II* was mid-ocean, President Wilson delivered his Third Annual Message to Congress. With belligerent interference in U.S. affairs in mind, he spoke of "citizens of the United States . . . born under other flags but welcomed under our generous naturalization laws . . . who have poured the poison of disloyalty into the very arteries of our national life," and he asked Congress to enact laws to crush out "such creatures of passion, disloyalty, and anarchy." Leader of a country surrounded by war and suffering from ongoing turmoil within, he spoke of Americans' passion for peace—and advanced a plan for expanding the county's armed forces.[116]

CHAPTER 2

JANUARY 1916 – JANUARY 1917

"HE KEPT US OUT OF WAR"

The world is on fire and there is tinder everywhere.
—President Woodrow Wilson,
Preparedness speech, Cleveland, Ohio, January 29, 1916

W ar, for Europe, is meaning devastation and death; for America a bumper crop of new millionaires and a hectic hastening of prosperity revival," business statistician J. George Frederick effervesced in the January 1916 issue of the *American Review of Reviews*. "It is as though an energetic doctor had pumped oxygen or a salt solution into a limp patient and turned him into a jumping jack." In a brisk survey of the nation's businesses, from gunpowder and barbed-wire production to car manufacturing and the horse-and-mule trade, Frederick celebrated the reinvigoration of the American economy with the near-gleeful tone of one safely removed from the catastrophic root cause of the nation's growing prosperity. In the year since J. P. Morgan & Company had begun acting as the official purchasing agent for the British, and the eight months since it commenced the same

service for the French, its export division had crafted myriad contracts for American goods on behalf of those governments. Russia had also become a stellar American customer, ordering millions of pounds of ammunition and thousands of railroad cars, so vital for the movement of troops and equipment. As the pace of war orders increased, Allied technical experts arrived in the United States to advise American manufacturers on production methods, the design of new factories, and security arrangements for the shipment of finished products.[1]

Still, economic relations were not all sunshine and roses. Resentments grew as the Allies tightened their blockade of the Central Powers, adding to the list of contraband goods and further inhibiting American trade with other neutral countries through which supplies might reach Germany. Insult was added to injury when, in December 1915, the British began searching mailbags being shipped between the United States and neutral ports and confiscating first-class mail and parcel-post packages containing contraband. That same month, Parliament passed Britain's Trading with the Enemy Act, which, among other provisions, authorized proclamations banning trade with organizations or individuals in neutral countries believed to be providing aid to the enemy—legislation that, as Secretary of State Lansing protested on January 25, was "pregnant with possibilities of undue interference with American trade." The American mood was not brightened by intermittent news of Allied ships stopping American vessels to remove German and Austrian passengers. "The situation here, so far as politics are concerned, has not improved in favor of the Allies," Britain's ambassador to the United States, Cecil Spring-Rice, wrote Foreign Minister Edward Grey in mid-January 1916. "Congress was opened in stormy meetings in which violent attacks were made upon our commercial policy." Yet American ire posed little danger of provoking a true rift with Britain and France, since Allied trade was increasing American prosperity. Throughout 1916, war-related orders, chiefly from the Allies, would almost double the value of American agricultural and industrial exports from 1915's total of nearly $3 billion to $5.7 billion.[2]

A move into markets, particularly in South America and Asia, previously monopolized by firms in belligerent nations was another factor in this American boom, despite the continuing challenges imposed by a dearth of American cargo ships. In January 1916 President Wilson

and Secretary McAdoo tried once again to remedy that problem, persuading Congressman Joshua Alexander to introduce new legislation that would establish a government-supported and -regulated U.S. merchant fleet, an idea they had first floated in 1914. As another months-long legislative tussle ensued between those still opposed to government interference in the private sector and those who had begun to see the creation of such a fleet in the positive light of "commercial preparedness," a few leading American banks established foreign branches, and some of the nation's most influential commercial leaders combined forces to exploit opportunities opened to them by the war. "One of the signs that point unmistakably to the sure grasp and firm faith which American businessmen now have regarding the future of business, after the war clouds clear off," George Frederick wrote, "is the formation of the American International Corporation (AIC), capitalized at $50,000,000 to finance and conduct large constructive industrial and commercial enterprises in foreign lands." Formed late in 1915, the AIC was an expression of its members' ambition, as declared by the banker Frank Vanderlip, to make the United States "the wellspring of capital for the world." In March 1916, AIC vice-president Willard Straight, a former officer of J. P. Morgan & Company with significant overseas business and consular experience, went to Europe to discuss possibilities with Allied bankers and political leaders, including plans for heavy American investment in postwar reconstruction of the devastated areas of Belgium and France.[3]

Postwar reconstruction and economic recovery were growing concerns of Europe's political leaders, optimists on each side believing, despite ample evidence to the contrary, that 1916 would finally bring victory and a favorable peace. In firm control of the surface of the world's seas, their naval blockade of the Central Powers increasingly effective, the Allies had deprived Germany of nearly all its colonial holdings and, despite their bitter loss at Gallipoli, as of January 1916 had stymied the Ottoman Turks in the Russian Caucasus and British Egypt and penetrated the Turks' Arab possessions in Mesopotamia. On the major fronts, however, the Allies themselves had been stymied. In the East, Russia's huge army had suffered major defeats at Tannenberg in 1914 and Gorlice-Tarnow in 1915 and, despite intermittent successes, had been forced to surrender territory to their German and Austrian opponents, while gaining yet another enemy when Bulgaria joined the Central Powers in October 1915. On the Western Front, Allied leaders had repeatedly hurled their armies across No Man's Land and against defenses the Germans were continually strengthening, expending huge amounts of blood and ordnance yet failing to achieve any lasting breakthrough.[4]

By December 1915 the combined casualties of all the warring armies numbered in the millions. Because trench warfare favored defenders over attackers and German generals had been more carefully husbanding their troops, Allied losses were significantly greater. Yet the Allies had more manpower resources than the Central Powers. New conscripts from the czar's massive empire filled the gaping holes in the Russian forces, which still proved full of fight; 1.5 million Italian troops had joined the Allied ranks; colonial

troops added to the strength of French forces; troops from Britain's globe-spanning empire were constantly mustering in; and Britain itself more than compensated, in numbers at least, for the awful losses its comparatively small regular army had suffered by pouring Territorial (reserve) troops and new volunteer units onto the Continent, to be followed by draftee units raised after the country broke with tradition and initiated conscription in March 1916.[5]

With their more limited manpower and painfully constricted access to imports, the clock was ticking for the Central Powers, a fact that, in late 1915, led German Chief of Staff Erich von Falkenhayn to reverse his previous opposition to unrestricted U-boat warfare. This added heat to the continuing debate among Germany's military and political leaders as to how best to use this increasingly important naval weapon and whether it remained crucial to employ U-boats in a manner that would keep Germany in the relatively good graces of the United States, whose farms and factories were supplying the enemy. Falkenhayn also convinced the kaiser to back a new offensive, to start in February, aimed at eviscerating the battle-worn French forces on the Western Front. Telling his supreme commander that "France has arrived almost at the end of her military effort," Falkenhayn planned to attack a vital point, the fortifications around the city of Verdun, which would compel the French "to throw in every man they have. If they do so," he declared, "the forces of France will bleed to death," and the British, deprived of their most valuable ally, would also be broken. Across No Man's Land, meanwhile, Allied leaders made plans to break the Central Powers by launching coordinated attacks in the three major theaters of war—Western, Eastern, and Italian—so that the enemy could not transfer forces from one theater to help meet an emergency in another. French commander in chief Joseph Joffre prevailed in a disagreement with the new British commander, Douglas Haig, over whether to launch the Western Front attack in Belgium, as Haig preferred, or north of Paris, near the river Somme. The Somme Offensive, in concert with attacks in the other theaters, was to begin in the summer. In their strategy sessions, leaders of both sides failed to heed a rule of military conflict succinctly expressed decades later by British historian John Keegan when he wrote, of 1916, "Plans made without allowance for the intentions of the enemy are liable to miscarry."[6]

In January, as Falkenhayn surreptitiously mustered forces to surprise the French at Verdun, the eccentric American peace offensive financed by Henry Ford and launched in early December 1915 continued. Ill and possibly irked by factional disputes among the 163 peace advocates

Chef des Generalstabes des Feldheeres.

who had traveled with him to Europe, Ford himself returned to the United States in early January and announced a change in his assessment of who was to blame for the European cataclysm. "Before going to Europe I had the view that the bankers, militarists, and munition manufacturers were responsible," Ford told reporters. "I come back with the firm belief that the people most to blame are the ones who are getting slaughtered. They have neglected to select the proper heads for their Governments." Moreover, he averred, they had become so afraid of the leaders they had chosen that they failed to write "and let them know their views." His peace expedition, he said, "got the people thinking"—and it was continuing with his support, if not his actual presence. The peace advocates he had left behind traveled to Norway, Sweden, Denmark, Switzerland, and, finally, to The Hague. At every stop they spent

The Evening Sun 4. 12. 1915

"300 Wise Men at Sea in a Bowl—"

Ford's money on programs and lavish dinners to win local support, while countering criticism of their mission from politicians, the press, and unsympathetic American diplomats. By the time they returned home toward the end of January, they had achieved their primary objective. Peace advocates in the neutral countries they visited, as well as in the United States, had selected delegates to a Neutral Conference for Continuous Mediation, which aimed to draw the belligerents into arbitrated discussions that would eventually result in peace. Its first formal meeting occurred in Stockholm on February 10, eleven days before a nine-hour storm of German artillery shells opened Falkenhayn's vaunted offensive, shattering trees into tinder, battering fortifications, and shaking the souls of the Frenchmen protecting Verdun.[7]

"I am against preparedness of any kind," Ford had declared when he returned from Europe. "If [the American people] want to arm, they know what they will get—what Europeans are getting now." Since President Wilson's December 1915 Third Annual Message to Congress, in which he called for a modest increase in U.S. armed forces, alarm had been growing among Americans who were opposed to what they viewed as the nation's slow drift toward militarism and involvement in the European war. "Our war contagion is like the case of a man living in Kansas," Woman's Peace Party president Jane Addams said in testimony before the House Committee on Military Affairs on January 13, "who, hearing that there were a great many burglaries in New York City, immediately armed himself against burglars, although

there were none in Kansas." Her testimony suffered from unfortunate timing. While European armies, fully involved in trying to annihilate each other, might pose little immediate threat to the United States, violence continued to fester in Mexico, where forces loyal to Pancho Villa had just outraged Americans by committing what came to be known as the "massacre at Santa Ysabel."[8]

Stung by the Wilson administration's recognition of the government of Venustiano Carranza in October 1915, Villa was further incensed when he learned that American logistical support had helped Carranza defeat his army at Agua Prieta in November, one of several damaging defeats Villa's forces suffered that month. Now regarded on both sides of the border as a bandit, his once-proud army reduced to the level of a guerrilla band,

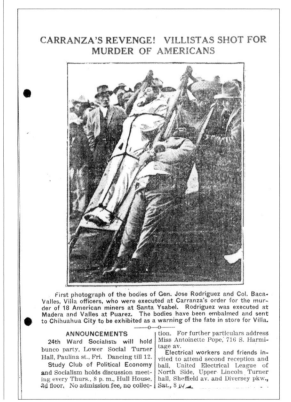

CARRANZA'S REVENGE! VILLISTAS SHOT FOR MURDER OF AMERICANS

First photograph of the bodies of Gen. Jose Rodriguez and Col. Baca-Valles, Villa officers, who were executed at Carranza's order for the murder of 18 American miners at Santa Ysabel. Rodriguez was executed at Madera and Valles at Puarez. The bodies have been embalmed and sent to Chihuahua City to be exhibited as a warning of the fate in store for Villa.

——o—o——

ANNOUNCEMENTS

24th Ward Socialists will hold bunco party, Lower Social Turner Hall, Paulina st., Fri. Dancing till 12. Study Club of Political Economy and Socialism holds discussion meeting every Thurs., 8 p. m., Hull House, 3d floor. No admission fee, no collec-

tion. For further particulars address Miss Antoinette Pope, 716 S. Harmitage av.

Electrical workers and friends invited to attend second reception and ball, United Electrical League of North Side, Upper Lincoln Turner hall, Sheffield av. and Diversey pkw., Sat., 8 p/

On January 27, 1916, *The Day Book* (Chicago) published a photograph of the bodies of two recently executed Villa officers, graphic proof that the Carranza government was bent on punishing those who murdered the Americans at Santa Ysabel.

Villa plotted revenge, although he and his troops had melted so effectively into the hills that General Álvaro Obregón, a Carranza loyalist, declared the Mexican states of Sonora and Chihuahua "pacified." Thus reassured, the American owners of the Cusi Mining Company in Chihuahua sent Mexican workers and seventeen American mining engineers into Chihuahua to resume operations. On January 10, 1916, a band of Villistas stopped the miners' train, robbed the Mexicans, then methodically murdered the Americans, stripping and mutilating some of their bodies. One American, Thomas Holmes, survived to stumble, mauled and shaken, into Chihuahua City hours later.[9]

A furor almost as great as that following the *Lusitania* sinking briefly convulsed the American public. In Washington, Senator James Hamilton Lewis of Illinois and Representative Hunter Moss Jr., of West Virginia introduced resolutions calling for armed intervention, while Idaho's Senator William E. Borah blasted the "compromising, side-stepping, procrastinating, apologizing and un-American policy of leaving the American citizen to struggle for himself against the bandits of an adjoining country." Theodore Roosevelt joined in condemning Wilson's Mexican policies and predicted, "If we do not do our duty in Mexico, one or all of" the nations currently warring in Europe would turn westward once the war was over and "seize Mexico themselves."[10] The most rabid reaction to the murders occurred in the border city of El Paso, Texas, where the bodies of the murdered Americans arrived on January 13, and some Anglo citizens threatened cross-border vigilante action. In the evening, tensions between Anglos and El Paso's Mexican inhabitants, which had increased with each turn in the Mexican Revolution, exploded into violence. Mobs of armed Anglos hunted Mexicans; Mexicans armed themselves to fight back. Calm was only restored when General John J. ("Black Jack") Pershing, commander at nearby Fort Bliss, sent the Sixteenth Infantry into the city, which he placed under martial law.[11] Calm also settled over the country at large as the Wilson administration coolly addressed the crisis, pacific Americans contemplated the possible repercussions of an invasion of Mexico, Carranza speedily responded to American demands for action, and Villa himself disappeared into the hills once again—followed by rumors that he intended to go to Washington to deny responsibility for the murders.[12]

The Santa Ysabel massacre confronted President Wilson less than two weeks after he and his new bride, Edith Bolling Galt Wilson, returned from their honeymoon in Hot Springs, Virginia. "Edith reveals new charms and still deeper loveliness to me every day," Wilson had written to friends midway through the wedding trip, "and I shall go back to Washington feeling complete and strong for whatever may betide." Much of great moment betided. As the Mexican crisis ebbed, Wilson was able to turn closer attention to three complex diplomatic campaigns aimed at the European belligerents, one of them cloaked in pretense. On January 5, the president's friend and confidant Edward House arrived in England, the central destination

in a journey that would also take him to Paris and Berlin. "His mission is unofficial, of course, and is announced to be for the purpose of conferring with the different American Ambassadors," a U.S. embassy staffer in Paris, John Gardner Coolidge, wrote in his diary. "Probably the President has sent him over to see whether this is not an opportune moment for the United States to proclaim peace to the world." A Boston Republican and experienced diplomat, Coolidge undoubtedly knew that a United States proclamation of peace would be futile. Both House and Wilson had come to believe, however, that the time was ripe to invite both sides to a peace conference chaired by Wilson as leader of the most powerful neutral nation and the world's most enlightened democracy.[13]

During two months of quiet diplomacy with leaders of both warring alliances, House displayed to Allied leaders his distinct leaning toward their cause,

something revealed in what has become known as the "House-Grey Memorandum," initialed by Britain's Foreign Secretary, Edward Grey, on February 22. Distilling what Grey had understood from his conversations with House, the three-paragraph memorandum stated, in part, that "President Wilson was ready, on hearing from France and England that the moment was opportune, to propose that a Conference should be summoned"; that "should the Allies accept this proposal, and should Germany refuse it, the United States would probably enter the war against Germany"; that if the conference did occur, Colonel House believed "it would secure peace on terms not unfavorable to the Allies; and if it failed to secure peace, the United States would [probably] leave the Conference as a belligerent on the side of the Allies." (The word "probably" was later inserted, without brackets, at President Wilson's insistence.) The president subsequently supported the memo without consulting either his cabinet or Congress.[14]

———————————

Both Wilson and House initially believed the memorandum portended more progress toward a peace conference than it actually did. Neither the Allies nor the Central Powers were eager to make peace when it still seemed possible to achieve a military victory. One telling indication of that attitude was the February 1916 Declaration of Sainte-Adresse, in which Britain, France, and Russia pledged to go on fighting until Belgium was restored to its prewar status and had been indemnified for war damages. Most political factions in Germany, meanwhile, continued to adhere to a 1915 declaration that negated any peace settlement that did not guarantee "Germany's military, economic, financial, and political

interests . . . to their full extent and by all means, including the necessary territorial acquisitions." Governments on both sides were also well aware that public sentiment, influenced by propaganda, ever-lengthening casualty lists, and home-front sacrifices, increasingly favored pushing on to defeat the enemy. Pressure was building in Germany for wholly unrestricted submarine warfare, despite the danger that the action would incite the United States and perhaps other neutrals to declare war. Pressure was building in Britain to further tighten the naval blockade, no matter how much outrage that might cause among neutrals, even America, vital supplier of funds and equipment. Moreover, while the Allies were ever more dependent on American resources, they were often uncertain of the judgment and intentions of the American president. At the same time House was touting the peace conference in Europe as beneficial to the Allies, Wilson

and Lansing were engaged in separate negotiations with Germany, some of which seemed almost calculated to harm the Allied cause.[15]

The crisis over the 1915 *Lusitania* sinking—which had once seemed to threaten the outbreak of war between the United States and Germany—had by the end of February drifted into diplomatic limbo, Berlin expressing regret but still not admitting, as Washington wished, that sinking the ship without warning and without removing its passengers had been illegal. In part, this stalemate resulted from the Wilson administration's unwillingness to push the matter to a breaking point. As Secretary Lansing wrote in a private memorandum in January, "We are not yet ready to meet the submarine issue squarely. Our people are not aroused to a sufficient pitch of indignation at the barbarism of the Germans." His tepid mid-February announcement that "any settlement of the Lusitania case must depend on how German submarine warfare will be conducted in the future" was generally regarded as prudent by war-averse Americans, but there were some dissenters. "The Lusitania affair seems to have blown over, the President to have backed down," John Gardner Coolidge grumbled to his diary in Paris, "with the result that again Germany has been able to slap us in the face."[16]

"The whole question of submarine warfare is again under consideration by our government," Lansing declared in his *Lusitania* statement, an assertion verified by a proposal the Americans had just made to the belligerent nations. Allied merchant vessels equipped with guns had begun appearing in American ports. Arming merchantmen had been a common practice in previous wars when navies fought only on the surface of the seas. In this new age of submarine warfare, however, it seemed to Lansing that the practice invited further *Lusitania*-like tragedies, which might plunge the United States into war with Germany before the American people were psychologically prepared. "If some merchant vessels carry arms and others do not," he wrote President Wilson, "how can a submarine determine this fact without exposing itself to great risk of being sunk?" And didn't that provide a "strong reason" why submarines, slow and vulnerable on the surface, should strike without prior warning? Thus Lansing, with Wilson's approval, asked both sides to agree to a new modus vivendi: "Submarines should be caused to adhere strictly to the rules of international law in the matter of stopping and searching merchant vessels, determining their belligerent nationality, and removing the crews and passengers to places of safety before sinking the vessels as prizes of war and . . . merchant vessels of belligerent nationality should be prohibited and prevented from carrying any armament whatsoever."[17]

As the president and Lansing went on to suggest that the United States might treat offensively armed merchantmen as warships, excluding them from American ports, and debated how to judge whether a commercial vessel's artillery should be considered offensive or defensive, they were overtaken, and taken aback, by the political and diplomatic furor provoked by the modus vivendi proposal. At home,

German naval artist Willy Stöwer (1864–1931) created the original painting reproduced in this 1916 print of a U-boat destroying an armed British trawler. Problems presented by arming merchant ships in the new age of submarine warfare vexed the Wilson administration in 1916.

Massachusetts Republican senator Henry Cabot Lodge and his colleague from North Dakota, Thomas Sterling, were prominent among the pro-Allied critics who castigated the suggestion as a violation of international law and a surrender to Germany. German authorities, unwilling to be restricted to the rules of surface warfare, mustered evidence they said proved that the Allies had directed all armed merchantmen to fire on U-boats, and announced on February 11 that German submariners would thereafter regard armed merchant vessels as warships to be attacked without warning. From London, a deeply concerned Edward House, still trying to arrange a peace conference and unnerved by British consternation at the American proposal, begged the president not to take any further action on the matter until they talked. Britain's foreign secretary Edward

Grey, meanwhile, deemed it "incredible" that "the United States Government would propose to justify and legalize wholesale sinking of merchant vessels by German submarines and to deprive British vessels of the chance of defense which the United States Government have hitherto recognized as legitimate." The modus vivendi proposal, he declared to the British cabinet, was "an attempt to readjust the balance of sea power in favor of our enemies" and was "if not unfriendly, at least unneutral."[18]

The modus vivendi idea quickly sank in this storm of protests—but it did not go down without giving a fresh boost to the U.S. congressional debate over whether Americans should be officially warned against traveling on vessels of belligerent nations. Former secretary of state William Jennings Bryan, long an advocate of such a

Leslie's
Illustrated Weekly Newspaper
Established in 1855

JULY 6th 1916

Price 10 Cents

WHAT ARE YOU DOING FOR PREPAREDNESS?

warning, rushed to Washington to support congressional resolutions to that effect introduced in the House by a Texas Democrat, Atkins Jefferson ("Jeff") McLemore, and in the Senate by Oklahoma's Thomas P. Gore. In a letter to Teddy Roosevelt, journalist and preparedness advocate John Callan O'Laughlin, who had helped organized the 1914 Christmas ship Americans sent to Europe, called those who favored such legislation "sneaking cowards [who] were willing to surrender any right in the belief that it would preserve peace. The democratic party is split up as a result of this situation," O'Laughlin observed, "and a great deal of feeling has been aroused against the President." Yet it was a presidential election year, and, whatever their differences, Democrats were eager to retain the White House. This undoubtedly contributed to the president's success in preventing passage of the two resolutions and related precautionary measures—in the process both reaffirming his political leadership and defending a principle he expressed in a widely publicized letter to Democratic senator William J. Stone of Missouri, a principle with which O'Laughlin and Roosevelt almost certainly would have agreed. "To forbid our people to exercise their rights for fear we might be called upon to vindicate them would be a deep humiliation . . . [and] a deliberate abdication of our hitherto proud position as spokesmen, even amidst the turmoil of war, for the law and the right."[19]

As that crisis abated, Wilson continued urging Congress to pass a law that would suitably strengthen and reorganize the U.S. armed forces, while energetically seeking greater support for such measures from the American public. During January and February, he made quick trips away from Washington, the Santa Ysabel crisis, and the delicate negotiations with the European belligerents to make pro-preparedness speeches before huge crowds in Pittsburgh, Cleveland, Milwaukee, Chicago, Des Moines, Topeka, Kansas City, and St. Louis. Each speech more deeply alarmed members of the Anti-Preparedness League and others opposed to what they saw as the country's drift toward militarism.[20]

"I am bound to tell you that the danger is constant and immediate," Wilson told an audience in St. Louis. "One reckless commander of a submarine, choosing to put his private interpretation upon what his government wishes him to do, might set the world on fire." As for the anti-preparedness spokesmen: They were "hopelessly and contentedly provincial." He suggested that the sensible people of St. Louis "listen to them with indulgence, and then absolutely ignore them," and he challenged anti-preparedness advocates to hire halls around the country so that their "folly" might be exposed for all to hear.[21]

Accepting that challenge, the

Anti-Preparedness League changed its name to the American Union Against Militarism (AUAM), its members then arguing their case before large audiences in New York, Buffalo, Cleveland, Detroit, Chicago, Minneapolis, Des Moines, Cincinnati, Pittsburgh, and Detroit. "Extraordinary and unprecedented measures have been taken to promote a public demand for military and naval expansion," social reformer and AUAM chairman Lillian Wald told those assembled in New York, "and these have brought in their train hysteria and the camp-followers of self-interest. But the serious cost to the nation . . . is the cost to democracy in this sinister reversion to the war system which Europe herself is, as we hope, on the verge of repudiating."[22]

"You have laid upon me the double obligation of maintaining the honor of the United States and of maintaining the peace of the United States," Wilson told an audience in Chicago. "Is it not conceivable that the two might become incompatible?" "New circumstances have arisen," he declared in Pittsburgh, "which make it absolutely necessary that this country should prepare . . . for adequate national defense."[23]

"We are not preparing to defend our country," pacifist Helen Keller announced to a crowd at a January event sponsored by the Women's Peace Party and the Labor Forum in New York's Carnegie Hall. "We have no enemies foolhardy enough to attempt to invade the United States." She called on the assembled working people to "strike against manufacturing shrapnel and gas bombs . . . Strike against preparedness that means death and misery to millions of human beings. Our flourishing industry in implements of murder is filling the vaults of New York's banks with gold."[24]

"It is being . . . spread abroad in this

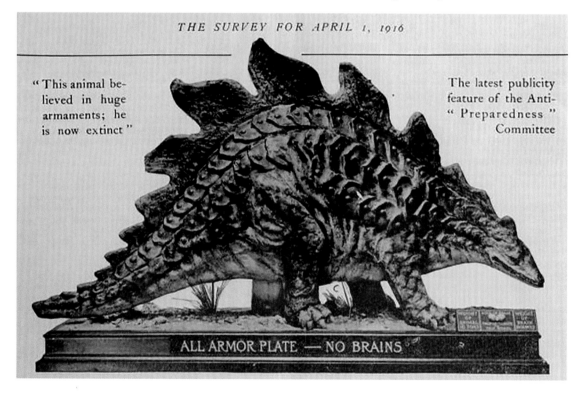

THE SURVEY FOR APRIL 1, 1916

"This animal believed in huge armaments; he is now extinct"

The latest publicity feature of the Anti-"Preparedness" Committee

ALL ARMOR PLATE — NO BRAINS

In April 1916, *The Survey* magazine published this small image of "Jingo," a large papier-mâché Stegosaurus that accompanied American Union Against Militarism speakers around the country.

country that the impulse back of all this is the desire of men who make the materials of warfare to get money out of the Treasury of the United States," Wilson retorted in Milwaukee. "Let no one suppose that this is a money-making agitation . . . All the rest of the world is on fire, and our own house is not fireproof."[25]

To start fireproofing the American house Wilson favored a gradual buildup of ships and men that, by 1921, would provide the country with "a navy fitted to our needs and worthy of our traditions." As Congress considered this prospect, Assistant Secretary of the Navy Franklin D. Roosevelt was advocating an additional component for the modest naval reserve funded by the Naval Appropriations Act that had passed in March 1915. With the Plattsburg Movement army civilian training camps as a model, Roosevelt proposed providing naval training to civilian volunteers already familiar with ships, engines, and radios, as well as organizing a fleet of private vessels that could be activated, when necessary, as auxiliary patrol boats. He then set out to recruit volunteers, a successful endeavor that resulted, in August 1916, in the launch of the navy's first civilian training program. This four-week "John Paul Jones Cruise," as Secretary of the Navy Josephus Daniels called it, saw 1,928 volunteers between the ages of nineteen and forty-five embark from ports along the Atlantic and Pacific coasts aboard eleven elderly warships, each volunteer having paid a $30 fee for the privilege.[26]

While the navy's civilian training program would never match the army's, the navy did take the lead in acquiring civilian technical assistance. Daniels had reportedly read with great interest a lengthy interview that revered inventor Thomas A. Edison gave to the *New York Times* a few weeks after the *Lusitania* sinking. "If any foreign power should seriously consider an attack upon this country a hundred men of special training quickly would be at work here upon new means of repelling the invaders," Edison said. "I would be at it myself." Furthermore, he declared, "the Government should maintain a great research laboratory, jointly under military and naval and civilian control . . . [to] keep abreast with every advanced thought in armament, in sanitation, in transportation, in communication." Within a few months, Daniels succeeded in establishing an unofficial advisory body, the Naval Consulting Board, headed by Edison and including a stellar roster of inventors and engineers. Supported at first entirely by private funds, the new board was initially regarded with skepticism by some in the naval hierarchy, including Assistant Secretary Roosevelt. Yet it set to work immediately and enthusiastically on a task Edison had also suggested in the interview: organizing an elaborate nationwide network of experts that in 1916 launched a five-month survey of all manufacturing facilities in the country capable of producing, or being converted to produce, the materials of war. "The war in Europe has taught us," Daniels wrote to state survey directors, "that industrial preparedness is the foundation rock of the national defense."[27]

Expansion of the navy, while fiercely debated, enjoyed smooth sailing compared with the proposed expansion of the nation's

land forces. In his request for an increase of the regular army to roughly 280,000 men, augmented when necessary to 500,000 by a regular reserve made up of army veterans, President Wilson was following recommendations included in a fall 1915 report published by the army's War College Division.[28] That proposal, which by itself excited concern among pacifistic Americans, was accompanied by another Wilson-backed War Department recommendation that was almost universally condemned. The small, ill-equipped, state-controlled National Guard—a force supported by many civilians but disparaged by army regulars as disorganized, ill-trained, and untrustworthy—was to be replaced with a new, federally controlled 400,000-man volunteer reserve to be called the Continental Army. Secretary of War Lindley Garrison was so firmly behind creation of

this new, more centralized volunteer reserve and demotion of the National Guard to a sort of auxiliary home-front police force that he informed Wilson he would resign if the president bowed to the Continental Army's many opponents. The president was so firmly determined to get adequate support for improving the army

that he told Virginia representative James Hay, chairman of the House Committee on Military Affairs he was not "irrevocably or dogmatically committed to any one plan of providing the nation with . . . a [military] reserve."[29]

Previously unconvinced that military improvements were necessary for a nation that was, he declared in January 1915, "safe in our vastness," Hay had grown more amenable to "practicable" military legislation as citizen support for preparedness strengthened and the European war and the Mexican Revolution grew more threatening to the country. Early in 1916 he seized the initiative, not only advising Wilson on what would be workable but also helping to formulate and guide through Congress a bill that would be palatable to the required number of members—a task that involved sailing gingerly between a Scylla and Charybdis of objections. Wisconsin's

insurgent Republican senator, Robert La Follette, who had developed a wary respect for Democrat Woodrow Wilson, spoke for anti-militarist progressives of both major parties when he worried aloud that the move to enlarge the armed forces meant the country would soon have "a permanent military system, a permanent market for war traders." Conservative Republican preparedness booster Henry Cabot Lodge, who had no respect whatsoever for the Wilson administration, excoriated the president's preparedness plan as "partly shams and wholly inadequate." Yet it was the Hay-Wilson plan that was incorporated in the June 1916 National Defense Act, a legislative turning point that increased the strength of the regular army to 175,000, created a Reserve Officer Training Corps (ROTC) program for college students, and provided for a volunteer army to be raised only in time of war. The act also enlarged

the National Guard to 475,000 men, now to be equipped, trained, and paid while in training by the federal government. Further, it authorized the president to federalize the guard for the duration of a war or other national emergency and, in a departure from past policy, to deploy the guard overseas.[30]

In another move toward preparedness, the army appropriations bill passed in late August supported creation of the Council of National Defense, comprising the secretaries of war, navy, agriculture, commerce, labor, and the interior. A Civilian Advisory Commission, undoubtedly inspired by the Naval Consulting Board and including some of its members, was set up to assist the council. Comprising men prominent in transportation, business, finance, labor, and medicine, the advisory commission, President Wilson said, "marks the entrance of the non-partisan engineer and professional man into American governmental affairs on a wider scale than ever before."[31]

Meanwhile, as it became obvious that the National Defense Act would not include the proposed Continental Army he so passionately favored, Secretary of War Garrison resigned. In early March, Wilson chose as Garrison's replacement a former mayor of Cleveland, Newton D. Baker, who in his years of public service had forged a reputation as a "reliable radical and a prudent progressive." Given the state of world and hemispheric affairs, this seemed an odd choice to those who were aware of Baker's pronounced pacifist bent. Yet Baker saw his new role as much greater than marshaling and deploying troops. "I think the War Department has, as its primary ideal, making America a strong and virile people," the new secretary wrote to an editor of the *Survey* magazine. "The accidental use of a part of that strength for war, when it is unavoidable, is an important aspect . . . but the primary thing is that we should be strong for the arts of peace, strong industrially, socially and morally."[32]

Baker arrived on the scene in the midst of another heated legislative debate, this one over how best to meet the considerable expenses involved in developing and maintaining strengthened armed forces without going into debt. ("The industry of this generation," President Wilson insisted, "should pay the bills of this generation.") Tariff revenues were not adequate to cover the cost. The emergency War Revenue Act passed in fall 1914, which chiefly mandated new or increased taxes on goods and services, had been renewed, but only until December 1916. Income tax, made possible by the Sixteenth Amendment to the Constitution, ratified in 1913, had as yet had little impact: it applied to only about 400,000 (out of 100.5 million) Americans and had accounted for only 17 percent of federal tax revenues the previous year. Yet income tax began to emerge as a key to the pay-as-you-go military expansion—and as a measure for dealing with a pressing social problem.[33]

To reform-minded progressives, a more widespread, graduated income tax system seemed a perfect instrument to help close the gaping divide between the 10 percent of Americans who owned 90 percent of

Surprising some, President Wilson chose the pacifistic progressive Newton Diehl Baker (1871–1937) to be secretary of war after Lindley Garrison resigned. Photograph by Harris & Ewing, 1917.

the country's wealth and the remaining 90 million citizens. "Let the millionaires and multi-millionaires whose incomes are beyond the dreams of Croesus chip in half of their annual incomes for this protection they are demanding against an imaginary enemy," thundered Nebraska Democrat Dan V. Stephens. Majority Leader Claude Kitchin, who was no friend of military expansion but was resigned to it, privately agreed with Stephens.[34] The Ways and Means Committee, which Kitchin chaired, assigned the task of drafting what would become the Revenue Act of 1916 to a Tennessee Democrat, Cordell Hull, and that initial draft launched months of debate, emendations, and negotiations among factions within and outside of Congress. No party to the negotiations was perfectly happy with the bill President Wilson signed into law on September 9, which, among its many provisions, included a special tax on munitions. Although it extended the reach of the income tax, thus transforming it into the largest single source of U.S. tax revenues, few at the time realized that it marked a turning point in American fiscal history, providing, among other things, a resource for expanding the federal government. Wilson backers touted the Revenue Act as a reform measure during the fall presidential campaign, millionaire Henry Ford praising both the legislation and the Wilson administration for "compelling the wealthy to bear a fair share of the load which has hitherto rested all too heavily on the backs of the poor."[35]

Representatives of American workers, some of whom sent Congress suggestions regarding the use of income taxation as the Revenue Act took shape, would almost certainly have agreed with Ford. Compelling wealthy owners who controlled the nation's large businesses to ease the burdens on their workers remained a common theme in the labor unrest that continued to ripple through the country in 1916. Strikes by Arizona copper miners and New York City garment workers were remarkable for peaceful resolutions that won some gains for the laborers; but an equally peaceful five-month strike by New York City transit workers aggrieved by fifteen-hour work days and arbitrary firing yielded the workers nothing. Other labor-management struggles were far from

Opposite: In this 1916 cartoon, Robert W. Satterfield (1875–1958) reflected the effort, renewed during the Revenue Act of 1916 debates, to make income tax an instrument for correcting the country's massive income inequality. The seal at upper right shows that an agent of the German government clipped the cartoon from an unidentified newspaper.

Right: Well-dressed and decorous cloak makers participate in the peaceful New York garment workers strike. Other labor protests in 1916 met violent resistance.

peaceful. A strike for an eight-hour work-day that began among electrical workers in East Pittsburgh spread to other local industries before it was broken by a surge of violence, mainly perpetrated by company men armed with clubs and rifles, that killed several workers. From May to November, lumber workers based near Everett, Washington, staged a series of protests against low wages. Their efforts were crushed by company-organized vigilante groups and local police, who forced some of the protesters to run a gauntlet of men armed with spiked clubs and initiated a lethal gun battle for which the workers were initially blamed. Strike breakers and armed company guards thwarted the aspirations of some eight thousand iron-ore miners in Minnesota during a violence-pocked three-month strike protesting dangerous conditions and the exorbitant prices the company charged workers for the tools and powder necessary for them to do their jobs. In the company town of Bayonne, New Jersey, whose mayor happened also to be legal counsel to the Standard Oil Company, oil workers protesting low wages had no success against the combined efforts of the company and civic authorities.[36]

Across the country, in San Francisco, businessmen supported in 1916 by a new "Law and Order Committee" had long been in contention with labor. The second of two bitter longshoremen's strikes that had resulted in several deaths ended just five days before tens of thousands of people poured into the city's streets for a parade supporting preparedness. One of several preparedness parades held around the country this year, and among the largest parades

ever held in the city, the July 22 event reportedly included more than fifty thousand marchers. At 2:06 P.M., about half an hour after the start of the parade, an innocent-looking suitcase suddenly exploded with incredible force, sending brick shards, nails, cartridges, and other missiles tearing through the crowd, killing ten people and maiming forty. "When the panic was over marchers and spectators surged back as rescuers," the *New York Times* reported the following day. "Bodies of men, women, and children lay scattered about the street." Though initially presumed to be the work of "anarchists" who had earlier sent warning postcards to newspapers and city authorities, the Law and Order Committee soon had many convinced that labor agitators were to blame. Two of those arrested, Tom Mooney and Warren Billings, were eventually convicted; Billings was sentenced to life imprisonment and Mooney to death. The extremely questionable character of the evidence and witnesses against the two men led some legal authorities immediately to question their convictions and sparked protests in the United States and abroad. A commission appointed by President Wilson to study the Mooney case concluded that he had not had a fair trial, and in 1918, at Wilson's urging, the governor of California commuted his death sentence to life imprisonment. A campaign to exonerate both men would continue for more than two decades.[37]

Largely restricted to labor organizations and a few others concerned with a probable miscarriage of justice, the international movement to free Mooney and Billings began in the midst of a U.S. military campaign that had much broader popular support in the United States. In the predawn darkness of March 9, 1916, Pancho Villa had emphatically disproved rumors that he was planning to seek reconciliation with the Wilson administration when he led hundreds of his men three miles north of the Mexican border to attack the town of Columbus, New Mexico. Sweeping through outlying areas, the Villistas raged through the main section of town, shooting, burning, and looting. Faulty intelligence had led Villa to believe that the U.S. Army garrison at Columbus was a small one. In fact, 350 soldiers, including a machine-gun troop, were in Columbus that night and, after recovering from their initial surprise, they fought back with deadly effectiveness. Within two hours of launching the raid, the Villistas had retreated, leaving behind them the bodies of dozens of their fellows, much of their

loot, seventeen dead Americans, including nine civilians—and a U.S. Army garrison hungry for revenge.[38]

Fifty-six troopers immediately engaged in a limited cross-border pursuit that killed more of Villa's men before the Americans, tired, short of ammunition, and aware that the Carranza government had not given permission for their cross-border pursuit, withdrew from Mexican soil. Meanwhile, George Seese, an Associated Press correspondent who happened to be staying in Columbus, telegraphed news of the raid, and soon the hunger for revenge was spreading through the rest of the United States. Meeting immediately with his cabinet, including Newton Baker, who officially began his tenure as secretary of war the day after the raid, President Wilson agreed that public sentiment and political considerations made it necessary to send a small force into Mexico to punish Villa, and he set those wheels in motion before leaving for a weekend cruise on the presidential yacht. On Monday he returned to a capital city boiling with rumors that the Carranza government would resist the presence of American troops on Mexican soil, with attendant calls for activating the National Guard and raising an additional 400,000 volunteers to prepare for a full-scale conflict. "There won't be any war with Mexico if I can prevent it," the furious commander in chief told his secretary, Joseph Tumulty. "It is easy for me as President to declare war. I do not have to fight, and neither do the gentlemen on the Hill who now clamor for it . . . I will not resort to war against Mexico until I have exhausted every means to keep out of this mess."[39]

The president of the United States and the first chief of Mexico, Venustiano Carranza, were each in a delicate position. Carranza had a tenuous hold on power in a strife-torn country, many of whose citizens bitterly resented the United States and would be incensed at the presence of an American army in Mexico, no matter what their feelings about Villa. Wilson suspected that self-interest stemming from heavy American investment in Mexico was inspiring at least some of the strident pleas for military intervention. At the same time, he was all too aware that the German government had long been working behind the scenes to provoke all-out war between the two Western Hemisphere neighbors as a means of diverting American attention and resources from the European conflict. As the military force that would embark on what was to become known as the Punitive Expedition began assembling at Columbus and Hachita, New Mexico, the

Wilson administration and the Carranza government engaged in wary negotiations from which each drew certain inferences that would lead to difficulties in the ensuing months. The Americans assumed that the expedition could move forward and proceed as far into Mexico as necessary "with the single object of capturing [Villa] and putting a stop to his forays"—at least until it was clear to U.S. authorities that the Mexican government had the Villa menace well in hand. Representatives of the Carranza government assumed that the expedition would be of short duration and not penetrate too deeply into Mexican territory.[40]

The Punitive Expedition, led by General John Pershing, began when six thousand troops crossed the Mexican border in the early morning of March 16. The initial phase brought great credit, if little satisfaction, to the hard-riding and hard-marching veteran cavalry, infantry, and support troops penetrating the inhospitable terrain where Villa and his men were reportedly hiding. It also brought home the epic problems the U.S. Army would face should it become involved in a full-scale war.[41] An emergency appropriation of some $400,000 helped alleviate the army's woeful lack of motorized trucks, which could help transport troops and supplies across the border (though in such rough country, horses and mules were often more efficient). But there was no quick fix for the benign neglect that had characterized development of the army's motorized aircraft. The entire, theoretically combat-ready,

army air force—eight fragile planes of the First Aero Squadron—arrived in Columbus on March 15, disassembled and transported by rail. Soon after the squadron's commander, Captain Benjamin Foulois, made the first aerial reconnaissance over foreign territory ever conducted by the U.S. military in his reassembled plane, two of the squadron's aircraft were lost through accidents. "By the end of our first ten days of operations it was obvious that our six planes were incapable of fully performing the [expedition support] task assigned," Foulois later wrote in a memoir. "Their low-powered engines and limited climbing ability with the necessary military load made it impossible to operate them safely in the vicinity of the mountains. In addition, the dry atmosphere was hard on the wooden propellers, causing them to warp." Few such problems plagued the much more numerous, more sophisticated, and specialized aircraft that were then operating over the battlefields of Europe and the Near and Middle East. This reflected a disparity in investment. As one historian has reported, despite America's being the progenitor of motorized flight, "The U.S. government had spent less than half a million dollars for aeronautics between 1908 and 1913, a period during which Germany spent $28 million." In August, with the Mexican experience and preparedness firmly in mind, Congress began to make up for that lag by appropriating $13 million for military aviation.[42]

Germany had also been investing millions to expand its fleet of combat submarines. As Pershing's troops moved deeper into Mexico, one of the smaller

coastal-patrol U-boats, *UB-29*, captained by Herbert Pustkuchen, caused another dangerous crisis in U.S.-German relations. On the afternoon of March 24, while his boat was patrolling the English Channel, Pustkuchen launched a torpedo at an approaching vessel without surfacing or warning the ship, which he believed was a mine layer. The explosion blew away much of the vessel's bow, although, miraculously, the ship did not sink. "The bridge is covered with people," Pustkuchen wrote in his log after observing the damaged vessel through his periscope. "It is a [troop] transport." In fact, the British-registered SS *Sussex* was an unarmed commercial Channel steamer traveling its usual route between Folkestone and Dieppe. Eighty of the vessel's 325 civilian passengers were killed or wounded by the explosion; 4 of the 25 Americans aboard were among the injured.[43]

Basic facts about the attack, and some erroneous assumptions, reached the United States late that same day. To the country at large, President Wilson displayed a life-as-usual demeanor through the weekend of March 25–26. By Monday, however, currents of alarm over a new crisis with Germany radiated throughout official Washington, enhanced in the following days by reports that U-boats had damaged or sunk four other British ships, all merchantmen, three of them with Americans aboard. Confusion reigned on both sides of the Atlantic as both the Wilson administration and German authorities tried to ascertain the exact circumstances under which all the attacks had occurred, with the passenger vessel *Sussex* being the central focus of American concern. At first German authorities reported that none of their U-boats had attacked the *Sussex*—an assumption based on the German navy's

muddled information and not corrected until after American authorities had definitive evidence to the contrary. "Part of a torpedo has been found in the hull of the Sussex," John Gardner Coolidge, in Paris, wrote in his diary on March 30. "That ought to be sufficient to prove that she was torpedoed."[44]

Coolidge and other U.S. embassy staff had spent several days after the attack taking depositions from American survivors, documents that arrived in Washington on April 15 aboard the American steamer *St. Paul*. In the meantime, the Germans had accurately determined that the other ships in question had been properly warned before being attacked, while in Washington Wilson and Secretary Lansing had begun the slow process of sifting through the information trickling in and drafting an official protest to the Germans. That process was further slowed by some alarming news from Mexico, received about the same time that the *Sussex* depositions arrived. A hundred-man squadron of the Thirteenth Cavalry had been attacked by a mob of civilians and some three hundred troops loyal to Venustiano Carranza in the town of Parral, about three hundred miles south of the border. In the running battle that ensued, two troopers of the Thirteenth Cavalry were killed and several wounded, while the retreating cavalrymen killed more than forty Mexicans. With each mile the Punitive Expedition had penetrated into Mexico, tensions between Pershing's men and local troops and civilians had been increasing. Now Pershing was so incensed at the attack on his men that on April 17 he recommended in a telegram that his troops take temporary control of the entire Mexican state of Chihuahua—an action that would surely have meant all-out war.[45]

Carranza was increasingly adamant that the Americans should withdraw from his country; Washington was equally determined not to do so until Villa's power in

Bijvoegsel van

De Nieuwe Amsterdammer

onafhankelijk nederlandsch weekblad
onder redactie van Mr H·P·L·Wiessing

No. 70 29 April 1916

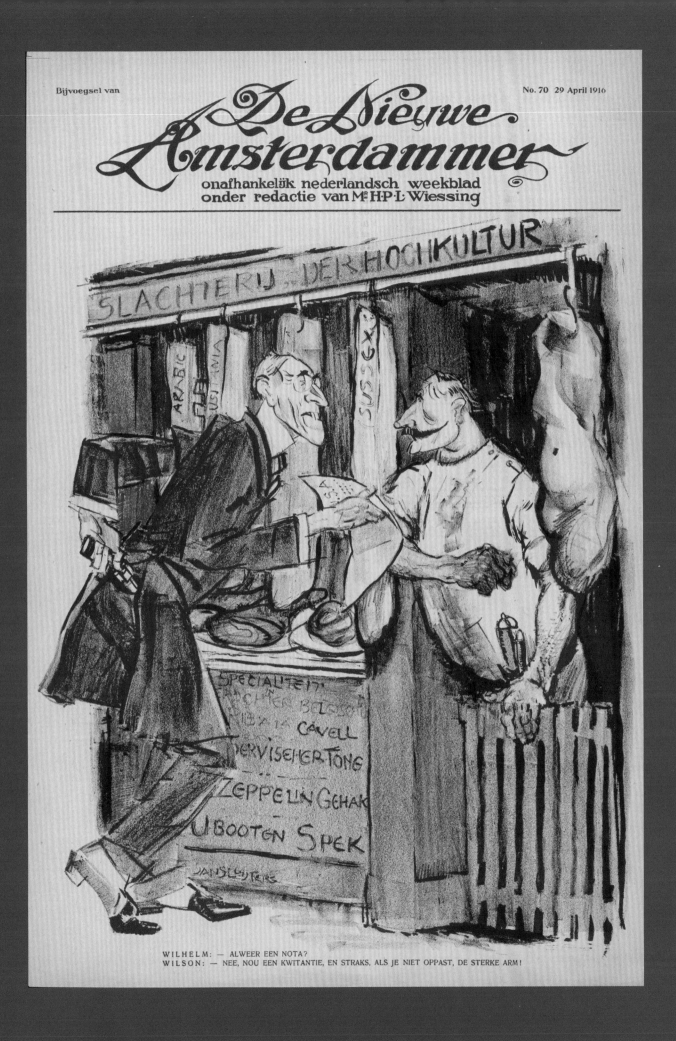

WILHELM: — ALWEER EEN NOTA?
WILSON: — NEE, NOU EEN KWITANTIE, EN STRAKS, ALS JE NIET OPPAST, DE STERKE ARM!

northern Mexico was completely shattered. Yet each government strove to avoid actually going to war. During weeks of long-distance negotiations between the Carranza and Wilson administrations and consultations between Wilson and the U.S. military leaders involved, the president accepted a recommendation made by General Frederick Funston, commander of the army's Southern Department, and Army Chief of Staff Hugh Scott that the American troops should pause in their active pursuit of Villa and concentrate around Pershing's headquarters near the Mormon colony at Colonia Dublán, about 110 miles south of the border. In an attempt to further ease tensions with Carranza, Funston and Scott were to meet with Carranza's representative, General Álvaro Obregón, somewhere along the U.S.-Mexican border.[46]

As all this was occurring, on April 18 Lansing transmitted to Ambassador James Gerard in Berlin Wilson's note protesting the attack on the *Sussex*. Intended to bring the whole question of Germany's submarine warfare to a head, it ended with an ultimatum: "Unless the Imperial Government should now immediately declare its purpose to abandon its present methods of submarine warfare against passenger and freight-carrying vessels, the Government of the United States can have no choice but to sever diplomatic relations with the German Empire." The following day the president addressed a joint session

Opposite: General John J. Pershing and staff at U.S. field headquarters near Casas Grandes, Mexico. From left: Colonel L. G. Berry, Colonel De R. C. Cabell, Lieutenant M. C. Schellenberger, Pershing, Lieutenant George S. Patton, Major J. C. Clayton, and Captain W. B. Burt.

Right: One of General Pershing's notebooks from the Punitive Expedition.

of Congress. "The Government of the United States has been very patient . . . It has of course accepted the successive explanations and assurances of the Imperial German Government as given in entire sincerity and good faith," he told the assembled legislators. Yet that government "has been unable to put any limits or restraints upon its warfare against either freight or passenger ships," one terrible result being that the toll of Americans killed in U-boat attacks had by now "mounted into the hundreds." Although the decision to send the ultimatum caused him "the keenest regret," the president deemed it necessary and was confident of congressional support. "We cannot forget," he said, "that we are . . . by the force of circumstances the responsible spokesmen of the rights of humanity and that we cannot remain silent while those rights seem in process of being swept utterly away in the maelstrom of this terrible war."[47]

Formally delivered by Ambassador Gerard on April 22, the American note sparked general resentment in Germany along with deeper reactions ranging from gloom to outrage. "*Hungerwar* against all noncombatants—women and children—in Central Europe, is absolutely *not* '*inhuman*' in Wilson's eyes," Kaiser Wilhelm snarled. "But that Germany should by *all means possible* parry this diabolical plan . . . even at the expense of some American passengers who have no right to get in its way—that is inadmissible and *very wrong* in the eyes of Wilson . . . Either starve at England's bidding or war with America!" Yet overall sentiment in his country still did not favor adding the

United States to the roster of Germany's enemies—especially now, when there seemed true promise of victory over the Allies. An entire British army, primarily made up of Indian soldiers, had been surrounded for weeks without food or medicine at Kut-al-Amara (a town south of Baghdad) and would surrender on April 29; on the Italian front and despite German disapproval, the Austro-Hungarians were planning to launch an attack; and the two-month-old Verdun Offensive continued to hold promise, although it was plagued by bad weather and French intransigence, and was producing almost as many German casualties as French. Moreover, the prototype of a new "commerce submarine," designed to thwart the British blockade by sailing under it, was nearly ready for its maiden voyage to America, and an ongoing program of

anti-British subversion was at that moment promising to come to fruition in one troubled area of King George V's globe-spanning realm.[48]

From the opening days of the war the German government had been providing assistance to nationalist factions of two major jewels in the British crown of possessions, supporting unrest that would divert resources from Britain's struggle against the Central Powers—and in the process sometimes treading on American neutrality. Money sent to Indian nationalists based in California helped support publications urging independence for India and, in 1915, paid for a shipment of surplus American rifles. Destined for separatists in India, the weapons left San Diego aboard the schooner *Annie Larsen*. After a series of maritime misadventures, the vessel was seized by American authorities, an episode that eventually resulted in a well-publicized months-long trial of U.S.-based Indian nationalists. The Germans were also doing their best to exploit the ongoing unrest in Ireland, which, given the long history of Irish immigration to the United States, also was of keen interest to many people in the United States. William Howard Taft and Theodore Roosevelt were among the many thousands of Americans who supported the movement for Ireland's independence. Political support was one thing, however; advocacy for revolution quite another.[49]

Relatively few ardent Irish Americans were cooperating clandestinely with hard-line Irish separatists determined to

Opposite: The French artist known as Weal (1878–1962) specialized in caricatures of men in power and captured in this portrait the dark view most French people and many Americans had of Kaiser Wilhelm by 1916.

Below: American children protest British behavior in Ireland. Photograph by Harris & Ewing ca. 1916.

take advantage of Britain's preoccupation with the Great War to win independence by force. Yet these few Irish Americans raised substantial funds that helped procure arms for rebels in Ireland; paid for the Irish nationalist Sir Roger Casement's travel to Germany from the United States, where he had been visiting in 1914, and supported Casement while he sought money and weapons from the authorities in Berlin. John Devoy, a New York–based Irish American journalist and fervent separatist, received a coded message in February 1916 notifying him of a pending uprising in Ireland, and in April 1916, as authorities in Berlin began contemplating President Wilson's *Sussex* protest, the plan came to unhappy fruition. A German submarine delivered Casement to Ireland, where he was promptly captured, as was a German vessel disguised as a Norwegian

merchantman and loaded with captured Russian arms. A portion of the German surface fleet did manage to elude the Royal Navy long enough to bombard the English coast, an action timed to coincide with the Irish rising. Yet that was of no help at all to the rebels whose leaders stood outside the General Post Office in Dublin on April 24 and announced their rebellion in a proclamation that pointedly noted the support of Ireland's "exiled children in America."[50]

A bloody affair confined to one city, the Easter Rebellion was quashed by the British in less than a week. In the rest of Ireland and among most Irish Americans and millions of others in the United States sympathetic to the quest for Irish independence, the rising was generally regarded as tragic and ill conceived. There the matter might have rested had the British not

determined to exact a terrible retribution on the leaders of the rebellion. Executions began almost immediately, with a ruthlessness that appalled even some American anglophiles. "Nothing more lamentable in the course of the war now raging has come to pass than this act of bloody vengeance by the English Government," William Dean Howells, a leading man of American letters, wrote to the *New York Evening Post* on May 6. "The shooting of the Irish insurrectionists is too much like the shooting of prisoners of war . . . England has roused the moral sense of mankind against her." "The *muddle of Ireland*," editors of the *New Republic* wrote, "has made America question the liberalism of Britain and the sincerity of her talk about [honoring the interests] of small nationalities." Among Irish Americans, particularly, sentiment hardened against Britain. A new organization, Friends of Irish Freedom, held public meetings denouncing British conduct. Petitioners descended on Congress asking members to pass resolutions sparing Irish prisoners slated for execution, particularly Roger Casement, who in his prewar diplomatic career had been hailed for his humanitarianism. When Casement was executed in August, on the very day that a U.S. resolution pleading for clemency arrived in London, it was not only Irish Americans who were outraged.[51]

As tensions increased between the United States and the Allies, the danger of war with Germany receded. On May 5, while the Irish executions were in progress, the White House received the German reply to Wilson's *Sussex* protest. It contained what has come to be known as

the "*Sussex* pledge," that U-boats would thenceforth adhere to accepted international rules requiring prior warning to merchant and passenger vessels. But it also contained a condition: the United States must compel the Allies to observe international law in the conduct of their maritime blockade, which was now beginning to cause German civilians serious distress. If that did not occur, Chancellor von Bethmann Hollweg warned Wilson via Ambassador Gerard, it was probable that within a month to six weeks there would be an irresistible countrywide clamor for a return to unrestricted submarine warfare.[52]

Wilson's formal reply to Berlin, published and applauded in American papers, seemed to dismiss the German condition as wholly inappropriate. Yet the president was aware that the United States could not press one side of the European war to adhere to international law without also pressing the other and still maintain credible status as a truly neutral power, something essential to realizing his still-vibrant hope of brokering an end to the war. With the advice and assistance of the ubiquitous Colonel House, Wilson renewed efforts at convincing the Allies to agree to peace talks, as outlined in February's House-Grey Memorandum, and to the development of a postwar convention that would effectively prevent future wars. Yet Allied actions and attitudes seemed increasingly at odds with that Wilsonian objective.[53]

On the day the Easter Rebellion began, Foreign Minister Grey finally replied to the forceful October 1915 American note protesting the Allies' "ineffective, illegal, and indefensible" blockade methods by

politely but firmly denying both the blockade's illegality and the assertion that it was harming American commerce. The British had also all but ignored repeated American protests against Allied confiscation of mail from U.S. vessels, which, like their methods of blockade, they deemed important to defeating the Central Powers. Encouraged by the German army's failure to break the French at Verdun, although that campaign was still in progress, Allied governments remained determined to push on to victory, to retake territory now occupied by enemy forces, and to destroy Germany's power to launch a future war—and they were extremely wary of any American action that might allow Germany to keep conquered territories or otherwise end the war in a position of strength. On May 12, Grey, replying to a message from House, stated that any peace moves at that time would be regarded as premature. Ten days later the French ambassador to the United States, Jules Jusserand, personally informed State Department officials that "anyone trying at this time to bring about peace would be considered a friend of Germany."[54]

Distressed and discouraged by the failure of their private peacemaking efforts, House and Wilson collaborated on a speech that would mark a turning point in America's wartime diplomacy. Delivered on May 27 before some two thousand members of the League to Enforce Peace at Washington's Willard Hotel, the speech unequivocally declared United States membership in the troubled community of nations. "We are participants, whether we would or not, in the life of the world," Wilson said. "What affects mankind is inevitably our affair as well as the affair of the nations of Europe and Asia." Briefly outlining American principles that he would also include among his Fourteen Points in 1918, including the right of both large and small nations to choose "the sovereignty under which they shall live," the president went on to announce that "the United States is willing to become a partner in any feasible association of nations formed in order to realize these objects and make them secure against violation." Just touching upon his hope that Americans could initiate a movement that would bring peace to the warring nations, he concluded by expressing his belief that "some common force will be brought into existence which shall safeguard right as the first and most fundamental interest of all peoples and all governments, when coercion shall be summoned not to the service of political ambition or selfish hostility, but to the service of a common order, a common justice, and a common peace."[55]

Reflecting widespread American approval of the president's speech, The *New Republic* headlined its review MR. WILSON'S GREAT UTTERANCE. Harry Garfield, the president of Williams College and son of the assassinated president James A. Garfield, told Wilson that the speech "directs us and the world in a new path." In Britain, the *Westminster Gazette* opined that the speech "brings the United States definitely into world politics and makes her from henceforth one of the nations that must be reckoned with." But that fact remained far from comforting to the belligerent nations. German authorities were happy to reap what propaganda benefit they could from

BATTLE OF JUTLAND

Location: The North Sea, 70 miles west of Denmark's Jutland Peninsula

Date: May 31–June 1, 1916

Objectives: The sequestered, outnumbered German navy sought to lure and cause significant damage to the British Royal Navy's Grand Fleet (its main fleet) and battle cruiser squadron.[1] For their part, the British, once the battle was engaged, hoped to wipe out the German Imperial Navy's High Seas Fleet.

Synopsis: A culmination of decades-long naval armament programs,[2] Jutland was the largest sea battle of the war with 251 ships and some hundred thousand men participating.[3] It was also the only combat encounter between British and German state-of-the-art battleships called dreadnoughts.[4] Neither side accomplished its objectives, creating initial confusion as to who was the victor.

Casualties: British deaths: 6,094; ships lost: 14. German deaths: 2,551; ships lost: 11.[5]

Outcome: Despite key failures, the Royal Navy remained supreme and emerged as the victor, but the British press and public were aghast at the death toll. The retired French admiral M. G. Paul Hautefeuille lent his perspective the following month: "This great victory was dearly bought; but if 5,000 British sailors perished on May 31, the lives of just as many French soldiers have been sacrificed daily for months near Verdun."[6] After the battle, the Germans retreated and did not put their surface fleet at risk for the rest of the war. Instead, they pursued unrestricted submarine warfare beginning in early 1917, a move that soon brought the United States into the war. Meanwhile, the British responded with new ship convoy tactics, use of hydrophones (underwater listening devices), and improved underwater mines and obstacles.[7]

Commentary: "During a few hours' fighting the other afternoon, the British lost a greater number of ships than the naval appropriation bill, now before the Senate, will add to the American navy . . . The action in the North Sea stands [as] a solemn warning to the United States. It shows that a young nation like Germany, with no traditions at all behind its navy, can inflict heavy punishment on even a superior enemy. It should open the eyes of our people."[8] —Henry Reuterdahl, naval expert and later a lieutenant commander in the U.S. Naval Reserve, June 6, 1916

Allied reluctance to enter peace negotiations, but they saw little reason to entertain peacemaking overtures made, as Foreign Minister Gottlieb von Jagow wrote on June 7, "by one whose instincts are all favorable to the English point of view, and who . . . is so naïve a statesman as President Wilson." Rock-hard resolve on each side to achieve its definition of victory kept the guns firing, the blood flowing, and the war spreading like an incurable plague. In March, Germany had declared war on Portugal; Romania would declare war on Austria-Hungary at the end of August.[56]

P eace closer to home continued to be elusive as well. In early May, growing disorder in the Dominican Republic, so close to the Panama Canal and entwined with American interests, caused Wilson to dispatch U.S. forces to occupy that nation, a neighbor to Haiti, which American troops had occupied the previous year. Contemplating the possibility that Germany might win the war and coerce Denmark into ceding to it the Danish West Indies, the site of harbors that would make excellent naval bases, the Wilson administration was also negotiating with Denmark to buy that Caribbean holding; it became the United States Virgin Islands in 1917. Most vexing of all: Relations with Mexico were rapidly deteriorating.[57]

The same day that Germany's "*Sussex* pledge" reached the White House, Mexican bandits crossed the border into Texas and attacked the towns of Glenn Springs and Boquillas, killing four Americans, wounding several others, stealing a payroll, and taking hostages (who were soon released). The raid sparked a two-week pursuit through Mexican territory by American soldiers unattached to Pershing's Punitive Expedition. It also moved President Wilson to activate forty-five hundred National Guardsmen from the Southwest and send four thousand additional regular army troops to the border. Considered prudent by the Americans, these actions exacerbated Mexican resentment of their northern neighbor, resentments constantly fed, as Americans in Mexico attested, by Heinrich von Eckhardt, the German ambassador to Mexico. Further evidence of German involvement in Mexico reached Washington in a stream of apparently reliable reports regarding the influence of Mexico-based German banks, businesses, and propaganda societies. One particularly ominous dispatch noted that German reserve officers then in the United States had been ordered to register at the nearest Mexican consulate, presumably so they could be called to join the ten German officers then serving in Carranza's army in case anti-American feeling exploded into war. American hopes for an accommodation with the de facto Mexican government began to die. Mexican troops were deploying in a manner strongly suggesting plans for offensive action, and on May 31 the State Department received a twelve-thousand-word note from the Carranza government reviewing American impositions and calling for Pershing's troops to leave the country immediately.[58]

In the midst of the barrage of disquieting international bulletins, the Republican Party held its national convention

in Chicago from June 7 through June 10. Dubbed a "reconsecration" of the party, the convention reflected little of the political drama and backstage maneuvering that surrounded it. Teddy Roosevelt, by now a fervent advocate of American intervention in Mexico and the European war and furious with Wilson's attempts to prevent both, had first declared himself out of the running, then quietly encouraged the work of Roosevelt-for-President organizations that sprang up across the country. "What I am really trying to do," he wrote California's governor, Hiram Johnson, "is . . . get the Republicans and Progressives together for someone whom we can elect and whom it will be worthwhile electing." Moving to be that someone, he encouraged the leadership of the dwindling Progressive Party to meet in Chicago during the convention, chiefly as a reminder to the Republican leadership of the divided election of 1912. Even

from afar (Roosevelt remained at home), he quickly realized that the Republicans needed no reminder. Precisely because of what they considered his rogue candidacy in 1912—and also because they knew the public would not embrace his aggressive plans for preparedness and intervention—they had no intention of allowing him to head their 1916 ticket. On June 10, the convention voted overwhelmingly for the man who had been the favorite from the beginning, Supreme Court Justice Charles Evans Hughes, who promptly resigned from the Court.[59]

Having drifted away from his earlier progressive views and wishing to return to the Republican fold, Roosevelt not only rebuffed all efforts to get him to run once more as the Progressive Party presidential candidate, he brusquely severed his ties with that party and announced his support for Hughes. An effective reformer when he served as governor of New York from 1906

until his Supreme Court appointment in 1910, Hughes had thereafter refrained, because of his judicial position, from making political statements. He thus entered the campaign unsullied by political controversy and respected for his integrity—but hampered by a lack of warmth and personal magnetism. ("I do wish the bearded iceberg had acted a little differently during the last six months so as to enable us to put more heart into the campaign for him," Roosevelt grumbled to a friend.) Hughes's letter accepting the Republication nomination saluted both the need for adequate preparedness and America's devotion to "the ideals of honorable peace," gave broad nods to both capital and labor, declared his support for "unflinching maintenance of all

of the rights of American citizens on land and sea," and decried the "weak and vacillating course which has been taken with regard to Mexico."[60]

On June 15, relations with Mexico deteriorated further when about sixty Mexican irregulars attacked San Ignacio, Texas, killing four soldiers and wounding six. As U.S. troops pursued the bandits back across the border, skirmished with unidentified Mexicans, and then withdrew, Carranza's military commander in Chihuahua, General Jacinto Treviño, informed General Pershing that he had been instructed "to prevent, by the use of arms, new invasions of my country by American forces and also to prevent the American forces that are in this State from moving to

Above: Though the U.S. Constitution had not yet been amended to grant women the vote, many were involved on both sides in the 1916 presidential campaign, as reflected in this Bain News Service photograph of Hughes supporters in action.

Right: A cartoon by William Allen Rogers (1854–1931), published in the *New York Herald* on March 24, 1916, gives a decidedly American view of Mexican-American relations.

the south, east, or west of the places they now occupy." Treviño's notification and Pershing's reply—that the U.S. government had placed no such restrictions on his troop deployments—ignited a flurry of activity in Washington. Secretary of War Baker called up the hundred thousand members of the National Guard not previously activated, Army Chief of Staff Hugh Scott ordered staff to plan for a full-scale invasion of Mexico, Secretary of the Navy Daniels sent more gunboats to Mexican waters, and Secretary of State Lansing made arrangements to evacuate any American civilians then south of the border who wished to return to the United States. "It looks to me as if the war will be on in a few days," Chief of Staff Scott wrote to a friend on June 20.[61]

All this overlapped equally frenzied activity in St. Louis, site of the three-day Democratic National Convention, which had convened on June 14. With the renomination of Woodrow Wilson a foregone conclusion, remaining out of war was the chief focus of delegate passions. In his keynote address, former New York governor Martin H. Glynn ignited a rousing call-and-response reaction by reciting past instances when the United States had refrained from settling a dispute by force of arms. After each example, the delegates roared, "What did we do? What did we do?" And Glynn roared back, "We didn't go to war!" He was followed to the podium by Senator Ollie M. James of Kentucky, a man of sonorous voice and oratorical prowess, who launched the assemblage into a tumultuous twenty-one-minute demonstration by concluding his speech with a thundering summary of Wilson's skillful avoidance of conflict with Germany. "Without orphaning a single American child, without widowing a single American mother, without firing a single gun, without the shedding of a single drop of blood, he wrung from the most militant spirit that ever brooded above a battlefield an acknowledgement of American rights and an agreement to American demands."[62]

Observing precedent, Wilson was not there to witness the demonstration. He had, however, been deeply involved in preparations for the convention and

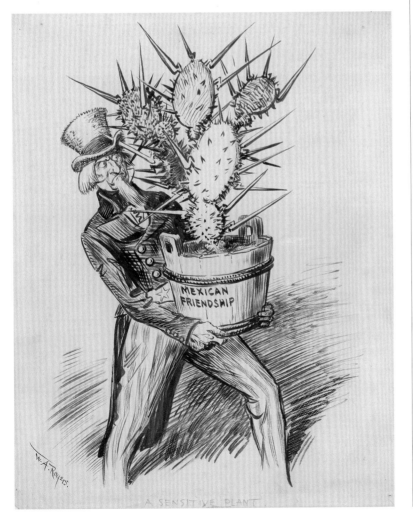

A SENSITIVE PLANT.

formulation of the Democratic platform. As amended and adopted by the party, that document outlined the administration's accomplishments to date; reaffirmed the party's commitment to Wilsonian domestic reforms and to a pending shipping bill that would provide for a new American merchant marine; underlined the president's and the party's new commitment to internationalism; condemned as "subversive to this nation's unity and integrity . . . the activities and designs of every group or organization . . . that has for its object the advancement of the interest of a foreign power"; and declared that American troops would remain in Mexico "until, by the restoration of law and order therein, a repetition of [recent cross-border] incursions is improbable." One phrase in the platform—"he kept us out of war"—later became the party's campaign slogan, although it made Wilson himself

uncomfortable. He was all too aware how fragile that statement might be.[63]

On June 21, while National Guard units were mobilizing across the country, the president heard newsboys outside the White House shouting about Mexico, the first inkling he had of a new crisis. U.S. CAVALRY IN BLOODY BATTLE, TWELVE AMERICAN NEGRO SOLDIERS MASSACRED

Opposite, top: The 1916 Democratic National Convention in St. Louis. Bain News Service photograph. *Bottom:* Senator Ollie James, arms outspread, moves the convention with his oratory as Martin Glynn (seated in dark suit at back of platform) listens.

Below: Troopers of the 10th U.S. Cavalry and their translator, Lemuel Spilsbury (white hat, center of troops) in El Paso, Texas, after being released by the Mexicans. Photograph by Underwood & Underwood, July 3, 1916.

IN MEXICAN AMBUSH, THE COUNTRY HOVERING ON THE BRINK OF WAR were among the banner headlines that appeared in papers over the next few days, as Wilson gathered information through military channels about an encounter between seventy-six troopers of the venerable Tenth Cavalry and two hundred to four hundred Carrancista soldiers at the garrison town of Carrizal. Leading a scouting mission, Captain Charles T. Boyd had ordered his men to go through Carrizal rather than around it, despite General Pershing's orders to avoid garrisoned settlements and similar advice from Boyd's own staff. During the fierce two-hour battle that resulted, fourteen Americans, including Boyd, were killed. Carranza's men took as prisoners twenty-four troopers and the Tenth Cavalry's Mormon guide, Lemuel Spilsbury.[64]

The afternoon of June 25, the Wilson administration sent Carranza's de facto government a message demanding the return of the prisoners as well as a clear explanation through official government channels of Mexican intentions, and a speedy reply to his message. Three days later, no reply having been received, the president finished drafting a speech asking Congress to grant him authority to use American armed forces in any way he deemed necessary to resolve the Mexican situation. A frustrated but hopeful Teddy Roosevelt, thinking that this time, possibly, Wilson might actually be forced to go to war, wrote Secretary of War Baker for permission to recruit a division and lead it in Mexico if a full-scale conflict did occur. Roosevelt's eagerness to see military action, however, did not reflect the prevailing American mood. Almost as soon as news of the Carrizal clash appeared in the papers,

the White House began receiving telegrams and letters appealing for arbitration rather than war. Yet experience had taught both Wilson and Lansing to be wary of negotiating with Carranza. "My heart is for peace," the president wrote Jane Addams on June 28, "and I wish that we were dealing with those who would not make it impossible for us." As if the wish had traveled southward as well as to Addams, that same day Wilson received word that the Mexicans were releasing the captive troopers. He shelved the speech to Congress, his administration began months of tortuous negotiations with Carranza's government, and the possibility of war with Mexico gradually receded.[65]

Not so the reality of war in Europe. On the Western Front, General von Falkenhayn's Verdun Offensive ground on. "The battle . . . has raged now for 127 days," the *Philadelphia North American* noted on June 27. "In expenditure of life and ammunition, in remorselessness of attack and heroic stubbornness of defense, this combat dwarfs to insignificance the greatest campaigns in history." The paper's editors went on to question German motivations for their epic assault. American volunteers serving with the French defenders were undoubtedly more interested in how they might survive it. San Antonio attorney Frank Musgrave became one of Germany's first American prisoners when his French infantry company was cut off and surrounded early in the campaign. David Wooster King of Rhode Island, in the ranks of the French 170th Infantry,

the "Swallows of Death," passed "an endless procession of stretchers" moving to the rear as he headed toward the frontline trenches, some carrying men reduced to "mere trunks, both arms and legs shot off." Badly wounded, but still possessing his limbs, machine gunner Eugene Bullard, also with the 170th, was removed from Verdun to a hospital in Lyon. During his long recovery he befriended the U.S. consul, a white southerner who was initially shocked to find that the wounded American he had come to check on was black, and American correspondent Will Irwin. "He had fought at Arras . . . he had been wounded in the blasted terrain of Champagne," Irwin wrote of "Private Gene" in a July 1916 *Saturday Evening Post* article. "But all memories of those . . . actions seemed to have been dimmed by that terrific fighting at Verdun, and especially by that day when his company held off a German charge . . . 'It was like mowing grass, only the grass grew up as fast as you mowed it . . . Every time the sergeant yelled, "Feu!" I got sicker and sicker. They had wives and children, hadn't they?'"[66]

German casualties sometimes became mixed with French in Allied frontline first aid posts, where the wounded waited for motorized ambulances to carry them back to hospitals. Americans were prominent among the men who drove the cars back and forth along narrow shell-pocked roads, traveling without lights at night to lessen their chances of drawing fire. Ambulances of the organization that, in July, was officially renamed the American Field Service (AFS) arrived at Verdun in February; cars of Richard Norton's American Volunteer

Motor Ambulance Corps arrived on the scene in June, later reinforced by vehicles of the Morgan-Harjes Unit, with which Norton's group soon merged.[67] Drivers of the small but dauntless Model T's operated on their own; men driving larger ambulances often had partners who could help load the wounded, push an ambulance stuck in knee-deep mud, or walk ahead of the car at night giving directions by waving a white handkerchief so the car would not fall into a hole or smash into the detritus of war. The forward posts from which the ambulance crews retrieved the wounded were often chambers of horrors, even without the near constant rain of artillery shells. "I shall never forget the feeling of scared helplessness that was with me all the time," New Yorker Coleman T. Clark wrote in his diary. "The shriek of a shell coming your way goes thru you like

a dentist's drill." Rear installations where drivers awaited the cover of darkness to make their forward runs were a huge relief, though they were often damaged and plagued by rats, flies, fleas, and mosquitoes. In early fall 1916, one was the scene of a widely reported baseball series between AFS and Norton ambulance teams. Left- and right-field action was hampered by protective barbed wire, the teams had only one bat between them—and at one point they suspended play to keep a wary eye on a damaged German plane, spewing propaganda leaflets as it plunged toward the earth.[68]

The planes that were constantly scouting, fighting, and dropping bombs over Verdun included a new French squadron, or escadrille, officially designated N 124, but more widely known in its first few months of operation as the Escadrille Américaine—and later, after German objections that the name violated American neutrality, as the Lafayette Escadrille. The brainchild of a wealthy lawyer and Harvard graduate, Norman Prince, one of the Americans who had joined the French air service early in the war, the squadron was formally organized in April 1916 and went on duty over Verdun in May. Under the command of an experienced French officer, Captain Georges Thénault—whose orders his eager American subordinates tended to disobey—the squadron was regarded by the French high command more as a ploy to gain favorable American attention than an effective addition to their air power. The squadron's pilots did not share that view. Flying without parachutes, as all pilots did at this time, they tore through

AMERICAN FIELD SERVICE

Left: Josef Pierre Nuttens (1885–1960) captured the formidable challenged faced by frontline ambulance drivers in this 1917 American Field Service poster.

———

Right: Captain Georges Thénault (second from left, foreground) briefs members of the Escadrille Américaine (Lafayette Escadrille). Bain News Service photograph, date unknown.

1-K. ROCKWELL   3. NORMAN PRINCE   5-SGT ~~J.R.MCCONNELL~~E.COWDIN   7-J.R.MCCONNELL
2-CAPT.THENAULT   4-LIEUT.DELAAGE   8-VICTOR CHAPMAN   6-SGT BERT HALL

the sky hunting German planes with an avidity that bordered on recklessness. On May 23, 1916, five escadrille planes attacked a dozen Germans and suffered more damage than their targets. At about the same time, a former ambulance volunteer, James McConnell, attacked six German craft single-handed and miraculously survived (he would be killed in an air battle ten months later). "A smoky pall covers the sector under fire," McConnell wrote of patrolling over Verdun. "Now and then monster projectiles hurtling through the air . . . leave one's plane rocking violently in their wake. Airplanes have been cut in two by them." In October the American squadron left Verdun and traveled some

120 miles northwest, where the Battle of the Somme had been raging for more than three months.[69]

Partly to relieve the pressure on the French from Falkenhayn's offensive, the Allies had launched that long-planned offensive on July 1, after alerting their enemies to the impending assault with a week-long storm of artillery fire calculated to destroy the German defenses. The first wave of British attackers discovered how badly their commanding generals had miscalculated the artillery's damaging effects. German barbed wired remained intact, and the fortifications behind it, the strongest on the Western Front, easily withstood the bombardment. When it lifted, German

BATTLE OF THE SOMME

Location: Northeast of Amiens, on the Somme River, France

Date: July 1–November 18, 1916

Objectives: An Allied offensive led by the British, the effort was yet another attempt to break the stalemate on the Western Front and to pull German forces away from Verdun.

Casualties: British (including dominion troops): 420,000 (96,000 dead). French: 200,000 (51,000 dead). German: 500,000 (164,000 dead).[1]

Synopsis: The British opened with an enormous but relatively ineffective week-long bombardment of entrenched German lines followed by major infantry attacks. The largest battle of the war in numbers of participants and casualties, the Somme was also notable for the first use of tanks in combat. On September 15 at Flers-Courcelette, the British deployed more than thirty of these ironclad weapons, surprising their own infantry and astonishing German troops.[2] Called the "steel-shelled armadillos of the Somme" and "travelling forts," the tanks went "over the German trenches and enfiladed them with machine fire," reported a British officer a day after their first appearance.[3] However, almost all the 36 tanks the British deployed were almost immediately disabled by malfunction or enemy fire. Tanks would not fully demonstrate their effectiveness in combat until late 1917, at the Battle of Cambrai. The Battle of the Somme, meanwhile, became a costly battle of attrition and what historian John Keegan has termed Britain's "greatest military tragedy."[4]

Outcome: The Allies advanced only about seven miles,[5] at a staggering cost, but the effort did force the Germans to move from Verdun. Overall, the Battle of the Somme achieved little besides providing some small relief to the French at Verdun and inspiring the Germans to developed more sophisticated defense systems.

Commentary: "[The tanks] came trundling across shell craters and over tree stumps, cutting down many small trees on their way toward the German trenches, on to the second line and even to the thrill line. The return to earth of ichthyossaurs [sic] or dinosaurs sprouting bullets from their nostrils could not have been more amazing." —*Detroit Free Press*, September 17, 1916

"We have sold about one thousand caterpillar tractors to the British government . . . We have sent some to France and some to Russia . . . It is true that these tractors can go over almost anything or through almost anything." —M. M. Baker, vice president of Holt Manufacturing, whose Peoria, IL, plant produced the vehicles that the French and Germans converted to produce their first tanks.[6]

machine guns cut down rank after rank of the advancing Britons. By the end of that first day, forty thousand British soldiers had been wounded and twenty thousand had been killed—the worst one-day loss of life in British military history. Undeterred, the Allied commanders continued the campaign until late November, gaining at best seven miles of ground at a cost of some 1.2 million men killed and wounded on both sides.[70]

Serving in the British Army, American Arthur Guy Empey was among the wounded in the first days of the Somme carnage. Taken to the American Women's Hospital in England, he would live to write about his experiences and become an effective patriotic propagandist once the United States entered the war. In the French sector of the line, Alan Seeger's French Foreign Legion unit attacked its Somme objective, the village of Belloy-en-Santerre, on July 4. The tallest man in his section, the young American poet was an easy target for the machine guns that swept the advancing French units from hidden emplacements. "War is another kind of life insurance," Seeger had written to his mother one month before. "Whereas the ordinary kind assures a man that his death will mean money to someone, this assures him that it will mean honor to himself." After the surviving legionnaires had taken their objective, stretcher bearers retrieved Seeger's body and buried it in a mass grave that was later obliterated by artillery.[71]

The French honored Seeger's sacrifice by posthumously awarding him the Croix de Guerre and the Médaille Militaire. Americans at home, acquainted with Seeger

through his wartime pieces in the *New York Sun* and the *New Republic*, learned more of the man, his work, and his views of the war through *Poems by Alan Seeger* (December 1916) and *Letters and Diary of Alan Seeger* (1917), part of a rising tide of published and filmed memoirs, testimonials, and pleas for assistance that were bringing the Great War ever closer to Americans. Edith Wharton followed her March 1916 letter to the *New York Times*, in which she asked her fellow Americans to support her charities in France, with an elegant tome, *The Book of the Homeless*, "sold for the benefit of the American hostels for refugees and of the Children of Flanders Rescue Committee." A compilation of artistic contributions by such notables as Jean Cocteau, Sarah Bernhardt, Charles Dana Gibson, and Wharton herself, the book also featured an introduction in which Theodore

Roosevelt included a few sharp digs at neutrality with his pleas for supporting Mrs. Wharton's good works.[72] July 1916 saw the debut of an hour-long silent documentary film, *Our American Boys in the European War*, consisting primarily of footage of AFS ambulance units in action. Brief coverage of the Escadrille Américaine (later the Lafayette Escadrille) included shots of Victor Chapman, who on June 23 had become the first American aviator killed in action. "The pictures are doubly interesting because they show more clearly than has previously been done America's contribution to the great war," the *New York Times* observed. Shown throughout the country, the film brought donations of money and ambulances and inspired college students to volunteer for the AFS.[73]

Americans also continued to support the relief effort coordinated by Herbert Hoover and his Commission for Relief in Belgium and a burgeoning number of other philanthropic organizations, including the BFB Blind Fund for the relief of war-blinded British, French, and Belgian soldiers; Duryea War Relief, founded by an American Francophile, Nina Larrey Duryea; and the Chicago-based German and Austro-Hungarian Relief Society. The brilliant pianist and Polish patriot Ignace Jan Paderewski visited U.S. government offices and gave concerts to support the Polish Victims Relief Fund. The Palestine-Syrian Committee and the American Committee for Armenian and Syrian Relief (later renamed Near East Relief) sent aid to the region where Armenians were still being persecuted by Ottoman authorities and where the Allied blockade and Ottoman food confiscations

were contributing to widespread starvation. By August 1916 food shortages had reportedly led to the deaths of between sixty thousand and eighty thousand people in northern Syria alone. In addition to aiding Jews in Europe, the Central Committee for the Relief of Jews and its sister organization, the American Jewish Relief Committee, collected money and goods to help Jews, Christians, and Muslims in the war-torn Holy Land, where members of the long-established American Colony in Jerusalem also provided medical and other relief services to people of all political and religious persuasions. In June, New York City's Grand Central Palace was the scene of a huge Allied Bazaar benefiting nearly a hundred war relief organizations.

Above: While Americans donated to various war relief funds, they also dug deeper into their pockets to feed their own families as food prices continued to rise, as noted by Clifford Berryman (1869–1949) in this cartoon created ca. 1915.

Right: Members of Duryea War Relief.

Duryea War Relief -

Mrs. Duryea, Mrs. Dixon, Peggy French, Hope Williams, Grace
Bristed, Miss Porter, Mrs. Harry, etc.

Featuring exhibitions and sales booths, the bazaar also drew the services of the stage and film star Marie Dressler, who clambered into an empty barrel and shouted that she wouldn't get out of it until the space around her was "filled with money for the Allies."[74]

Even as that barrel was repeatedly filled, members of the Wilson administration were worrying about the curb on America's current and postwar overseas enterprises portended by the Allied Economic Conference held in Paris in mid-June. Prompted by rumors of German plans to create and control a postwar trading bloc of Central European countries, delegates to the Paris conference planned to establish a similar trading bloc comprising Allied nations and their colonial holdings. All this threatened to reverse American expansion into new markets opened by the war and thwart postwar trade with the countries of both proposed blocs. Yet President Wilson refused to countenance Secretary Lansing's proposal to create a third bloc, this one of neutral nations, to "fight combination . . . by combination." The president believed an

The commerce submarine *Deutschland*, which drew crowds of the curious on its two wartime visits to the United States, remained a popular draw postwar. The vessel is shown here while on view in Yarmouth, England, September 15, 1919.

open world economy was infinitely preferable to what would amount to constant economic warfare. He held to this principle through a crisis that began in July, when first the British, then the French, the Japanese, the Australians, and finally the Italians blacklisted more than eighty American firms and individual businessmen suspected of aiding the Central Powers. Denounced even by the pro-Allied *New York Times* as "tactless, foolish, and unnecessary," and by State Department Counselor Frank Polk as "extraordinarily stupid," the blacklist sparked creation in New York of the Association to Resist British Domination of American Commerce, a steady stream of irate politicians and blacklist victims into the State Department, and a furious reaction from the president. "I am . . . about at the end of my patience with Great Britain and the Allies," he wrote to Colonel House. "This black list business is the last straw . . . I am seriously considering asking Congress to authorize me to prohibit loans and restrict exportations to the Allies."[75]

Despite a formal protest from the U.S. government, regarded by some Allied leaders as election-year posturing, the Allies were slow to comprehend the depth of American ire—their powers of appreciation possibly dulled by distress over America's warm welcome to the German commercial submarine *U-Deutschland*, which had successfully sailed under the Allied blockade. Captained by the charming and propaganda-astute Paul König and packed with dyestuffs badly needed by American industry, *U-Deutschland* arrived in Baltimore on July 9. As the boat was inspected and

declared an ordinary merchantman by U.S. officials, its cargo unloaded and the vessel reloaded with South American rubber and nickel required by German industry, the people of Baltimore and the national press treated König and his crew as celebrities. The glow of possibilities that attended *U-Deutschland*'s first visit faded, however, after a second commercial sub, *U-Bremen*, disappeared without a trace on its first voyage to the United States.[76]

Other events increased American wariness of German intentions. At 2:08 A.M. on Sunday July 30, as *U-Deutschland* was preparing to leave Baltimore harbor for home, a massive explosion disintegrated Black Tom Island, New Jersey, a large shipping depot directly across from New York City that was packed with munitions destined for the Allies. The first explosion, felt in Maryland, Pennsylvania, and Connecticut, was followed by six hours of chaos in which three people died and hundreds more were injured as shells exploded, fires raged, thousands of windows shattered, and shrapnel gouged holes in homes, businesses, and the Statue of Liberty. Though it was assumed at first that the cataclysm was an accident, suspicion soon turned to German sabotage. Investigations had begun and repairs were still in progress on October 7 when a 213-foot fully armed German long-range combat submarine, *U-53*, astonished the residents of Newport, Rhode Island—and personnel aboard thirty-seven U.S. Navy vessels anchored in Newport harbor—when it sailed up to a pier and docked. The boat's dapper captain,

Lieutenant Hans Rose, emerged with a smile, asked if someone would mail a letter he was carrying for Ambassador von Bernstorff, and conducted tours of his boat until *U-53* departed at 5:17 P.M. Moving about fifty miles off Nantucket, the U-boat then proceeded to sink six Europe-bound Allied and neutral vessels during the night—after giving proper warning and letting each vessel lower its lifeboats. Anxiety levels hit a new high along the East Coast and marine insurance rates instantly skyrocketed as American naval vessels scrambled to rescue the people Rose and his crew had left adrift. Allied governments were outraged when the U.S. government failed to condemn *U-53*'s action, which had followed procedures outlined in the *Sussex* pledge, while the German government, alarmed by Americans' negative reactions to the boat's abrupt appearance in a homeland harbor, determined not to send any more belligerent U-boats into United States waters. It did, however, dispatch *U-Deutschland* on what proved to be that vessel's final commercial voyage. When the merchant sub docked on November 1, this time in New London, Connecticut, it was greeted with less celebratory publicity and a great deal more suspicion.[77]

The day *U-Deutschland* arrived, the U.S. presidential campaign was entering its final frenetic week. The Republicans had launched their attempt to regain the White House and control of Congress on July 31, when Charles Evans Hughes formally accepted his nomination before a capacity crowd in New York's stifling hot Carnegie Hall. Almost upstaged by Teddy Roosevelt, though the former Bull Moose was in the audience rather than on stage, Hughes responded to the notification address made by Ohio Senator Warren G. Harding with a speech that

EXPOSITION
DU 1ER AU 30 OCTOBRE 1917
CHEZ GEORGES PETIT, 8, RUE DE SÈZE
ORGANISÉE PAR LA LIGUE SOUVENEZ-VOUS
167, RUE MONTMARTRE

DOCUMENTS - PHOTOGRAPHIES - AFFICHES
TABLEAUX - DESSINS RELATIFS AUX CRIMES ALLEMANDS

Prix d'Entrée : Dimanche 0F.50 - Semaine 1F. - de 10 h. à Midi et de 2 h. à 5 heures
AU PROFIT DE L'ŒUVRE DE PROPAGANDE DE LA LIGUE

lambasted the Wilson administration's "confused chapter of blunders" in Mexico, its "weak course" in dealing with the European belligerents, and its policies that left the nation "shockingly unprepared" to meet any great military crisis. With cleanup still in progress from the explosive night of July 30, Hughes declared "utterly intolerable . . . the use of our soil for alien intrigues," then concluded on a positive note, declaring strong support for woman suffrage, nodding vaguely to labor, and renewing the party's "pledge to the ancient ideals of individual liberty, of opportunity denied to none because of race or creed." A month later, Roosevelt opened his promised campaign supporting Hughes, his rousing rhetoric a sharp contrast to Hughes's cautious oratory, his avid interventionism a discomfort to Republicans who understood that most Americans were still determined to cling to peace.[78]

The Democrats were not yet formally on the hustings. As Wilson slowly crafted his nomination acceptance speech, he faced both international and domestic distractions. In August, he appointed members to a Joint (American-Mexican) High Commission formed to resolve points of contention with the Carranza government, a process complicated in September by a revivified Pancho Villa, who raided Chihuahua City, his expanded force of some four thousand men again a threat to Pershing's army. Yet Wilson held Pershing in check and allowed commission negotiations to continue toward an agreement as Mexican forces pursued Villa. At the same time,

the president continued to deal with reverberations from the Allied blacklist, which seemed far more important to Americans than a late-August change in the German high command brought about by the continuing failure of the Verdun Offensive, a stunningly successful Eastern Front offensive by Russian general Alexei Brusilov, and Romania's declarations of war against Germany and Austria-Hungary. Yet the replacement of General von Falkenhayn as chief of the general staff by the stolid hero of the Eastern Front, Paul von Hindenburg, and his perfervid associate, Erich Ludendorff, would eventually have a far greater impact than the blacklist on Americans' struggle to maintain their country's neutrality. Soon overshadowing even the kaiser, the two German officers began tightening the entire German nation's organization for war. By the end of the year, with Romania essentially defeated, the Allies' Somme Offensive a failure, and an aggressive new chapter in the U-boat blockade of Great Britain achieving promising results—even, ostensibly, under the rules of surface warfare—Hindenburg and Ludendorff began to look favorably on a resumption of unrestricted submarine warfare as the best and quickest means to defeat Great Britain.[79]

Chancellor von Bethmann Hollweg believed its resumption would bring America, and possibly other neutrals, into the war against Germany. Desperate to prevent that, he engaged in a series of backstage maneuvers which he hoped would inspire a new peace initiative from Wilson—something the president was unwilling to undertake before the November election. Rumors of a peace initiative nevertheless

On August 27, 1916, Romania declared war on the Central Powers. By December, its armies were in deep trouble. American artist Edward Penfield (1866–1925) created this art to accompany an article in the February 10, 1917, edition of *Collier's* magazine.

circulated through the Allied capitals, where the British, both alarmed and irritated by American reactions to their war policies, launched a study to determine just how dependent their alliance had become on loans and goods from the United States. The result was sobering. "For numerous articles," the British Board of Trade reported, "America is an absolutely irreplaceable source of supply." In the financial realm, "The sums which this country will require to borrow in the U.S.A. in the next six or nine months are so enormous," John Maynard Keynes of the Treasury reported, "that it will be necessary to appeal to every class and section of the investing public. It is

hardly an exaggeration to say that in a few months' time the American executive and the American public will be in a position to dictate to this country on matters that affect us more nearly than them." Based on these facts, Foreign Minister Edward Grey recommended that, while making no concessions on matters of principle, "the greatest possible consideration, compatible with solid military requirements, should be given to American interests," and communications with Americans "should be revised where necessary in the direction of greater civility."[80]

Very little civility marked the gravest domestic crisis distracting Wilson from the presidential campaign. Negotiations with railroad owners and managers having come to naught, workers were threatening a nationwide strike to secure an eight-hour day and time-and-a-half pay for overtime. "A general strike on the railways would at any time have a most far-reaching and injurious effect upon the country," Wilson wrote officials on both sides on August 12. "At this time the effect might be disastrous," for the nation's rail network was the central means of distributing food and goods across the country and to ports for shipment overseas. He then brought negotiations into the White House in a series of tense meetings in which he supported a compromise: adoption of the eight-hour day, with overtime and other demands being subject to arbitration. Labor proved willing, management did not. With the strike only days away, Wilson appealed to Congress, which worked with him to enact, on September 3, a bill establishing an eight-hour day for all railroad workers

Rumania
learns what
War is
by
Arthur Ruhl

engaged in interstate commerce, the first American labor law to provide for oversight of nongovernment employment. Four days later, Wilson achieved another legislative victory when he signed the Shipping Act, which created a federal Shipping Board to own and operate commercial vessels and an Emergency Fleet Corporation to buy and build merchantmen. A governmental boost to America's capacity for international trade, the bill also protected free enterprise by stipulating that some elements of the Shipping Board's authority would end five years after the end of the European war.[81]

As the railroad crisis ebbed, Wilson launched his election offensive, formally accepting his nomination on September 2 during ceremonies attended by some fifteen thousand people at his imposing new summer residence, Shadow Lawn, in Long Branch, New Jersey. He proceeded to give a series of weekly "front porch" addresses there to various groups, interspersing these with campaign speeches away from home on the general themes of peace, prosperity, and progressivism. Other Democratic speakers, taking their lead from Wilson's oratory, fanned out across the country—including the eloquent William Jennings Bryan, who now regarded Wilson as the candidate least likely to involve the United States in the European War. "Wilson and Peace with Honor?" one Democratic newspaper ad asked, "or Hughes with Roosevelt and War?" Despite the continuing American hunger to avoid military conflict in Europe and Mexico, the election battle was perilously close, owing in part to lopsided

Above: A stamp used by organized labor to promote the eight-hour day, reproduced in *The Survey* magazine, April 1, 1916. *Left:* A crowd gathers at President Wilson's imposing summer residence at Long Branch, New Jersey, to hear him accept his nomination for a second term, September 2, 1916. Photograph by Harris & Ewing.

Opposite: German Foreign Secretary Arthur Zimmermann (1864–1940). Bain News Service photograph, date unknown.

corporate support for Hughes as a result of the business community's anger over Wilson's support for the eight-hour-day, a bill to regulate child labor, and other progressive measures. By the evening of Election Day, November 7, with East Coast and some Midwestern votes counted, the *New York World* and the *New York Times* both declared Hughes the winner. But results from states west of the Mississippi River kept trickling in, until on the morning of November 10, Wilson learned, finally and officially, that he had been reelected.[82]

His confidence bolstered by the election results, the president turned his attention once again to leading the European belligerents to peace. Yet events were conspiring against him. In November, Gottlieb von Jagow's deputy, Arthur Zimmermann, replaced Jagow as foreign minister of Germany, an event initially applauded by Americans, who believed that the personable Zimmermann would be much more amenable to peace than his dour predecessor. In truth, Zimmermann had joined the growing ranks of German officials pushing for the resumption of unrestricted U-boat warfare. On the Allied side, David Lloyd George succeeded Herbert Asquith as Britain's prime minister on December 7, and Arthur Balfour replaced Edward Grey as foreign minister. Completely divorced from his prewar aversion to armed conflict, Lloyd George had told an American correspondent in September that Britain would press on with the war "until Prussian military despotism is broken beyond repair."[83]

Through the rest of December and into early 1917, possibilities for a negotiated peace became the subject of intense

official and informal exchanges between the United States and the major belligerent nations. On December 12, as Wilson was preparing his own peace initiative, von Bethmann Hollweg asked Wilson to pass on to the Allied governments a proposal for negotiations devoid of any specific terms that Germany might require. The note evoked instant unfavorable responses from the Allies, who then suspected German influence on the message Wilson dispatched to all the belligerent leaders on December 18. Declaring that he was "not proposing peace . . . not even offering mediation" but "merely proposing that soundings be taken in order that we may learn . . . how near the haven of peace we may be," Wilson asked the leaders to state their specific war aims and definite terms that might lead to a negotiated peace. The note's assertion that, up to this time, "the objects which the statesmen of the belligerents on both sides have in mind in this war are virtually the same, as stated in general terms to their own people and to the world" further roiled, rather than calmed, the angry international waters. Wilson's words "disparage our cause, they dishonor our dead . . . in the name of perfect neutrality they render exclusive service to the enemy," the *London Observer* declared. German press reaction ranged from thunderous condemnation to cautious approval, while in official circles, reception was decidedly cool. "When the president wants to put an end to the war, he needs only to threaten the English blockade pirates with a munitions embargo and a blocking of the market for loans," Kaiser Wilhelm growled, adding later, "The note has undoubtedly been prepared in collusion with England." Nevertheless, in their official answer the Central Powers, while still not publicly disclosing terms, expressed willingness to meet somewhere on neutral ground. (Privately, Kaiser Wilhelm was adamant that only the *belligerent* powers should meet and the irritating Wilson should be excluded.) The Allied response, in mid-January, did outline war aims, including restoration of Belgian and Serbian sovereignty, evacuation of France, Russia, and Romania, and payment of reparations by the Germans—aims to which the Germans would never have agreed.[84]

As delicate official and unofficial peace probes continued—and with the people rather than the governments of the belligerent nations foremost in mind—on January 22 Wilson delivered what came to be known as the "Peace without Victory" speech before the U.S. Senate. After asking whether the war was "a struggle for a just and secure peace, or only for a new balance of power," the president declared, "There must be, not a balance of power, but a community of power; not organized rivalries, but an organized common peace." But how could that occur if one side vanquished the other? "Victory would mean peace forced upon the loser . . . and would leave a sting, a resentment, a bitter memory upon which terms of peace would rest, not permanently, but only as upon quicksand. Only a peace between equals can last." He outlined bedrock "American principles, American policies" on which such a peace might be built—including government by the consent of the governed, freedom of the seas, moderation of armaments, and avoidance of entangling alliances—ideas that "must prevail" as the principles of mankind.[85]

Applauded in the United States (except by interventionists) and by factions within the belligerent nations favoring a negotiated settlement, the speech made little impression on the principal belligerent military and political leaders and millions of their people who believed that years of blood and sacrifice could only be vindicated by victory. But victory remained elusive, and the Germans, their manpower waning and the bite of the Allied blockade increasingly felt at home, had decided, two weeks before Wilson's speech, to bring victory within reach by returning to unrestricted submarine warfare. "Things cannot be worse than they are now," Field Marshal von Hindenburg stated. "The war must be brought to an end by whatever means as soon as possible." Admiral Henning

Holtzendorff estimated that by sinking as much as six hundred thousand tons of Allied merchant shipping every month, Germany's expanding U-boat fleet could bring Great Britain to its knees within six to eight months. Thus, beginning February 1, 1917, Holtzendorff announced, "Every enemy and neutral ship found in the war zone is to be sunk without warning . . . If we fail to make use of this opportunity, which as far as can be foreseen, is our last, I can see no way to end the war so as to guarantee our future as a world power."[86]

As for the United States, "We are counting on the possibility of war" with that country," Hindenburg said, "and we have made all preparations to meet it"—although, according to the Naval Minister, Admiral Eduard von Capelle, military preparations need not be excessive. "As far

as the financial and economic situation is concerned I have always laid great stress on the importance of America's entrance into the war," the admiral stated. "But from a military point of view, her entrance means nothing . . . I am convinced that almost no Americans will volunteer for war service . . . And even if many enlist, they must first be trained. This will take time . . . And when the men have been trained, how are they to cross the ocean? . . . And . . . should America be able to provide the necessary transport ships, our submarines could not wish for a better piece of hunting."[87]

To support the high command's decision and place a roadblock in America's path if the United States chose to declare war, in mid-January Foreign Minister Arthur Zimmermann encoded a proposal to the Carranza government and sent it to

During the presidential campaign many Americans were more concerned with domestic problems than foreign affairs. On October 20, suffragists in Chicago demonstrated across the street from a Chicago auditorium where President Wilson was speaking. Photograph by Burke & Atwell.

Ambassador von Eckhardt in Mexico by three different routes, including via a U.S. State Department cable the Americans had allowed Germany to use for certain important traffic. British Naval Intelligence, which had long been hiding the fact that it had broken German diplomatic codes, intercepted all three messages. In its top secret Room 40 in the Admiralty Building, decoders began their work, finding a particular challenge in one passage that was to resist their efforts for weeks.[88]

At four ten P.M. on Wednesday January 31, 1917, as the British began to realize the importance of Zimmermann's message, Germany's veteran ambassador in Washington, Johann von Bernstorff, arrived at the State Department. "When he entered my room . . . I noticed that, though he moved with his usual springy step, he did not smile with his customary assurance," Secretary Lansing wrote in a private memo four days later. Reminding Lansing "how constantly I have worked for peace" and expressing regret at the drastic step his government must now take, von Bernstorff gave Lansing a note, which stated in part:

> Germany will meet the illegal
> measures of her enemies by forcibly

preventing after February 1, 1917, in a zone around Great Britain, France, Italy, and in the Eastern Mediterranean all navigation, that of neutrals included, from and to England and from and to France, etc., etc. All ships met within that zone will be sunk. The Imperial Government is confident that this measure will result in a speedy termination of the war and in the restoration of peace which the Government of the United States has so much at heart.

Stunned not by the announcement, for he had long been braced for such a move, but by its midwinter timing, when submarine navigation was particularly difficult in northern waters, Lansing concluded that "the food situation in Germany had reached such a pass that the Imperial Government had to do something to satisfy public opinion." Yet "to give only eight hours' notice without any previous warning," he told von Bernstorff, was in his personal opinion "an unfriendly and indefensible act."

He immediately forwarded the note to the White House, telling the president in his covering note, "We are face to face with the gravest crisis presented since the war began."[89]

CHAPTER 3

FEBRUARY – DECEMBER 1917

"THE YANKS ARE COMING"

The world must be made safe for democracy. Its peace must be planted
upon the tested foundations of political liberty.
—President Woodrow Wilson
Speech to a Joint Session of Congress, April 2, 1917

We are about to put the dollar sign upon the American flag . . .
We are committing a sin against humanity and against our countrymen.
—Senator George Norris
Speech during debate over the war resolution, April 4, 1917

A bitter chill enveloped Washington, D.C., in early February 1917 as Americans reacted to Germany's shocking declaration of unrestricted submarine warfare in huge swaths of the Atlantic Ocean and the Mediterranean Sea ordinarily regarded as international waters. "Apparently the whole coast of France and Italy are now declared in the zone," American diplomat in Paris John Gardner Coolidge wrote in his diary on February 1, "and Norway and Sweden are also cut off except in the North . . . How long are we to stand this insolence?" Editors of the *New York World* agreed with Coolidge and hosts of other irate Americans that something had to be done. "To acquiesce in a resumption of ruthless submarine operations is to subject ourselves to the losses of war while depriving ourselves of the means of self-defense," the *World*'s editorial writers declared, proposing not war with Germany, but a break in diplomatic relations. If the president "had a spark of manhood about him," Teddy Roosevelt grumbled to a relative, "he would take such action that Germany would either have to respect us, or face war."[1]

Yet many who viewed the German action as reprehensible still saw no reason to abandon neutrality. "The national honor of the United States is not at stake," the *Seattle German Press* stated. "The people do not want war, they want peace." Wilson's former secretary of state, William Jennings

Bryan, agreed, telling an audience of five thousand called together on February 2 by the American Neutral Conference Committee that Americans should fight to the last man if their own country was invaded, but that all other problems should be solved by arbitration. "It is our own first duty to our country and to the stricken people of the world to keep this nation out of war," the group he addressed then stated in a message to President Wilson, expressing their faith that "in the new emergency that confronts us you will still succeed in combining peace with honor and justice." Avoiding war would indeed be the best course, former president William Howard Taft said in a speech that same night. "We are not prepared for it . . . Our prayer is for some escape from it in this critical hour, consistent with our national honor and vital interests. But we must face the facts," he added, acknowledging the possibility that if not now, then soon, Germany would push the United States too far.[2]

Looking out from the White House at his agitated country and the roiling world, the president was besieged by circumstances—the abrupt and offensive German note, the growing push for belligerent action among millions of Americans increasingly angered by Germany's actions, the relative impotence of America's military establishment, a population that included myriad people with strong ties to belligerent nations on both sides of the conflict, the determination for peace among millions of citizens who believed that neutrality should remain the nation's

course, his own determination to lead the warring nations to the negotiating table—and he was unsure of what action to take. He told his cabinet on February 2 that he still did not favor either belligerent alliance. Both the Allies and the Central Powers had been "indifferent to the rights of neutrals—though Germany had been brutal in taking life, and England only in taking property."[3] Moreover, to react in a manner that jeopardized or abandoned American neutrality might place in peril his own faltering program of domestic reforms while deepening the rifts in America's ethnically and philosophically diverse society. The country had to remain united, progressive, and strong, ready to guide war-shattered European nations away from the evils of the past and toward a postwar civilization that would be democratic rather than militaristic—with world affairs still dominated, he made clear to his cabinet, by the "white race."[4]

Remaining progressive, in the view of such antiwar reformers as Jane Addams and Senator Robert La Follette, meant finding a nonbelligerent solution to this new dilemma. As the cabinet met, members of the American Union Against Militarism were prominent among those sending both public and private messages to the White House urging Wilson to maintain the country's neutrality. Yet to demonstrate strength, other progressives and many conservative Americans believed, the country must be both able and willing to defend its rights. "If we acquiesce [to Germany's action], we ought not to pose as a nation or as a free people," Secretary of Agriculture

April 19, 1917, on the anniversary of the 1775 Revolutionary War battle at Lexington, Massachusetts, dozens of American cities held parades, many featuring impersonators of Paul Revere, who warned the colonists "The British are coming!" James Montgomery Flagg created this promotional poster.

WAKE UP AMERICA DAY

APRIL 19
1917

JAMES MONTGOMERY FLAGG

David F. Houston asserted during the February 2 cabinet meeting. "We ought to invite the Kaiser to set up as our permanent dictator." Most cabinet members agreed that the government had to respond firmly; few, however, favored going as far as a declaration of war.[5]

The next day the president revealed the path he had chosen. Speaking before a hastily called joint session of Congress, with the House of Representatives galleries filled to overflowing, Wilson formally severed diplomatic relations with Germany—while still embracing the possibility of reconciliation. "I refuse to believe that it is the intention of the German authorities to do in fact what they have warned us they will feel at liberty to do," the president said after announcing the break. The people of the United States were still "the sincere friends of the German people," he

added, "and earnestly desire to remain at peace with the Government which speaks for them."[6]

Fortified by overwhelming press approval for his action and a formal resolution of support from the U.S. Senate, President Wilson was determined that no American action would provoke hostilities and expressly forbade any troop movements that the Central Powers might construe as belligerent. At the same time, he and the secretaries of war and the navy continued doing what little they could to reinforce the nation's defenses. Concern for homeland security had been a contributing factor in the recall of the Punitive Expedition from Mexico in late January, after Carranza's forces had dealt Pancho Villa some damaging blows. Though the Americans had not caught or crushed Villa, the incursion, which ended officially on February

The Washington (D.C.) Times published this announcement of a peace rally to be held on April 2, 1917, the same night a special session of Congress was to begin. Its first order of business: to consider a declaration of war.

5, accomplished something potentially more valuable. "I have learned more useful soldiering while in Mexico," cavalry lieutenant George Patton, Jr., wrote to his wife, "than all the rest of my service put together."[7]

Only a few thousand American soldiers benefited similarly from the Punitive Expedition. Despite recent steps toward preparedness, the bulk of the regular army had little if any recent campaigning experience, while much of its high command remained inefficient and resistant to change. In the weeks of tense uncertainty after the break in relations with Germany, many civilian organizations were able to prepare for the possibility of war more effectively than either the military or the federal government.

The same frigid day that Wilson addressed Congress, staff of the American Red Cross (ARC) moved into their grand new headquarters on Seventeenth Street in Washington, D.C. Bolstered by a contributing membership that had jumped from 28,000 to more than 280,000 during the previous crisis-fraught year and energized by the prevailing national reliance on volunteerism, they leapt into action as soon as they learned that the United States had broken diplomatic relations with Germany, bringing the possibility of U.S. belligerence a giant step closer. Telegrams went to 267 local chapters: Form committees! Establish training detachments! Eager responses came pouring in from local chapters whose members had two years of experience providing aid to war-torn nations and to American troops involved in the Mexican incursion. Throughout

1916 ARC had also organized, at its own expense, some twenty "base hospitals" across the country that would be transferred to government control in case of war. Counting base hospital staff and additional nurses' aides ARC had been training, acting chairman Eliot Wadsworth stated on February 9, "We are prepared today to give expert nursing service to an army of one million men."[8]

One million men would be an eightfold increase of February 1917's 128,000-man U.S. Army, a force that Peyton March, the wartime army chief of staff, would later describe as of "no practical military value as far as the fighting in France was concerned."[9] With the military and naval expansion authorized in 1916 proceeding at a decidedly nonemergency pace, sympathetic civilian organizations continued to do what they could to bolster preparedness. Men who supported the Plattsburg civilian training camp movement—in February 1916, they had also established the Military Training Camps Association (MTCA)—continued to push for an increase in officer training for civilian volunteers. Colleges across the nation had, by 1917, established about one hundred units of the Reserve Officer Training Corps (ROTC), a cooperative civilian-military enterprise authorized under the 1916 National Defense Act. By 1917 the National Research Council (NRC), comprising scientists from many disciplines, had joined the previously established Naval Consulting Board and the Civilian Advisory Commission of the Council of National Defense to expand areas of civilian-government-military coordination, which the European catastrophe had shown to be essential in this new age of total war.[10]

Many women's groups, too, were prepared for possible belligerence. Members of the National American Woman Suffrage Association (NAWSA) announced in February their readiness to "serve our country with . . . zeal"—a sentiment echoed that month in a wire to President Wilson from the General Federation of Women's Clubs (GFWC). Many of GFWC's member organizations were already active in war relief and could easily refocus on an American war effort. The GFWC membership was predominantly white, but black women's groups, too, had been contributing to war relief, as well as helping African Americans who had been drawn out of the repressive South to work in northern factories that were scrambling to fill Allied war orders. That Great Migration continued to accelerate, spurred anew in February by the announcement of plans for a spring "Great Northern Drive" in the *Chicago Defender*, a black newspaper that was so forthright about the travails African Americans faced below the Mason-Dixon Line and so active in urging black workers to move north that it had to be distributed clandestinely in the South. As the black populations of some northern cities grew threefold, fivefold, and more, exacerbating racial tensions, women of the Phyllis Wheatley Clubs, the fifty-thousand-member National Association of Colored Women, and similar organizations helped avoid interracial confrontations by providing new arrivals with housing, health, and educational services—honing skills that would prove invaluable to a nation at war.[11]

As was the case with so many elements of America's disjointed preparedness movement, the myriad women's groups remained basically autonomous and uncoordinated. In January 1917, in Washington, D.C., the National Security League Congress of Constructive Patriotism endorsed a new organization, the National League for Women's Service (NLWS), which aimed to develop a comprehensive, centralized, and efficient scheme through which women could contribute to national security. Inspired by Britain's Voluntary Aid Detachments and founded by women who anticipated and supported American belligerence, by February the NLWS was marching toward its goal with military efficiency, adopting uniforms, engaging in military drills, and establishing divisions devoted to home economics, motor driving, and signaling and map reading.[12]

The NLWS division devoted to agriculture reflected Americans' growing appreciation of food-supply problems faced by countries at war, and by neutral countries striving to help feed them. Overseas war-relief shipments, coupled with a sharply reduced 1916 wheat harvest, had already created one food crisis in the United States. In late February skyrocketing prices provoked food riots in the poorer sections of New York, Chicago, Boston, and Philadelphia—people raged through the streets, overturned food carts, and looted grocery stores. The crisis ebbed when local authorities vowed to take action and food shipments reached the affected areas. Still, prices continued to rise, strengthening demands that the country stop exporting food. Yet ending exports might mean starvation to millions of people largely dependent on America for sustenance, including the people of occupied Belgium and northern France served by the Commission for Relief in Belgium (CRB). The commission's head, Herbert Hoover, now one of the country's most celebrated citizens, was visiting the United States when the break with Germany came. Two days after the unrestricted U-boat campaign began he learned that U-boats had sunk

without warning two plainly marked CRB relief ships. Temporarily suspending further shipments, Hoover engaged in tense negotiations with both belligerent alliances, seeking some way to resume deliveries with minimum danger of loss.[13]

Within three weeks CRB ships were guaranteed safety as long as they sailed around the British Isles using an extreme northern route. No such guarantee applied to neutral vessels moving through the vastly expanded maritime war zones. Thus, many American ships clung to the safety of East Coast ports. "The enforced idleness of American ships is costing American exporters, and indirectly all American producers, enormous amounts of money," the *New York Times* said on February 15, as goods piled up on American wharves, "and experts on economy declared today that to permit it to continue would disastrously affect American markets."[14]

In the midst of the Washington social season and preparations for his second inauguration, Wilson considered the benefits and dangers of defending the country's rights, and reassuring the nation's ship owners, by defensively arming the nation's commercial vessels. By late February, he decided to ask Congress to pass an armed-ships bill as soon as the volatile political climate calmed enough to favor its passage. The pro-war American Rights Committee (ARC), which had been pressing for some such remedial action, would certainly favor the bill. Yet the ARC's limited lobbying efforts and those of other like-minded Americans were at this point still more than countered by the activities of peace advocates, who in February staged a march to the U.S. Capitol and huge rallies in New York, Minneapolis, and Chicago. They also sent delegations to the White House, where, as Jane Addams later recalled, Wilson "still spoke to us as fellow pacifists."[15]

In fact, the president was still attempting to bring the belligerent nations to the negotiating table, now concentrating on Germany's badly battered chief ally, Austria-Hungary. Yet the Austro-Hungarian government proved unwilling to make a separate peace or to act in any manner that might be offensive to Germany; and Germany was betting that its U-boats would quickly defeat the Allies.[16] The Allies, too, remained focused on victory. Their manpower depleted from the war's horrendous casualties, teetering precariously on the edge of bankruptcy, and aware that loans from private American sources would not be enough to sustain them much longer, they were doing everything they could to bring America and its full range of both private and government resources into the war on their side. In meetings arranged by Wilson's longtime supporter and friend Florence Harriman, the eminent French philosopher Henri Bergson pled the Allied cause to Wilson administration members and, on February 19, to the president himself. Wilson also received that month a long message from Prime Minister David Lloyd George averring that the British wanted Wilson to declare war "not mainly [for] the military nor naval nor economic nor financial pressure that the American Government and people

might exert . . . against Germany" but to earn the right for Wilson to sit at the postwar peace table, where, as the leader of a country only interested in "justice and an ordered freedom," he would exert "the greatest influence that any man has ever exerted." There is no record of Wilson's reaction to that extraordinary note. There is, however, ample evidence that a message the British forwarded to Washington on February 24 did much to color the president's subsequent attitude toward the German government.[17]

Intercepted and decoded by British Intelligence, the forwarded message comprised the text of the lengthy January 16 telegram that Foreign Minister Arthur Zimmermann had dispatched to the German ambassador in Mexico. In the telegram, Zimmermann instructed the ambassador to propose to Carranza's government that, should the United States enter the war against Germany, Mexico and Germany become allies "on the following basis: make war together, make peace together, generous financial support, and an understanding on our part that Mexico is to reconquer the lost territory in Texas, New Mexico, and Arizona" (ceded to the United States after the Mexican War of 1846–1848). The telegram also suggested that Carranza urge America's ambitious Far-Eastern rival, Japan, to abandon the Allies and enter negotiations with Germany. Indignant in the extreme when he read the message, Wilson did not immediately disclose its contents to the public. Yet it may well have added steel to his voice as he addressed a joint session of Congress on February 26 to request an armed-ships

WESTERN UNION TELEGRAM

CLASS OF SERVICE DESIRED

Fast Day Message
Day Letter
Night Message
Night Letter

NEWCOMB CARLTON, PRESIDENT

Send the following telegram, subject to the terms on back hereof, which are hereby agreed to

via Galveston

JAN 19 1917

GERMAN LEGATION
MEXICO CITY

130	13042	13401	8501	115	3528	416	17214	6491	11310
18147	18222	21560	10247	11518	23677	13605	3494	14936	
98092	5905	11311	10392	10371	0302	21290	5161	39695	
23571	17504	11269	18276	18101	0317	0228	17694	4473	
23284	22200	19452	21589	67893	5569	13918	8958	12137	
1333	4725	4458	5905	17166	13851	4458	17149	14471	6706
13850	12224	6929	14991	7382	15857	67893	14218	36477	
5870	17553	67893	5870	5454	16102	15217	22801	17138	
21001	17388	7446	23638	18222	6719	14331	15021	23845	
3156	23552	22096	21604	4797	9497	22464	20855	4377	
23610	18140	22260	5905	13347	20420	39689	13732	20667	
6929	5275	18507	52262	1340	22049	13339	11265	22295	
10439	14814	4178	6992	8784	7632	7357	6926	52262	11267
21100	21272	9346	9559	22464	15874	18502	18500	15857	
2188	5376	7381	98092	16127	13486	9350	9220	76036	14219
5144	2831	17920	11347	17142	11264	7667	7762	15099	9110
10482	97556	3569	3670						

BERNSTORFF.

Charge German Embassy.

For Myself
For California
For Nevada (?)
For New Mexico
ARIZONA NEW MEXICO
TEXAS
PACIFIC OCEAN
MEXICO

bill. "I am not now proposing . . . war or any steps that need lead to it," he assured his listeners. "I merely request . . . that you will authorize me to supply our merchant ships with defensive arms . . . and with the means of using them, and to employ any other instrumentalities . . . that may be necessary . . . to protect our ships and our people in their legitimate and peaceful pursuits on the seas."[18]

Due to adjourn on March 4, Congress moved quickly to draft the legislation, spurred by popular approval of the president's speech—and by public concern over the February 25 sinking of the British liner *Laconia*, with two Americans, Mrs. Mary Hoy and her daughter Elizabeth, among the dead. Very quickly, however, the bill was caught in an eddy of arguments. Some congressmen wished to give the president greater powers than he had asked for; others were concerned that the requested authority would put too much power in the chief executive's hands and that arming ships would almost guarantee "a plunge into war."[19]

With the legislation apparently foundering, Wilson authorized release of the Zimmermann telegram. When it appeared in newspapers on March 1, a tsunami of indignation engulfed the country—accompanied by expressions of incredulity. Members of New York's elite Round Table Dining Club, generally sympathetic to Britain, believed it too absurd to be true. Prominent German-American journalist George Sylvester Viereck agreed, calling the telegram a "brazen forgery planted by British agents." Responding to a Senate resolution asking for verification, the

White House said the message was real but provided no evidence. That, incredibly, came from Zimmermann himself, when on March 3 he confirmed to reporters that he was, indeed, its author. His reminder that the arrangement with Mexico would only activate if the United States entered the war did little to mollify American public opinion. "Germany is at war with the United States now and has been for months," the Cleveland *Plain Dealer* raged. "It remains for Congress and the Administration to say what America's answer to this latest effrontery shall be—a Congress which for days has been hair-splitting over the kind and degree of power it shall confer upon the President to meet the gravest national crisis since the civil war."[20]

Moved by the furor, members of the House of Representatives quit splitting hairs and passed the Armed Neutrality (armed-ships) bill in a trice. In the Senate, however, it bumped up against a small group of legislators who were concerned that placing guns on U.S. commercial vessels could lead to full-scale belligerence, without due congressional consideration or a proper declaration of war. "Shall we, to maintain the technical right of travel and the pursuit of commercial profits, hurl this country into the bottomless pit of the European war?" Wisconsin's Robert La Follette thundered. Furthermore, these senators believed that allowing the president complete discretion to take further measures to defend U.S. shipping, measures that also might result in full-scale conflict, would violate a crucially important constitutional requirement. "Under this bill the President can do anything," George W. Norris of Nebraska declared. "The Constitution says that Congress has the sole power to declare war. This [bill] in effect is an amendment of the Constitution, an illegal amendment." Norris, La Follette, and the few who agreed with them successfully prevented the bill's passage before Congress adjourned—though they did not prevent the arming of merchantmen, which Wilson accomplished by executive action on March 12. In the meantime, this "little group of willful men," as Wilson quickly dubbed the anti-bill senators, were subjected to a wave of vilification as public opinion turned toward confronting Germany, a nation now shown to be conspiring against the American homeland itself. "I have no doubt that you feel as keenly as I do the treason committed by the eleven senators in fighting against the Armed Neutrality bill," journalist and 1914 Christmas ship organizer John Callan O'Laughlin wrote Teddy Roosevelt. "I am glad to say that all over the country there are expressions of indignation at their shameful conduct."[21]

In this contentious atmosphere, Wilson was sworn in for his second term in a private ceremony on Sunday, March 4, the date designated by law, then returned to the Capitol on March 5 for his public inauguration. Traveling through rainy streets lined with cheering crowds and bristling with security, he delivered his short inaugural address before about forty thousand people, speaking into a cold wind that made his words inaudible to all but those standing near him. After making a brief nod to the benefits created by his

THE ONLY ADEQUATE REWARD.

Branded "a little group of willful men" by an angry President Wilson, the senators who prevented the armed-ships bill from passing received Germany's Iron Cross from Rollin Kirby (1875–1952) in a March 7, 1917, political cartoon.

domestic progressive program, he spoke of the European war, which had marked every aspect of national life. "We stand firm in armed neutrality," he said, but acknowledged that the country might be drawn by uncontrollable circumstances into "a more immediate association with the great struggle." Whatever occurred, it was important that the people of the United States "stand together. We are being forged into a new unity amidst the fires that now blaze throughout the world."[22]

The new unity was a work in progress. Old divisions remained and new ones were appearing, even as indignant patriotism spurred the growing consensus for war. Most woman suffragists, represented by NAWSA, were prepared to divert their

energies to war work, both for patriotic reasons and because they believed that doing so would further their cause. Alice Paul and other militant suffragists disagreed. Determined to keep pushing for the right they had been trying to secure for decades, they continued picketing the White House, a heretofore unheard-of practice they had begun in late January and saw no reason to discontinue, even in the event of war. In mid-August they would even unlimber a sign referring to the president as "Kaiser Wilson," which did little to endear them to patriotic passersby.[23]

Within the African American community, opinions also differed, although the Tuskegee Institute principal, Robert Russa Moton, undoubtedly reflected prevailing sentiment when he wrote President Wilson in mid-March, "You and the Nation can count absolutely on the loyalty of the mass of the negroes." W. E. B. Du Bois, the editor of the NAACP's *Crisis*, believed that, should the country abandon neutrality, participation in the war effort would not only demonstrate loyalty but might also further black Americans' continuing quest for the full rights of citizenship. By early 1917 he had endorsed white NAACP board member Joel Spingarn's campaign to have the War Department establish a camp for training black officers. The call for *separate* training, a reflection of the country's unhealthy racial climate, initially offended many in the NAACP. Other African Americans were more generally offended by the idea of fighting for a country that seemed always to be fighting against *them*. "Should a black man shoulder a gun and go to war and fight for this country . . . which denies him the rights of citizenship under a flag which offers him no protection, strips him of his manhood by enacting laws which keeps [*sic*] him from the ballot box . . . segregated . . . lynched, burned at the stake, Jim Crowed and disarmed?" one R. K. McWoodson wrote to the *New York Sun* in mid-February. "If he fight, and fight he must, for what does he fight?"[24]

Parting ways with their pro-preparedness brethren, militant antiwar socialists and unionists were convinced that the country would be fighting in the interests of big business and against the continuing struggle to better the lives of ordinary workers—and they would have none of

it. "Eugene V. Debs last night urged the workers of the county to declare a nationwide general strike if the United States goes to war," the *New York Times* reported on March 8. "Speaking to an audience that packed Cooper Union to the doors, the veteran Socialist . . . declared he would rather be backed up against a granite wall and shot as a traitor than 'go to war for Wall Street.'" Conversely, the canny pro-preparedness labor leader Samuel Gompers of the American Federation of Labor viewed support for preparedness as an opportunity to accommodate workers' interests in the nation's war plans. Appointed to the Advisory Commission of

Unlike their more moderate sisters, militant suffragists campaigned for the vote throughout the war in ways that many Americans considered unpatriotic, including protests in front of the White House. Harris & Ewing photograph, ca. 1918.

the Council of National Defense in 1916, Gompers summoned labor representatives to a March 1917 meeting in Washington to determine and announce labor's role in formulating defense plans. That same month he backed President Wilson's successful effort to avoid a threatened strike by railroad workers, who had not yet been granted the eight-hour day promised them five months before.[25]

Events seemed to accelerate. As the navy began installing guns on American merchantmen, the Connecticut legislature became the first in the nation to appoint a state Military Emergency Board and to authorize formation of a home guard and a state census of manpower and materials "for use in event of war." The Emergency Peace Federation, meanwhile, deluged the White House with letters and petitions and dispatched twelve "apostles of peace" to speak on behalf of neutrality. Hostile receptions and hecklers apprised the apostles

of the changing mood of the country—especially after Americans learned, on March 18, that German submarines had sunk the American ships *City of Memphis*, *Illinois*, and *Vigilancia*. The latter two had not been warned; fifteen crewmen died.[26]

This tragic American loss occurred as many Americans were celebrating what seemed an astonishing gain for the cause of democracy. After a series of civilian food riots and mutinies within Russia's long-suffering military units, Czar Nicholas II had been forced to abdicate on March 15 and had been replaced with a more liberal provisional government, one that pledged to continue fighting against the Central Powers. THE CZAR HAS BEEN DROPPED. GOOD! the *Tacoma (WA) Times* exulted in a statement also predicting that Kaiser Wilhelm would go. "No more kings, no more war . . . A different day is dawning." "The democratic nations of Western Europe have

Above: After W. E. B. Du Bois urged African Americans to help make the world safe for democracy, A. Philip Randolph (1889–1979) wrote in his magazine, *The Messenger*, "We would rather make Georgia safe for the Negro." Photograph, ca. 1911.

Right: Czar Nicholas II of Russia, shortly after his abdication from the throne, 1917.

been emancipated from the handicap of Czarism," the *Nation* stated, "and have won a new ally—democratic Russia." These celebratory articles made little mention of continuing civil and military unrest in democratic Russia or the growing factionalism within the country's new regime. From London, meanwhile, Ambassador Page reminded the president that Britain and France, while emancipated from an autocratic ally, had not been freed from the probability of bankruptcy and that Allied resentment continued to rise over what the British, especially, perceived as America's inadequate response to Germany's new U-boat campaign.[27]

On March 20, Wilson convened a cabinet meeting, "the influence of which may . . . determine the destinies of the United States and possibly of the world," Secretary of State Lansing wrote in his notes. Undoubtedly stirred by the revolution in Russia and the recent ship losses, for the first time all cabinet members agreed that war with Germany was inevitable. Yet Secretary of the Treasury McAdoo and Secretary of Agriculture Houston stated that, as a combatant, the United States could best aid the Allies financially, with naval assistance, and by continuing the flow of supplies. With many others in government and across the land at this time, they believed the country could not and should not field an army overseas.[28]

The following day, Wilson called Congress into a special session, to begin on April 2, when the legislature would "receive a communication concerning grave matters of national policy." Though a decision for war remained uncertain, the president ordered Ambassador Brand Whitlock and American relief workers to leave occupied Belgium. He also instructed Secretary Daniels to establish a means of cooperating with the British Royal Navy and to do so quietly, to avoid raising either expectations or alarm. Daniels chose Admiral William S. Sims, head of the Naval War College, to act as liaison, and by March 31 Sims was bound for London— in civilian clothes and under an assumed name—aboard the recently armed liner *New York*. When the naval crewmen manning the ship's guns recognized him, the admiral quickly impressed on them the importance of keeping his secret.[29]

On March 22, news that many crewmen were killed when a U-boat sank the American tanker *Healdton* fueled the ardor with which twelve thousand people cheered for war at an American Rights Committee meeting in New York's Madison Square Garden. More thousands gathered at Carnegie Hall the following day in the first of several mass meetings held to celebrate and support Russia's turn toward democracy. For half an hour, however, the celebration deteriorated into what the *New York Times* termed a "violent clash between patriots and pacifists," pro-neutrality attendees loudly protesting New York mayor John P. Mitchel's assertion that America was about to go to war for democracy. Mitchel retorted, "Tonight we are divided into only two classes, Americans and traitors."[30]

As March turned to April, pro-war mass meetings occurred in Philadelphia, Chicago, Boston, Denver, and Manchester, New Hampshire. On April 1, as the National Security League sent two spokesmen,

Opposite: A map of the expanded zones of unrestricted U-boat operations established by the Germans in February 1917. Reproduced from *Kelly Miller's History of the World War for Human Rights,* 1919.

THE BLOCKADE ZONES.

Frederic Coudert and Henry L. Stimson, on a two-week tour to tout universal military training (UMT), a mob of nearly a thousand people surged into a Baltimore building where former Stanford University president, David Starr Jordan, now an "apostle of peace," was speaking. Jordan was only saved from a mauling when his audience stood and sang the "Star-Spangled Banner," temporarily halting the intruders and allowing him to retreat. "The Germans have behaved like sin, for such is the nature of war," Jordan wrote to a friend that day, "but the intolerance and tyranny with which we are being pushed into war far eclipses the riotous methods which threw the Kaiser off his feet and brought on the crash in 1914."[31]

Both peace advocates and pro-interventionists were among the throngs that gathered in Washington on April 2, a crowded day that saw the Sixty-fifth Congress organize its leadership; the swearing in of the nation's first congresswoman, Jeannette Rankin of Montana; an exchange of blows between Senator Henry Cabot Lodge and one of his Massachusetts constituents, a pacifist named Alexander Bannwart, over the senator's intent to support a war resolution; and, in the evening, the convening of a joint session of Congress. "That night at the Capitol everything seemed unreal," Florence Harriman, who observed the session, later recalled. "The white Capitol with the young moon over it and the playing searchlights . . . the guard of cavalry [that] surrounded the building . . . and the odd expectant crowds milling through the corridors and galleries were . . . something out of opera."[32]

The president arrived just after eight thirty. In his solemn thirty-six-minute address, he asked that Congress "formally accept the status of belligerent which has . . . been thrust upon" the people and government of the United States. What entering the war would mean to Americans was "clear" only in the most general sense. Wilson listed some measures the country must definitely take, among them counseling with and supporting the Allies; immediately providing the navy with all required equipment, especially that needed for antisubmarine warfare; and building an army of at least five hundred thousand men, preferably selected "upon the principle of universal liability to service." To do this, and more, would require "the organization and mobilization of all the material resources of the country"—and absolute dedication. "If there be any disloyalty," he said, to approving applause, "it will be dealt with with a firm hand of repression."

Only a few who attended, among them Robert La Follette, did not join in the wild cheers and flag waving that erupted at the end of the speech.[33]

The following day, as newspapers headlined both the president's speech and the sinking of the armed American merchantman *Aztec*, La Follette managed to postpone the Senate's consideration of a formal declaration of war by citing a rule requiring a one-day delay before voting on such a momentous measure. When debate began at ten A.M. on April 4, emotion and numbers overwhelmingly favored the war resolution, and its fervent supporters had little patience with the few who argued against it. Cries of "Treason!" greeted Senator George Norris's assertion that the nation was going to war chiefly for financial reasons. Senator John Sharp Williams called La Follette's ardent four-hour antiwar speech—during which the Wisconsin progressive criticized Wilson's uneven treatment of the belligerents and stated that most Americans still did not favor war—not just pro-German but "pretty nearly pro-Goth and pro-Vandal." (La Follette took his seat looking, one observer reported, "like . . . a person who had failed to keep his child from doing itself an irreparable harm.") At eleven minutes past eleven P.M., the war resolution passed by a vote of eighty-two to six. The House began its debate at ten thirty-five A.M. on April 5, as Washington received news that a U-boat had sunk the American vessel *Missourian*. The momentum for war by then seemed unstoppable, even though many were torn. There was "something in the air," Representative Frederick Britten said, "forcing us to vote for this declaration of war when away down deep in our hearts we are just as opposed to it as are our people back home." Through the day and into the night eighty congressmen spoke in favor of the war resolution; twenty spoke against it—including Jeannette Rankin, who said, with tears in her eyes, "I want to stand by my country, but I cannot vote for war." The resolution passed, 373 to 50, at three twelve A.M. on Good Friday, April 6. At one eighteen that afternoon, after President Wilson affixed his signature to the document, the United States was at war with Germany.[34]

Allied nations greeted news of the declaration with heady relief; Americans absorbed the news with confusion and conflicting emotions. The evening of April 6 in New York, as Metropolitan Opera star Geraldine Farrar ended a performance of *Tosca* by leading the audience in the "Star-Spangled Banner," police raided an antiwar meeting that they said "bordered on treason." Yet other city police simply stood by as a U.S. Army veteran delivered a street-corner speech urging men *not* to enlist in the armed forces, the police telling an inquiring reporter that "they knew of no law under which they could interfere." Despite the veteran's words and a Socialist Party pronouncement that the war declaration was "a crime against the people of the United States," most Americans seemed prepared to embrace the sentiment in a recently penned song, "America, Here's My Boy": "America, I raised a boy for you," the lyrics went, "You'll find him staunch and true/ Place a gun upon his shoulder/ He is ready to die or do." A Montana newspaper reported a dip in the Missoula County high school's hopes for victory in an interscholastic track meet after several star athletes declared their intention to quit school and

enlist. In Chicago, scores of applicants, many accompanied by their mothers, besieged military recruiting offices, where more than 300 enlisted in the navy, 252 in the army, and 42 in the Marine Corps on April 10 alone. Whether in anticipation of being called for military service or in hopes of evading it, at the same time an even greater number crowded into the city's marriage license bureau. A newspaper account of this surge in matrimonial enthusiasm noted, "Federal agents also obtained the names of the 2,000 recent applicants for licenses," although the agents gave no reason for their interest.[35]

This early rush to volunteer for the military notwithstanding, the president on April 2 had called for expanding the army by conscription, thus belatedly falling in step with the National Security League, General Leonard Wood, and other military leaders who for years had favored universal military training. In peacetime, UMT's proponents believed, this obligation would create a reservoir of men prepared to spring to the colors at times of national emergency. Perhaps more important, it would help break down class barriers—workers and the wealthy, immigrants and native-born serving side by side—and would instill a sense of loyalty and national pride and an appreciation for the obligations of citizenship among the country's polyglot population. With the nation now at war, universal (or at least widespread) liability to service seemed the most practical means to muster and monitor the human resources necessary for military expansion—a decision informed by the British experience before

that nation broke long tradition and instituted the draft in 1916. Unregulated by any coherent system, hundreds of thousands of Britons had deserted their civilian pursuits for military service, leaving great manpower gaps in vital businesses and industries. So many of these eager volunteers were slaughtered on the Western Front in the war's early years, among them many of Britain's best-educated and brightest young men serving as frontline officers, that the country's later war effort was seriously damaged. "The idea of the draft is not only the drawing of men into the military service of the Government," Wilson wrote to a friend on May 4. "Its central idea was to disturb the industrial and social structure of the country just as little as possible."[36]

Conscription legislation was presented to the appropriate congressional committees almost immediately—and was quickly enmeshed in violent arguments, as both pro- and anti-draft factions were bolstered by rafts of constituent mail. "Don't stand for any conscription," Pennsylvanian J. B. Eastwood wrote to his congressman. "Leave it to those who wanted the war and brought it about to continue their advocacy and be consistent by doing the fighting and foot[ing] the bills." Their own convictions fortified by such letters, anti-draft congressmen cited the country's proud tradition of volunteerism, evoked memories of Civil War draft riots, and called conscription "Prussianism" and draftees the equivalent of slaves or convicts sent to war to help solve "European squabbles." Many proponents of a volunteer military were also thinking of the division

In May 1917, artist Henry Glintenkamp (1887–1946) created this protest against the proposed national conscription, which would, his drawing suggests, make slaves of labor (at left), ravage democracy (strapped to the wheel), and sacrifice the nation's youth (tied to the cannon's mouth). Published in the August 1917 edition of *The Masses*, the drawing was declared treasonous by the U.S. government.

Conscription

H. J. Glintenkamp.

of volunteers Teddy Roosevelt had been organizing for months, repeatedly offering its services to Secretary Baker and, on an April 10 visit to the White House, to the president himself. But Roosevelt's lust for frontline service had little effect on those opposed to relying solely on volunteers to build the required wartime army. "History has proven that Universal Service is the only fair and efficient system and that the volunteer system in war against a first class power is a failure," wrote Henry Bryant of Milwaukee. Such letters inspired pro-draft congressmen to characterize conscription as the most "scientific" way to expand the army, while repeating many arguments previously used by advocates of UMT. "I cannot bring myself to . . . [believe] that defense of the nation is a question of will," Representative George Lunn of New York declared. "I say it is a question of obligation upon every citizen."[37]

While wrestling over conscription, Congress also began months of complex wrangling over the best ways to pay for the country's own war effort while maintaining financial support to the Allies. Echoing fiscal arguments made during the preparedness surge in 1916, much of the debate centered on effective use of the federal income tax. To progressive reformers such as Amos Pinchot, "effective" income taxation involved spreading the burden in a manner that would help narrow the daunting divide between the country's superrich and the remaining 95 percent of the population. In March, Pinchot co-founded the American Committee on War Finance (ACWF), which by April was trumpeting a fiscal program of progressive

taxation, limited net profits on "war supplies or war service," and a cap on wartime net income. The chief purpose, Pinchot wrote to a friend, was "to keep the people from being exploited and to get an income tax started which, when once in operation, will be hard for the privileged interests to tear down after the war." Through such progressive taxation, which would "tap and reduce the great fortunes," Pinchot's fellow reformer, the newspaper magnate E. W. Scripps, averred, "we may draw the greatest reform and the greatest blessings to our people." The blessings of taxation were much less evident to those not so keen for social reform. As local committees supporting the ACWF program sprang up across the country, a steady procession of individuals and delegations appeared on Capitol Hill, each one claiming to support the war effort but begging for exemptions from various proposed taxes.[38]

Debate on what would become the War Revenue Act of 1917 continued for months. The final version, signed in early October, did further expand income and other taxes—another plateau in the government's growing reliance on taxation for revenue. Yet war-cost estimates ballooned so much during the lengthy debate that the Wilson administration chose to rely much more heavily on loans than on taxes to secure the needed funds—a major defeat for Pinchot and like-minded progressives. In fact, the first Liberty Loan Act was passed as the War Revenue Act debate was just getting started, zipping through Congress in less than three weeks. Signed by President Wilson on April 24, it authorized the issue of $5 billion in

"RECRUIT" -UNION SQ.   4211-13

Men gather around the USS *Recruit*, a wooden battleship built by the U.S. Navy in New York City's Union Square (ironically, within view of the Germania Life building in the background). Its purpose: to recruit seamen and sell Liberty Bonds. Bain News Service photograph, ca. 1917.

bonds to cover both immediate American war expenses and a round of loans to the Allies.[39] Its timing was propitious: that same week two special Allied political-military missions arrived in the country to hold policy discussions and to assess America's ability to make war. The British mission, headed by the foreign secretary, Lord Arthur Balfour, arrived in the country on April 21 to a reception that, while extremely cordial, was muted by lingering resentment over the harm British blockade policies had done to American commerce, concern over Britain's continuing refusal to grant independence to Ireland, and the general distrust that had long simmered beneath the surface of British-American relations.[40]

No such difficulties tempered the reception of the French mission, which arrived in Washington on April 25 "amidst the wildest excitement," Florence Harriman reported. Its political leader, Minister of Justice René Viviani, was far overshadowed, in American eyes, by the head of the military contingent, Marshal Joseph Joffre, hero of the 1914 Battle of the Marne, which had saved Paris and prevented the Germans from attaining their planned quick victory over France. "The leathery General in bright blue regalia dissolves with a smile," Harriman wrote in her diary, "and he becomes 'Grandpapa Joffre,'—a kindly French visitor, who is most humanly pleased at the way we adore him and frankly adores back." His reputation battered in his own country by the military reverses of 1915 and 1916, Joffre remained to Americans a symbol of the French nation's heroic defense of democracy and a reminder of the vital assistance France had provided to the fledgling United States during its revolution against Great Britain. Mobbed at public appearances around the country, Joffre made his most valuable contribution to the French mission in closed-door meetings with U.S. military and political leaders, where his recommendations were often at odds with those of the British.[41]

That both countries needed the U.S. government's financial support came as no surprise. In fact the Wilson administration had just agreed to lend the British $200 million and the French $100 million—the first of what would by 1919 amount to more than $10 billion in American treasury loans to Allied nations. Almost half that total would go to the British—with the stipulation that loan funds must be spent in the United States, thus boosting the American economy. The Wilson administration was also aware that, with shipping losses increasing, the Allied need for supplies was becoming desperate. As the missions arrived in Washington, Herbert Hoover, then on a fact-finding mission in Europe, cabled Secretary of State Lansing that the Allies' food supplies were at a critical level, and to alleviate the situation the United States and Canada would have to export one hundred million bushels of wheat in the coming months. Admiral Sims, now wearing his uniform and officially established as the U.S. naval liaison in London, was also reporting on the huge dent U-boats were making in British food and shipping resources. While asking the Navy Department to send as many American destroyers and patrol craft as possible, he also added his voice to those of the British officials urging the Royal Navy to adopt a convoy system aimed at cutting Allied losses (a practice the British would finally adopt in May).[42]

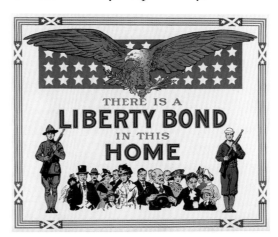

Far left: Britain's foreign secretary, Lord Arthur Balfour (waving top hat), with American diplomat Hugh Gibson (far right) in New York City during the British mission's visit to the United States. Bain News Service photograph, May 11, 1917.

Left: A Liberty Loan placard to be displayed in bond purchasers' windows.

Top: Marshal Joseph Joffre (center, large medal on chest) with other members of the French Mission and an honor guard of African American soldiers at the State Department in Washington, D.C. Photograph by Harris & Ewing, spring 1917.

Bottom: Admiral William S. Sims (1858–1936), the United States Navy liaison to the Royal Navy.

American officials were taken aback, however, when the British and French pressed to have American troops in Europe at the earliest possible moment. Both nations were continuing to hemorrhage men in ultimately futile campaigns on the Western Front. A British offensive at Arras that made some headway when it began in early April had devolved into a battle of attrition by the time the British Mission reached Washington; before it ended it would inflict 130,000 casualties for little appreciable gain. The French suffered at least as many losses when a smashing attack launched on April 16 along the Aisne River, and guaranteed by General Robert Nivelle to rupture German lines, lost all momentum within the first few days. Continuing attacks through the end of the month, Nivelle only managed to rupture the morale of French troops. Joffre knew the offensive was in trouble before he arrived in America. He did not know

La Tête de l'Armée

Abel Faivre

176/600

of the "acts of collective indiscipline" that were spreading through the bone-weary French army, contributing to Nivelle's replacement as general-in-chief by General Philippe Pétain on April 29. Even so, Joffre understood what a boost the arrival of even a small force of Americans would give to his long-suffering countrymen. (France is "sore distressed and bleeding," U.S. ambassador William Graves Sharp reported to Washington during the French Mission's visit. "The exhaustion is . . . much greater than the world knows—for no other of her Allies has suffered such a drain in men and resources.")[43]

Joffre also grasped something about the Americans that his counterpart on the British Mission failed to appreciate: that if Americans were to fight in France, they would want their own discrete army. "No great nation having a proper consciousness of its own dignity—and America perhaps less than any other—would allow its citizens to be incorporated like poor relations in the ranks of some other army and fight under a foreign flag," he was to write in his memoirs. Pressing the Americans to send a token force directly to France as soon as possible, with other units to follow as soon as they were organized, he tempered his request with certain assurances. Though the French would assist with equipment and advanced training, the United States would build and maintain its own army, which would serve on the Western Front close to that of the French. British general Tom Bridges, meanwhile, was calling for the immediate dispatch of five hundred thousand raw U.S. recruits to Britain for nine weeks' training, after which they would be "amalgamated," or dispersed as needed, in the British lines to serve under the Union Jack. Joffre and the Americans emerged victorious from this first skirmish in what was to be a long struggle over possible amalgamation of American troops, as British—and French—pressure for that policy ballooned with every negative fluctuation in the fortunes of war.[44]

Joffre's diplomatic pressure, with that of the British, undoubtedly influenced the Wilson administration's decision to send troops to Europe.[45] The French marshal was delighted to learn that the administration was already pushing another measure he favored. He was at a lawn party on April 28, talking with Florence Harriman and Teddy Roosevelt's daughter, Alice Roosevelt Longworth, when someone announced that the Senate had approved conscription. Joffre greeted the announcement with a smile, Harriman wrote in her diary, after which the old soldier said that this was "the beginning of the end"—presumably for the Germans. The end of the conscription debate did not come until the two houses of Congress reconciled their differences, however, and passed the final bill that President Wilson signed into law on May 18. It authorized bringing the regular army to full strength and federalizing the National Guard, with volunteer enlistments allowed to augment both those forces; registering all male citizens age twenty-one to thirty, as well as aliens who had taken out their first citizenship papers; and an initial draft selection of five hundred thousand men, which could be augmented by a second five hundred thousand, if needed. These draftees would

chiefly populate what would be called the National Army, a supplementary force raised because of the war emergency. Ardent lobbying by moral-reform groups resulted in a provision that forbade houses of ill repute and liquor near army camps, the ban on liquor giving a giant boost to the increasingly powerful national prohibition movement. The act also included a somewhat vague provision exempting from combat service—though not from induction into the military, where it was unclear what alternate duties they might perform—members of any established and "well-recognized religious sect or organization . . . whose then existing creed or principles forbid its members to participate in war in any form." One small section of the act, tussled over for weeks, allowed but did not require the president to accept Teddy Roosevelt's volunteer

unit. "It would be very agreeable for me to pay Mr. Roosevelt this compliment, and the Allies the compliment of sending to their aid one of our most distinguished public men," the president wrote in a diplomatically worded refusal. "But this is not the time . . . for any action not calculated to contribute to the immediate success of the war. The business now at hand is undramatic, practical, and of scientific definiteness and precision."[46]

The business of transforming the United States into an active combatant nation definitely had practical and scientific aspects, but it would prove to be far from undramatic. The country was entering uncharted waters in which lurked treacherous shoals. The president himself had reportedly sketched a dramatic picture of what might happen to the ship of state in a conversation with *New York World* editor in chief Frank Cobb shortly before the declaration of war. Entering this bitter conflict, Wilson had predicted, would cause Americans to abandon the country's core ideals and any notion of tolerance. "To fight you must be brutal and ruthless, and the spirit of ruthless brutality will enter into the very fiber of our national life, infecting Congress, the courts, the policeman on the beat, the man on the street," Cobb recalled the president saying. "He thought the Constitution would not survive it; that free speech and the right of assembly would go." Conformity would be the only virtue, Wilson told Cobb, and anyone who refused to conform would pay the penalty.[47]

Yet at this early stage, it was difficult to know precisely what "conformity" might mean beyond general support for the war effort—and no one yet knew what the American war effort was to include. The conscription bill had passed, but was the country truly to send a great force overseas? If so, how great was it to be? How was it to be trained and supported? On April 10 a never-to-be-explained explosion that killed more than 130 employees at the Eddystone (Pennsylvania) Ammunition Works raised memories of the Black Tom explosion in 1916 and a similar catastrophe in January in Kingsland, New Jersey, feeding fears of more home-front espionage. President Wilson did nothing to allay those fears when he said in his April 2 war message, "The Prussian autocracy . . . has filled our unsuspecting communities and even our offices of government with spies and set criminal intrigues everywhere afoot," and newspaper articles were already asserting that German agents were trying to foment rebellion among African Americans in the South. But must Americans truly disregard constitutional rights and

the democratic principles for which, the president asserted, the nation was fighting to guard against such dangers? "The will of the majority of Congress has declared war and it is the duty of all Americans to accept this mandate," peace and education advocate Fannie Fern Andrews wrote to the teachers of the United States on April 10. Yet in this national emergency "there will be none of the old passions of war . . . A cult of hatred has no place in free America, for tolerance is the first principle of democracy."[48]

As that statement circulated in pamphlet form, Congress considered a proposed Espionage Act, which had been percolating within the Wilson administration for months but which the legislature had previously refused to consider. "We are without adequate federal laws to deal with . . . creatures of passion, disloyalty, and anarchy dwelling within the United States," Wilson had told Congress in his Third Annual Message in December 1915. "They are infinitely malignant," the president said, "and the hand of our power should close over them at once." The bill now under consideration was designed for that purpose. Despite the overwhelming congressional and public support for the war declaration and attendant concern over security, however, the proposed Espionage Act did not sail through the legislature. Three of its sweeping provisions, in particular, caused weeks of intense and agonizing debate.[49]

As East Coast peace activists hired Fannie Mae (Frances) Witherspoon to head a legal aid bureau for "conscientious objectors and persons who had been deprived of

their right of exercising free speech, free assemblage and free press" by war-related intolerance, the press censorship provision of the nascent Espionage Act came under congressional scrutiny. Making illegal the publication of any material the president deemed "of such character that it is or *might be* useful to the enemy" (emphasis added), the provision died in a fusillade of criticism from legislators and newsmen concerned with the power it would place in presidential hands, the damper it would

With debate raging within and outside Congress on provisions of the proposed Espionage Act, on May 2, 1917, the *New York American* declared its opposition to the measure in this cartoon by Winsor McCay (1869–1934) showing Congress using the act to drive Liberty away from the United States Capitol.

THIS MUST NOT BE!

put on their own ability to criticize the Wilson administration, and the damage it would do to fundamental American rights. The proposed censorship was "outrageous, shameful and tyrannical," California's progressive senator, Hiram Johnson, wrote to a friend. The provision not only assailed the people's freedom of speech, the American Newspaper Publishers' Association declared, but also sought to "deprive them of the means of forming intelligent opinion. In war, especially, the press should be free, vigilant, and unfettered."[50]

While subscribers to Max Eastman's left-leaning magazine, the *Masses*, were reading its April edition, containing radical journalist John Reed's essay "Whose War?" (his answer: "not mine"), legislators struggled with the broad wording of the "nonmailability" provision of the proposed Espionage Act. After rejecting the terms "treasonable" and "anarchistic" as too broad and subject to individual interpretation, they gave the postmaster general the power to withhold from the mails material "containing any matter advocating or urging treason, insurrection or forcible resistance to any law of the United States" or that, in his judgment, violated any provision of the overall bill. (In fact, the Postal Service was already on alert. On April 25, First Assistant Postmaster General J. C. Koons ordered all local postmasters to report on "suspicious characters, disloyal and treasonable acts and utterances" and anything else "which might be important during the existence of the present state of war.")[51]

What would prove to be the proposed Espionage Act's most potent provision in restricting freedom of speech did not inspire as much congressional debate, though it was the subject of testimony by concerned citizens before the House Committee on the Judiciary. As worded, attorney Gilbert Roe of the Free Speech League told the committee, the ban on making or conveying false reports or statements that might "promote the success of" America's enemies, and the prohibition against willfully causing or attempting to cause "disaffection in the [U.S.] military or naval forces," could be so broadly interpreted that *any* discussion or criticism of the war could be deemed criminal. Emily Balch, a peace activist and Wellesley College professor, agreed, adding that even criticism intended to right some wrong or error in the prosecution of the war could be deemed by authorities as an attempt to create "disaffection." To a congressman's observation that juries, not prosecutors, would make the ultimate determination of criminality, Balch replied that, with the country immersed in the international conflict, jury members would be no less prone to "war hysteria" than anyone else. Such arguments moved Congress to eliminate the term "disaffection," from this provision, substituting "cause or attempt to cause insubordination, disloyalty, mutiny, or refusal of duty"—which still left ample room for interpretation.[52]

On Flag Day, June 14, 1917, President Wilson delivered a speech on the grounds of the Washington Monument in which he again declared friendship for the German people while forcefully condemning their government and its ongoing plot to dominate the world. "That Government has many spokesmen here, in places both high and low," Wilson averred. "They have learned discretion, they keep within the law. It is opinion they utter now, not sedition." These people "seek to undermine the [American] government with false professions of loyalty to its principles," the president said. "But they will make no headway." The Espionage Act of 1917 passed the following day. The first federal law since the widely detested (and quickly abandoned) Sedition Act of 1798 to be aimed at curbing seditious speech,[53] it became a powerful tool for suppressing any suspect or unpopular opinion, allowing fines up to ten thousand dollars and imprisonment for up to twenty years for those convicted under its elastic terms. Overzealously enforced, the act would facilitate the very abandonment of tolerance the president had so darkly predicted. Yet without the press censorship provision and with some of the language originally proposed tightened to deal with various concerns (see discussion above), neither the president nor Attorney General Thomas Gregory considered the Espionage Act sufficiently strong.[54]

Gregory also believed that the Justice Department and duly constituted federal law enforcement institutions were not sufficient to monitor the loyalty and activities of the country's hundred million people. In March 1917 his department's own Bureau of Investigation (BI, later to become the FBI) had only about three hundred agents. Army and navy intelligence operations were as yet rudimentary, and State Department, Post Office, and Treasury intelligence groups were similarly unprepared

for what Gregory perceived as a home-front emergency. Moreover, at this time, all these agencies were competing rather than coordinating with each other. Thus, as soon as the country was officially at war, Gregory assumed the initiative, urging all federal attorneys to be constantly vigilant and asking the nation's police chiefs to keep watch on pacifists and German-Americans. His request that all "citizens . . . bring their suspicions to the . . . Department of Justice" initiated a tidal wave of often self-serving accusations. By the end of April, Gregory was boasting to President Wilson that he had "several hundred thousand private citizens . . . keeping an eye on disloyal individuals and making reports of disloyal utterances." Prominent among this growing army of untrained and unrestrained snoopers were members of the American Protective League (APL), a vigilance organization founded in March 1917 by a Chicago advertising executive, Albert M. Briggs, who offered its services to BI chief A. Bruce Bielaski. Both Bielaski and Gregory embraced the league, Gregory authorizing it to print on its letterhead, "Organized with the Approval, and Operating under the Direction of the United States Department of Justice, Bureau of Investigation." He also allowed its members to carry badges bearing the legend SECRET SERVICE DIVISION, which understandably concerned Treasury Secretary William McAdoo, whose department housed the genuine United States Secret Service. Such official backing undoubtedly helped boost APL's membership, which by mid-June stood at more than 100,000 individuals in six hundred branches nationwide. As

President Woodrow Wilson delivers a Flag Day address on the grounds of the Washington Monument. Secretary of State Robert Lansing is visible on the extreme right, in the dark suit and hat. Harris & Ewing photograph, June 14, 1917.

DON'T TALK

THE WEB IS SPUN FOR YOU WITH INVISIBLE THREADS

KEEP OUT OF IT
HELP TO DESTROY IT
STOP = THINK
ASK YOURSELF IF WHAT YOU WERE ABOUT TO SAY MIGHT HELP THE ENEMY

SPIES ARE LISTENING

INTELLIGENCE OFFICER NORTHEAST HQ DEPT U.S. ARMY

"The Vigilantes"

An Organization of Writers, Artists and Others for Patriotic Purposes

Executive Committee

Porter Emerson Browne   Thomas C. Desmond
Monroe Douglas Robinson   Hermann Hagedorn
Charles Hanson Towne   Julian Street

J. Harry Welling, Executive Secretary

it continued to grow, eventually enlisting some 250,000 volunteers, the league branched out from its original intent, to monitor enemy aliens, and began peering suspiciously at the behavior, statements, and finances of anyone suspected of disloyalty. Joined by other less-sanctioned but equally enthusiastic amateur spies—including members of the Knights of Liberty, the Sedition Slammers, the Terrible Threateners, and the Boy Spies of America—APL "agents" increasingly disregarded due processes of law, engaging in warrantless wiretapping, intercepting mail, and trampling all over the Bill of Rights in hot pursuit of disloyalty that was generally more imagined than real. "Between Wilson and his brigades of informers, spies, volunteer detectives, perjurers and complaisant judges," acerbic journalist H. L. Mencken would write before this particular wave of vigilantism finally died down, "the liberty of the citizen has pretty well vanished in America."[55]

Mencken's jaundiced eye concentrated on the dark side of support for the war, but millions of Americans were altering their normal life patterns to support their country and its allies in more positive ways. Civilians continued to brave the hazardous trip to Europe to join the volunteer ambulance corps still serving the French army, even as the Wilson administration entered delicate negotiations with the French to

transfer the ambulances to U.S. military control. Recent Harvard graduate Edward Estlin (later e.

Top: Kaiser Wilhelm is the spider whose tentacles reach far into the American homeland in this poster published in Boston by the Intelligence Officer, Northeastern Department, U.S. Army, ca. 1917.

Bottom: American vigilance societies and vigilantism proliferated during the war, but the organization of writers and artists called the Vigilantes was closer in nature to a patriotic propaganda committee. One major goal: to cultivate "a sense of public service and an intelligent interest in . . .national problems."

Inset: The frontispiece from *A History of Section 647, United States Army Ambulance Service with the French Army,* 1919.

e. or E. E.) Cummings left in late April to serve with the Norton-Harjes ambulance corps, his brief and decidedly atypical service culminating in his arrest and months-long confinement because, among other lapses, he refused to say he hated the Germans—an episode that inspired his postwar book *The Enormous Room.* Cummings's friend and fellow writer John Dos Passos, also a Norton-Harjes volunteer, embarked in June aboard the *Chicago,* a ship carrying other volunteers and laden, Dos Passos wrote, "with fear, patriotism, and young men in uniform." He encountered two of the better-known soldiers during the voyage: Theodore Roosevelt, Jr., and his brother Archie, both Plattsburg camp graduates and now reserve army officers, who were en route to join Pershing's staff. (Their brother Kermit would shortly travel to what is now Iraq to serve with the British, and the youngest Roosevelt son, Quentin, would arrive in France in July after completing pilot training.)[56]

W ell before the *Chicago* sailed, New York's commissioner of weights and measures, Joseph Hartigan, had suggested formation of a new home-front force. Men whose minor defects such as very poor eyesight disqualified them from military service could form an "agricultural army" to compensate for the continuing drift of farm workers into more lucrative industrial work. February's food riots might have inspired Hartigan's idea. They certainly inspired timber magnate Charles Lathrop Pack, who in March organized the National War Garden Commission "to arouse the patriots of America to the importance of putting all idle land to work," Pack

T in training with Chausseurs Alpins, 1917.

wrote in 1919, "to teach them how to do it, and to educate them to conserve by canning and drying all food they could not use while fresh." In March, too, the National League for Women's Service and the Women's National Farm and Garden Association agreed jointly to form a Land Service League to prepare for increased wartime production and help fight the high cost of food. With the nation officially at war, food-supply expert Herbert Hoover, back from his April fact-finding trip, engaged in a subtle behind-the-scenes turf battle with Secretary of Agriculture Houston while encouraging Congress and the Wilson administration to establish a separate wartime Food Administration staffed by individuals recruited from the private sector. Normal government bureaucracy was all very well in peacetime, Hoover told an interviewer for the *Saturday Evening Post* in late March, but "bureaucracy tends toward mediocrity," and the crisis of war demanded "the best brains of the country—which means its industrial brains." He intended to tap these brains, should his plan come to fruition.[57] Hoover's one-man lobbying campaign, and his stellar reputation for getting things done, did the trick. On May 19, well before a restive Congress passed the enabling legislation, Wilson informally established the Food Administration and named Hoover to head it, a position the wealthy businessman would fill without pay. The Department of Agriculture would continue with the duties it

Left: The Woman's Land Army of America brought thousands of volunteer "farmerettes" from urban areas into the countryside to replace male farmworkers. It was inspired by a similar organization in Britain, which used these stamps to promote participation.

Below: Children tend a garden donated by the Rockefeller Foundation at Sixty-fifth Street and Avenue A in New York City. Bain News Service photograph, May 1917.

regularly performed in peacetime, Wilson said, while Hoover's organization, under the president's direct supervision, would, with congressional approval, supervise "distribution and consumption . . . exports, imports, prices, purchase, and requisition of commodities, storing and the like which may require regulation during the war." By May 22, Hoover had moved into temporary offices at the Department of the Interior. Deluged with hundreds of offers of volunteer assistance, he began to build an organization intended, he said, to wisely administer rather than dictate wartime food policies.[58]

F ood for the body was essential but so was food for the mind, something American historian John Franklin Jameson well understood. In April he founded the National Board for Historical Services so that the country would benefit during the war from the knowledge of its historians, who would also assure that war-related materials would be preserved for posterity. The nation's leaders and future generations would be prime beneficiaries of Jameson's board. Librarian of Congress Herbert Putnam was more concerned with improving the minds and moral fiber of the growing body of American servicemen when he contacted his fellow bibliophile, Secretary of War Baker, who agreed that wholesome reading matter should be supplied to the armed forces. By the end of April, the American Library Association established a Committee on Mobilization and War Service Plans, with Putnam as the chair. Thus began a program that

Both the photograph taken by Able & Company, Washington, D.C., and the poster by artist Charles Buckles Falls (1874–1960) promote the "Books for Sammies" program. Initiated by the American Library Association, it supplied camp libraries and approved reading matter to armed forces in the United States and abroad.

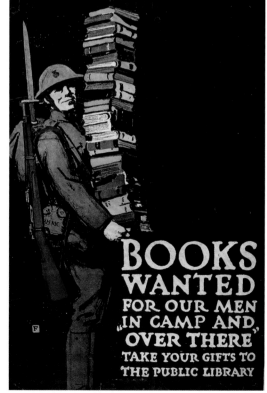

would construct thirty-six camp library buildings and distribute about 10 million books and magazines before the committee disbanded in 1920.[59]

Officials of the Military Training Camps Association (MTCA) also contacted Secretary Baker in April to suggest "that the citizens' military training camps be turned into officers' training schools" to help provide the leaders needed for the country's expanding armed forces. Using authority provided by the 1916 National Defense Act, the MTCA wire continued, the training camps could "be opened May first for two or three months of instruction . . . to be continued in relays." Aware that the army had minimal plans for officer training, Baker agreed to open discussions, and an MTCA delegation quickly appeared in Washington. At the War Department they encountered a military babel of plans, counterplans, questions, and uncertainty over how the camps would jibe with the conscription bill then being debated. By April 17, however, the army announced that sixteen training camps would be established across the country, and three-month training for civilian officer candidates would start on May 8. Two days later, the MCTA executive committee sent forty thousand hastily printed circulars and application forms to the association's state offices, and across the country, civilian members of the MCTA hired clerks, established recruitment offices, secured the voluntary services of doctors to perform medical examinations, and established what would become a long-term working relationship with the army.[60]

A 1917 poster by artist L. N. Britton requesting donations to support the many wartime services provided by the American Red Cross.

Judging from the atmosphere in Massachusetts, where Lieutenant George Patton was enjoying a furlough, recruitment of officer candidates would not be difficult. "All the people here are war mad," Patton wrote General Pershing on April 23. "Everyone I know is either becoming a reserve officer or explaining why he can't." Some three weeks later, a newly promoted Captain Patton joined Pershing in Washington, where the general had gone to assume command of the American Expeditionary Forces (AEF), still of indeterminate size, that would be sent to fight in France. Going into one meeting at the War Department, Pershing encountered Marshal Joffre, who was preparing to return home. Joffre "spoke of the serious situation in France," Pershing later remembered, "and expressed the hope of seeing American troops on the Western Front very soon"—a remarkable appeal, Pershing thought, from such a celebrated wartime leader to "the commander-in-chief of an army not yet in existence." Yet plans were afoot to fulfill Joffre's hope, at least in small measure: On May 17, President Wilson authorized the dispatch of one U.S. division as soon as possible, to boost Allied morale and as a sign of more help to come. Eleven days later, while that division was being organized, Pershing, Patton, and 186 other core staff embarked for England aboard the British ship *Baltic*. During the crossing, the Americans studied French, attended lectures on the dangers of venereal disease—and worried that U-boats would find their war-supply-laden ship a tempting target. On June 6, Patton noted in his diary, "everyone was more cheerful" when two American destroyers, *Tucker* and

Rowan, appeared on the *Baltic*'s flanks and escorted the ship for the last two days of its voyage. After warm welcomes in Liverpool and London, Pershing, like Admiral Sims before him, spent several days in meetings where he learned more details of the Allies' deteriorating situation before repacking to leave for France.[61]

"Movement" was the watchword in these early months of the American war. While Pershing was receiving his orders in Washington, the first American noncombat troops, the staffs of six Red Cross base hospitals now under armed forces command, set sail, on separate ships, for the Western Front: nurses, doctors, chaplains, and a bevy of enlisted men who would act as orderlies and clerks. "It is a mighty omen," an anonymous Red Cross writer declared, "that our first contribution as belligerents consisted of men and women from the American Red Cross who are ready to give their lives that others—friends or foes—may live."[62]

Proceeding in the opposite direction, a thirty-member U. S. mission to Russia, headed by former secretary of war Elihu Root, traveled by train to California, then boarded a ship bound for Vladivostok. Unlike the American railroad commission, sent to Russia at about the same time to provide technical assistance, the Root Mission's sole purpose was to impress upon Russia's shaky new government that to secure "the good will and financial support of this country," as Wilson's close adviser Edward House wrote, "they must compose their internal differences and not make a separate peace at this time." The greater the rifts among the country's

several political factions, the greater the danger that Russia would abandon the war to deal with its domestic problems. If that happened, Germany could transfer massive numbers of troops to the Western Front, break through the Allied lines before sufficient AEF reinforcements arrived, and sweep on to victory. With that opportunity in mind, in mid-April German officials arranged passage across Germany to Russia for Vladimir Lenin and a party of like-minded radicals who had been exiled in Switzerland, hoping that these adamantly antiwar and anticapitalism Bolsheviks would add to the Russian turmoil—although more disruption hardly seemed necessary. TALK OF DICTATORSHIP TO SAVE RUSSIA; WAR MINISTER RESIGNS IN DESPAIR, *New York Times* headlines shouted as the Root Mission was en route, while at the same time the paper reported hopefully on the increasing influence of the democratically inclined Alexander Kerensky. After becoming Russia's new minister of war in mid-May, Kerensky fired the army's

ineffective commander in chief, replaced him with the aggressive and accomplished general Alexei Brusilov, and ordered Russia's war-weary army—reportedly bleeding thirty thousand deserters a day—made ready for a major new offensive. In early June, when the Root Mission reached Vladivostok, the journalist Charles Edward Russell noted organizational chaos and uncertain support for the war among the Russians he met before he and the other mission members were whisked onto an elegant train for their five-thousand-mile journey to Petrograd.[63]

At the same time, a Russian political and military mission was heading to Washington, D.C., a city now filled with thousands of eager American war supporters bearing proposals on which they demanded immediate action. "They will have to learn how slowly the wheels of government grind," Florence Harriman wrote in her diary on April 30. A number of them turned to her to grease those wheels. "Like everyone else, I am having the most unique requests," she reported. "I have worn out my boot leather running between [my home] and the War Department." She was also conspiring with Colonel House and various State Department officials to thwart one eager volunteer's plans. Her friend Willard Straight, a Plattsburg camp graduate who in 1916 had gone to Europe representing the newly formed American International Corporation, was determined to enlist in the army. Harriman's efforts to divert him from possible battlefield service and into the

State Department, where his business and diplomatic experience would be useful, were unsuccessful. Straight was commissioned a major and assigned to the adjutant general's office in the War Department. By August, however, he received an assignment much more to his liking: adjutant to the Thirty-fifth Division, training in Oklahoma for deployment in France.[64]

Harriman herself was often in uniform. Having enlisted with her daughter Ethel in the local Red Cross Ambulance Corps, she was "learning to make all minor repairs to a motor, change tires, etc." Because of her earlier experience as a member of the Commission on Industrial Relations, she was also appointed to head the Women in Industry Committee, which had been established under the recently formed Women's Committee of the Council of National Defense (WCCND), a government-affiliated clearinghouse and information center for all forms of women's service. Working closely with Samuel Gompers, who headed the Council of National Defense labor committee as well as her own committee members, including many women trade unionists, Harriman directed efforts to formulate acceptable labor standards for women based on a sweeping investigation of wartime readjustments in women's work. One readjustment the committee and most new female workers were determined should not take place was the receipt of lower wages for the same work men had been doing. In mid-May, women auto-supply workers hired by a Chicago firm at $12 a week when the men

they replaced had earned $21 were out on strike—one of 4,450 strikes that would occur in 1917 as prices continued to rise while unskilled workers' wages stagnated, unfair management practices continued, and the nation struggled to meet its own and its Allies' needs.[65]

As Harriman juggled jobs and requests for assistance, some recent Washington arrivals sought out another new man in town. George Creel had been tapped by President Wilson to head the Committee on Public Information (CPI), which the president established by executive order on April 14, one day after cabinet members Lansing,

Baker, and Daniels suggested creating an agency that would provide Americans with the "feeling of partnership that comes with full, frank statements concerning the conduct of the public business." The CPI could combine the functions of "censorship and publicity . . . in honesty and with profit," the secretaries believed. It could be a means for safeguarding "all information of value to an enemy" while opening, as far as possible, "every department of government to the inspection of the people"—at best a precarious balancing act in a country swept by the volatile winds of war.[66]

Creel was game. The former muckraking

journalist and longtime Wilson supporter embodied the progressive belief that only a well-informed public could make wise decisions. Like those who were excoriating the Espionage Act's proposed censorship provision just as Creel assumed office, he objected to censorship by legislation. Yet he did believe in voluntary restraints on media in a nation at war and almost immediately issued a statement to that effect. "It will be necessary at times to keep information from our own people in order to keep it from the enemy," he acknowledged. Yet the stringent censorship the other belligerent nations had imposed had done more harm than good, inviting "insane and dangerous rumors" too easily believed by publics well aware that their governments were withholding information. Ignoring suspicions among many in the press that CPI censorship measures were meant to replace the failed Espionage Act provision, Creel promulgated and distributed to the nation's editors a list of eighteen types of information, such as the location of army camps and naval minefields, that should be kept secret. He titled the list "What the Government *Asks* of the Press" (emphasis added), an appeal to patriotic common sense that had plenty of steel behind it once the Espionage Act became law.[67]

While Major Douglas MacArthur, on loan from Secretary Baker, canvassed the city to find permanent office space for the CPI and the committee's censorship activities continued, Creel began building a many-faceted organization that would, in his words, "fight for the minds of men, for the 'conquest of their convictions'" in this international struggle between democracy and ruthless autocracy. Among those eager to help was a young Chicagoan, Donald Ryerson, who on April 17 burst into CPI's crowded temporary workspace, grabbed Creel by the lapels, and outlined a plan to have volunteers speak on war-related topics during the four minutes it took projectionists to change reels in the country's immensely popular movie theaters—a program Chicago businessmen had been supporting locally since April 1. Within the hour, Creel made Ryerson chief of a nationwide division to be called the Four-Minute Men that would grow to involve seventy-five thousand carefully monitored volunteers and reach into many more venues than movie houses. That same day renowned artist Charles Dana Gibson brought Creel a poster he wished to contribute to the cause, and by April 22 Gibson was heading CPI's new Division of Pictorial Publicity. An open letter to school principals from Guy Stanton Ford,

dean of the University of Minnesota graduate school, suggesting that upcoming high school commencements be turned into patriotic forums inspired Creel to create the Division of Civil and Educational Cooperation, with Ford at its head. Over the next nineteen months, its small staff directed the creation and wide distribution of 105 war-related works ranging from pamphlets to the 321-page *War Cyclopedia: A Handbook for Ready Reference on the Great War*. Posters, cartoons, photographs, advertisements, films, pamphlets in multiple languages, news releases to guide the nation's editors, war exhibitions, and the somewhat dull but informative *Official Bulletin*, which outlined the daily activities of every government agency— these and more streamed from the ever-expanding CPI, whose reach eventually extended overseas. The battle for men's minds was raging, Creel wrote, in "every home in every country," and as that battle grew more desperate, CPI's high standards for the distribution of accurate, if restricted, information would begin to slide into the murky and strident realm of propaganda.[68]

Nothing murky was to invade the ranks of the country's armed forces, however. On April 17, well before the conscription bill passed and the government decided to send troops to Europe, the War Department established the Commission on Training Camp Activities (CTCA), one expression of the continuing zeal for (sometimes clashing) progressive reforms that embraced America's foreign and domestic war efforts. CTCA was also a response to respected reformer Raymond B. Fosdick's August 1916 report to the War Department on the easy access to alcohol and prostitution enjoyed by soldiers stationed in towns along the Mexican border, and to longstanding civilian concern over immorality in the heretofore ill-regarded armed forces.[69] "We are willing to sacrifice our boys, if need be, to die to make men free," Marcia Bradley, of Oregon, wrote Secretary Baker in May 1917 as conscription neared passage, "but we rebel and protest against their being returned to us ruined in body and ideals." Appointing Fosdick to head the CTCA, Baker declared that the organization should provide the nation's soldiers with "an invisible armor," a moral shield that would reflect the values of enlightened America. "The eyes of all the world will be upon you," President Wilson later wrote to embarking AEF troops. "Let it be your pride . . . to show all men everywhere not only what good soldiers you are, but also what good men you are, keeping yourselves . . . pure and clean through and through." Creating ties with seven established civilian organizations, including the YMCA, the YWCA, and the American Library Association, the CTCA built an elaborate network to assure wholesome recreation *within* army camps (libraries, sing-alongs, lectures, and literature on social hygiene) and suppression of unwholesome activities in "moral zones" it established *around* them—a network that for many months failed to live up to the CTCA's pledge to provide separate but equal services for African American troops.[70]

The CTCA would eventually have many more men to shield from moral decay than were at first anticipated, including

Opposite: The 321-page *War Cyclopedia* was among the multimedia flood of materials released by the Committee on Public Information. Operating under the Commission on Training Camp Activities, the War Camp Community Service, devoted to the welfare of soldiers and sailors on leave, published *A Primer on "Catching Diseases."*

WAR
CYCLOPEDIA

A HANDBOOK FOR READY REFERENCE
ON THE GREAT WAR

18-26144

ISSUED BY
THE COMMITTEE ON PUBLIC INFORMATION

THE SECRETARY OF STATE
THE SECRETARY OF WAR
THE SECRETARY OF THE NAVY
GEORGE CREEL

Price : 25 Cents

WASHINGTON : GOVERNMENT PRINTING OFFICE : 1918

Monograph

the regular armed forces and National Guard, volunteers who joined after April 6, and 2.8 million draftees. Even before the conscription act was signed, the War Department had printed millions of draft registration forms and distributed them secretly to the nation's forty thousand sheriffs. As conscription became law, Secretary Baker and Army Provost Marshal Enoch Crowder, the chief architect of the Selective Service System, laid plans to prevent the bloody resistance to registration that many politicians and anti-draft activists were predicting. Tying the draft to the rights and obligations of citizenship, registration was to occur at local polling places. Area officials—county sheriffs, medical

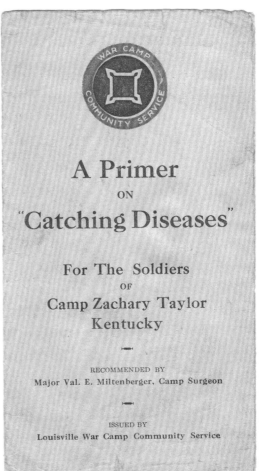

A Primer
ON
"Catching Diseases"

For The Soldiers
OF
Camp Zachary Taylor
Kentucky

RECOMMENDED BY
Major Val. E. Miltenberger, Camp Surgeon

ISSUED BY
Louisville War Camp Community Service

officers, and clerks—were to make up the boards overseeing registration, lending an air of local control to a process defined and directed from Washington. Preregistration publicity emphasized both patriotic duty and penalties for failing to comply. A week before the nation's first Registration Day, local police arrested some draft denouncers, and Secretary Baker asked state governors whether they wanted federal troops to help keep order (none did). On June 5, 1917, predictions of widespread disorder proved unfounded as 9.6 million men twenty-one to thirty years of age signed up with Uncle Sam, cheered on by their fellow citizens. West Coast governors proclaimed a holiday. In Oklahoma City, every whistle in the city blew as registrants marched to the polls. In St. Louis and Philadelphia

parades encouraged both registration and investment in the First Liberty Loan, and both were the subject of patriotic speeches in churches, halls, and squares throughout New York City.[71]

On Governor's Island, off Manhattan,

REGISTER

"A great day of patriotic devotion and obligation."
Woodrow Wilson

JUNE 5th

ISSUED BY COMMITTEE OF PUBLIC SAFETY OF PENNSYLVANIA, DEPARTMENT OF MILITARY SERVICE, SOUTH PENN SQUARE, PHILADELPHIA

meanwhile, General William Sibert and his new aide, Captain George Marshall, were bringing together four understrength army regiments, the Sixth Field Artillery, and many raw recruits to create the First Division of the American Expeditionary Forces.[72] At precisely the same time, AEF commander John Pershing and his staff were experiencing firsthand the desperate eagerness with which the French awaited American reinforcements. Heartily cheered when they arrived in the port city of Boulogne on June 12, the Americans went on to Paris the same day and were welcomed by Marshal Joffre, U.S. ambassador William G. Sharp, and a host of French political and military leaders before driving slowly to their hotel through streets clogged with flag-waving French people. "Men, women, and children absolutely

packed every foot of space, even to the windows and housetops," Pershing later remembered. "Cheers and tears were mingled together . . . Women climbed into our automobiles screaming, 'Vive l'Amérique,' and threw flowers until we were literally buried." Two days later, the First Division embarked for France in four separate convoys. As yet unable to function as a cohesive unit, lacking essential equipment, and completely unprepared for Western Front combat, these troops would nevertheless fulfill the government's pledge to Marshal Joffre. As the initial group of troop transports and warships moved out, George Marshall was relieved to see a gun crew on his ship, *Tenadores*, expertly unlimber their weapon—until he heard one of them say that they had no ammunition. "I thought, My God," he later remembered, "even the naval part isn't organized."[73]

When Congress declared war, the naval part was actually quite well organized— for an entirely different conflict than the one it was facing. The Navy Department's only contingency plan, War Plan Black, envisioned duels between surface fleets. Instead, the navy would be jousting with U-boats while shepherding troops, animals, and equipment on the long voyage to Europe and maintaining their transatlantic supply lines, duties that would call for a complete naval retooling. In late March, as sailors left clerical and other shore duty to man new naval vessels and the guns on merchantmen, concern over maintaining administrative operations led Secretary of the Navy Daniels to open the Naval Coast Defense Reserve Force to women enlistees, which he deemed allowable under a

REGISTRATION CERTIFICATE.

To whom it may concern, Greetings:

THESE PRESENTS ATTEST,

That in accordance with the proclamation of the President of the United States, and in compliance with law,

Clarence C. Bauer, _Cleveland_,
(Name)   (City or P. O.)

Precinct _R_ County of _Cuyahoga_, State of _Ohio_,

has submitted himself to registration and has by me been duly registered this _5th_ day of _June_, 1917.

No. _8_
(This number must correspond with that on the Registration Card.)

_1660_

6—4227

R. C. Riley
Registrar.

Men between ages twenty-one and thirty who registered for the draft on June 5 received certificates like this one, issued to Clarence C. Bauer of Cleveland. A private with A Company, 58th Infantry Regiment, on May 23, 1918, Bauer survived the sinking of his troopship, HMS *Moldavia*, on the way to France (fifty-six AEF soldiers died) and saw action at Château-Thierry and Soissons, where he was wounded.

provision of the Naval Expansion Act of 1916. Within days, newspapers were carrying pictures of Loretta P. Walsh, the first of twelve thousand women officially to enlist in the navy during the war to perform recruitment, clerical, and similar duties. Acquiring a sufficient number of appropriate ships proved somewhat more complicated. Battleships, the bedrock of both War Plan Black and the plan for naval expansion, would be of little use against U-boats (in fact would make juicy targets). "O for more destroyers!" Navy Secretary Daniels wrote in April. "I wish we could trade the money in dreadnaughts for destroyers already built." Three months later he temporarily halted battleship construction and secured approval for building 250 destroyers, rather than the 50 specified in the 1916 naval expansion plan, but few of these would be launched before November 11, 1918. For anti-submarine work, the navy would rely on its existing

fleet of destroyers and other sub hunters, on Allied assistance, and on small patrol craft bought, borrowed, or rented from private citizens (including J. P. Morgan, who charged Uncle Sam one dollar a year for the use of his yacht).[74]

Though off to a rocky start, the transport of troops and supplies became a "noteworthy example of American ingenuity and zeal," the navy's wartime convoy operations commander, Admiral Albert Gleaves, wrote after the war. "The Army . . . developed an efficient system for loading and unloading the ships . . . The Navy transported the troops and safeguarded them en route." While the Emergency Fleet Corporation, authorized under the Shipping Act of 1916 and established in April 1917 to buy and build merchantmen, dithered for months in organizational confusion, the government converted to troopships some of the German vessels that had taken refuge in American ports in 1914 and were seized when America went to war. The navy also procured existing American vessels through its new Committee on Merchant Naval Auxiliaries, chaired by Franklin D. Roosevelt (who overcame more than a few problems with price gouging). Despite these efforts—and given Wilson's reluctance to divert U.S. merchantmen from the lucrative South American and Japanese trade—throughout the war only 46 percent of the approximately 2 million men sent overseas sailed in American bottoms; British vessels carried 48 percent; French and Italian ships conveyed the rest.[75]

Plane production would also fall short, to a degree even greater than that anticipated by Raynal C. Bolling, an aviation enthusiast who was U.S. Steel's general counsel and a Plattsburg training camp graduate. In May 1917, as a reserve army major, Bolling headed a War Department

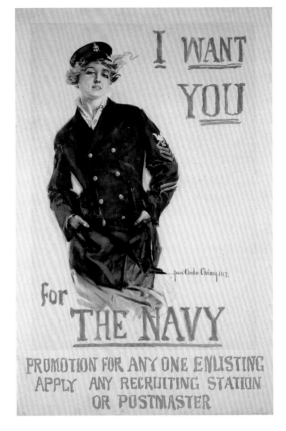

Top right: After Secretary of the Navy Daniels opened the Navy to female recruits, artist Howard Chandler Christy (1873–1952) created this recruitment poster, 1917.

Right: Lieutenant Colonel George C. Marshall (1880–1959), U.S. Army Signal Corps photograph, ca. 1923. A highly effective AEF operations officer with the rank of captain during the Great War, Marshall learned lessons that would inform his service as U.S. Army chief of staff during World War II. As U.S. secretary of state (1947–49), he proposed the highly effective Marshall Plan for European recovery from that second devastating conflict.

commission sent to Europe to study the air war and select an Allied airplane design for American production; the winner was Britain's De Havilland DH-4. Praised by General Pershing for his "ability and expert knowledge," Bolling remained in France to help develop AEF aviation after his commission determined that no American-built planes could be ready for European service until summer 1918. This contradicted an earlier prediction by auto executive Howard Coffin, chairman of the Aircraft Production Board, that Americans would produce 3,500 military aircraft in 1917 and double that number each year thereafter—an exceedingly ambitious goal for a country that at the time had no effective military aircraft and had produced only 411 planes in 1916. To manufacture planes and observation balloons and develop an air corps of 110,000 men to fly and maintain them, in July Congress appropriated a whopping $640 million— while a worried Germany embarked on the Amerika Programm to double its Western Front air defenses. When few planes appeared by the end of the year, and those that did were of less than stellar quality, Congress launched multiple investigations that uncovered corruption, mismanagement, and incompetence born of inexperience (many plane manufacturers had previously built cars). Remedial measures, further hampered by strikes and shortages, did little to improve the rate or quality of production. While most American aviators took to the heavens in French, British, or Italian planes, the United States began turning out its one major contribution to Great War aviation: the twelve-cylinder, 440-horsepower "Liberty engine."[76]

Aircraft production—and comparably sluggish production of artillery, machine guns, and other implements of war—were only a few among many problems plaguing the War Department in 1917. The army's first two wartime chiefs of staff were distracted by special assignments: Hugh Scott went to Russia with the Root Mission before retiring in September; Tasker Bliss traveled to France on various missions. The army's chief coordinating apparatus, the general staff, endured months of organizational confusion, expanding exponentially even as it lost many of its most talented officers to overseas or training commands. Without adequate restraint from high up in the chain of command, the army's several bureaus, always competitive, ran completely amok. By July there were more than 150 separate purchasing committees as each bureau vied with the others to corner the market on everything from hats to howitzers. Attempts by the Advisory Commission to the Council of National Defense to bring some order to production and procurement by establishing "cooperative committees" of businessmen and military

Left: USS *Nokomis*, a yacht the navy purchased from automobile magnate Horace E. Dodge on July 1, 1917, helped protect American troop transports approaching the French coast.

Opposite: Multiple failures in the production of American military aircraft prompted this graphic comment from cartoonist Nelson Harding (1878–1944), published in the *Brooklyn Daily Eagle* on August 2, 1917.

THE EAGLET

Nelson Harding

officers resulted in new difficulties as army bureaus defended their prerogatives and excluded businesses complained. In late July, President Wilson established a new coordinating entity, the War Industries Board (WIB), which included one army and one navy representative and three civilian members responsible for raw materials, finished products, and establishing priorities, respectively. The board's heavy responsibilities were not accompanied by sufficient enforcement powers, however, and it muddled along ineffectively until Wilson reorganized it in March 1918 and placed at its head Wall Street's astute "Lone Eagle," Bernard Baruch.[77]

In the meantime, the need for an efficient supply system was growing. By early July the army had more than doubled in size. (Among the 301,000 volunteers who had joined the ranks since April: a future commander in chief, Harry Truman, whose Missouri field artillery regiment would be federalized in August as part of the AEF's Thirty-fifth Division.) On July 11 General Pershing's staff sent Washington the General Organizational Plan with an initial call for 1 million men, approximately thirty divisions, to be in France "in time for a 1918 offensive." Given the current dearth of trained officers, men, equipment, and transport, reaching that goal would require fast and intensive action. On July 20 (while Pershing and his staff toured Allied lines and met British Expeditionary Force commander Douglas Haig) in Washington, D.C., a blindfolded Secretary Baker drew from a glass jar a slip bearing the number 258, the first of 10,500 draft numbers (10,500 being the highest

number of registrants in any draft district). Fourteen hours later, with the last number drawn, the War Department telegraphed the resulting "order of call" to the nation's 4,647 draft boards, which proceeded to fill the first quota of 687,000 men, who were to be ready for training by September 1. Between July 20 and the end of August, as sites were selected and work began on building thirty-two training cantonments across the country, these civilian boards examined selectees and heard pleas for deferments with widely varying degrees of fairness and efficiency.[78]

Militarily, economically, and socially, the war was causing seismic shifts in the American nation. With the draft in place, new war-related laws and agencies aborning, and more emphasis on income taxation, the federal government was affecting more deeply than ever before the lives of ordinary Americans—some of whom objected to its tightening embrace. While millions of men marched dutifully to draft boards, training camps, and ports of embarkation, a significant number pivoted and ducked. The Selective Service would later estimate that some 338,000 of those who registered for the draft failed to report when called; as many as 3 million may have avoided registration altogether. Most draft resistance was subtle, but there were some exceptions. In Oklahoma opposition to conscription revitalized the Working Man's Union, an organization of sharecroppers and tenant farmers. In early August, hundreds of its white, black, and American Indian members, determined to end what they saw as a rich man's war in which poor men would do all the fighting, embarked on a march to Washington, planning to dine on barbecued beef and roasted green corn on the way. Hastily

Opposite: American aircraft and (presumably) American artillery loom large in this watercolor drawing by Edward Penfield, cover art for *Collier's* magazine, August 4, 1917. In fact American airmen mainly flew Allied planes and depended heavily on the Allies for artillery.

Right: A draft lottery drawing photographed by Harris & Ewing, Washington, D.C., 1917.

assembled posses brought this "Green Corn Rebellion" to a swift and inglorious halt, killing three and arresting more than four hundred, of whom 150 were jailed for up to ten years.[79]

Many farmers and wage earners who remained on the home front—especially those affiliated with Samuel Gompers' American Federation of Labor—did benefit from increased wages and job protections during the period of American belligerence. For others, however, the war created setbacks and tragedies. In the West, where the war declaration accelerated booms in the copper and lumber industries, mine owners and lumber magnates turned deaf ears to workers' pleas for livable wages and adequate safety precautions, even as profits soared. On June 8, during round-the-clock operations at the Speculator Copper Mine in Butte, Montana, a shift boss, Ernest Sallau, accidentally touched a frayed electrical cable with a carbide lamp, setting a fire that quickly spread, trapping miners in flames and suffocating smoke that incinerated two workers and asphyxiated 166. Rescuers later discovered bodies piled near bulkheads that lacked the required iron escape doors, some men's fingers worn to the bone from frantic clawing. Through weeks of anguished recovery from this deadliest metal-mining disaster in U.S. history, area miners who had abandoned union activities as futile came together again to push for better conditions. Members of the radical International Workers of the World (IWW), called Wobblies, constituted only one element in this outraged reaction to tragedy, as they were in strikes threatening to cripple the Northwest's lumber industry

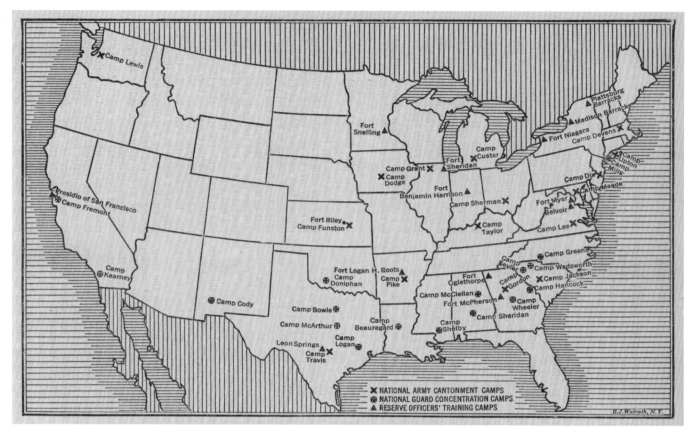

and copper strikes in the neighborhood of Bisbee, Arizona. Yet the IWW's uncompromising positions and threatening rhetoric made it a particular target as mine owners, lumbermen, and the newspapers they controlled linked all labor unrest, however well-founded, to Wobbly-inspired anarchism—and to dark German plots."[80]

With little effective federal presence in any of the strike-torn states, owners also encouraged vigilantism to deal with strikers. In Jerome, Arizona, on July 10, members of a mine-owner-sponsored "loyalty league" rounded up sixty-seven IWW members, shoved them in freight cars, and "deported" them to California. Two days later and 260 miles away, well-armed vigilantes in Bisbee repeated and expanded the process, packing cattle cars with twelve hundred suspect miners—including, an investigation later

determined, hundreds with no union affiliation and many who had loyally registered for the draft. After a blistering journey of 173 miles, the train arrived at Columbus, New Mexico, where officials refused to accept the men, who then languished in the desert outside nearby Hermanas until rescued by the army. Shocked by this brutal new tactic but unable to assist in Bisbee, where vigilantism remained the law for months, labor advocates, including fiery IWW organizer Frank Little, flocked to Butte, where the strike was beginning to flag under unremitting pressure from mine owners. Without proof (none ever surfaced), city newspapers declared that German funds were supporting the protesters. Rumors spread that Sallau, a German American, had started the fire on purpose— an accusation he could not refute since he had returned to the mine after escaping and died trying to save others. On August 1, less than a month after a flagrantly anti-union Montana newspaperman, Will Campbell, published an editorial titled "Declare an Open Season on IWW," Frank Little was torn from his rooming house by unknown assailants, dragged behind a car, and then beaten to death, his body left hanging from a bridge. His anonymous murderers attached a placard to the body: OTHERS TAKE NOTICE, FIRST AND LAST WARNING.[81]

Representative Jeannette Rankin, Montana's U.S. Attorney Burton K. Wheeler, and other federal and state officials condemned the murder. Most state newspapers did as well, but placed more blame on the government for not being hard enough on labor "agitators," who, with owners still unmoved, continued their agitation. In this turbulent atmosphere, biased local reporting, war news filtered through the CPI, rumors of German plans to disrupt the American homeland, and earnest patriotism combined to create in Montana a prime example of the war hysteria Emily Balch cited during her testimony on the Espionage Act. Accusations of sedition whizzed back and forth, generally based on little more than personal dislike or offhand comments that, in any objective light, could not be construed as harmful to the war effort. Yet several cases wound up in Montana's U.S. District Court. In this, the state was not unusual; by late summer Espionage Act cases were in process all over the country.[82]

In Vermont, a court tried and convicted Pentecostal minister Clarence Waldron and sentenced him to fifteen years in federal prison for distributing pacifist

literature and allegedly stating, "A Christian can take no part in the war." Thirty North Dakota German Americans were awaiting trial after their arrest for "signing a petition of an intimidating nature" in which they threatened to vote against the governor if he did not pursue reforms in Selective Service procedures. In California, marshals arrested film producer Robert Goldstein on charges that his film on the American Revolutionary War, *The Spirit of '76*, was German propaganda because it included a scene showing British Loyalists and their Indian allies dealing mercilessly with defeated revolutionaries in the 1778 Battle of Wyoming Valley. Goldstein was convicted, fined five thousand dollars, and sentenced to ten years in prison, the judge stating that, while the film might be factual, this was no time for anything that might sow "want of confidence between us and our allies." As Balch predicted, neither judges nor juries were immune to wartime passions. Nationwide, they acquitted only 6 of the 180 defendants brought to trial under the Espionage Act before January 1918.[83]

During the same period, there were no convictions under the Espionage Act in Montana, a state that was unusual in its two federal judicial officers. Both Burton Wheeler and Federal District Judge George Bourquin interpreted the act strictly and stoutly defended individual rights. Though patriotism, like religion, was an indispensable virtue, Bourquin would say after the war, "when . . . it descends to fanaticism, it is of the reprehensible quality of the religion that incited . . . the tortures of the Inquisition . . . In its name,

as in that of Liberty, what crimes have been committed!" Determined not to abet any such crimes, he carefully considered the eight Espionage Act cases that came before him in 1917, acquitted three of the defendants, and dismissed charges against all the others. Outraged at the two federal officers' refusal to bend their principles to the winds of wartime emotion, in February 1918 Governor Sam V. Stewart and an overwrought state legislature passed a sweeping state law that deemed seditious any wartime criticism of the government and any act or statement that could be interpreted as resistance to the war effort. Echoing the hated 1798 Sedition Act, the Montana law also resembled legislation introduced in the U.S. Congress on August 15, 1917, by Montana's senior senator, Henry L. Myers. Myers's Senate Bill 2789 remained in committee for months as the nation's war effort, and attendant patriotic fervor, grew more intense.[84]

White employers in the South, blind to the conditions suffered by most of the region's black citizens, began blaming agitation by German agents for the continuing migration of black residents to the North. Southern migrants, meanwhile, discovered that northern cities were not trouble-free zones. In East St. Louis, Illinois, where thousands of southern blacks had settled since 1915, prejudice and labor unrest proved a deadly combination. Recruited by city employers, who correctly calculated that their restive white workers would never ally with these new arrivals to stage an effective strike, black workers quickly felt the wrath of white unionists and others who resented their presence.

In a late-May outbreak of violence, angry whites randomly attacked blacks on the streets, the first of several violent episodes that continued through June. Then, on July 2, months of tension exploded in a full-scale riot. White gangs encouraged by mobs of cheering spectators rampaged through parts of the city, beating and killing blacks and burning hundreds of their homes and businesses. "People were being shot down & thrown back into fire if they tried to escape," one survivor wrote to a friend. Though the chaos made an exact figure impossible, it was later estimated that forty black people were killed and hundreds injured; nine whites also died, some by "friendly fire." As National Guardsmen arrived in force and slowly restored order, news of the carnage shocked the nation. "The German press will, doubtless, gloat with ghoulish glee over the atrocities of . . . East St. Louis," Howard University dean Kelly Miller wrote on July 7. "The principle of democracy is on trial before the world today as it has never been before . . . A democracy that will not stand the acid test of race and color is no democracy at all."[85]

The largest and ugliest of several racial clashes that occurred in 1917, the East St. Louis tragedy occurred in the wake of a triumph for African Americans hoping that full participation in the war would aid their quest for equality. On June 15, the War Department opened the long-sought training camp for black officers, with many college graduates and 250 noncommissioned officers from the army's four African American regiments among the complement of 1,250 trainees.[86] Shaken by the news from East St. Louis as they embarked on a grueling three-month training regime that kept them busy from five forty-five A.M. to nine forty-five P.M., men of the Seventeenth Provisional Training Regiment were also affected by a late-August incident in Houston, Texas. Black soldiers of the Third Battalion, Twenty-fourth Infantry Regiment, proud veterans of Philippines and Mexican-border service who had recently arrived to help build a training cantonment, angered white Houstonians by resisting the city's strict Jim Crow regulations. After city police pistol-whipped two soldiers on various pretexts, about a hundred enraged infantrymen marched into the city, shooting indiscriminately, rousing white civilians into a frenzy of confused resistance until the black soldiers' anger dissipated and a National Guard unit arrived. In what came to be called the

In "The I.W.W. and the Other Features That Go with It," 1917, cartoonist H. T. Webster (1885–1952) captured a view of the radical labor organization held by an overwhelming number of businessmen, newspapers editors, and agencies of the U.S. government.

The I. W. W. and the Other Features That Go With It

Houston Mutiny, seventeen whites were killed and two of the mutineers died, one by his own hand. As alarm at this uprising by well-trained black soldiers spread through the South and into the halls of Congress, the White House, and the War Department, authorities disarmed the entire battalion and sent it to New Mexico. Official retribution thereafter was swift, uncompromising, and alarming to African Americans. Between November 1917 and April 1918, the army court-martialed 118 soldiers, found 110 guilty, hanged 19 without opportunity for appeal, and imprisoned 63 for life. No white civilian was ever tried for harassing or beating black soldiers.[87]

Amid a cacophony of protesting voices—southern congressmen insisting that all black troops be removed from their states, black activists and their white allies demanding fair treatment for African American soldiers—Secretary Baker temporarily suspended induction of black soldiers, delayed for a month commissioning the 639 black officers who had completed training in Des Moines, and convened a Washington conference of "men interested in the Negro question." Meanwhile, training of existing black units continued. In October, famed musician turned military volunteer, Lt. James Reese Europe of the Fifteenth New York National Guard, narrowly averted another riot in Spartanburg, South Carolina, when he kept soldiers from rushing to aid a comrade, Noble Sissle,

who had been attacked by a white man. (By the end of the month, men of the spit-and-polish Fifteenth were on their way to New York; six weeks later they embarked for France.) In the fall, too, with new rules in place for training African Americans, including strict segregation and at least a two-to-one ratio of white to black soldiers in camps billeting both, Baker announced resumption of African American inductions and agreed to the formation of a black combat division. Designated the Ninety-second Infantry Division, it included draftee enlisted men, black officers up to the grade of captain, and white senior officers. With Houston fresh in mind, the unit's various elements were trained at seven separate facilities, making impossible proper division cohesion, a problem that would become evident in 1918, when the Ninety-second finally assembled in Europe. As all this was occurring, Baker brought Emmett J. Scott, an educator and former assistant to Booker T. Washington, into the War Department as special assistant for Negro affairs. Given prevailing attitudes and his own careful approach, Scott could only affect to a limited degree the fates of more than four hundred thousand black soldiers, the vast majority of them draftees, who served in U.S. armed forces during the war. Nearly 75 percent of these servicemen were relegated to labor units, in which they chiefly battled mistreatment, bad weather, boredom, and fatigue while completing a multitude of menial jobs.[88]

"Let me give you the list of fellows who sleep in cots around me," a white draftee, Private John F. Callahan, wrote to a new acquaintance, Clara Morehouse, late in 1917. "We have . . . truck driver, fireman, jeweler, gun man from the East Side of N.Y. now on a 'French' leave, bookkeeper, truck chauffeur, Nebraska farmer, Jewish shoe salesman, bartender, Italian laborer, and a chauffeur who worked for a Pittsburg millionaire." Himself a New York fireman, Callahan was describing what advocates of universal military training had long cited as one of the prime benefits of required national service—Americans and aspiring Americans who would not ordinarily intermingle coming together to further a common national cause. The well-educated Callahan did not mention in his letter a problem the army began grappling with in September as thousands of draftees crowded into unfinished and severely underequipped training cantonments: a significant number, perhaps 25 percent, were illiterate or barely literate. Moreover, many of the half million recent immigrants from forty-six nations who would serve during the war neither spoke nor understood English. In a December report to the War Department, a multilingual officer, Lieutenant Stanislaw A. Gutowski, described visiting a Massachusetts cantonment where tearful non-English-speaking Polish recruits told him of trying to learn under officers and noncoms with whom they had no way to communicate effectively: "After three months' training . . . most of the men had learned absolutely nothing." A small part of the language-barrier problem evaporated on December 7, when the United States formally declared war on the Austro-Hungarian Empire; Czechs, Slovaks, Hungarians, and others still technically citizens of the empire were instantly reclassified as enemy aliens ineligible for service. To remedy the larger problem, over the following months the War Department established a system of linguistically grouped "developmental" units with bilingual officers who could teach trainees the rudiments of soldiering as they also learned English.[89]

The entire country was leaning to cope, often by trial and error, with the war's monumental challenges—and centralization seemed one key to total-mobilization success. In August, after heated debate over the growth in government powers, Congress passed the Lever Food and Fuel Control Act, which provided Herbert Hoover's Food Administration with a firm legislative foundation and allowed President Wilson to establish a similar Fuel Administration as well as the Grain

Polacy! Idźcie na bój na prawy- za ziemię Polską, za pokrzywdzoną!

POLES! UNDER THE POLISH FLAG ON TO THE FIGHT "FOR OUR LIBERTY AND YOURS!" ENLIST TO-DAY

Corporation and the U.S. Sugar Equalization Board to regulate trade in those essential commodities. In late December, when operation of the nation's vital railroads flagged because of poor maintenance, inadequate equipment, insufficient coordination among the nation's several rail lines, and the competing interests of labor, management, and freight shippers, the federal government intervened. Presidential Proclamation 1419 established the U.S. Railroad Administration, with Secretary of the Treasury McAdoo at the helm, to operate all railroad lines and related companies seized by the government in the interest of national defense. Applauded by those progressives who had long believed that a nationalized rail system would best protect consumers from unfair pricing and practices, the measure elicited howls from railroad owners. The noise subsided after the Federal Control Act of March 1918 guaranteed both financial compensation and a postwar end to federal control. Meanwhile, disappointed progressives, shippers, and the general public began yelping with distress as rail rates skyrocketed to compensate for the monies the new agency was paying railroad management and labor to assure efficient and uninterrupted service.[90]

Focusing on wartime regulation of international commerce, in October Congress passed the Trading with the Enemy Act, which made it illegal, except when allowed by the president, to trade with an enemy of the United States or any ally of an enemy. In December, the War Trade Board established under the act made official a policy the United States had been following sub rosa for several months, when it publicly issued the first of several commercial blacklists. Outdoing Great Britain, whose blacklist of American individuals and firms during the period of U.S. neutrality had so outraged Americans, the United States forbade its citizens, for the duration of the war, to trade with any of more than five thousand people or firms in neutral countries around the world because of suspected ties with the enemy. To deal with enemy assets within the United States, the president appointed Pennsylvania attorney A. Mitchell Palmer alien property custodian. Initially empowered to identify, hold, and administer enemy money and property only for the duration of hostilities, Palmer pressed for and in March 1918 received via amendments to the act the authority *permanently*

to deprive German owners of much of their substantial investments in U.S. businesses and to sell many German-owned patents, all to the benefit of American commerce and industry.[91]

Stretching the definition of international trade and reflecting growing intolerance of criticism and fear of subversion, Section 19 of the act required the nation's many foreign-language periodicals to submit to the Post Office Department any war-related articles (broadly defined) before publication, thus augmenting the already substantial monitoring powers Postmaster General Albert Burleson was overzealously wielding under the Espionage Act. Already swamped with accusations from local postmasters that hosts of English-language newspapers, periodicals, and other printed matter should be deemed "nonmailable," Burleson's department added yet a another duty to its growing

roster of responsibilities in November when it gained a seat on the government's new Censorship Board. Also including representatives from the War Department, the navy, the War Trade Board, and George Creel's Committee on Public Information, this advisory and coordinating body had some difficult issues to contemplate, for the war in Europe was not going well for the Allies.[92]

In a southern sector of the Eastern Front in early July, the offensive promised in May by Russia's war minister, Alexander Kerensky, fell apart within days. Whole sections of the Russian lines simply disintegrated under an Austro-Hungarian counterattack, and thousands of ill-equipped and war-weary Russian troops headed for home, pillaging as they went. In the wake of this disaster, Prince Gregory Lvov resigned as prime minister and Kerensky moved into that post, while Lenin's Bolsheviks and their political allies exploited their countrymen's growing unrest. Disquiet grew in September, when German troops in the Baltic region gained enough ground to threaten Petrograd, then exploded in early November into a second Russian revolution from which the Bolsheviks emerged in control. As Kerensky and a few of his loyalists escaped, some of them in a car borrowed from the American embassy, Lenin's new communist government embarrassed the Allies by publishing excerpts from their secret wartime agreements. The Bolsheviks also fulfilled Allied fears by declaring a three-month armistice, during which they commenced negotiations with Germany—while the German high command, confident now that Russia could be held in check with a much smaller force, began transferring selected divisions from the Eastern Front to France.[93]

On the Western Front, meanwhile, as General Philippe Pétain worked to restore morale and fighting spirit in French forces, the British took the initiative, launching on July 31 the Third Battle of Ypres (Passchendaele). Despite a strong start, this two-month clash gradually descended into catastrophe, torrential rains and torrents of artillery shells stirring the battlefield into a glutinous morass through which Allied troops repeatedly struggled to attack, some soldiers simply disappearing into deep pockets of mud or drowning in water-filled shell holes. On the Italian Front, in October, Austro-Hungarian and German troops routed Italian forces at the Battle of Caporetto, taking at least 275,000 prisoners as they pushed the Allied troops back more than fifty miles. Staggered by these new setbacks on different fronts, Allied leaders decided to take a

KERENSKY EXHORTING A REGIMENT   4-281-8

Von der Isonzo-Offensive: Abtransport gefangener Italiener auf der Vormarschstraße im Isonzotal.

Bild- und Film-Amt.

recommendation, Wilson appointed General Tasker Bliss as permanent U.S. military representative to the council. Then in Europe with House, Bliss was intensely aware of the Allies' deepening troubles—and the status of AEF deployment. "It is pitiful to see the undercurrent of feeling that the hopes of Europe have in the United States," he had written to his wife in November as the Kerensky government collapsed, "pitiful because it will be so long before we can really do anything, although the very crisis seems to be at hand."[94]

When the Supreme War Council met at Versailles in early December there were five AEF divisions in France: The First Division, which arrived in June, had been joined by the Second, which included both soldiers and U.S. Marines; the Twenty-sixth "Yankee" Division, principally comprising National Guardsmen from New England; the Forty-first, designated as "depot" or support troops; and the Forty-second "Rainbow" Division, the sobriquet reportedly bestowed by its chief of staff, Colonel Douglas MacArthur, because the division drew men from many U.S. states and thus spanned the country "like a rainbow." All told, Pershing had 176,655 soldiers under his command as 1917 came to an end—far short of the million men he believed necessary to launch the AEF's first offensive in mid- to late 1918. Dissatisfied with the rate at which troops and supplies were arriving from America and occasionally impatient with the speed at which AEF units absorbed training once they arrived, Pershing pressed Washington and negotiated with the British to provide more troop transports and blasted First Division

coordinative measure they had previously resisted. "France, England, and Italy have agreed to form a Supreme War Council and believe that it is imperative that we should be represented in it because of the moral effect that it will have here," Edward House wired Wilson from Europe. The council was to include heads of state or their political representatives as well as military advisers from each nation, but Wilson agreed with House that participating in political discussions at this time might compromise the president during postwar peace talks. American representation in the group's military strategy discussions was important, however, and, at House's

commanders for the unit's poor showing during an early October inspection (he later replaced the division commander). He also defied protocol to establish a separate AEF General Purchasing Board, which procured munitions, horses, mules, steel helmets, and thousands of French planes and engines while American manufacturers grappled with stateside problems.[95]

As Pershing fretted, German commanders watched the slow but inexorable influx of American troops and tried to calculate how long they had before Allied strength reached the point where Germany would have little chance of shattering enemy lines and sweeping to victory. Across No Man's Land, Allied commanders, increasingly worried about German divisions arriving from the East, intermittently pressed for the amalgamation of U.S. troops to shore up their own forces, sent battle-tested instructors to training cantonments in America, and did their best to prepare the Yanks in France for the trials of trench warfare. In mid-October, after the First Division completed behind-the-lines training with their French tutors, its commanders sent elements of the division to a quiet sector of the French front line to gain practical experience. In the early hours of November 3, men of the Second Battalion, Sixteenth Infantry who were manning a remote outpost were nearly overwhelmed by a German raiding party. During the intense hand-to-hand encounter, the Germans killed Corporal James B. Gresham and Privates Thomas F. Enright and Merle D. Hay, wounded five others, and captured twelve—the American army's first front-line casualties from the only combat-ready division the AEF then had. "With Russia out of the war it is possible for the Central Powers to concentrate 250 to 260 divisions on the Western Front," Pershing wrote to Secretary Baker one month later. "Against those German and Austrian divisions the Allies have 169 . . . It is of the utmost importance to the Allied cause that we move swiftly."[96]

Many aspects of the American war effort were, in fact, speeding along. Builders worked nearly nonstop, if sometimes sloppily, on thirty-two training cantonments where hundreds of thousands of men were learning the arts of war. American civilians were donating time, money, and goods to support the troops; buying war bonds (the Second Liberty Loan was launched with great hoopla in October); and accepting sacrifices the government's new war agencies were beginning to call for—restrictions on the use of coal and gas, meatless and wheatless days to stretch the food supply—while keeping weather eyes on their neighbors to make sure they sacrificed, too. In October, after Congress, in an unprecedented action, expanded the 1914 War Risk Insurance Act, passed to protect U.S. international shipping, to cover American servicemen, the War Department ordered Major Willard Straight to leave his post with the Thirty-fifth Division, then training in Oklahoma, and report to Washington, where he drew on his business experience to develop an implementation plan in near-record time. By December 11 he and his hastily assembled sixty-five-man command were aboard a ship bound for Europe to seek out and sign up all 176,655 members of the AEF in France for insurance that provided modest compensation for service-related death or disability and might provide, under certain circumstances, payments to dependents of men who were in service.[97]

Straight's friend Florence Harriman had left for Europe one month earlier in her dual capacities as head of the WCCND's Women in Industry Committee and a Red Cross volunteer. Stopping in England to tour munitions factories and assess support programs for women workers, Harriman described in her diary the stoicism and unfailing cheerfulness she encountered in a country where every household had endured some terrible loss. In her conversations with Britons, she learned of the hopes, expectations, and fears that were focused on her American countrymen. "The English

can't bear to have us break our hearts," she wrote, "by wasting time on mistakes or false motions as they did at first."[98]

In Washington shortly thereafter, anger rather than heartbreak ruled congressional investigations into mistakes and false motions impeding the production and procurement of vital war supplies. Where were the rifles needed for training draftees, many of whom were drilling with wooden sticks? Where was the artillery? Where were the planes? As committees quizzed witnesses, fuel shortages, transport problems, and organizational muddles in both government and industry were exacerbated by a bitterly cold winter. In the Northeast, normally upstanding men formed gangs and stole coal to keep their families warm. In New York City, 263 people died of pneumonia in one week alone. Soldiers in overcrowded and unfinished training cantonments fell victim to flu, pneumonia, meningitis, measles, and mumps—often because they were inadequately protected. "We found, in the dead of winter, tens of thousands of men without overcoats, tens of thousands lacking woolen breeches, tens of thousands without woolen blouses," one Senate investigator stated. In France, where the winter was equally bitter, the AEF also faced shortages despite Pershing's efforts to fill supply gaps. AEF horses and mules were starving. There weren't enough blankets, gloves, or coats for the men, and some soldiers could not find boots that fit. On a forty-seven-mile Christmas Day march through a blizzard, badly shod men of the Rainbow Division left bloody tracks in the snow.

Congressional critics of the Wilson

administration were far from reluctant to express outrage at the overall state of the nation's war effort after nine full months of belligerence. "We are still unprepared, without a definite war program and still without trained men," George Chamberlain, chairman of the Senate Military Affairs Committee, roared in a public speech. "The military establishment of the United States has broken down. It has almost stopped functioning."[99]

Even as Teddy Roosevelt and others in the audience at this National Security League event stood to applaud, Kaiser Wilhelm's chief strategist, General Erich Ludendorff, was bending over maps at his headquarters in the German spa town of Bad Kreuznach, weighing three possible Western Front targets for a massive early-spring offensive, and battle-tempered German divisions continued moving from Russia to France.[100]

CHAPTER 4

1918

FOR VICTORY AND LASTING PEACE

I have the terribly depressing sense of the waste of life occasioned by this war.
We mark time, mark time, waiting to be allowed to live again.
—Brand Whitlock, American diplomat living in France, March 4, 1918

Retreat? Hell—we just got here!
—Captain Lloyd W. Williams (1887–1918), U.S. Marine Corps
Retort to a French officer, June 2, 1918

For the first time during the present war, a year begins with no legitimate reason for expecting victory, decisive victory during its course," veteran American journalist Frank H. Simonds wrote in January 1918. "Unless all signs fail, the end of the year will see the war still in progress; and there is every prospect that it will see Germany able to make headway against her enemies and in possession of Allied territory on the Western Front." The unhappy status of military operations, uncertainty about Russian intentions as the Bolshevik government continued intermittent negotiations with Germany, and frustration over domestic muddles inhibiting America's own war effort made early 1918 for many in the United States a winter of deep discontent, distress over war-related matters

exacerbated by the continuation of December's foul weather. Freezing temperatures reached as far south as central Florida, snow fell in southern Mississippi, and the worst snowstorm in half a century enveloped the Midwest, where municipal officials nervously monitored ebbing coal supplies as area rail traffic slowed to a crawl. To aid Eastern Seaboard cities already shivering through a coal famine, and to ease rail-traffic congestion inhibiting the flow of troops and matériel to East Coast ports, Treasury Secretary McAdoo in his new role as director-general of the country's recently federalized railroads (see chapter 3) temporarily restricted passenger traffic on eastern rail lines to get more freight trains through. Naval vessels also pitched in, shuttling coal north from Virginia, while the navy simultaneously diverted resources

CESARE in New York Evening Post

TWO WINTERS

Washington, 1917   Valley Forge, 1777

to aid an American neighbor suffering through a devastating natural disaster. Since mid-November, earthquakes had been wracking Guatemala, all but razing its capital city, particularly destructive shocks occurring on January 3 and 24. "In this unfortunate place conditions exist akin to those in the devastated portions of France," American archaeologist Marshall H. Saville wrote after returning from the stricken country. Noting that Guatemala had been the first Latin American nation to sever diplomatic relations with Germany and the Guatemalan government was carefully monitoring the activities of thousands of Germans living in that country, he called on the United States to provide as much aid as possible. "Already the work of the Red Cross is fast drawing this people closer to us . . . and we have now an opportunity to cement this union into a lasting friendship."[1]

Tents, medicine, and food sent to Guatemala in the following months constituted a minute portion of the tremendous outflow of American foodstuffs and goods as the country strove to increase its support for the Allies, civilian victims of the war, and its own rapidly growing armed forces—while continuing to exploit commercial opportunities the war had created, particularly in South America and Asia. To meet all these demands, conservation had become the home-front watchword. "In the national interest [I] take the liberty of calling upon every loyal American to take fully to heart the suggestions which are

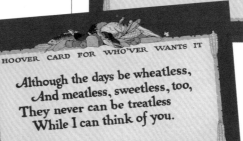

being circulated by the Food Administration," President Wilson urged in a mid-January proclamation.[2] The spirit of federal food administrator Herbert Hoover seemed to possess the nation, his myriad suggestions for stretching food supplies echoing forcefully through the mighty megaphone of George Creel's Committee on Public Information, which also reinforced calls for fuel conservation, donations to war-related charities, and subscriptions to Liberty Loans. Most Americans tried their best to respond. Some did so grudgingly, aware they were watched by critical neighbors, but most sacrificed willingly and, at times, with creative good humor. In early January, a Minnesota newspaper highlighted a bit of

inspired doggerel titled "O. U. Hoover," by St. Louis resident Cable Gray:

My Tuesdays are meatless,
My Wednesdays are wheatless,
    I am getting more eatless each day.
My home it is heatless
My bed it is sheetless,
    They're all sent to the Y.M.C.A.
The bar rooms are treatless,
My coffee is sweetless.
    Each day I get poorer and wiser.
My stockings are feetless,
My trousers are seatless.
My God, but I do hate the kaiser![3]

Germany's ruler briefly took a back seat to an American official as a target of ire on January 17, however, when federal fuel administrator Harry A. Garfield abruptly announced a drastic measure to deal with the coal-distribution crisis, which in addition to causing civilian suffering had stranded in U.S. ports dozens of coal-powered ships packed with materials badly needed in Europe. With the exception of munitions plants, every factory fueled by coal in states east of the Mississippi River was to shut down for five days beginning January 18. Moreover, all businesses requiring heated buildings were to close every Monday for the following ten weeks. CONGRESS IN GREAT FUROR, SENATE IN AN UPROAR, WHITE HOUSE IS FLOODED WITH PROTESTS were just a few of the January 18 headlines reflecting the bedlam of complaints hurled at Garfield and President Wilson. New York Chamber of Commerce president E. H. Outerbridge expressed the feelings of myriad business leaders affected

LIGHT CONSUMES COAL
SAVE LIGHT   SAVE COAL
UNITED STATES FUEL ADMINISTRATION

by the shutdown when he claimed that the order gave "the greatest aid and comfort to the enemy" and was "quite as great a disaster as the one it is sought to clear up." Labor leader Samuel Gompers, usually a stalwart Wilson supporter, told reporters that the order "seemed a very radical measure" and cited the many telegrams he had received from labor representatives protesting the loss in pay the shutdowns would undoubtedly inflict on wage earners already hard-pressed by the high cost of living. Because the order had been issued without any warning or many details, confusion reigned. Questions poured into

Garfield's office: Could other factories be exempted from the five-day shutdown? Which businesses could remain open on Mondays? "No one of the belligerent nations in Europe, except Russia, has been forced to admit such incompetence in public administration," former Harvard University president Charles W. Eliot fumed in the midst of the uproar.[4]

Incompetence in conducting the war effort had become a central theme for critics of the Wilson administration during the congressional investigations that began in December and were still going strong. Political agendas mixed with patriotic concern as congressmen lambasted what they deemed government-wide inefficiency in prosecuting the war, though they concentrated on two topics guaranteed to draw maximum public attention: shoddy conditions in many of the hastily constructed training cantonments and the Wilson administration's apparent inability to build ships (after ten months and millions of dollars the Emergency Fleet Corporation had yet to launch even one) or supply the nation's armed forces with sufficient American-made artillery, aircraft, machine guns and other vital war matériel. The two topics had merged in late-December testimony by several training cantonment commanders. After riveting attention by describing how eighteen hundred sick soldiers had been crammed into a hospital built for eight hundred before adequate winter clothing reached his Texas cantonment and the rate of sickness declined, General Edwin Greble added rifles, pistols, bayonets, and haversacks to the lists provided by other camp commanders of equipment still in short supply. When Oregon's Democratic senator George Chamberlain asked General William Wright, commander of Camp Doniphan, Oklahoma, whether the "shortage of rifles and of machine guns and trench mortars retards . . . proper training," the general simply replied, "Yes it does."[5]

Though a member of the president's political party, Chamberlain had become one of the harshest critics of federal mobilization shortcomings during the trying winter of 1917–1918. In early January, the senator had raised presidential hackles when he proposed creation of a new cabinet department headed by a "secretary of munitions," who would assume responsibility for "arms, ammunition, food, clothing . . . and any other materials the

Opposite: Artist Coles Phillips (1880–1927) had the bright idea for this poster touting the Fuel Administration's conservation campaign, published in Chicago, ca. 1918.

Right: In 1917, the publications section of the United States Shipping Board Emergency Fleet Corporation produced this reminder that the war effort depended heavily on civilian workers at home. John E. Sheridan (1880–1948) provided the artwork.

president shall designate as munitions of war," which would have removed from the War and Navy departments control over matériel vital to their operations. Then, in the midst of the fuel-distribution crisis, Chamberlain graduated from Wilsonian irritant to particular target of presidential ire by formally proposing creation of a separate "War Cabinet" comprising "three distinguished citizens of private ability" to oversee the American war effort—a body that, if created, would essentially demote Wilson to the level of a figurehead in that crucial area of national affairs. "The roll of red tape has grown with the ages," Chamberlain told an audience at the Republican Club in justifying his unprecedented proposal, "and it can only be destroyed in the same way that a tank destroyed the barbed wire in front of the enemy trench."[6]

The president fired back with an unusually strong verbal barrage aimed directly at the senator, whose "statement as to the present inaction and ineffectiveness of the Government," Wilson declared, "is an astonishing and absolutely unjustifiable distortion of the truth." Admitting that there had been "delays and disappointments and partial miscarriages of plan," the president charged that these had been "exaggerated" by the congressional investigations, which themselves had "contributed a great deal to such delay and confusion as had inevitably arisen." Furthermore, by the time of Chamberlain's latest proposal, "effective measures of reorganization had been thoughtfully and maturely perfected." Recently approved by Secretary of War Newton Baker, these reforms included establishing five major War Department

divisions to reduce the chaos created by multiple, uncoordinated supply orders made by the many army purchasing committees and bringing a Wall Street businessman, Edward R. Stettinius, Sr., into the department to help monitor army procurement. Calling Baker "one of the ablest public officials I have ever known," Wilson proceeded to demonstrate his confidence in the secretary by sending him back to Capitol Hill on January 28 to defend the administration and deflect Chamberlain's proposals. Through four and a half hours

Senator George Chamberlain (1854–1928), at right, a severe critic of Wilson administration war policies, posed with Senator Warren G. Harding (Rep.-OH, 1865–1923) on a winter's day. Bain News Service photograph, date unknown.

of testimony and interrogation, Baker remained forthright and imperturbably diplomatic, outlining current and future remedies for the continuing problem of shortages, defending the War Department's considerable achievements to date, and acknowledging the American people's impatience for his department, and the nation, "to do as much as we can. And," he told his interrogators, "we are doing it."[7]

"Jesus, you ought to see that little Baker," Kentucky's Democratic senator, Ollie James, chortled to Wilson during a rushed lunch-break visit to the White House. "He's eating 'em up!" News reports and CPI publicity about what George Creel termed Baker's "forceful accounting to the people" temporarily defused a politically dangerous situation. But Chamberlain's proposals were still circulating. As another of Wilson's Democratic critics, Nebraska senator Gilbert Hitchcock, opened a ten-day debate on the War Cabinet bill with a bitter attack on Baker (for misleading the public) and Wilson (for expanding federal power and acting like a king), the president called a small group of more supportive Democratic senators to the White House and outlined a plan that would, he believed, do much to disarm the administration's critics while providing a mechanism to cope more effectively with domestic war-effort problems. Strong central authority seemed to be proving its worth. The federalized railroads were beginning to operate more smoothly, and the tumult over Fuel Administrator Garfield's recent edict was receding as his measures proved effective. Wilson now asked the senators to back a new bill giving the

president authority and sole discretion, until shortly after the conclusion of hostilities, to enlarge, merge, or reorganize existing executive agencies and transfer funds and responsibilities from one agency to another. This quest for a further extension of executive power unchecked by congressional oversight disquieted many in the room. Eventually, Senator Lee Overman of North Carolina agreed to sponsor the bill, which he introduced on February 7.[8]

One week later, after a battle within the Republican Party leadership, Indiana politico Will H. Hays became national party chairman, replacing William Willcox, who was considered too friendly to the Wilson administration. Counseled and encouraged by Teddy Roosevelt, the youthful and charismatic Hays immediately began a round of visits to prominent Republicans aimed at strengthening party unity before the November midterm elections, when Hays was determined to wrest control of Congress from the Democrats. The Republicans would need to underline their wholehearted support for the war and persuade the electorate that voting for Republican candidates would help, not impede, the war effort. Democrats would have to convince voters that the administration was overcoming the early muddles and mismanagement Republicans had done so much to point out and was vigorously prosecuting the war.[9]

Overseas, meanwhile, American troops continued arriving in France—at a pace that failed to satisfy Allied commanders or General Pershing. Some 48,000 partially trained "Sammies," a.k.a. "doughboys," debarked in January (as the U.S. First

Division took over a quiet portion of the French line). These new arrivals immediately moved inland for combat training, unlike one unit that had arrived in late December. The first black combat regiment to arrive in France, one of four African American combat regiments that were not part of the Ninety-second Division (see chapter 3), the Fifteenth New York National Guard was immediately sent to a camp near the port city of Saint-Nazaire, in Brittany, where men of the regiment were to help build a vast storage depot. "This pick and shovel work was most destructive of the morale of men who had enlisted to fight," one of the regiment's white officers, Arthur W. Little, later wrote. "We put up with it, and the incidental indignities . . . but the condition was not one to be endured indefinitely." In February, at least some of the men got to put down their shovels. The regimental band, led by the renowned musician and composer Lieutenant Jim Europe (see prologue) and twice as large as most such bands, received orders to tour France. For thirty-seven days the band played marches, anthems, ragtime, and "le hot jazz" for soldiers and civilians, introducing thousands of applauding Frenchmen to a new American music. The tour ended when the band received orders to rejoin its regiment, which had been liberated from depot construction, formally redesignated the 369th U.S. Infantry, and assigned to the Sixteenth Division of the French army. With three other black combat regiments that would arrive in France over the next few months (the 370th, 371st, and 372nd), the 369th was now part of the U.S. Ninety-third Division

(provisional). Never physically united as a division, regiments of the Ninety-third would serve with distinction under French command for the rest of the war.[10]

While the 369th Infantry band was still touring, about 49,000 more American troops had arrived in France (as both the Forty-second Division and the Twenty-sixth, whose roster included "Stubby," a soon-to-be-famous canine, assumed front-line duties). By the end of February the AEF's strength was 252,000, appreciably less than the estimated number of British *casualties* from the 1917 Third Battle of Ypres (Passchendaele). This slow progress, the need to train and equip the Americans once they landed, and the continuing buildup of German forces on the Western Front moved the Allied high command to consider ways of reactivating the Eastern Front in order to stop, or at least retard, the transfer of German troops to France. In February, the Allied Supreme War Council began developing plans for a movement into Siberia by the United States' Far East rival, Japan. Those in the Wilson administration who most distrusted Japan spoke out against such an incursion unless U.S. troops also participated and there were some guarantee that the Japanese would later withdraw. President Wilson countered that there were no ships to send an American force to Siberia. Moreover, he told his cabinet, "If we invade Russia, will not Germany say we are doing exactly what she is doing? We will lose our moral position." There the matter rested, at least in Washington. Yet the Wilson administration took careful note when, on March 6, the British warship *Hood* landed 130 Royal Marines in the northwest Russian port city of Murmansk to protect the large cache of supplies the Allies and the United States had shipped there while Russia was still actively at war. This action, taken with the full cooperation of both local and national Bolshevik authorities, would later be regarded as a precedent for further Allied action in both north and southeastern Russia (Siberia), as various Russian factions were organizing to oppose Bolshevik rule.[11]

Reopening the Eastern Front remained at best a distant possibility, while the German threat on the Western Front was immediate and growing. Since late 1917, the Allies had renewed pressure on Pershing, Baker, and Wilson to amalgamate small

groups of American soldiers into the ranks of battered French and British divisions. In Washington, Wilson and Baker seemed prepared to acquiesce, even before General Tasker Bliss sent word from Paris in late January that Allied leaders appeared "badly rattled" and had shown him "information indicating that the Germans have already secured a decided superiority in men and guns on the Western Front." "We do not desire loss of identity of our forces," Baker had cabled General Pershing in December, "but regard that as secondary to the meeting of any critical situation by the most helpful use possible of the troops at your command." Still, the general was to "act with entire freedom in making the best disposition and use of your forces," and Pershing stood fast against amalgamation. He believed that a strong, separate American army, adequately trained and adhering to U.S. military doctrine—which gave a central role to the rifleman, discounted the importance of heavy artillery, machine guns, and automatic rifles, and favored open-field warfare—would inspire Allied troops to leave their trenches and engage in a war of movement that would finally destroy the kaiser's war machine.[12]

Building the AEF would take precious time, and nervous Allied leaders were not certain when Germany would launch its anticipated spring offensive, how well they could withstand that onslaught with so few Americans ready for combat, or how a new wave of losses would affect increasingly war-weary civilians. "There is no doubt that the spirits of England are at present at a low ebb," journalist and semiofficial American observer Ray Stannard Baker

wrote in his diary during a long visit to Britain early in 1918. "The submarine losses are terrific and the food supply grows ever shorter . . . America [is] not yet in the fighting. London is being bombed and the city is full of wounded men. No end is in sight." Though most British civilians remained absolutely unwilling to tolerate a German victory, the Lloyd George government worried that they might accept a negotiated settlement. Veteran politician Lord Lansdowne had suggested as much in a published letter the previous November, and in May 1917, after the Russian Revolution but before the Bolshevik coup, the Petrograd Soviet [i.e., Council] of Workers' and Soldiers' Deputies had suggested a basis for ending the war: "peace without annexations or indemnities on the basis of the self-determination of peoples." With that "Petrograd formula" in the air, home-front labor troubles abounding, and a dangerous year ahead, British leaders believed it imperative to remind their people of the country's war aims. "It is only the clearest, greatest and justest of causes that can justify the continuance even for one day of this unspeakable agony of the nations," Lloyd George told an audience of trade unionists on January 5. Britain fought in self-defense, he said, to defend the public law of Europe and against the German rulers' quest for military domination. It fought to establish a just and lasting peace that would include "a territorial settlement . . . based on the right of self-determination or the consent of the governed" and creation of an international organization that would make future wars less likely. Looking eastward, where there had been a break in the Bolsheviks' negotiations with Germany in the city of Brest-Litovsk, Lloyd George said that the Allied nations would "be proud to fight to the end side by side with the new democracy of Russia . . . But if the present rulers of Russia take action which is independent of their Allies we have no means of intervening to arrest the catastrophe which is assuredly befalling their country. Russia can only be saved by her own people."[13]

Russia was also on Woodrow Wilson's mind as he worked on his own war aims address on January 5, as yet unaware of the British prime minister's speech. Conflicting recommendations had been reaching the White House from Russians and Russian sympathizers in the United States and from some of the many Americans in Russia: diplomats, staff of the Red Cross, YMCA, YWCA, and CPI, as well as newsmen, bankers, and businessmen—despite growing chaos in the country, the Singer Sewing Machine Company and International Harvester were still active there. Most agreed on one point: that the United States should maintain at least informal relations with the Bolshevik government, which, in addition to controlling tons of Allied and American goods stockpiled in both north Russia (Murmansk-Archangel) and Vladivostok (southeastern Siberia), also controlled Siberian mines that produced some 95 percent of the world's supply of platinum, an element required for munitions production. Moreover, a promise of more American aid might help bring Russia back into the war, for the huge, struggling nation certainly needed all sorts of assistance. "Before anything else the Russian people have got to have food," American journalist John Reed wrote from Petrograd on January 6, "especially canned stuff, shoes, clothes and cloth, and enormous amounts of milk for the babies—*immediately.*" Thus, concern for Russia and its people became a leitmotif in Wilson's "Fourteen Points" war aims speech.[14]

Crafted without consulting his cabinet and delivered before a hastily arranged joint session of Congress on January 8, the speech included brief praise for the Lloyd George address and a succinct outline of the president's own vision for world peace. Among the major requirements: "open covenants of peace, openly arrived at"; absolute freedom of the seas; removal of economic barriers and equality of trade

John Reed (1887–1920), journalist, activist, pacifist, and a co-founder of the Provincetown Players. Fascinated with Russia, Reed's most famous work is an account of the Russian Revolution, *Ten Days That Shook the World* (1919). Photograph by Pirie MacDonald, 1914.

conditions among nations; reduction of national armaments; the right of affected peoples to have a say in any territorial adjustments; and creation of "a general association of nations" to guarantee the rights of both great and small countries. Points dealing with particular populations and territories were drawn from recommendations the president received from a group of academic experts he had established the previous September, under the loose direction of his close adviser Colonel House, for the express purpose of preparing for peace negotiations. Known informally as the "Inquiry," the group suffered at first from a dearth of expertise on geographical areas previously of little interest to the American academic community, including Turkey, the Balkans, and most of Africa. For those areas, journalist and Inquiry member Walter Lippmann noted, "we have been compelled practically to train and create our own experts"—something extremely difficult to achieve in a short time and under high pressure.[15]

Yet the Inquiry forged ahead, compiling information and devising reports on countries, colonies, and ethnic groups as the text of Wilson's Fourteen Points traveled around the world via regular news services and the CPI's foreign division. In Russia, Americans rapidly translated and circulated the speech, and the CPI's Edgar Sisson headed a small delegation that personally delivered a copy to Bolshevik leader Vladimir Lenin, who read it immediately. Telling the Americans the speech was "a great step ahead toward the peace of the world," Lenin sent a copy to Leon Trotsky, then resuming negotiations

THE FOURTEEN POINTS

These were defined by President Wilson in an address to Congress on January 8, 1918. Summarized they are:

1. " Open covenants of peace, openly arrived at."
2. Freedom of the seas, in peace and war.
3. Equality of trade conditions.
4. Reduction of armaments.
5. Adjustment of colonial claims with reference to the wishes of the governed population.
6. Evacuation of all Russian territory.
7. Evacuation and restoration of Belgium.
8. Evacuation of French territory, restoration of Alsace-Lorraine.
9. Readjustment of Italy's frontiers along lines of nationality.
10. Autonomous development for the peoples of Austria-Hungary.
11. Independence of Roumania, Servia, and Montenegro.
12. Relinquishment of Turkish control over non-Turkish populations.
13. Erection of an independent Polish state, with free and secure access to the sea.
14. A League of Nations to guarantee independence and territorial integrity to great and small states alike.

with the Germans at Brest-Litovsk. Any hope that the speech itself would help bring Russia back into the war dimmed in February, however, when Trotsky walked out of the Brest-Litovsk negotiations, prompting German troops to renew their advance toward Petrograd. The threat to Russia and Bolshevik rule became so intense that Lenin's government signed the Treaty of Brest-Litovsk on March 3. A note from President Wilson that arrived in the new Russian capital, Moscow, some ten days later, as the Fourth All-Russian Congress of Soviets met to consider ratifying the treaty, generated much less enthusiasm than had the Fourteen Points. Though wishing the Russian people well, Wilson specifically stated that the U.S. government was "not now in a position to render the direct and effective aid it would wish to render." With the Germans at the door, and no hope of further substantial help from any of the Allies, the Russians ratified the treaty, officially taking Russia out of the war, surrendering vast territories whose resources would benefit Germany—and creating a deeper rift between the Bolsheviks and the American government and people.[16]

In Allied nations still actively at war, meanwhile, Wilson's stock, which had been high before the Fourteen Points speech, was soaring ever higher as millions of people embraced his plan for a better postwar world. Allied leaders did have some reservations: The British, whose powerful navy was proving so effective in its blockade of Germany, were unhappy with Wilson's insistence on freedom of the

seas. The Italians were dissatisfied with point 9, which pertained to readjusting their borders. And while the French were delighted with Wilson's call for returning to France the province of Alsace-Lorraine (annexed by the Germans in 1871, after the Franco-Prussian War), French Premier Georges Clemenceau reflected an undercurrent of Gallic disdain for Wilsonian idealism when he growled, after learning of the president's Fourteen Points, "God only needed ten." In the United States, the president's progressive vision for world peace generally won plaudits, although some Republicans grumbled about his apparent endorsement of a postwar free trade policy that would benefit Germany along with everyone else. The *New York Tribune* called the speech "one of the great documents in American history"; prominent Socialist Eugene Debs, a past and future candidate for president, declared that it deserved "the unqualified approval of everyone believing in the rule of the people, Socialists included."[17]

Unlike some leading socialist theorists who now supported the U.S. war effort, including the muckraking novelist Upton Sinclair, Debs remained with the antiwar faction when the Socialist Party split after the declaration of war. In early February the antiwar Socialists issued a proclamation calling for "an immediate and democratic peace with full representation of the working class at the peace conference." Though it approved of Wilson's call for open covenants of peace openly arrived at, the proclamation expressed concern over what it termed a growing threat to "the civil and political freedom of our country" from vigilantism and government spying and censorship.[18]

Socialists were not the only Americans alarmed at increasing home-front repression. On January 13 the recently formed National Civil Liberties Bureau, an offshoot of the American Union Against Militarism and precursor to the American Civil Liberties Union, sponsored a mass meeting at New York City's Liberty Theater to discuss the general topic "American Liberties in Wartime." One of the speakers, Reverend Herbert Bigelow of Ohio, a former state representative and president of the Ohio Constitutional Convention, had been kidnapped by hooded men on his way to give an antiwar speech the previous October, gagged, handcuffed, and tied to a tree deep in the woods while his back was flayed into ribbons "in the name of the women and children of Belgium." Later, while recovering at home, Bigelow was told by an anonymous caller that he would only be allowed to stay in the vicinity if he remained "loyal." (His remarks at the New York meeting were, understandably, subdued.) The NCLB had been keeping track of such incidents; their list for January through March 1918 alone included a Connecticut man of German extraction who had been beaten and forced to kiss the American flag; six alleged pro-Germans beaten, forced to kiss the flag, and thrown into jail in Hartford, Arkansas (they were later declared loyal by the Justice Department); a Socialist attorney in West Virginia who had been tarred and feathered for alleged disloyalty; and a labor organizer and his attorney beaten by a mob inside a police station in Staunton, Illinois. The NCLB also listed dozens of convictions under state sedition laws and the Federal Espionage Act. It somehow missed, however, the late-March arrest of wealthy Socialist and

Social activist Rose Pastor Stokes (1879–1933) with a companion identified only as J. Elster. Bain News Service photograph, date unknown. Stokes fought her conviction under the Espionage Act and was finally exonerated in 1921.

social activist Rose Pastor Stokes for violating the Espionage Act. Stokes would be sentenced to ten years in prison for stating, before a Kansas City, Missouri, women's group—with no supposedly corruptible uniformed or draft-eligible men anywhere in sight—"No government which is for the profiteers can also be for the people, and I am for the people while the Government is for the profiteers." With the tide of such episodes rising, on January 24, an NCLB official, Roger N. Baldwin, asked, in a letter to Colonel House, that the president "indicate clearly . . . the line which in his mind can properly be drawn between those matters which can be fully discussed without prejudice to the country's interest, and those which cannot."[19]

The president issued no guidelines, however, leaving decisions regarding restrictions on freedom of expression to the Post Office Department (now authorized to deny mailing privileges to any publications it deemed suspicious) as well as the Justice Department and other elements of the rapidly expanding U.S. intelligence network, which relied heavily on dubious information provided by the quasi-official nationwide American Protective League (APL). Most states and many cities also formed vigilance societies, many of which embraced monitoring their fellow citizens with an excess of enthusiasm that often bordered on vigilantism. Early in 1918 the Citizens' Patriotic League of Covington, Kentucky, convinced that a sixty-six-year-old shoemaker and longtime community leader, Charles Bernard Schoberg, was expressing disloyal sentiments in personal conversations, hired private detectives who installed a dictograph (a device that magnified sounds) in the base of a grandfather clock in Schoberg's shoe store, telling Schoberg it was an electric meter. Establishing a listening post in the basement of a nearby bank, for more than four months they tried to ignore the constant, magnified ticking of the huge clock as they took notes on generally innocuous conversations Schoberg had with two longtime friends, J. Henry Kruse, fifty-six, and Henry Feltman, sixty-five. All three were subsequently sentenced to prison—Schoberg to ten years, Kruse to five, and Feltman to seven, plus a forty-thousand-dollar fine—for, among other things, causing and inciting "insubordination, disloyalty, mutiny and refusal of duty" in the armed forces of the United States, although the men, all of whom purchased Liberty Bonds and otherwise supported the war, had uttered their supposedly seditious statements only to each other.[20]

In the whirlwind of America's first great overseas conflict and all the attendant domestic suspicions and uncertainties, prominent private citizens and organizations not generally associated with the term "vigilance" also monitored the behavior of their constituents and fellow citizens. On January 30, Teddy Roosevelt delivered a typically energetic speech to five thousand soldiers at Camp Merritt, New Jersey, a training cantonment and assembly point for men about to be transported to Europe. Calling such camps "the great universities of American citizenship," Roosevelt spoke in favor of universal military training and against conscientious objectors, who, he thought, should be placed on naval minesweepers or be assigned to dig frontline trenches. There was no room in the wartime United States, he said, for "fifty-fifty" citizens. Two days later, in a speech that marked the end of the New York Federation of Women's Clubs' annual convention, Mrs. Thomas Massey created a stir by stating that she had overheard disloyal sentiments during the convention and proposing a formal resolution to "put . . . out of our clubs"

anyone who "during the period of the war, favors pacifism or expresses sentiments of a disloyal or treasonable character," "disloyal" and "treasonable" apparently to be defined case-by-case. After that resolution sailed through with only two dissenting votes, Mrs. J. Hungerford Milbank, a longtime preparedness advocate who since 1914 had formed or inspired a number of women's military drill teams, reminded the clubwomen that when New York State enacted woman suffrage in 1917, they had been "given liberty with one hand and obligation to serve with the other." Many military men she had talked with believed that the Germans would eventually reach the American East Coast, she said. Thus the federation should form its own regiment, for "You will need to know how to handle a gun either to kill an enemy or yourself."[21]

As interested clubwomen followed Milbank's instructions and went to 104 Broad Street for more information, a convoy of Allied ships on the last leg of the dangerous journey from the United States turned into the channel between Ireland and Scotland bound southward to Liverpool. More than two thousand American soldiers aboard the British liner *Tuscania* and the crew

of the U.S. Navy tanker *Kanawha* were among those breathing more easily as the convoy neared its destination—until, on the night of February 5, a torpedo from *UB-77* coursed through the water. "As I ran up the ladder to the bridge I could see the *Tuscania* . . . ahead of us, give a lurch and then list to starboard," *Kanawha*'s chief electrician, Harold Dunne, later wrote. "The lights flashed on, flooding the *Tuscania*'s sides and we could see the boats being lowered and the troops lining the side and putting their life belts on." *As Tuscania* sent out an SOS, "I am torpedoed and sinking fast," Dunne and his mates watched their countrymen (and two women passengers) leap into the water or slide down the listing ship's sides— many of them singing, Dunne reported with pride, "that popular song, 'O Joy, O Boy, Where do We Go from Here?'" Most of them went into lifeboats or onto the

welcoming decks of British destroyers escorting the convoy, but two hundred Yanks were killed. A shocking disaster for Americans not yet accustomed to casualty lists touching their own homes, the *Tuscania* sinking made headlines across the country. This tragic news boosted determination, among millions of ardent war supporters, to strengthen the nation's war effort, defeat the networks of German agents still rumored (with little factual basis) to be in the country, and root out all "disloyalty," however that might be defined. That determination surged anew with war news that began appearing in papers across the country on Friday, March 22.[22]

At four forty A.M. on March 21, more than 6,400 heavy guns and 3,500 trench mortars unleashed an unprecedented storm of steel, fire, and gas on Allied troops of the British Fifth and Third armies along a forty-three-mile line at approximately the center of the Western Front, near the point where British lines met those of the French. For nearly five hours the lethal rain swayed back and forth in a calculated pattern, completely obliterating portions of the frontline trenches and the men within them, pummeling second-tier trench lines, tearing into communications hubs and artillery positions, then moving back to pound what was left of the front lines. At nine thirty A.M., in a mixture of smoke and fog, German troops rose and moved forward, beginning Operation Michael, the long-feared spring offensive. Employing a phenomenally effective tactic relatively new to Western-Front warfare, small groups of soldiers preceded the main body of troops, infiltrating and exploiting the many weak points the bombardment had created in the British lines. Having amassed a two-to-one advantage in manpower, General Erich Ludendorff had developed a multi-stage plan, choosing this first point of attack with the hope of separating the British and French armies, pushing the British back toward the English Channel to protect the ports that were their gateways home, and forcing the French Sixth Army, on the southern edge of the onslaught, back toward Paris.

The initial success was stunning: The British Third Army, closest to the English Channel, fell back slowly, putting up strong resistance, but the Fifth Army was in full and disorganized retreat, ceding mile after mile to the Germans, which forced the French to fall back as well.

Caught in the midst of the chaos: three hundred men of the U.S. Sixth Engineers, the first element of the Third Division to arrive in France. Completely untrained in combat, these Yanks abandoned their bridge-building project, took up whatever weapons they could find, joined in the retreat, and then became part of an ad-hoc British-Canadian contingent, dubbed "Carey's Force," which formed a defensive line near the hinge of the two British armies. In two weeks of fighting, before action shifted away from their sector, twenty-eight of the Americans were killed.[23]

On March 26, not far from the engineers' action, Colonel Raynal C. Bolling—former head of the 1917 American Aeronautical Mission to Europe who was now helping to build an AEF air arm—went to reconnoiter near the city of Amiens, accompanied only by his military chauffeur. Though they had been assured by British and French officers that the Germans were three to five miles away, within a mile the two Americans ran into a German unit that raked their car with machine-gun fire, sending the bullet-riddled automobile careening off the road, where its two occupants dove into adjoining shell holes. Armed with a pistol, Bolling shot and killed a German who was trying to kill his driver—and was immediately shot through the heart by one of the slain German's comrades, becoming the first high-ranking American officer to be killed in the Great War. That same day, Major Paul H. Clark, the AEF liaison to French General Headquarters, was with General Philippe Pétain and his staff in their temporary command post in a railroad car near Chantilly. "We have

Left: Some wartime German postcards featured this image of General Erich Ludendorff (1865–1937).

———

Right: A native of Scotland, Sergeant John C. Laing was one of the U.S. Sixth Engineers who fought alongside the British during the opening days of the German Offensive. He survived to proudly become an American citizen immediately after the war.

had terrible days," Clark wrote to General Pershing that evening. "The situation is very grave . . . Several of the [French] staff look like they had been hit in the belly with a baseball bat. That is a result of loss of sleep and the intense anxiety through which they have passed since [the] night of [March] 20th–21st."[24]

Anxiety was not confined to the military. "Last night our line was sixty miles, in some places, west of where it had been on the morning of March 21st," American writer Mildred Aldrich, long resident in France, wrote in despair to a friend on March 28. "In the lost land are the scenes of so much hard fighting, land over which the Allies had crept inch by inch . . . and oh! how many tragic hilltops, and how many spots where our beloved dead lie buried." More distressing to Aldrich than even the Allied retreat and the distant artillery fire, so heavy that "the very ground seemed to tremble under me," were the streams of refugees passing by her home, the looks on their faces, the things they said. "Fear seemed suddenly to have taken root everywhere, a thing I have never seen here before—fear that the Germans were too strong in numbers still, and the Americans not only unprepared, but not yet numerous enough to turn the balance."[25]

By this time General Pershing had six complete AEF divisions under his command, with more troops arriving as quickly as limited shipping could bring them. Four of the huge 28,000-man divisions—the First, Second, Twenty-sixth, and Forty-second—were considered combat-ready, though their training continued.[26] The Forty-first Division remained well behind the lines as a supply and replacement unit, and additional elements of the Third Division, comprising regular army units, and the Thirty-second Division, chiefly National Guardsmen from Michigan and Wisconsin, were among the 85,000 U.S. troops that arrived in France during March.[27] Secretary of War Baker was also on hand, having left Washington in late February on his first trip to the European front. Meeting Baker at the train station in Paris on March 25, as the secretary returned from a London meeting with the deeply worried David Lloyd George, Pershing, too, noted what he described as the "pathetic scene" created by refugees crowding into the city. Still convinced that the Americans could best help these displaced people and the

10. They invited me to have lunch with them
in the train but I declined though the
invitation was repeated with urgence. ~~good~~
It seemed to me though that it would
have been an intrusion so I persisted in
declining and said I would call again
during the afternoon to get more
information.

Several of the staff look like they had
been hit in the belly with a base ball
bat. That is a result of loss of sleep
and the intense anxiety through which
they have passed since night of $20^{th}-21^{st}$

At Compiègne the arty. fire was close
enough to make windows rattle noisily.
The city is largely emptied, the roads were
crowded with fleeing inhabitants for
20 kilometers south of Compiègne.

Paris is quiet and the truth does not
seem to be generally known. The streets

overall war effort by continuing to build a strong and separate AEF, Pershing and Baker negotiated with the British for more ships to transport the troops that Lloyd George was begging Washington to rush to Europe *now*. Determined to provide more immediate help in the crisis, on March 28, the AEF commander traveled along roads clogged with troops and supply convoys to a farmhouse outside the town of Clermont-sur-Oise, headquarters of the newly named commander in chief of all Allied Western Front armies, Marshal Ferdinand Foch. There, in a quiet garden, Pershing made a morale-boosting pledge widely publicized in both French and American newspapers. "I have come to tell you that the American people would consider it a great honor for our troops to be engaged in the present battle . . . Infantry, artillery, aviation, all that we have are yours; use them as you wish."[28]

Initially, however, the four U.S. combat divisions remained in less active but still dangerous sectors. The First Division, now under the command of General Robert Bullard, was in a section of the French lines about 140 miles to the southeast of the Operation Michael fighting, on the south side of the Saint-Mihiel salient, a hilly protrusion in the German lines that the French had dubbed the "hernia." The sector had been relatively quiet before the Americans arrived, but under Bullard's aggressive leadership his doughboys began lobbing some four thousand shells a day into the salient, the Germans responding with shrapnel and explosive shells—and with phosgene gas, which alone killed eight Yanks and caused the evacuation of seventy-seven more who were suffering the agonies of exposure. These early U.S. gas casualties added another layer of difficulty to questions already troubling American censors, the AEF high command, and the War Department in Washington: how much detail should be included in casualty

Left: One page of the March 26, 1918, report to General Pershing by Major Paul H. Clark, AEF liaison to French General Headquarters, in which Clark notes some effects of the German offensive.

Right: Some American doughboys pose in the proper gear for surviving lethal gas attacks. National Photo Company, date unknown.

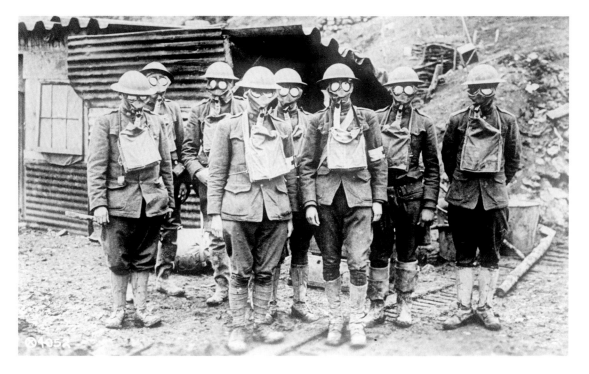

reports (too much, too soon might assist enemy intelligence), and how much should be allowed in public descriptions of combat, especially when it involved chemical weapons. ("A real gas case was a pitiable sight to see," one American soldier would write to a friend in 1919. "Imagine a human being trying to tear his own throat with agony.") After these early gas casualties, therefore, AEF censors sought to exorcize from letters and correspondents' reports any language that would "cause unnecessary apprehension and pain" to the affected soldiers' friends and relatives. The division's persistent artillery bombardments, meanwhile, may well have contributed to the German high command's choice of its sector as the target for a heavy raid. The kaiser's well-oiled propaganda machine had been portraying doughboys as reluctant and incompetent soldiers. But as the trickle of Yanks arriving in Europe became a steady stream, it was deemed necessary to provide some proof of these assertions. Yet the raid would not hit the First Division. In early April, before the raiders were ready, the Twenty-sixth ("Yankee") Division, under General Clarence ("Daddy") Edwards, replaced Bullard's men, and also stretched its resources to take over nine miles of trenches previously held by the French.[29]

As the Yankee Division assumed its new duties, General Peyton C. March, recently returned to Washington from France, where he had been Pershing's artillery commander, was stirring things up at the War Department as the new U.S. Army chief of staff. The general had assumed his duties on Monday, March 4 (as the army was recruiting qualified women to operate the AEF telephone system in France and the War Department was beginning to receive disturbing reports of an unusually virulent flu striking some of the larger stateside training cantonments). After meeting with department personnel on his first day, General March returned in the evening to find only one officer on duty and many of the darkened corridors heaped with unopened mail sacks—conditions that he apparently considered unsatisfactory. "The next night

the entire General Staff were on duty," he later reported, "and they stayed on duty at night until the end of the war. All the other offices and bureaus of the War Department took up the work without regard to hours, and in a very short time the piles of unopened mail sacks vanished." A man of erect military bearing and impressive field experience, March "lived, breathed, and slept efficiency," one subordinate attested, and he did not much care whose toes he stepped on to get results. Immediately embarking on a reorganization program, he built on the reforms that President Wilson and Secretary Baker had noted during the congressional hearings in January to further centralize procurement and other processes. "With General Peyton C. March as Chief of Staff," Pershing would write in his postwar memoirs, "the General Staff and the supply departments began to exert more energy."[30]

Energy infused a speech President Wilson gave in Baltimore's Fifth Regiment Armory on April 6 to kick off the Third Liberty Loan campaign. "This is the anniversary of our acceptance of Germany's challenge to fight for our right to live and be free," he said, "for the sacred rights of freemen everywhere. The nation is awake"—awake to the need for sacrifice, for opposing the German militarists' campaign to "everywhere impose their power and exploit everything for their own use and aggrandizement," as they had with their "cheap triumph" over the "great people" of Russia. "I am ready, ready still, ready even now, to discuss a fair and just and honest peace at any time that it is sincerely purposed," Wilson said. But Germany was once again demonstrating its determination that "force alone, shall decide whether justice and peace shall reign in the affairs of men" and there was, "therefore, but one response possible from us: Force, force to the utmost, force without stint or limit, the righteous and triumphant force which shall make right the law of the world and cast every selfish dominion down in the dust."[31]

Some American officials also favored using greater force against shirkers and those of dubious loyalty at home. In early March, with the blessing and encouragement of Attorney General Thomas Gregory, Pittsburgh's public safety director, Charles Pritchard, launched a roundup to catch the many draft dodgers ("slackers") he believed were lurking in his city. Collaborating with bona fide federal agents in the city as well as quasi-legal "agents" of the American Protective League, he instigated a Saturday-night sweep of city streets, hotels, cafés, and assorted entertainment

Beat back the HUN with LIBERTY BONDS

venues that hauled in any man who could not immediately produce a valid draft registration card. The raids continued for several nights, cramming Pittsburgh's jails with hundreds of men detained without warrants—most of whom proved innocent of any wrongdoing. At the end of the month, with news of the German offensive filling the nation's newspapers, 120 APL "agents," assisted by a local army detachment, staged more of these "slacker raids" in Minneapolis. Again, most of the men detained proved to be innocent. But that did not dampen the APL's enthusiasm for this new extralegal but officially condoned practice, which quickly spread to other league chapters across the country.[32]

In Washington, just after Wilson's forceful April 6 speech, Senator George Chamberlain introduced a bill requiring military courts-martial for all civilians accused of the broad range of offenses the bill defined as seditious, even though the nation's criminal court system was operating efficiently. Although the bill had many supporters, Chamberlain withdrew it after President Wilson publicly stated that the measure was "unconstitutional [and] . . . would put us nearly upon the level of the very people we are fighting and effecting to despise." Detestation of all things German had by then reached a near-fever pitch in the country, spurred by German gains on the battlefront and increasingly frenzied home-front propaganda, including a just-released Hollywood potboiler, *The Kaiser, the Beast of Berlin*. The country's millions of German Americans walked cautiously through thickening clouds of suspicion, but they were not alone, as witnessed by the diverse victims of the country's growing plague of vigilantism and the equally broad list of those accused under the Espionage Act. Yet even that potent act was not deemed sufficient. As the president condemned Chamberlain's court-martial bill, Attorney General Gregory was pressing Congress to give the Espionage Act more "teeth" by adding several amendments. Echoing in many respects the stunningly repressive Sedition Act the Montana legislature had enacted in February (see chapter 3), the amendments were necessary, Gregory said in an appearance before the American Bar Association, to afford greater "protection of the nation against the insidious propaganda of the pacifist." A more drastic act would also constitute a public service, he continued, for "unless the hysteria, which results in the lynching of men, is checked" by government enforcement of more stringent laws, "it will create a condition of lawlessness from which we will suffer for a hundred years."[33]

As if on cue, on April 4, a mob that grew to more than two hundred people raged through the streets of Collinsville, Illinois, hunting a thirty-year-old German immigrant, Robert Prager, a former baker who had just begun work in the local coal mines. Collinsville had experienced intermittent strikes and labor disputes since the declaration of war, labor unrest that had brought with it accusations of disloyalty. It had also bucked the country's increasing bent toward prohibition, saloons being among its most prominent features. Drunk on both alcohol and patriotic fervor, the mob found and seized Prager, stripped off his shoes and clothing, wrapped him in an American flag, and dragged him out of town, accusing him of all sorts of disloyal acts that Attorney General Gregory later said there was no evidence he had ever committed. Far from being disloyal, Prager had secured his first citizenship papers and tried to enlist in the U.S. Navy, but was rejected because he had one glass eye. That did not deter the increasingly excited mob, which at least allowed him to pray and

write a short note to his parents before they hanged him. Lynching of African American men and women (sixty-four people, including two pregnant women, would be lynched in 1918) had thus far done little to arouse a majority of the country's white citizens or the mainstream press to condemn the practice—and despite pleas from the NAACP and others representing black Americans, President Wilson had also refused to speak out against it. The president also remained silent about the Prager hanging, but as news of this latest act of war-related mob violence against a white registered alien spread across the country, many others did react, condemnation generally outweighing statements that seemed to dismiss the execution as understandable patriotic excess in time of war. "A fouler

wrong could hardly be done America," the *New York Times* stated. "We shall be denounced as a nation of odious hypocrites." Senator Lawrence Sherman of Illinois agreed. Damning Collinsville's mayor and four-man police force for their "abject cowardliness" in failing to stop the lynching, he cited Prager's death while arguing on the Senate floor against passing the Espionage Act amendments. "Such laws as the one proposed here will not . . . make less frequent mobs of that kind and the consequent tragedies."[34]

Sherman was among several senators who opposed the amendments, now collectively known as the Sedition Act of 1918. "Yes . . . [this] is war," California's Hiram Johnson thundered. "But, good God . . . when did it become war upon

the American people?" Senator Joseph France of Maryland declared the Western world had not seen "since the dark ages any criminal statute so repressive." But these legislators were swimming against an overwhelming current, for by then war hysteria had thoroughly infiltrated the halls of Congress. Even the staunchly pro-war Republican senator Henry Cabot Lodge complained, as the debate continued, that he had "become a little weary of having Senators get up here and say to those of us who happen to think a word had better be changed [that we] are trying to shelter treason."[35]

War hysteria deepened as more alarming news arrived from the Western Front. On April 9, Ludendorff's grand offensive entered its second phase, German divisions turning east toward the Lys River and the English Channel beyond, smashing into the British First Army, easily shattering Portuguese regiments and overrunning trenches held by two British divisions, then hitting and pushing back the badly outnumbered British Second Army on April 10. Alarmed and unwilling even to countenance losing the Channel ports, now only some twenty-five miles behind his retreating troops, on April 11 the British Western Front commander, General Douglas Haig, distributed an unprecedented message to the armies under attack, its main import contained in one unyielding line: "With our backs to the wall, and believing in the justice of our cause, each one of us must fight on to the end." Just as Wilson's "force to the

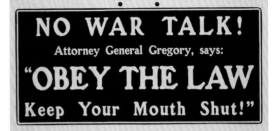

utmost" speech quickly appeared in British newspapers to widespread approval, so Haig's "backs to the wall" order inspired concerned and admiring headlines across the United States.[36]

Day by day, Americans read how the British were holding, though their situation remained desperate: "The men are . . . so tired after weeks of fighting," British correspondent Philip Gibbs reported in the *New York Times* on April 15, "that they can hardly stagger up to resist another attack. Yet they do so," even as "the enemy still storms against them with fresh men, always fresh men, in overwhelming numbers." With Gibbs's somber article underlining the crisis, General March and his staff in the War Department scrambled to comply with an agreement that President Wilson had recently confirmed with Allied chiefs (after incorporating changes recommended by General Pershing): With the assistance of British transports, the Americans would rush headquarters staff plus infantry and machine-gun components of the Third, Fifth, and Seventy-seventh divisions to Europe, artillery and supplies to be provided by the Allies. The same components of three more divisions were to be dispatched in early May. All these units were to be deployed as needed, but to remain under Pershing's control. Secretary Baker had helped formulate the agreement, and when he returned to Washington in mid-April, he found the dispatch of troops in motion: A total of 116,642 would be sent across that month, 245,945 in May.[37]

After giving a gaggle of eager reporters a rosy, if not completely accurate, report of the Allies' high regard for the AEF, the war secretary held a closed-door briefing in the White House for the president and an informal body of advisers established in February at the suggestion of Food Administrator Herbert Hoover. Dubbed Wilson's "war cabinet," but not to be confused with the body Senator Chamberlain had proposed in his War Cabinet bill (which was dying quietly from lack of support), this small group comprised heads of agencies that regularly dealt with questions related to the conduct of the war. In addition to Baker and Hoover, those attending its Wednesday sessions included Secretary of the Treasury McAdoo; Secretary of the Navy Daniels; Fuel Administrator Garfield; Edward N. Hurley, chairman of the Emergency Fleet Corporation; Vance McCormack, chairman of the War Trade Board; and the newly appointed chairman of the War Industries Board, Bernard Baruch. This group quickly became the center of war planning, which frustrated the excluded members of the president's regular cabinet. "Nothing talked of at Cabinet that would interest a nation, a family, or a child," Secretary of the Interior Franklin

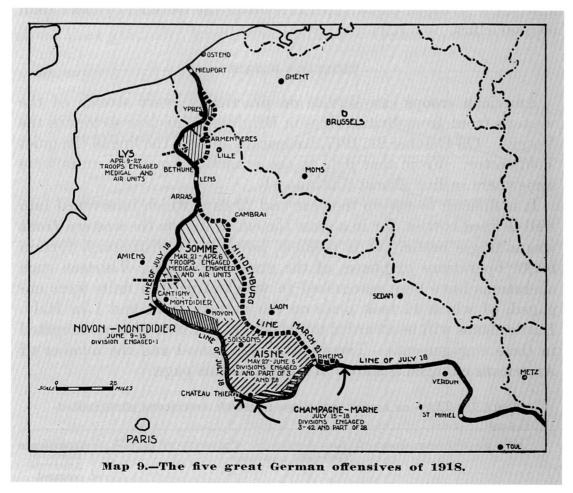

Map 9.—The five great German offensives of 1918.

Left: Map 9 from *The War with Germany: A Statistical Summary* by Leonard P. Ayres showing the scope of what the author describes as the "five drives of unprecedented violence" through which the Germans "sought to break the Allied line and end the war."

Opposite: Color lithograph showing the Japanese cavalry taking Khabarovsk, a city about five hunderd miles north of Vladivostok. Published by Shobido & Co., Tokyo, ca. 1919. Japanese ambitions regarding China and Russia concerned the Wilson administration.

THE ILLUSTRATION OF THE SIBERIAN WAR. №14   *Our Cavalrys Corupied Khabarovsk And March Past Took Place in Front of the Enemys Gun Boats.*

Lane grumbled in a mid-March note. "No talk of war. No talk of Russia or Japan."[38]

Japan and Russia were prominently mentioned in American newspapers in April, however, when Bolshevik authorities protested the landing at Vladivostok, without Russian permission, of four hundred Japanese marines, ostensibly to protect their countrymen in that increasingly chaotic city, where a Japanese soldier had recently been murdered. Although the *New York Times* reported that the Japanese move was "not regarded by the American Government as possessing political significance," that was not entirely true—though President Wilson still resisted sending any American troops to Siberia to curb Japanese ambitions. But as pressure for direct U.S. military involvement in Russia continued to build among presidential

advisers and Allied war planners, the president did allow the cruiser USS *Olympia* to transport a British general, Frederick Poole, to Murmansk, where Poole was to assume command of the small contingent of Allied troops stationed there with the (increasingly grudging) approval of the Bolsheviks.[39]

Olympia received its orders on April 19. The following day, Germans on the Saint-Mihiel salient launched their long-planned heavy raid, 2,800 men, 600 of them specially trained shock troops, surging through holes the initial artillery bombardment punched in a two-mile sector of the Twenty-sixth Division's front line. Pouncing on two companies of shocked Yankee Division soldiers, often in brutal hand-to-hand combat, the Germans battled more than a mile into American territory, pushing 400 Americans out of the town of Seicheprey, then leveling the town while battling the displaced Yanks, who were struggling to reorganize so they could mount an effective counterattack. Finally withdrawing on their own initiative, the Germans took with them 136 prisoners and left behind more than 600 American casualties, 81 of them dead. American newspapers framed the clash as a demonstration of American grit in the face of superior numbers. German propagandists cited it as proof of American military incompetence—and some Allied leaders agreed. "This kind of result is bound to occur on an enormous scale," British Prime Minister Lloyd George asserted, "if a largely amateur United States Army is built up without the guidance of more experienced [British and French] General Officers." General Haig considered the encounter evidence that it would be "criminal" to count on serious assistance from the AEF for many months.[40]

Pershing was well aware of Allied skepticism about AEF capabilities before Seicheprey. Visiting the First Division on April 16, in a rear area about 140 miles northwest of Saint-Mihiel, he joined a bevy of French officers to watch the Americans smartly engage in an open-warfare test maneuver, then called the First Division officers together for an Americans-only meeting. Each of them knew the situation: With the British stubbornly hanging on some twenty-five miles east of the English Channel, the Allies were anticipating a third phase of the Ludendorff offensive, quite possibly an attack in the French sector the First Division would soon be

helping to defend. "You have just had a test of efficiency and met it," Pershing said of the just-completed maneuver. "You are now to go against a victorious enemy under new and harder conditions. All our Allies will be watching to see how you conduct yourselves." By the end of April, the division, flanked by French forces, was under constant bombardment by dozens of enemy artillery batteries firing from higher ground within and around the German-occupied town of Cantigny. As American and French artillery returned fire and rattled First Division infantrymen tried to shore up their line under constant enemy bombardment, American commanders began planning the first (limited) American offensive of the war: The First Division was to take and hold Cantigny.[41]

General Pershing, meanwhile, traveled

Opposite: Captain Douglas MacArthur (1880–1964) on duty in San Antonio, Texas, 1916. MacArthur later helped form the Forty-second (Rainbow) Division and became one of the most distinguished and decorated officers of the AEF in France—occasionally startling soldiers by wearing somewhat less-than-military garb, as in this photo.

Right: As baseball fans were seeking to exclude ballplayers from the May 1918 "work or fight" order, former major league player Edward (Harvard Eddie) Grant was taking his place on the Western Front with the Seventy-seventh Division. Captain Grant would be killed by artillery fire on October 5, 1918, during the Meuse-Argonne Campaign. He is buried in France.

to the city of Abbeville for a two-day meeting of the Supreme War Council. "Extreme pessimism prevailed regarding present crisis. Everybody at high tension," he wrote in his diary on May 2. Amalgamation was a chief item on the agenda, and Pershing described those discussions as "at times very lively." In fact, the British were distraught and the French nearly beside themselves at the AEF commander's continuing refusal to scatter his doughboys through the ranks of badly mauled Allied armies. When General Foch asked him if he was "willing to risk our being driven back to the Loire," Pershing answered "Yes . . . the time may come when the American Army will have to stand the brunt of this war, and it is not wise to fritter away our resources in this manner."[42]

At home, the government was also focusing on effective use of war-support resources. On May 20, Congress passed the bill that Senator Lee Overman had introduced in February, allowing the president during the war crisis to reorganize executive agencies at will. A milestone in the accretion of presidential power, the Departmental Reorganization (Overman) Act also put Wilson's relations with Congress on a permanent downward slope, more legislators now agreeing with Senator Hitchcock, who in February had accused the president of acting like a king. Yet the bill's immediate effects were beneficial. It facilitated restructuring of the War Department and allowed Wilson to transform the War Industries Board from an arm of the Council of National Defense to an independent agency, which, under

the guidance of Bernard Baruch, became increasingly effective in coordinating the nation's sadly lagging war production.[43]

An army of workers was essential to maintaining production, and three days after the Overman bill passed newspapers alerted the country to a new Selective Service regulation, quickly dubbed the "work-or-fight" order, aimed at shoring up the workforce and reassuring the nation's business community regarding the labor supply. "One of the unanswerable criticisms of the draft has been that it takes men from the farms and from all useful employments and marches them past crowds of idlers and loafers away to the army," stated the army's judge advocate general, Enoch Crowder, a chief architect of Selective Service. "The

remedy is simple . . . to require that any man pleading exemption on any ground shall also show that he is contributing effectively to the industrial welfare of the nation." The regulation listed occupations that could no longer shelter men from military service, including waiters, gamblers, clairvoyants, domestic servants, soda counter workers, bellboys, and elevator operators—all of which the country accepted with relative equanimity. The inclusion of ballplayers was another matter. Irate baseball fans lobbed so many complaints at the War Department that Secretary Baker appealed to the president, who would not agree to remove ballplayers from the list, but did agree to postpone drafting any until after the World Series.[44]

The work-or-fight regulation did not list any organized trades included under the umbrella of Gompers' administration-friendly American Federation of Labor, and it excluded other occupations, deemed essential, in which workers were still struggling to achieve better conditions. With food prices 63 percent higher than in 1914, clothing costs up 77 percent, and war profiteering by the nation's businesses and corporations often in the news, workers were shifting disruptively from job to job or resorting to strikes when otherwise thwarted from getting adequate pay—for, as Secretary of Commerce William Redfield had written to President Wilson in December 1917, "Patriotism is a cold thing when the breakfast is scant and a strike seems the only way to make it sufficient." To help deal with continuing discord, the Wilson administration in late March had established a War Labor Board

(WLB), co-chaired by former president William Howard Taft and attorney Frank P. Walsh, that comprised representatives of industry, the workforce, and the public. In arbitrating a steady stream of disagreements and strikes, the board, following the president's instructions, attempted to steer a course between the aspirations of labor and the demands of capital, allowing workers to organize without interference but under conditions employers would not find objectionable (e.g., no coercion of non-union employees, no objections to existing open shops). Government policies thus gave unionization a modest boost in 1918—with one glaring exception. Members of the radical antiwar IWW were

everywhere under siege by federal, state, and municipal authorities, businessmen, and most mainstream newspapers. On May 16, as the first of three mass trials of Wobblies accused of "conspiracy against the war program of the United States" was getting under way in Chicago, Congress widened the scope of possible antiwar prosecutions, passing the Sedition Act by a vote of 48 to 26 in the Senate and 293 to 1 in the House (New York Socialist Meyer London cast the single dissenting vote). It was now illegal in time of war to "willfully utter, print, write, or publish any disloyal, profane, scurrilous, or abusive language about the form of government . . . the Constitution . . . the military or naval forces . . . the flag . . . or the uniform of the Army or Navy of the United States" or to "use any language intended to bring" any of the above "into contempt, scorn, contumely or disrepute." What constituted "disloyal," "scurrilous," or "abusive" language remained open to broad interpretation.[45]

While Congress was voting the Sedition Act into law, on the other side of the Atlantic Ocean Privates Henry Johnson and Needham Roberts of the 369th Infantry, no strangers to scurrilous and abusive language that had nothing to do with the war, were engaged in a desperate struggle in the dead of night with more than twenty German soldiers who were attempting to eliminate their outpost in front of the French lines. Propped up against the door of a dugout, the badly wounded Roberts hurled grenades as Johnson grappled with the invaders, taking several wounds but inflicting many more with his rifle butt and a bolo knife. The Germans finally retreated, leaving a bloody trail from their wounds; the two doughboys survived to be celebrated as heroes on both sides of the Atlantic. "There is just one way the American people as a whole could recognize the valor of Privates Johnson and Roberts, colored, in a manner worthy of the nation," the *New York Evening World* editorialized on May 22: "to make the lynching of a negro an abhorred and obsolete crime." One week later, as the New York City-based African American newspaper the *Amsterdam News* reported that more than 230 black Americans had been murdered by mobs since April 1917, Major Joel Spingarn assumed new duties in the Washington, D.C., offices of the U.S. Army's Military Intelligence Branch (MID). While still an official of the NAACP, Spingarn had been instrumental in establishing the Des Moines training camp for black officers (see chapter 3). Now assigned to investigate left-wing radicalism, in particular, subversion among African Americans, he did his best to implement, as the NAACP magazine the *Crisis* would soon note, a "far-reaching constructive effort to satisfy the pressing grievances of colored Americans." Spingarn lobbied Congress

for an anti-lynching law, encouraged Secretary Baker to press President Wilson for an anti-lynching declaration, and, with the War Department's liaison to the black community, Emmett Scott, organized a three-day conference of influential African Americans. Among its several recommendations, that conference, too, called for "the immediate suppression of lynching," adding to the pressures that would, in late July, finally result in a presidential proclamation against mob violence.[46]

Days before Johnson and Roberts had their near-fatal encounter in France, Wilson issued another proclamation, this one designating the week of May 20 Red Cross Week, which sparked huge parades in cities across the country. Traveling to New York City to help launch the drive for contributions there, he drew wave after wave of cheers from a massive crowd as he marched at the head of more than seventy thousand Red Cross supporters before moving onto the reviewing stand. (Among the marchers who passed by him: a new Red Cross volunteer, Ernest Hemingway, who reported to friends that he was able to get a "fine look" at the president. A few days later, Hemingway was aboard ship heading for France, the first leg of his journey to a post in Italy and experiences he would fictionalize in his 1929 novel, *A Farewell to Arms*.) Wilson returned to Washington with the burgeoning financial costs of the war on his mind. On May 27, as the House was considering a bill that would allow the War Department to raise an army of unlimited size, he addressed a joint session of Congress. With the war now at its "very peak and crisis," he said, American might must be increased "until there can be no question of resisting it"—and that would require more funds, a significant portion of which should come from increased taxes on incomes, luxuries, and excessive war profits. Though the summer recess and fall midterm elections were looming, these things must wait "until we have done our duty to the full. Politics," Wilson declared, "is adjourned."[47]

Congress reluctantly remained in session to start months of wrangling over the Revenue Act of 1918. But as Wilson well knew, politics was not adjourned. Democrats had already suffered a double defeat in a Wisconsin special election where three candidates vied to fill the U.S. Senate seat left vacant by the death of Senator Paul Husting. Not only had a Republican, Irvine Lenroot, won, despite Wilson's (widely resented) intervention on behalf of Democrat Joseph Davies, but Socialist Victor Berger, recently indicted under the Espionage Act for his antiwar statements, had received an unusually large percentage

of the vote. When the president addressed Congress on May 27, the Republican National Committee had already completed a model platform for a full-fledged fall campaign, emphasizing Republican support for the war effort and condemning Democrats in the national government for harming that effort through political partisanship.[48]

That same day, forty-one German divisions stormed through a twenty-five-mile-wide sector of the Allied line that had been torn to pieces by another devastating bombardment. Launched in the area between the cities of Soissons and Reims after a massive nighttime gathering of forces that the Allies had failed to detect until far too late, this third phase of Ludendorff's grand offensive, Third Battle of the Aisne, was to be a mere feint toward Paris to draw Allied units there so that the Germans could turn back to Flanders and finally destroy the British defending the Channel ports. Ludendorff had instructed his commanders to penetrate no farther than twelve miles, assuming that would take at least several days. But German troops roared forward at such an astounding pace, shattering French and British divisions as they went, that they reached the twelve-mile limit in less than twenty-four hours—and Ludendorff decided to let them keep going. Postponing his plan to turn again toward the Channel, he called for reinforcements to help exploit this new triumph.[49]

The next day, thirty miles to the west of the German push, the Twenty-eighth and Eighteenth infantry regiments of the U.S. First Division moved on Cantigny. Supported by French planes, tanks, flamethrowers, and heavy artillery (until the French hauled their big guns away to aid in the defense of Paris), the doughboys fought their way into the town in just a few hours. Despite nerve-shattering bombardments and seven German counterattacks over the following few days, the Yanks held on to Cantigny. A small action by Great War standards, it was an important one for the Americans. "Here was the first decisive proof that the American soldier could fight and the American officer could lead him," AEF general officer Hunter Liggett wrote in 1928. "It bucked up the morale of our own troops immensely . . . and it strengthened the hand of General Pershing." The French were at that moment extending their own hands to Pershing, requesting AEF units to help defend Paris. On May 30, German troops reached the north bank

of the Marne, a riverine avenue leading directly into the French capital, and if they secured both banks, the city might fall.[50]

While the French government prepared to evacuate to Bordeaux should Ludendorff's army move any closer, the German navy was creating general alarm in the United States. U-BOATS RAID U.S. COAST and 15 CRAFT OFF ATLANTIC COAST SUNK BY GERMAN SUBS were among the headlines announcing a new chapter in the U.S. naval war. On June 3, after a spate of sinkings off New York and New Jersey, the Navy Department was under siege, phones ringing, telegrams pouring in, hallways filled with worried shippers, shipowners, and relatives of merchant crews. Reporters bombarded Navy Secretary Daniels with rapid-fire questions: "'What is the Navy doing to protect shipping?' 'Why

U-boat attacks along the U.S. East Coast made headlines across the country. The *Tacoma (WA) Times* included a dramatic illustration with the news on June 3, 1918.

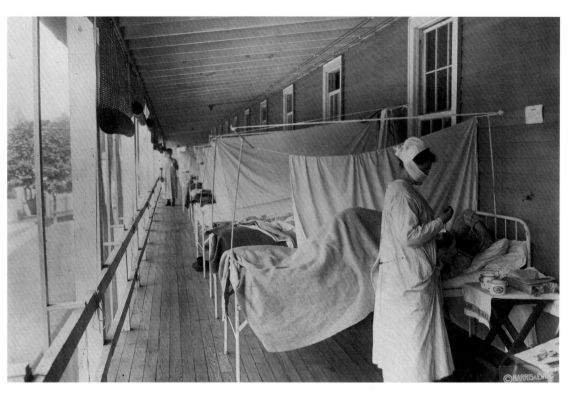

did it let the submarine sink those vessels?' . . . 'Will you recall our destroyers from Europe?'" Daniels did not recall any ships. The navy simply implemented defense plans it had already prepared (coastal watch stations, sea and aerial sweeps), and these largely frustrated the few U-boats that continued to lay mines and stalk shipping in North American waters.[51] Defense against submarines between the United States and Europe had already been greatly enhanced by adoption of the convoy system. The lives that were lost when U-boats got through and sank convoyed ships could not, of course, be replaced. But American and Allied shipbuilders were further reducing U-boat effectiveness by replacing many of the lost vessels—the output of private shipyards and both domestic and foreign purchase and charter agreements helped to boost U.S. merchant tonnage. Meanwhile, the best defense being a good offense, in

June the U.S. Navy, in cooperation with the British, embarked on an epic and controversial mine-laying program far away from American shores. Largely financed by the United States and employing a newly developed American mine, this slowly unfolding "North Sea mine barrage" added a

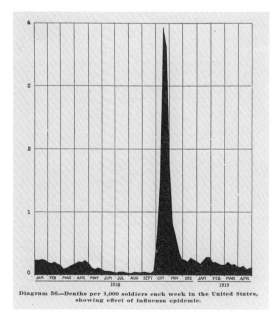

Diagram 56.—Deaths per 1,000 soldiers each week in the United States, showing effect of influenza epidemic.

new measure of destruction to the Allies' multifaceted anti-submarine defense.[52]

Neither the U.S. government nor the country's medical profession had effective plans to defend against an even stealthier enemy. The virulent flu that had appeared in several army training cantonments and a number of cities in March and April was puzzling pathologists. Not only were there peculiarities in the lung tissue of its victims, but an unusual percentage of those who died were previously healthy young adults, rather than infants or the elderly. Still, flu was a common affliction, the number of deaths from attendant pneumonia had not been unusual in this era before sulfa and penicillin, and by late May the disease seemed to have run its course. But it had infected some fourteen of the largest cantonments during the accelerated transport of soldiers to Europe, and not all of the doughboys embarking for France were free of the disease. Six men of the Fifteenth Cavalry died aboard ship in March; Private Cid Allen, who left Fort Dix, New Jersey, still feeling ill, died on the voyage in April. That same month, AEF doctors reported flu in a camp near Bordeaux, and British soldiers began falling ill. In May, as travelers carried the sickness into Italy, neutral Spain, and by ship to ports around the globe, flu swept through the U.S. Twenty-sixth and Forty-second divisions. At the end of May, AEF liaison to French headquarters Major Paul Clark noted his own recent bout with the "Grippe" and reported to Pershing's headquarters, "I have been told that there is an epidemic of it among many French divisions and also among the Boche [Germans]." At the time,

these reports raised no special alarm. The flu was not causing an unusual number of fatalities, and the Allies had much more pressing worries.[53]

To help stem the German advance, Pershing had ordered two AEF divisions into the French front lines. In early June, the Third Division dug in and held fast on the south bank of the Marne, at the farthest point of the German penetration toward Paris, facing enemy troops holding the nearby town of Château-Thierry. The army regulars and U.S. Marines of the Second Division deployed to the First Division's left, in a line south of the German-held towns of Vaux and Belleau and a small, densely forested hunting preserve called Belleau Wood—though at first, it was uncertain that they would stay

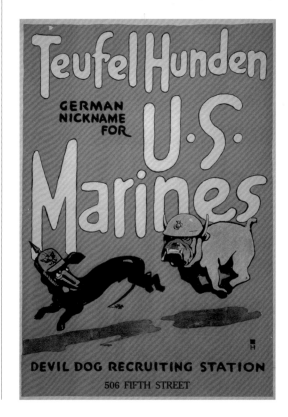

there. "Retreat?" one incredulous Yank bellowed at an exhausted French officer whose shaken troops the division had come to support. "Hell, we just got here!" And, after intense Franco-American consultations, there they stayed. Advancing in old-fashioned line formation, until German machine guns began teaching them lessons the Allies had learned long before, Marines took high ground near Belleau Wood and, after three weeks of bitter, often hand-to-hand fighting, wrestled the wood itself from the Germans, while the division's army regulars took Vaux. Once again, Americans had proved they would fight, with a stubborn and reckless valor that both awed and appalled their allies and enemies and wholly refuted German propaganda. But the Second division had paid a terrible price: more than 8,200 men wounded, missing, or killed. German divisions were also suffering, their battle and flu casualties aggravated by logistical problems. Yet Ludendorff attempted another thrust forward on June 8, several miles to the west of the fierce fighting in Belleau Wood. It met with little success: French ground and aerial forces under Charles Mangin engaged the Germans in a bloody slugfest that brought the German advance to a halt in just five days.[54]

There seemed no end to this struggle, and Allied human resources were growing thin. France was hard-pressed for replacements. Britain was drafting men up to age fifty-one, age fifty-six for qualified medical practitioners and perhaps other specialists as the crisis worsened. "It should be most fully realized at home that the time has come for us to take up

the brunt of the war," Pershing cabled Secretary Baker and General March on June 3. "France and England are not going to be able to keep their armies at present strength much longer." In July 1917 he had asked that a thirty-division American Expeditionary Force of 1 million men be in place by the summer of 1918. By June 1918, with nearly 700,000 U.S. troops in Europe and the Germans even deeper into France, he asked first for sixty-six, then eighty, and finally one hundred divisions—a force of more than 3 million men to be ready to mount an American offensive by June 1919. "Every American must do his duty in this great crisis," Judge Advocate General Enoch Crowder told home-front newspaper reporters on June 4. "Those who . . . actively oppose themselves against our enemy on the European battlefields are indeed privileged." The following day the country added more than 750,000 men to its 10-million-man recruitment well with a second draft registration for those who had turned twenty-one during the previous year.[55]

"The master class has always declared

Eugene V. Debs (1855–1926). Photograph by Harris & Ewing, 1912. Sentenced to ten years in prison for anti-war statements, Debs made his fifth run for the U.S. presidency in 1920, while still incarcerated. He won more than 900,000 votes.

the wars; the subject class has always fought the battles," Eugene Debs roared during a speech to a Socialist meeting in Canton, Ohio, eleven days later. "They have always taught and trained you to believe it to be your patriotic duty to go to war and to have yourselves slaughtered at their command . . . If war is right let it be declared by the people." APL agents from both Canton and Cleveland were in the audience taking copious notes, and within two weeks Debs was arrested and indicted under the Espionage and Sedition acts; he would be sentenced to ten years in prison. On June 18, two days after Debs's speech, the sheriff in Lexington, Mississippi, arrested an African American, Charles Mason, founder of the fifteen-thousand-member Church of God in Christ, for advising draft-eligible church members to avoid registration. "I feel that it is wrong for me to kill my fellowman," Mason declared. "I counselled them not to fly in the face of the government, but I told them if God showed them a way, to take it." Black newspapers around the country reported the incident: The *Chicago Defender* noted that Mason had "distributed a large amount of disloyal literature of religious savor"; the *New York Age* dismissed rumors that Mason was a German spy. Church of God in Christ congregants came under close government scrutiny.[56]

Support for the war and the nation's war leader was the central theme of the Indiana State Democratic Convention, which began the day of Mason's arrest. Delegates laughed as Vice President Thomas Marshall ridiculed Teddy Roosevelt and the Republican national chairman, Will Hays, then

cheered when Marshall described President Wilson as the man "without whom the world's hope must perish . . . Captain General of the armies of freedom, Admiral of the seven seas." Applauding the suggestion that Wilson be awarded an unprecedented third term in 1920 to guide the nation through war's end and into reconstruction, they adopted "Win with Wilson" and "Stand by the President" as national party slogans, implying that votes for Republican candidates in 1918 would be antiwar and unpatriotic. The *New York Times* excoriated the meeting as an exercise in bad taste. Echoing the recently adopted Republican Party platform, its editorial also censured the Democrats for unseemly partisanship when the war crisis demanded national unity, an accusation for which President Wilson was at that moment providing additional ammunition. Trying to ensure that the post-election Senate would continue to support his policies, Wilson personally and publicly convinced Henry Ford to become a candidate for U.S. senator from Michigan. Though he was now an avid war and administration supporter, the eccentric auto magnate was better known—and roundly criticized, particularly by Republicans—for his active and outspoken pre-American-belligerence antiwar stance. Moreover, as one irate anti-Ford commentator declared, "He admits he hasn't voted but twice in twenty years, and he knows nothing of history, affairs of state, or anything to qualify him for the office." Wilson's urgent plea that Ford enter the contest, Republican senator Charles E. Townsend said, was an "absolutely uncalled for and unjust meddling in politics at this time when politics by the Commander in Chief of the armies of the United States is inexcusable." Former Michigan governor Chase S. Osborn was less polite. Wilson, he snarled, was "the greatest political autocrat in the world" and was "seeking to dictate to the people of Michigan whom they should send to the Senate."[57]

The Ford furor, which would lead to his defeat, was only one in a growing list of Democratic political challenges. Republicans had also pounced on an issue troubling voters in the Midwest and West. The government's maddeningly uneven program of wartime price controls placed a strict (if generous) ceiling on the price of wheat, yet did nothing to control the skyrocketing price of cotton—a commodity grown, many noted sourly, in the South, the native region of the president, most

of his cabinet, and a number of powerful Democratic congressmen. While Republicans fanned the fires of Midwestern indignation, Teddy Roosevelt, General Leonard Wood, and Republican senator Albert B. Fall of New Mexico sought to make a campaign issue out of Selective Service age limits, which should be expanded, they said, so that the nation could build a bigger army. To add steel to their point, Fall held up the army appropriations bill—and got results: On June 26, Secretary Baker promised to submit new draft legislation to Congress within three months. Suffragists were also turning angry eyes toward the White House. Overjoyed in January when the House approved the Nineteenth Amendment to the Constitution, according women the right to vote, they became increasingly frustrated as it languished for months in the Senate—though the Republican senatorial caucus had endorsed the measure—while the Eighteenth Amendment, outlawing liquor, had sailed through both houses and had already been approved by fourteen of the required thirty-six states. Both the militant Alice Paul and the more moderate Carrie Chapman Catt vowed to campaign against anti-suffrage Democratic candidates in the fall if the president failed to see that the amendment was approved.[58]

Many of the country's ethnic minorities had political concerns that reached far beyond U.S. borders and intertwined with the president's wartime diplomacy. The president had pleased Polish Americans by calling for an independent Polish state in Point 13 of his January 8 Fourteen Points speech. He did not go that far in Point 10, which concerned the diverse peoples of

To Mr. Creel in remembrance of common work T. S. Masaryk Nyork, 16. November '8.

T. G. MASARYK
President of Czecho-Slovakia and members of Czecho-Slovak Legion that fought their way across Russia.

Austria-Hungary, stating only that they "should be accorded the freest opportunity of autonomous development." Yet this raised hopes among Czech and Slovak Americans that the United States would support Czech scholar Tomas Masaryk's quest to establish an independent Czechoslovakia. Since 1915 Masaryk had been working furiously to realize this dream, traveling among all the Allied capitals, and on June 18 he spoke with President Wilson in the White House, adding his thoughts to the increasingly heated debate regarding military intervention in Russia. Among the Czech leader's foremost concerns: the fate of the stranded Czech Legion. In 1917, Masaryk had traveled to Russia and secured Alexander Kerensky's agreement to create

a combat unit from Czech and Slovak soldiers whom the Russians had taken prisoner. At least fifty-thousand-strong, the Czech Legion had fought effectively against its former Central Powers masters on the Eastern Front until the Bolsheviks deposed Kerensky. Earlier in 1918, again in Russia, Masaryk had obtained the Bolshevik government's permission for the legion to travel by train across Russia to Vladivostok, from where it could embark for the Western Front to join another Czech force fighting in the Allied armies. Trouble along the way had turned the Bolsheviks hostile, and the Czechs, strung out over thousands of miles of Siberian railroad, were now fighting their way toward the sea—their marked success against

Bolshevik opposition sparking hopes in the Allied camp that the legion could be used to overthrow Lenin's government and bring Russia back into the war.[59]

At the same time, a variety of counterrevolutionaries collectively known as White Russians were mobilizing to overthrow the Bolsheviks, and one of their number was touring the United States. Celebrated as the leader of Russia's all-woman "Battalion of Death," Colonel Maria Bochkareva "is no visionary nor is she a patriotic fanatic," a Connecticut paper declared, "but a person of steadfast determination, and one who believes that the safety of Russia depends on the defeat of the Kaiser." The colonel also believed it depended on the defeat of the Bolsheviks. Arriving in Washington, D.C., in late June, she stayed at the home of Florence Harriman, who had just returned from touring industrial sites and military hospitals in Europe. Fascinated by Bochkareva's "magnetism and the vociferousness of her gestures," Harriman arranged a meeting between the colonel and President Wilson, an encounter that became, Harriman later remembered, "intensely dramatic." Her emotions building as she described the plight of the Russian people, Bochkareva "suddenly . . . threw herself on the floor and clasped her arms about the President's knees," Harriman wrote, "begging him for help, for food, for troops to intervene against the Bolsheviki. The President sat with tears streaming down his cheeks, and assured her of his sympathy."[60]

Sympathy was one thing, concrete and realizable plans another. Japan's growing presence in Vladivostok, the plight of the

Czech Legion, and continuing Allied pressure for American help in reopening the Eastern Front seemed to have convinced Wilson by July 6 to send several thousand troops to Siberia. Yet he was not overly firm in that conviction. Plans for a Siberian incursion remained up in the air for several weeks as action flared again on the Western Front. On July 15 Ludendorff made the fifth assault of his grand offensive (Second Battle of the Marne), hurling fifty-two divisions against thirty-four French, American, and Italian divisions arrayed along the south bank of the Marne between Château-Thierry and Reims. This time opening bombardments shot through the air in both directions, for the Allies had discerned the buildup of German forces and had prepared not only a solid defense but an offensive surprise of their own. July 15, 16, and 17 the two armies battered each

Colonel Maria Bochkareva (1889–1920). Celebrated as the leader of Russia's all-woman "Battalion of Death," Bochkareva petitioned President Wilson to help the White Russians. After her return to Russia, she was captured by the Bolsheviks, who executed her by firing squad on May 16, 1920.

other, Germans throwing portable foot-bridges across the river, Allied troops grappling with the south-bank invaders and in some places yielding ground. On the left of the Allied line, however, the American Third Division held fast, its Thirty-eighth Regiment, under Colonel Ulysses Grant McAlexander, taking brutal punishment over more than two days of solid fighting but refusing to give any ground. "The Americans kill everything," one survivor of the German assault on the Thirty-eighth later remembered. "That was the exclamation of terror that lay in the bones of our men . . . We left on the field, dead and wounded, more than 60 percent of the troops brought into the conflict on July 15." The Thirty-eighth Regiment thus earned the French Croix de Guerre, and the regiment, McAlexander, and the entire Third Division were all known thereafter as the "Rock of the Marne."[61]

On July 18, as the German push weakened, Marshal Foch launched the Aisne-Marne Offensive, a counterattack on the rear right flank of the enemy's push toward Paris. Unheralded by a preparatory bombardment, the assault was a surprise not only to the Germans but also to most of the Allied division commanders involved, who for the sake of secrecy had not been briefed until just before the assault. Advancing under a rolling barrage, with the U.S. First and Second divisions flanking the French Moroccan Division in the vanguard, Allied troops pushed the Germans back seven miles in four days of grueling combat that littered the countryside with thousands of dead and maimed soldiers. Ludendorff's troops were now all north of the Marne, continuing their fighting retreat, and the great German offensive, begun four months before with impressive élan, was over—at least for the time being. "Five times thus far during the war I had to withdraw my troops, and was still able, in the end, to beat the enemy," Ludendorff said to the alarmed Chancellor Count Georg von Hertling. "Why shouldn't I succeed a sixth time?[62]

A sixth success, if it were to occur, would require time and intense preparation. Before he could launch another offensive, Ludendorff would have to rebuild his army, which had suffered almost a million casualties over the previous six months. But the well of available men was running dry, as were other types of resources. The Allied blockade had not succeeded in completely strangling Germany, but it was causing grievous harm to both Germany and Austria-Hungary, and civilians were sacrificing to an enormous degree to keep their armies supplied. As a result, on the home front almost everything was in short supply, including metal, cotton, wool, leather, milk, meat, and soap. Hygiene was suffering, health had declined. Tuberculosis, which had been on the wane, had reappeared with a vengeance. By 1918 the civilian mortality rate in Germany was 37 percent higher than it had been in 1913. There was political fallout from this lengthy deprivation. The unrestricted U-boat campaign's failure to break Britain as promised and news of the Russian revolutions in March and November 1917 had fed growing civilian unrest. Strikes, political agitation, and a few mutinous episodes in the German navy had raised the specter

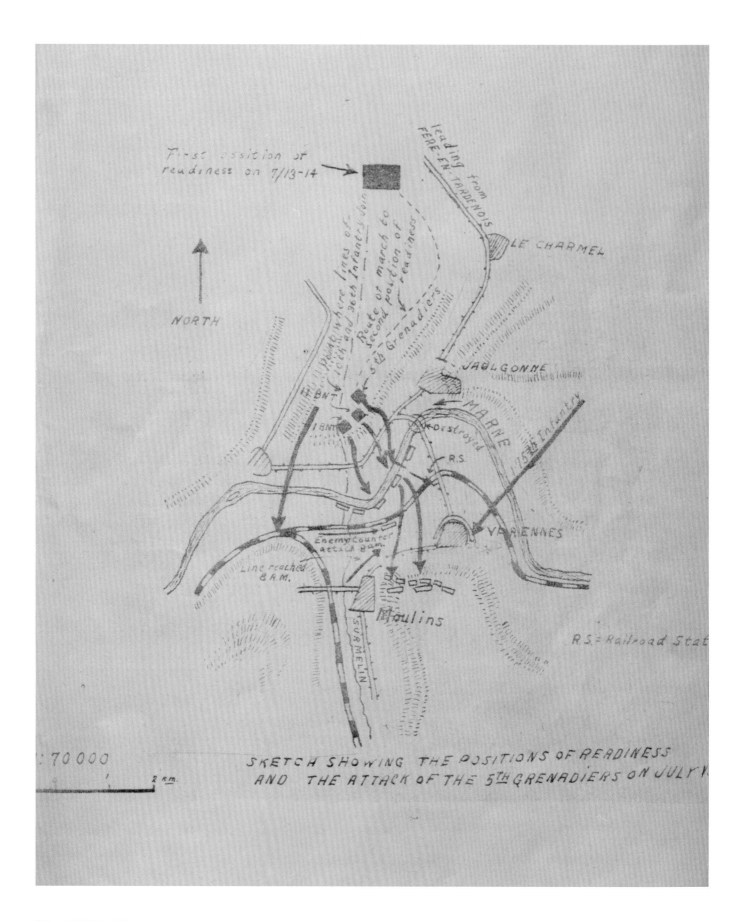

First position of
readiness on 7/13-14

leading from
FÈRE-EN-TARDÉNOIS

LE CHARMEL

NORTH

Position where lines of
10th and 30th Infantry join

Route of march to
second position of
readiness

5th Grenadiers

JAULGONNE

MARNE

1 BNT

1 BNT

Destroyed

R.S.

15th Infantry

VARENNES

Enemy Counter
attack 8 A.M.

Line reached
8 A.M.

Moulins

R.S. = Railroad Stat

SURMELIN

:70000

2 km.

SKETCH SHOWING THE POSITIONS OF READINESS
AND THE ATTACK OF THE 5TH GRENADIERS ON JULY 1

of revolution. The early success of Ludendorff's March offensive had raised morale; the retreat from the Marne sent it plunging again. Still, factories were operating (some with the help of forced labor from occupied countries), munitions were reaching the front, three hundred thousand eighteen-year-olds had just become available for the army, and men who had recovered from their wounds would also strengthen the ranks. While rebuilding and restocking, the army, still deep in Allied territory, could hold off enemy offensives, if necessary retreating behind the Hindenburg Line, the most formidable defenses on the Western Front.[63]

To prevent just that, and sensing the Germans' growing weakness, Marshal Foch gathered senior Allied commanders together on July 24 and outlined his plan for building on the success of the Aisne-Marne Offensive. Allied armies were to mount a continuous offensive through the summer and into the fall, hitting the Germans first here and then there, wearing them down, keeping them on guard and unable to shift troops easily from one point of attack to another or rebuild damaged units before the Allies hit them again. The ultimate goal: final victory in 1919. At first blush, the plan seemed overambitious. Generals Haig and Philippe Pétain said that the British and French armies were tired, their ranks depleted from months of nearly non-stop fighting; the Allies, too, were short of some vital supplies, including coal and iron; and Allied intelligence had learned that the Germans were calling seven divisions back to the Western Front from Italy and several more divisions from the Eastern

Front—one reason for growing Allied eagerness to see White Russians topple the Bolsheviks and bring Russia back into the war. Yet in the end, Foch's plan did seem worth the gamble, especially since the Allies had an ace protruding ever more prominently from their sleeve.[64]

By the end of July the American Expeditionary Force comprised 1.2 million officers and men. Few of the newer arrivals had ever experienced combat, almost all still needed training, and the training they received from American officers still suffered from the nineteenth-century roots of the current U.S. military doctrine, which discounted the value, and adverse effects, of machine guns, artillery, and tanks. Yet Pershing was beginning to recognize those flaws. With the tremendous AEF casualty figures from the Aisne-Marne Offensive in hand, he ordered a review of American combat methods, telling his chief of staff, Major General James McAndrew, "Perhaps we are losing too many men." He had more than enough men to achieve the goal toward which he had been working since June 1917, however, and on July 24 Pershing ordered, with Foch's approval, formation of the First Army, AEF, effective on August 10. This all-American fighting force would take its place on the right of the Allied lines, in the Saint-Mihiel sector, where it would prepare to launch the first major American offensive of the Great War. Of inestimable help in stymieing Ludendorff's drive toward Paris, the men of the AEF were battering the morale of German troops faced with their ever-increasing numbers and obvious determination to fight and were earning the United States and its president a seat at the postwar peace table.[65]

"The settlement must be final. There can be no compromise," Woodrow Wilson said in a soaring, idealistic speech at Mount Vernon on the Fourth of July. "The blinded rulers of Prussia have roused forces they knew little of—forces which, once roused, can never be crushed to earth again." Outlining for his audience once more the great principles on which a better postwar world must be founded, he then summed them up in a single sentence: "What we seek is the reign of law, based upon the consent of the governed and sustained by the organized opinion of mankind." "We stand for law and order," city editor G. Grant Williams of the *Philadelphia Tribune*, an African American newspaper, wrote two days later. "But knowing as we do . . . that our people are driven from pillar to post looking for houses to rent and that they pay more rent than whites for the same shacks, our patience runs out." In Philadelphia, as in many northern cities, the black population had exploded during the war, new arrivals now chiefly working in the huge new Hog Island shipyards. As the city grew more crowded and even inadequate housing became scarce, blacks looked outside the city's "colored sections" for shelter. Clashes occurred, tension increased. "While the world is being made safe for Democracy," Williams declared, "Philadelphia must be made a safe city wherein to dwell and if the law is insufficient we'll meet the rowdies of the town and give them shot and shell."[66]

Such statements reflected the "pressing

grievances" of African Americans that Major Joel Spingarn, of the Military Intelligence Branch, was seeking to alleviate in his assignment to detect and prevent black subversion, a mission in which he hoped to be joined by his former NAACP colleague W. E. B. Du Bois, the editor of the *Crisis.* On June 15, after Spingarn secured Du Bois's agreement to have *Crisis* content reviewed by a "designated person" in the government before publication, MID offered Du Bois a captain's commission. With that offer pending, Du Bois published an editorial, "Close Ranks," in the July *Crisis* urging African Americans to "forget our special grievances" and help defeat the German power that "spells death to the aspirations of Negroes and all darker races for equality, freedom and democracy." The editorial and Du Bois's pending commission in a government intelligence agency ignited a firestorm of criticism from many black spokesmen who saw no evidence that a German defeat would improve black lives in the United States—and events in Philadelphia did nothing to reduce their skepticism. On July 26, the day President Wilson issued his proclamation against mob violence, a white mob surrounded and hurled rocks through the windows of a home in their neighborhood that had just been purchased by African American municipal court probation officer Adella Bond, who fired a gun in the air to summon police. Like a spark on dry tinder, this small clash initiated four days of violence. Four people died and several hundred were injured before police, augmented by the city's wartime Home Defense Reserves and a contingent of U.S. Marines, restored a simmering calm.[67]

41

The Town Called After Him.

"THE TOWN OF BISMARCK, PA., HAS
CHANGED ITS NAME TO QUENTIN."
—Vide Newspapers.
Quentin, young Quentin Roosevelt
Has a town called after him!
Some way, as we read the word
It makes the eyes grow dim.

How brave they were, how young they
were,
Our boys who went to die!
Children who played in field and street
So short a time gone by,

Now reach the stature of the stars!
Ah, none of us can say
How many Heavenly places
Are named for such as they.

But romping children here, through
years
Secured from horrors grim,
Will speak the name of Quentin
In the town called after him.
MARY STEWART CUTTING.

AUX MORTS DE LA GRANDE GUERRE

TO THE MEMORY
OF
QUENTIN ROOSEVELT
FIRST LIEUTENANT, AVIATION SECTION,
SIGNAL OFFICERS RESERVE CORPS, 95TH U. S. AERO SQUADRON
WHO DIED IN THE CAUSE
OF
FREEDOM AND HUMANITY
JULY 14TH, 1918
WITH THE HOMAGE AND GRATITUDE
OF
THE FRENCH NATION

Quentin was buried by the Germans
with full military honors.
Left: his grave as they left it,
showing cross made of pine branches, and parts of his plane.

Opposite: July 1918 was a rending time for the family of Theodore Roosevelt. On July 14, T. R.'s youngest son, Quentin, an AEF pilot, was shot down and killed, an event commemorated in one of the Roosevelt scrapbooks. Shortly thereafter, Ted Jr. was badly wounded during the final German offensive, while Archie was still recovering from severe wounds he had suffered in the spring.

Below: Black and white workers pose together in the Virginia Shipbuilding Corporation shipyard at Alexandria, Virginia. U.S. Army Quartermaster Corps photograph, 1918.

Brief articles about this latest incident of racial violence shared newspaper space with salutes to ongoing war work by Americans of all backgrounds. Black and white workers at Philadelphia's grand new shipyard were BREEDING PATRIOTISM IN HOG ISLAND MUD, one feature-story headline declared, as they made it possible for President and Mrs. Wilson finally to launch in early August the first vessel built there by the Emergency Shipping Corporation. Full-page multiphoto spreads celebrated WOMEN IN WAR WORK. Other articles praised a pastor who gave up his safe home-front position to serve with the YMCA in France; gave a nod to Mrs. Clara Simmons of Massachusetts, who weathered incoming artillery fire running a canteen near Château-Thierry while her husband served with a YMCA unit in Siberia; acknowledged contributors to the American Red Cross and the Salvation

Army and Americans who adopted French orphans and equipped overseas hospitals; and honored a "hundred thousand Camp Fire Girls" whose war work included cultivating gardens, raising pigs, chickens, and calves, selling Liberty Bonds, and sending "comfort kits by the thousand to their big brother 'Sammies' on the fighting fronts."[68]

Newspapers were also publishing armed forces casualty lists, now lengthening as the AEF grew in size and engaged more in combat. In addition to fulfilling General Pershing's new request for more than 3 million men, the United States would have to replace those whom the war killed or permanently incapacitated, and compensate for hundreds of thousands who either evaded the draft or secured legitimate exemptions. Tolerance of slackers lowered; slacker raids became more frequent, with the added incentive now of a $50 government bounty for every actual draft evader bagged. Poorly paid police officers became intensely vigilant in their daily patrols; rural sheriffs went slacker-hunting. But it was the large multi-agency slacker raids in cities across the country that drew most attention, as thousands of suspects were herded into jails, auditoriums, and any other available facilities, some of them remaining in custody for weeks until their status could be verified—all without due process of law, though for months there were few public complaints. In mid-July, during a three-day roundup in Chicago, federal agents, U.S. navy sailors, municipal police, and APL agents accosted men on the streets, met incoming trains, stopped

Fighting in France for Freedom!--Are YOU Helping at Home?

NEW YORK STOP 61,000 MEN IN THEIR SEARCH FOR SLACKERS. PHOTO SHOWS A WAGON LOAD OF SUSPECTS.
As a result of a three days drive in New York special agents, soldiers and sailors "interviewed" over 61,000 men and made them produce registration cards and many were detained temporarily before they could be properly identified. About 1500 slackers were caught and sent to camps.

News Photo Poster No. 12
ISSUED FOR
Maine Committee
On Public Safety
BLAINE MANSION, AUGUSTA, MAINE.

ILLUSTRATED CURRENT NEWS,

DON'T BE CAUGHT NAPPING.
Every man registered under the Selected Service Law must
carry his registration card at all times.
Obey the law and save embarrassment.

automobiles, and swept through ballparks, movie theaters, and picnic grounds, detaining tens of thousands, including more than a thousand in a makeshift internment camp on the municipal pier. Of more than 150,000 suspects "interviewed," fewer than 1 percent were thereafter *legitimately* detained as either draft evaders or deserters. Police shot and seriously wounded one visiting New Yorker who tried to run away when they asked for a closer look at his draft registration card. Their unfortunate target, one Mr. Helge Gustavson, received but a tiny paragraph in a few newspaper accounts, while another shooting that occurred five thousand miles to the east, made front-page headlines across the country.[69]

On July 6, anti-Bolshevik Russians forced their way into the German embassy in Moscow and assassinated the kaiser's new ambassador, Wilhelm von Mirbach, while their comrades took possession of the Bolsheviks' secret police

headquarters elsewhere in the city. GERMAN AMBASSADOR MURDERED AT MOSCOW, RUSSIAN PEASANTS IN REVOLT AGAINST BOLSHEVIK RULE, American newspaper headlines shouted; one paper's hopeful headline read, RUSSIA MAY PLAY NEW PART IN WORLD CONFLICT. But the Bolsheviks, while shaken, were also stirred into making firm counterblows. As Lenin sent frantic conciliatory messages to the German government in Berlin, local units of what would quickly grow to be a strong and effective Red Army quickly put down the Moscow revolt. By then, however, Lenin was receiving other unhappy news. On July 11, elements of the Czech Legion defeated pro-Bolshevik forces and gained control of an important section of the Trans-Siberian railway and the city of Irkutsk, some two thousand miles west of Vladivostok, and their success encouraged other anti-Bolshevik factions. Claiming that the Czechs were part of a conspiracy to free Czar Nicholas, the Bolshevik leadership sanctioned the czar's execution on July 16, Russian reports assuring the outside world, incorrectly, that the czar's family remained safe.[70]

Faced now with a true civil war as well as a growing foreign presence in and around Vladivostok (predominantly Japanese, though there were some British and French-Indochinese troops, and thousands of Czech Legion soldiers had arrived there as well) the Lenin government was shaken once more at the end of July by news of what it at first believed to be a huge Allied landing in the northwest, at Archangel, near Murmansk. In fact the invasion force included only 1,200 British French, Canadian, and Serbian troops, plus fifty-four crewmen and officers from USS *Olympia*. Yet the small force speedily displaced local Bolshevik leaders and began an occupation of the city and surrounding countryside, while Lenin's government, busy building forces to meet multiple threats, could only fume. "We have done nothing to provoke this aggression," Foreign Minister Gregory Chicherin wrote U.S. Consul General DeWitte Poole on August 5. "Our people want nothing else but to remain in peace and friendship with all the toiling masses of all other countries." Fear that, should the Bolsheviks survive, they would incite revolution in toiling masses within their own borders might have been one motivation for the Allied incursions. But for the European Allies, close, now, to launching their continuous offensive on the Western Front, replacing Lenin's government with one that might abrogate the Treaty of Brest-Litovsk and rejoin the war remained the prime motivation—and their argument, plus the swelling Japanese presence in Siberia, finally persuaded President Wilson. On August 3, Secretary Baker rendezvoused secretly in Kansas City with Major General William S. Graves, commander of the newly formed California-based Eighth Division, and gave him orders that, by September 1, would see Graves and nine thousand

American troops in Vladivostok. At about the same time that Graves received his orders, 4,600 Michigan and Wisconsin doughboys who were completing a training course in England (a number of them of Polish and Finnish extraction and fluent in Russian) began to suspect they might not be heading to the hot, muddy Western Front when they were issued heavy winter clothing. By the end of August (as Germany and Russia signed agreements supplementing the Brest-Litovsk Treaty that, among other things, required the Bolsheviks to repulse all Allied incursions) the Yanks were jammed into British transports bound for Archangel—with a dangerous stowaway also on board.[71]

The intense flu that had made its first appearance in American stateside training cantonments in March had circumnavigated the globe, and in doing so had mutated into a truly savage disease. The number of people who had fallen ill in Spain in the spring had earned the evolving sickness the name Spanish influenza, yet there was nothing particularly Spanish about the virulent sickness, so often ending in a devastating pneumonia, that was spreading inland from heavily trafficked coastal ports in Africa, Europe and the United States. Extremely contagious, hard-hitting, and fast-moving, it attacked many of the Americans bound for Archangel, more than seventy of whom died either on board or after they arrived. By mid-August U.S. newspapers were carrying brief reports of the flu's progress in Europe: felling a thousand workers at the Krupp factories in Essen; killing six hundred Londoners in less than two months; racing through the malnourished peoples of Austria-Hungary. Then the news moved closer to home. On

Anna Coleman Ladd complemented the work being done in France by her husband, Dr. Maynard Ladd, by opening a studio in Paris under the auspices of the American Red Cross. There, following the example of British artist Francis D. Wood, she fashioned masks for soldiers who had suffered disfiguring facial wounds.

Opposite: A scene of devastation in Soissons, France. Photograph (incorrectly labeled Amiens) by William Lester King, 1919.

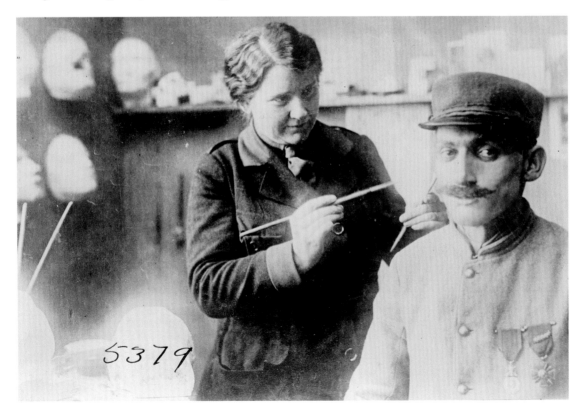

August 14, passengers suffering from "a strange disease" that might be the Spanish flu were taken from a recently arrived Norwegian-American passenger liner to a New York City hospital, while New York commissioner of health Dr. Royal S. Copeland reassured concerned citizens that there was little danger of an epidemic among sturdy well-fed Americans. At the end of the month, flu arrived at the crowded port facilities in Boston, quickly infecting more than two thousand naval personnel before moving into the city, with its crowded streets and capacious ballpark (soon to host games of the 1918 World Series), and then beyond. By early September it was thirty miles west in the overcrowded army cantonment, Camp Devens, where it spread like wildfire, as visitors and new recruits constantly came and went, carrying the bug along with them.[72]

"You haven't heard of our doughboys getting it, have you?" Dr. Copeland asked in his reassuring statement about American sturdiness. "You bet you haven't, and you won't." He was, of course, wrong. The new and more devastating flu was already moving through the ranks of doughboys, their allies, and their enemies in Europe.

But not even the flu could stop the war. On August 8, General Haig launched the first major assault of Foch's continuous offensive, the Battle of Amiens, hitting German forces along a line near the Somme River with a strong force spearheaded by six hundred tanks that overwhelmed the German front lines. The tanks led the way for Australian, Canadian, and British infantry, and Americans were there, too. Elements of the Thirty-third Division of the AEF, which had been training in the British sector, joined in the fight, which steadily, painfully, gained ground. By the end of August Haig's forces were near the outer works of the Hindenburg Line, having regained most of the ground lost during the first phase of the Germans' spring offensive. Thereafter referring to August 8 as the "black day of the German Army," Ludendorff lost much of his reassuring optimism, telling his staff that Germany could no longer win the war but must not lose it and advising the German Crown Council that peace negotiations should commence immediately. He would later vacillate, stating at times that the army could rebuild and sweep forward again in 1919, but others agreed with his first analysis. Crown Prince Rupprecht of Bavaria, one of Ludendorff's senior commanders, wrote Prince Max of Baden on August 15 that Germany's military situation had "deteriorated so rapidly that I no longer believe we can hold out over the winter. The Americans," he added, "are multiplying in a way we never dreamed of."[73]

One month later, on September 12, the American First Army—half a million Americans and four French divisions under U.S. command—smashed against the Saint-Mihiel salient that had been a thorn in the Allies' side for four years. Supported by fifteen hundred planes of French and British manufacture piloted by American, French, Italian, and Portuguese pilots and led by Colonel Billy Mitchell, the attack started with a massive bombardment by French artillery, as the Americans still had none of their own. Hitting all three sides of the salient simultaneously in frontal assaults consistent with American doctrine, the doughboys and their French comrades made speedy progress against curiously light German resistance. In less than four days, the salient was no more. Pershing was triumphant: the American army had again proved itself, this time in its own major offensive. Yet intelligence and a brief after-action analysis soon provided troubling information. On September 8, Ludendorff, consolidating his forces, had ordered the salient abandoned, and the Americans hit midway through that evacuation. Given the resulting comparatively light

En route to France as an observer when the war began, the U.S. military aviation pioneer Major William (Billy) Mitchell posed in flight gear that June with American major Millard Harmon and two French officers. In September, Colonel Mitchell would lead fifteen hundred planes in support of the American offensive at Saint-Mihiel. He would end the war a brigadier general.

resistance, the number of American casualties—seven thousand during the assault, three thousand more as the First Army established the new Allied line—seemed high. Coordination between attacking units had been poor, and staging areas for the assault had become scenes of massive traffic jams that would have inhibited the operation had it gone on much longer. All these problems and their implications were largely ignored, however, for Pershing and his staff were scrambling to organize a larger offensive that Foch had insisted be launched at the end of the month sixty miles to the northwest.[74]

On the American home front, other types of war-related operations were in progress. From September 3 to 5 in New York City, an estimated twenty thousand APL and government agents, city police, and soldiers and sailors staged the most intensive slacker raid to date, stopping cars and pedestrians, sweeping through dance halls and businesses, interrupting a Broadway performance of Sergeant Irving Berlin's musical *Yip Yip Yaphank*, as they interrogated more than three hundred thousand men and detained more than sixty thousand—of whom just 199 were actually guilty of some sort of draft dodging. The huge and intrusive raid, and the use of uniformed servicemen in conducting it, incited an angry clamor, most prominently in New York and Washington, where Woodrow Wilson's many congressional opponents, with the looming midterm elections in mind, were particularly vociferous. Republican

senator Reed Smoot of Utah called for an investigation. Democratic senator George Chamberlain denounced both slackers and the government's unseemly raids. "If the [Justice] Department would devote more time to catching pro-Germans and spies," he raged, "it would not have so much time to round up whole communities of innocent persons as draft evaders." The White House announced that President Wilson had asked Attorney General Gregory for a full report; privately, Wilson seemed pleased, telling Secretary of the Navy Daniels that the raid had "put the fear of God in others just before the new draft."[75] Legislation passed on August 31 made men from 18 to 45 eligible for the draft, and on September 12, as the American First Army charged the Saint-Mihiel salient, 13 million of these younger and older men marched to their local polling places to register. The American draft pool now stood at an amazing 24 million, 50 percent more than the total manpower of Britain and France combined—manpower that the Central Powers knew they had no hope of matching.[76]

One week later, the government launched the Fourth Liberty Loan campaign, in which patriotism and partisan politics immediately entwined. Republicans denounced Democrats for distributing circulars at loan rallies urging the citizenry to "vote with President Wilson for the Democratic ticket and hasten the end of the war." Democrats were furious when Teddy Roosevelt added condemnation of the president's peace proposals to his speeches pleading for funds to support the war. With the war news improving,

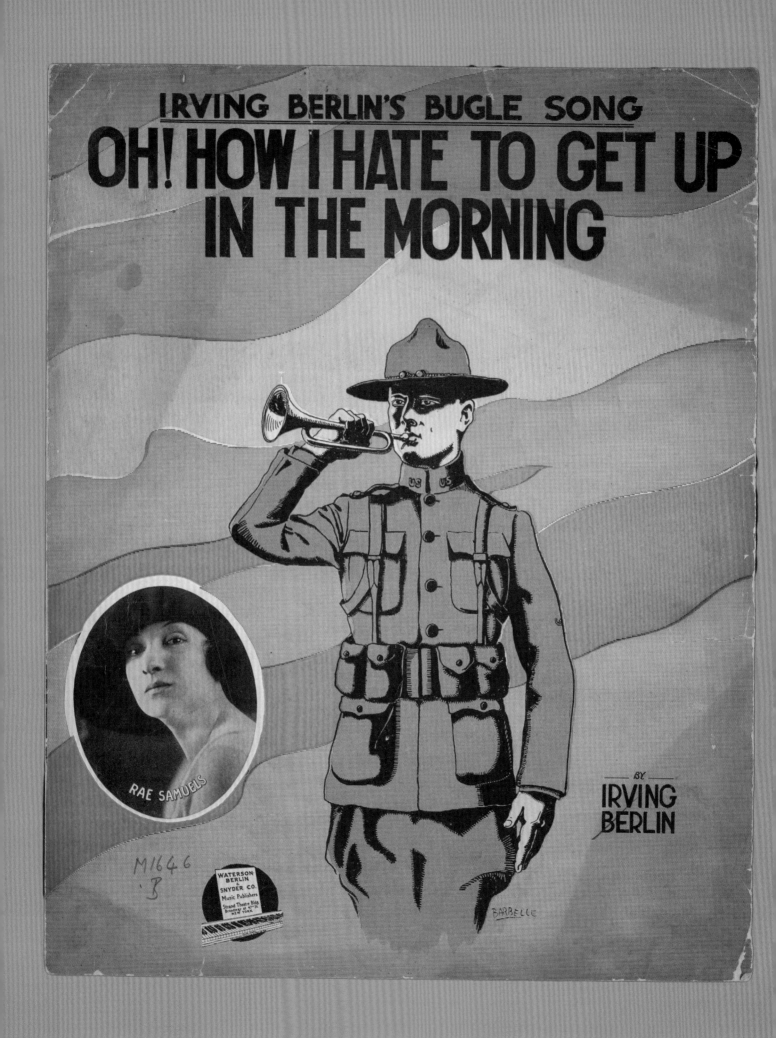

Republican Party leaders had changed from criticizing flaws in the administration's war effort to condemning any effort to make peace before Germany and its chief ally had been completely crushed and casting aspersions on the whole idea of a League of Nations. "We are not internationalists. We are American Nationalists," Roosevelt roared to an audience in Illinois. The country's strength was in its armed forces, he said, not the league or any other mechanism established to do away with war.[77]

As much as Wilson might have agreed with Roosevelt's nationalism, he had acknowledged more than two years before, in his much-applauded May 27, 1916, speech (see chapter 2), that Americans were also "participants, whether we would or not, in the life of the world," an interested partner in all that affected mankind, an assertion

with which the internationally celebrated Roosevelt might also have agreed in a non-wartime-election year. During the period of American neutrality, Wilson had sought to be an arbiter of peace. With America at war, he had expressed principles for a more humane postwar world that the war-weary world seemed to have embraced. Though both Allied and German leaders had at one time or another privately derided the president's naïve idealism, leaders of the Central Powers now began turning toward the Fourteen Points and the American president who expressed them to provide an avenue out of their deepening troubles. On September 15, three days after America's draft-eligible pool of men reached 24 million, Wilson received a note from the Austro-Hungarian government. Their empire riven by civil unrest, army desertions, and independence movements among many

Opposite: Drafted early in 1918, composer and lyricist Irving Berlin (1888–1989) was assigned to Camp Upton in Yaphank, New York. "Oh! How I Hate to Get Up in the Morning," expressing his distress over early-morning reveille, was included in his 1918 Broadway review, *Yip, Yip Yaphank*—one performance of which was interrupted by a slacker raid.

Right: The Naval Reserve band led by American "March King" John Philip Sousa (1854–1932), not pictured, parades in support of the Fourth Liberty Loan, which was launched in September 1918. Photograph by Harris & Ewing.

of its diverse peoples, the near-desperate Austro-Hungarians asked Wilson to help them initiate peace talks. Their timing was unfortunate. Given the unbending mood of Allied leaders and Republican fulminations against negotiating before the enemy was crushed, Wilson could do little but send a prompt negative answer—and then return to the business of prosecuting America's war. On September 27, he braved the flu epidemic that was now overwhelming medical facilities in multiple states and traveled to New York City to address more than five thousand Liberty Loan workers. Calling the world conflict a "people's war," he went on to irritate Republicans by stressing again the importance of a League of Nations through which the will of the world's peoples, rather than the special and secret interests of governments, could be expressed. The speech was enthusiastically applauded—as was a bulletin Wilson had just received from Europe: American forces had begun to advance "over a front of twenty miles, from the Argonne Forest to the valley of the Meuse."[78]

Launched in the early hours of September 26 after a barrage from 2,700 big guns, this new American operation was to smash through three lines of strong German defenses and then sweep to the northwest, taking the city of Mézières, which would deprive the Germans of a vital railway supply line. With six French and sixteen American divisions facing five German divisions, Pershing planned a fast-moving operation: His troops were to push the Germans out of the Argonne Forest, which occupied high ground to the left, capture Montfaucon, the high point in the center, and break the German defenses along the banks of the Meuse on the right, all before the enemy could bring in substantial reinforcements. It was a demanding timetable, and it was almost immediately thwarted, and not just by the Germans. Because Pershing had used his most experienced AEF divisions in the Saint-Mihiel operation, many of those he initially deployed at Meuse-Argonne had insufficient training and little or no combat experience. Resupply quickly became a problem as traffic piled up on the few inadequate roads into the sector, which became little

more than mud after it started to rain. Communication between fighting units was bad; coordination between infantry and artillery was worse. There were too few horses to pull the artillery, too few carrier pigeons for communications. George Patton's tank force steadily lost strength due to enemy fire and mechanical failure. Patton himself was wounded and had to leave the battleground. And there were not enough replacements for the many battle casualties and the tens of thousands of men now being felled by the flu; twenty-five hundred died in September alone. Nevertheless, the Yanks bludgeoned their way forward, sadly behind Pershing's optimistic schedule, until the AEF commander ordered a pause so that he could reorganize and bring in more experienced divisions.[79]

British and Belgian armies, meanwhile, were beginning the ground phase of an equally large offensive in northwestern France and Flanders, with the assistance of the American Twenty-seventh and Thirtieth divisions, serving under Australian command. Inexperienced but enthusiastic, the Yanks helped breach the Hindenburg Line at the city of Saint-Quentin, an operation in which the Twenty-seventh Division's 107th Infantry Regiment suffered more casualties than any other AEF regiment in the war. With the British and Belgians pushing the Germans back from the heretofore unbreachable Hindenburg Line in Flanders, on October 4 Pershing opened the second phase of the Meuse-Argonne Offensive. Advancing into the razor-sharp teeth of "one damn machine gun after another," as one doughboy growled, the Yanks made slow progress against ferocious German resistance, but as they advanced, gradually widening their front, they created some American WWI legends: the "Lost Battalion" of the Seventy-seventh Division battling it out with the Germans who had them completely surrounded in the Argonne Forest, only 195 of the 550 men caught in the trap emerging unscathed; Sergeant Alvin York, a former pacifist from Tennessee, using his hill-country marksmanship to kill 28 Germans threatening his men, then employing sheer bravado to capture 132 others; Acting Captain Sam Woodfill, single-handedly annihilating several machine-gun nests, then bringing his company up to the position he had secured—only to be ordered back because they were "too far out front." By the last week of October, the Americans had advanced about thirteen miles; Pershing, in charge of all American Expeditionary Forces, had relinquished command of the First Army to Hunter Liggett and organized a Second Army led by Robert Bullard; and the enlarged American attack force was set to embark on the third phase of the Meuse-Argonne Campaign on November 1.[80]

By that time, the world of the war had changed drastically. On September 29, Bulgaria deserted the Central Powers and signed an armistice with the Allies; the Ottomans capitulated on October 3; and on October 28 the Austro-Hungarians finally achieved at least a partial cessation of hostilities by initiating armistice negotiations with the Italians (the Armistice of Villa Giusti would become effective November

4). Its tired armies reeling from Foch's continuous offensive and the resignation of the nation's chief military strategist, Erich Ludendorff, Germany stood alone, its government in confusion, its sorely tested people trembling on the edge of revolution, its navy becoming mutinous. In early October the new German chancellor, Prince Max of Baden, looking to the Allied leader his country felt would be most reasonable, had sent a message to Woodrow Wilson, asking him "to take steps for the restoration of peace" and accepting the Fourteen Points as a basis for peace negotiations. Unwilling to risk prolongation of the war with the sort of abrupt refusal he had sent to Vienna, Wilson proceeded cautiously. His answer, delivered through Secretary of State Lansing, consisted primarily of questions framed to determine whether the request was sincere and authoritative. The ensuing exchange of messages accomplished little more than irritating the Allies and stirring the political pot at home. Republicans and some Democratic newspapers condemned the commander in chief for conducting a "war by correspondence" before the Germans were removed from occupied soil and decried the "abyss of internationalism" into which the president was leading the country. As the negotiations storm abated, Wilson created a new one on October 25 by asking Americans to confirm to the world their support for his war policies, and to extend that support by electing a Democratic Congress. Howling theatrically, irate Republicans used every means at their disposal to turn the president's appeal into a weapon against Democratic candidates.[81]

At the same time, much more lethal weapons were firing all along the Western Front, as the American First and Second armies initiated the third phase of the Meuse-Argonne Offensive; the French, British, and Belgian armies also kept pushing forward; and German forces continued to fall back, while political storms raged on the German home front. Every day more voices called for the kaiser's abdication, sailors at the navy base at Kiel had raised the red flag of revolution, and their mutiny was spreading. Aware of Wilson's exchange of peace notes with the German government, Allied commanders met while the fighting raged on to discuss armistice terms that should be imposed on the failing Germans. General Pershing's recommendations were among the most stringent. "I think that the damage done by the war to the interests of the powers with which the United States is associated

Opposite: As an acting captain, Samuel X. Woodfill (1883–1951) fought with such distinction during the Meuse-Argonne Offensive that he was awarded, among many other medals, the United States Medal of Honor. General Pershing declared him the most outstanding American soldier of the Great War.

Right: Rows of caskets adorned with flags for a memorial ceremony at the Brooklyn Navy Yard are one solemn reflection of the human cost of the war. Photograph by Elite Studio, ca. 1918.

against Germany has been so great," he told Foch, "that there should be no tendency toward leniency." In a memorandum to the Supreme War Council, he went further, recommending *against* an armistice because it would "revivify the low spirits of the German Army and enable it to reorganize and resist later on." It would, moreover, "deprive the Allies of the full measure of victory."[82]

On November 5, voters in the United States deprived their nation's commander in chief of any measure of domestic political victory by handing control of both houses of Congress to the Republican Party. The result of myriad factors—many of which, like the wheat growers' anger, the president had ignored or discounted—the election cast a heavy shadow over Wilson's grand plans for a better world. Yet in Europe, at long last, he could see some light, and his eyes were fixed more firmly on that. On November 7, a German delegation crossed into France under a flag of truce and was escorted to the Forest of Compiègne. As peace negotiations began there two days later—Foch told the Germans that fighting would continue until an armistice was signed—the kaiser finally acceded to demands for his abdication and went into exile in Holland. The following night the German government in Berlin accepted all thirty-five terms the Allies required. German armies would immediately evacuate Belgium, France, Luxembourg, and Alsace-Lorraine, surrender vast stores of munitions, and show the Allies where they had planted landmines and taken other measures to harm their enemies. Allied armies would occupy western Germany up to the Rhine as well as three bridgeheads across that river. Germany would surrender all of its U-boats and most of the navy's capital ships. And it would pay reparations for damages done in occupied Belgium and France.[83]

Fighting continued and men were killed through the morning of November 11, until, at eleven A.M. French time, the hour designated in dispatches to Allied commanders from Marshal Foch, the guns on the Western Front at last fell silent. The most destructive war in human history to that time was over—although the armistice, by definition, did not mean final peace. Treaties to achieve that end still had to be crafted, establishing bases for rebuilding a shattered world with new configurations and without more than 13 million soldiers' lives the war had destroyed and the millions of civilians who had perished from war-related causes. Millions of sick and starving people had to be cared for, farmland and industries repaired, economies resuscitated, the lives of tens of millions of those displaced, maimed, and mentally seared by the war somehow restored. And this would all have to be done in the midst of new crises, new conflagrations as old nations were reborn and new ones formed. Poles were already fighting Ukrainians. American soldiers in northern and southeastern Russia were bearing witness to that country's increasingly violent civil war.[84]

Physically untouched by the conflict, the United States was nevertheless a changed nation. The war had strengthened and increased the reach of the federal government, made America the world's

Crowds celebrating the November 1918 armistice surge along New York City's Wall Street under a rain of confetti. Photograph by W. L. Drummond.

GERMANY SURRENDERS
W. L. DRUMMOND
92 WALL ST.

General John J. Pershing pins decorations on officers of the U.S. Eighty-ninth Division at Treves, Germany. Stereograph by the Keystone View Company, ca. 1918.

leading economic and a premier political power, and demonstrated the country's potential for military might and for projecting that might beyond American shores. The vigilantism and intolerance incited by wartime passions, and now turning away from Prussianism toward other targets, had exposed some of the darker aspects of the American dream. But it was the brighter dream, the optimism inherent in the progressive principles Wilson and many of his supporters believed in, that marked the beginning of the president's immediate postwar mission. Surrounded by reports, charts, and experts from the Inquiry and armed with his Fourteen Points and an exalted vision for the postwar world, Woodrow Wilson would be the first sitting United States president to travel to Europe, where he would take the central seat at the peace table earned for him by millions of his countrymen.

EPILOGUE

Never I think was the world in such [a] plastic state, never such a sense
of receiving life and new possibilities.
—U.S. Paris Peace Conference Press Officer Ray Stannard Baker, December 27, 1918

Our supreme task is the resumption of our onward, normal way.
—President Warren G. Harding, Inaugural Address, March 4, 1921

First came the great surge of relief and astonishment at the rapid collapse of the German war effort. In Allied and neutral nations and the United States bells rang, artillery boomed in celebration rather than anger. Crowds gathered. Revelers danced, sang, and burned the deposed kaiser in effigy. Everywhere people wept, their tears a mixture of joy at the suspension of carnage and sorrow over four years of loss. Later came waves of anxiety, extravagant hopes, and uncertainty. "If I had dreamed that silencing the guns was to bring me instant peace, I was mistaken," American author Mildred Aldrich wrote to a friend from her home in France on November 15, 1918. "I can't help remembering that this is only an armistice, and wondering if, since Germany got it the first time she asked—saving her army, escaping invasion—we can really impose on her a punishing peace. First and last every one of the Allies has been a blunderer in diplomacy. Are they going to blunder in imposing peace terms?"[1]

Three days later the White House announced that President Wilson would leave for France in early December to participate in negotiating the treaty with Germany that would truly end the war.[2] He would be the first serving president since George Washington was inaugurated 129 years before[3] to make the long journey to Europe, a break with precedent accepted by most Americans but unsettling to a few. The president, some of these critics said, would be abdicating his many domestic duties; Senator Lawrence Sherman of Illinois even introduced a resolution that Wilson be declared "out of office" if he went. Democrat senator Key Pittman of Nevada reported to Wilson that about half the Senate thought it would be better if he remained in the United States and influenced the peace negotiations "as a superman residing afar off in a citadel of power beyond that of all nations." Yet Wilson was determined to follow his own inclinations and those of his most ardent progressive supporters who believed that his presence at the peace table was required, at least for a while. In France, the president could most effectively guide nations embittered by four years of blood and destruction toward establishing a more enlightened new order in Europe. "I want to tell Lloyd George certain things I can't

279

write to him," Wilson told a visiting Swiss politician, William Rappard, on November 20. "I'll tell him: Are you going to grant freedom of the seas? If not, are you prepared to enter into a race with us to see who will have the larger navy, you or we?"[4]

The makeup of the small American peace delegation he would lead ignited a much greater political furor. In addition to Wilson, the White House announced, the members would be the president's close adviser, Colonel Edward House; General Tasker Bliss, U.S. military representative on the Allied Supreme War Council; Secretary of State Robert Lansing; and veteran diplomat Henry White, a Republican but far from a party leader. All prominent Republicans were excluded, as were members of the Senate, the body responsible for ratifying treaties to which the United States is a party. No one in the delegation was likely to voice strong objections, the excluded parties worried, should Wilson agree to peace terms too weak to prevent Germany from again invading its neighbors or should he create a framework for his cherished League of Nations that might in some way impinge on American sovereignty. "Our delegation with the exception of Mr. White are merely mouthpieces of the President," Wilson's longtime enemy, Senator Henry Cabot Lodge, wrote Lord James Bryce on December 14, "and if Mr. White should differ he will be overridden."[5]

Hope and high expectations overrode criticism and doubt on December 4, however, when the American Peace Mission left the port at Hoboken, New Jersey, aboard the German-built liner SS *George Washington*, one of the vessels seized by the U.S. government when America entered the war. Small civilian craft crowded as close as they were allowed to the giant liner. Tugboats tooted, dirigibles and army planes cruised the skies above, and Secretary Lansing released a bevy of carrier pigeons bearing messages of hope for an enduring peace. More than ten thousand people crowding the shoreline across the river in Manhattan cheered as the ship eased away from the dock and was joined by its naval escort. Five hundred children on Staten Island waved a host of tiny American flags as the *George Washington* passed the Statue of Liberty. Wilson would be greeted by even greater, more ecstatic crowds in France, Britain, and Italy before

the peace conference officially convened. When that occurred, on January 18, 1919, Wilson enjoyed, in the words of British economist John Maynard Keynes, "a prestige and moral influence throughout the world unequaled in history."[6]

Author of the Fourteen Points, advocate for just democracy and a new kind of mutually supportive relationship among nations—"not a balance of power but a community of power," as he said in January 1917—Wilson had assumed the mantle of champion of mankind. As spokesman for European peoples whose governments, he believed, did not truly represent their interests, he would fight for a better world based on "American principles, American policies." Yet he had not yet disclosed to anyone, perhaps because he was not sure, specifically how he would seek to

apply his Fourteen Points amid the hosts of conflicting requests and demands that would undoubtedly be made by official and nonofficial delegations during the negotiations in Paris. Confident in his principles, he was less confident of a bright outcome. "You know and I know that these ancient wrongs, these present unhappinesses are not to be remedied in a day or with the wave of a hand," he said to George Creel during the voyage to France. "What I seem to see—with all my heart I hope I am wrong—is a tragedy of disappointment."[7]

Focused on the myriad problems attending international reconstruction, the president seemed to lose sight of the difficult challenges the abrupt transition to peace was also presenting to the people of the United States. Emotions fueled by the relentless wartime quest for national unity and "100 percent Americanism" as shields against domestic subversion during the great crusade against German militarism remained at fever pitch. Like those heightened emotions, the vast and intricate machinery of war, which had just recently reached full power, could not be abruptly shut down. And when the transition to peace was completed, how should the country use the experiences gained and the lessons learned in the war? Progressive hopes for building a better world applied equally, if differently, to the war-battered nations of Europe and the war-strengthened United States. Editors of the progressive magazine the *New Republic* spoke of the need to continue America's wartime progress in "social control" in order to subordinate "class and sectional interests to the interests of the nation, as well as an adjustment of these to the larger world interests." Prewar Socialist and fervent war supporter

Algie Simons, author of the 1919 book *The Vision for Which We Fought: A Study in Reconstruction*, rhapsodized about the potential of the now-more-potent federal government. It *could* be used, he believed when most optimistic, as an instrument "for the common good, to serve the common ends, to defend the common interest." "I feel that . . . the hour has come," social reformer Felix Adler said in November 1918, "when we have an opportunity, such as has never existed before in this country, to do great things."[8]

Possibilities for social reform abounded, but so did immediate problems, many of them pertaining to particular, rather than common interests. What should be done about businesses heavily invested in war production that was no longer needed? How could the country dispose of the many tons of war product now filling home-front warehouses and supply dumps

Left: The 803rd Pioneer Infantry Battalion aboard the troopship USS *Philippine* in the harbor at Brest, France, as they embark for home, ca. 1919.

Opposite: Cover art on the March 17, 1922, edition of *The American Legion Weekly* reflects a continuing battle for many U.S. Great War veterans: finding employment in a postwar period characterized by volatile economic conditions.

in Europe without severely shaking the American economy? What was the best way to guard against rampant unemployment as factories tooled down and millions of men returned to civilian life? What should be the fate of the new wartime federal departments, the nation's growing intelligence organizations, and civilian vigilance groups? And what should be done for those who sacrificed to support the war—including U.S. military veterans, resident aliens who joined the armed forces, women, and African Americans? How much and what sort of social change would the various elements of America's diverse society be demanding after nineteen months of patriotic endeavors and furious upheaval? How much would the country be prepared to accept? Charles W. Eliot, Harvard's venerable president, was more skeptical than the reform-minded Adler of a widespread thirst for permanent alterations in the nation's social fabric. "Americans as a rule are too well pleased with what they have got," he wrote in October 1918, "to venture on vast untried experiments in vague hope of getting more."[9]

One definite hope on which most Americans focused immediately after the armistice was for the rapid demobilization of the nearly four-million-man United States Army that had surged into existence with awe-inspiring speed and was now spread across two continents. More than 1.5 million doughboys were on duty or in training in the United States, two million more were "Over There," and not all

Save This Copy for Service Census Instructions—Page 15

Vol. 4, No. 11   MARCH 17, 1922   10c. a Copy

The AMERICAN LEGION Weekly

No Man's Land

American Legion Employment Day, Monday, March 20th—In Your Town—Everywhere

of those overseas were allowed to stand down after November 11. On November 17, the recently formed U.S. Third Army, flanked by the French Fifth and Tenth armies, began moving toward Germany in the wake of withdrawing German troops. As the Americans moved forward, passing liberated Allied prisoners of war heading in the opposite direction, Third Army intelligence officers made daily reports to AEF headquarters: Citizens of the Duchy of Luxembourg, now free after four years of German occupation, showered the Americans with flowers. It was evident that some of the withdrawing Germans "did considerable looting . . . but most of the German army passed through in an orderly manner." After crossing the German border on December 1, the 200,000-strong Third Army, now designated the American army of occupation, reached the Rhine River on

December 12 and established its headquarters in Coblenz.[10]

American Expeditionary Force troops in England, France, Italy, Vladivostok, and Archangel who were not required for occupation duty grew more anxious each day to return home (morale in frigid Archangel was particularly low), and their families were impatient to see them. With little likelihood that hostilities would recommence and the war still costing the United States $50 million a day, the War Department was also eager to bring troops home and reduce the size of the army. Yet it faced some formidable challenges. On November 11, 1918, no embarkation facilities stood ready to handle such a great crowd of returnees and, in any event, precious few ships were available to transport them. British, French, and Italian shipping, which had carried more than 50 percent of the doughboys to Europe, would be busy returning dominion and colonial troops to their homes—and attempting to reestablish commercial trade the war had diminished.[11]

The War and Navy departments quickly settled on solutions to these problems, and these were gradually realized. By mid-November the AEF Quartermaster Corps chose three French ports along the Bay of Biscay—Brest, St. Nazaire, and Bordeaux—as the major points of departure and began building a huge embarkation facility at the main port, Brest. At Le Mans, midway between Paris and the coast, a camp so massive that "a man could walk briskly for an hour in a single direction . . . and see nothing but tents, barracks, drill fields, and troops" was transformed from an assembly point for incoming doughboys to a center for troops

Left: The First Division of the AEF parades up Fifteenth Street, NW, in Washington, D.C., the front of the column turning left through a victory arch onto Pennsylvania Avenue before passing the White House in review. Photograph by Harris & Ewing, September 1919.

Opposite, top: Civilians greet wounded veterans who are waiting to view General Pershing and the First Division on parade in Washington, D.C. National Photo Company, September 1919.

Bottom: A multilingual ballot polling iron- and steelworkers about their willingness to strike should companies refuse their demands. Reproduced in William Z. Foster, *The Great Steel Strike and Its Lessons,* 1920.

celebrated band, large as it was, could hardly be heard "so great were the roars of cheers, the applause, and the shouts of personal greetings," Major Arthur Little later reported. By the end of June, there had been more than five hundred parades, although few quite so boisterous, and more were to come. Perhaps the grandest reception was given to General Pershing and the First Division as they marched in New York on September 10 and in Washington, D.C., on September 17.[13]

Most American troops were home by that time, a majority of the American army of occupation included; only a few thousand Third Army troops still stood their watch on the Rhine. After feverish lobbying by the people of Michigan, whose men were suffering in remote Archangel, and

heading home. German commercial vessels that were surrendered to the Americans immediately postwar, including *Imperator*, the largest passenger ship in the world, were converted to troop transports, as were American cargo vessels and some U.S. Navy warships. These and additional vessels leased from other nations were placed at the disposal of the newly formed Transportation Service, which ferried the AEF home at a steadily increasing pace that still left men impatient. "Lafayette, we are here," Captain Charles E. Stanton had famously stated at the Marquis de Lafayette's tomb on July 4, 1917. "Lafayette, we are *still* here," disgruntled doughboys scribbled on barrack walls as they waited their turn to go home.[12]

Thousands of returning doughboys paraded through America's streets before heading to their demobilization centers. On February 17, 1919, the now-famous African American regiment, the 369th Infantry, marched seven miles along Fifth Avenue and into Harlem, though its

by politicians critical of the whole Russian incursion, the doughboys in Archangel finally made it home in the summer—except for 144 who had been killed fighting Bolshevik troops and 100 who died of disease. American troops remained in Vladivostok until the spring of 1920, continuing to see elements of the Czech Legion safely aboard ships for their journey home, keeping track of vying anti-Bolshevik factions in the area, and reporting on the activities of the much larger contingent of Japanese troops, which would remain in Siberia after the Americans left.[14]

By then, the Bolshevik government, supported by the strengthening Red Army, seemed likely to outlast its disorganized opponents, leaving the largest nation on earth in fervently anti-capitalist hands and increasing the danger of communist revolutions in Russia's war-ravaged neighbors. Many Americans believed it increased the danger to their own country, too. By late 1918 "Bolshevism" had replaced "Prussianism" as the dark force to be blamed for disturbances in the American body politic—and in 1919 the United States endured a year of violent disruptions. From January to December waves of strikes shivered across the country: New England telephone operators struck as did Eastern Seaboard shipbuilders, Baltimore cigar makers, miners in several states, members of the International Brotherhood of Blacksmiths in Cleveland, streetcar workers in Indiana, theatrical actors in several cities, commercial telegraphers across the country. One in every five workers walked off the job, more than ever before in the nation's history, as labor sought to solidify and build on the gains it had made during the war. But capital, freed from the constraints of the wartime need for cooperation, fought back with a vengeance, often assisted by the government.[15]

When the Seattle Central Labor Council organized a peaceful four-day walkout by sixty thousand laborers, the first general strike in American history, Mayor Ole Hanson accused the strikers of being part of the Red menace that wanted "to take possession of our American Government and try to duplicate the anarchy of Russia" and called in federal troops. After Boston police unionized in August and struck in September, they were widely condemned as "deserters" and "Bolsheviks." Massachusetts governor Calvin Coolidge gained the national spotlight by declaring, "There is no right to strike against the public safety by anyone, anywhere, anytime," and the city replaced the striking officers. Later in September some three hundred thousand iron and steel workers, many of whom worked twelve-hour days in grueling conditions for low pay, walked off the job, demanding the right to collective bargaining. Managers labeled the walkout a revolutionary plot, and in a way they were correct, though the plot had nothing to do with Bolshevism. In August 1918, Samuel Gompers and thirty other union leaders, buoyed by the gains and apparent respect labor had achieved through its vital contributions to the Allied war effort, decided the time was ripe finally to unionize workers in the nation's bedrock, and most resistant, industry. "We have established democracy in politics," Gompers said, "and our present purpose is to establish democracy in the iron and steel industry." To industry leader Elbert Gary, however, democracy stopped at the steel mill gates; in August 1919 he refused even to meet with steelworkers' representatives. A month later, after the strike began, management set company police on the protesting workers and replaced them with strikebreakers, many of them African Americans—thus

The Burning of William Brown, Omaha, Nebraska, September 28, 1919

EUROPE AND ASIA MINOR IN 1914

EUROPE AND ASIA MINOR IN 1924

exacerbating postwar racial tensions. By January 1920, the strike had failed, and American labor, their wartime gains fast evaporating, faced a period of renewed struggle.[16]

As all this was happening, a congressional committee headed by Senator Lee Overman of North Carolina, originally formed to investigate German propaganda in the United States, began well-publicized hearings on real and rumored Bolshevik activities in America and concluded that Bolshevism was the "greatest current danger facing the Republic." Stories circulated of thwarted bombing attempts by radicals. Then on April 28, 1919, the stories gained substance. A mail bomb arrived at Mayor Hanson's office but did no damage. The next day a mail bomb addressed to former senator Thomas W. Hardwick at his Atlanta apartment blew off the hands of the maid who was opening it and injured Hardwick's wife. Insufficient postage led to

the discovery two days later of thirty-four more bombs addressed to other prominent figures, including Postmaster General Albert Burleson, Secretary of Labor William B. Wilson, Attorney General A. Mitchell Palmer, and Senator Overman. Banner headlines spread the news across the country of "a nationwide bomb conspiracy, which the police authorities say has every earmark of I.W.W.-Bolshevik origin," as the New York Times reported on May 1. That same day, angry mobs broke up May Day (International Workers' Day) rallies in several cities, as anti-radical fever spread. It became more intense a month later when bombs exploded in eight cities, one blowing off the front of Attorney General Palmer's Washington, D.C., home (and blowing to pieces the Italian anarchist who was delivering it).[17]

America's first great "Red Scare" was thus set in motion. While vigilantes and vigilance groups acted on their own against IWW members and others they deemed to be radical, Palmer created a new Radical Division within the Justice Department's Bureau of Investigation, and chose an eager twenty-four-year-old named J. Edgar Hoover to head it. Under Hoover's direction, the division started compiling information on hundreds of thousands of suspect resident aliens and American citizens, and it fed the growing anti-radical panic by spreading sensationalized and often wholly fabricated stories of nefarious Bolshevik actions. On November 7, 1919 (the second anniversary of the Bolshevik coup in Russia), the Justice Department launched the first of what became known as "Palmer raids," sweeping arrests and detention of aliens and citizens even vaguely suspected of radical activities or Bolshevik sympathies. Reminiscent of the wartime mass arrests of suspected slackers, the raids continued into the following spring, when it became evident

that, random acts of radical violence notwithstanding, the domestic threat from Bolshevism was minuscule. In May 1920, a group of respected attorneys published the painstakingly researched *Report upon the Illegal Practices of the United States Justice Department* documenting government excesses in conducting the raids. The following month, Judge George Anderson of the Massachusetts Federal District Court, in a decision releasing from custody twenty aliens falsely arrested, censured the Justice Department for its abuses. It was at this time, "in a reaction to the country's excesses," legal historian Geoffrey Stone later wrote, "that the modern civil liberties movement truly began."[18]

The threat of a Bolshevik revolution in America proved chimerical. For black Americans, however, the domestic threat from racism was all too real and, despite

Opposite: Two maps record major changes that the war, and the Versailles conference, brought to Europe and the Middle East. Reproduced from *International Conciliation,* May 1924.

Right: "Signing of the Peace Treaty at Versailles, June 28, 1919 at 3:12 P.M." Color print by William de Leftwich Dodge (1967–1935), ca. 1920.

African Americans' many contributions to the war effort, seemed to have grown even greater. Lynch mobs killed seventy-eight blacks in 1919, among them several Great War veterans. Between June and December there were race riots in more than twenty locations, from Texas and Arkansas to Chicago and Washington, D.C. (where the city commissioner blamed Bolsheviks). Yet now, almost everywhere white rioters attacked blacks, they faced strong resistance. "The outstanding feature remains, not that the Negro will fight," the emerging black author Jean Toomer wrote on July 29, "but that he will fight against the American white. It now confronts the nation, so voluble in acclamation of the democratic ideal, so reticent in applying what it professes, to either extend to the Negro (and other workers) the essentials of a democratic commonwealth or else exist from day to day never knowing when a clash may occur in the light of which the Washington riot will diminish and pale."[19]

Trouble and threats of trouble were also erupting abroad. Shattered Europe had become, in the words of Czech patriot Tomas Masaryk, "a laboratory resting on a vast cemetery," and all the elements in that laboratory were explosive. As military forces and militias battled each other in Russia, the Baltic region, and the remnants of the Austro-Hungarian Empire and governing factions formed and fell in new and aspiring nations, Herbert Hoover assumed yet another challenging role. Named director general of relief in Europe by President Wilson in January 1919 and head of the new American Relief Administration, Hoover, with the help of his dedicated staff, haggled, jury-rigged, negotiated, and begged his way around a host of obstacles to getting food to the millions of people facing starvation. Concerned for the threatened millions, Hoover was also convinced that food supplies and economic assistance were effective weapons against the menaces of anarchy and revolution—a conviction that would become a hallmark of American foreign policy during the 1920s.[20]

In Paris, meanwhile, peace delegations

argued over treaty terms, and supplicants from imperial colonies and collapsed empires strove to be heard, their hopes nourished by Woodrow Wilson's wartime eloquence. "Peoples are not to be handed about from one sovereignty to another by an international conference or an understanding between rivals and antagonists," the president had stated in February 1918. "Peoples may now be dominated and governed only by their own consent. 'Self-determination' is not a mere phrase. It is an imperative principle of action." But to what entities was that principle to be applied? "When the president talks of 'self-determination,'" Secretary Lansing wrote in December 1918, "does he mean a race, a territorial area, or a community? Without a definite unit which is practical, application of this principle is dangerous . . . It is bound to be the basis of impossible demands on the Peace Congress . . . It will raise hopes which can never be realized."[21]

Lansing proved prescient. Many supplicants were turned away either unheard or deeply disappointed in their reception—including Nguyen Tat Thanh, a young Vietnamese admirer of American democracy who would later change his name to

Ho Chi Minh, and W. E. B. Du Bois, chief organizer of and spokesman for the Pan-African Congress held in Paris in February 1919. As official delegates to the peace conference redrew the maps of Europe and the Near and Middle East (most decisions were made by the "Big Four," Lloyd George of Britain, Clemenceau of France, Vittorio Orlando of Italy, and President Wilson), peoples were, in fact, handed about from one sovereignty to another. Moreover, the system of "mandates" that evolved from the conference, under which designated Allied powers were given authority over former German and Ottoman territories, actually placed more of the world's area under imperial control than before the war.[22]

President Wilson did manage to realize his own hope for creating a League of Nations. Its covenant, or charter, became the first twenty-six articles of the Versailles Treaty. The product of six trying months of negotiation, argumentation, and compromise among the Allied powers, the treaty was signed with great ceremony in the crowded Hall of Mirrors of the Palace of Versailles on June 28, 1919, the fifth anniversary of the assassination of Archduke Franz Ferdinand. The two German officials who had reluctantly agreed to represent their country, Foreign Minister Hermann Müller and Minister of Transport Johannes Bell, were required to sign first, and their hands shook as they affixed their names to the document. They were all too aware of the terrible resentments two of the treaty's terms, in particular, had aroused in their countrymen. Article 231, quickly dubbed the "war guilt" clause, made Germany and its allies responsible for all war damages; Article 232 required that Germany "make complete reparation for all such loss and damage." Colonel House was among those unhappy with the elaborate ceremony and the treatment of the two German delegates. "I wish . . . there might have been an element of chivalry, which was wholly lacking," he wrote. "The whole affair was . . . made as humiliating to the enemy as it well could be." After the Allied representatives and President Wilson signed and the treaty was official, artillery boomed, setting off wild celebrations outside the palace and then all across France. Throughout Germany, flags were lowered to half-staff.[23]

Exhausted from his efforts in Paris, battered by criticisms of the sometimes secretive way negotiations had been conducted and compromises he had made that seemed to some a betrayal of his own Fourteen Points, Wilson returned to the United States to face a months-long struggle with Congress over ratification of the treaty. The League of Nations covenant was the biggest bone of contention. Some senators felt that, as designed, the League would perpetuate the corrupt prewar political order. Others believed membership in the League would hobble the United States in its international relations, and the requirement in Article 10 of the covenant, that members aid other members threatened with aggression, would inevitably drag the United States into another war. Things looked so dark for acceptance of the League, which Wilson believed was "the only possible guarantee against war," that the president embarked in early

Left: Delegates sign documents aimed at averting a postwar naval armaments race at the end of the Washington (D.C.) Naval Disarmament Conference. Held at the behest of the U.S. government, the conference was one indication of increasing United States influence in world affairs.

Opposite: The Aisne-Marne American Cemetery and Memorial, near the site of the Battle of Belleau Wood. Photograph by M. E. Wagner, 1991. Nearly 31,000 U.S. casualties of the Great War are interred in nine American cemeteries in France, where plaques also record the names of 4,452 Americans listed as missing in action.

September on a ten-thousand-mile speaking tour through the Midwest and West to gain public support that would sway the reluctant senators. The effort proved to be too much. After giving forty-two speeches in twenty-one days, Wilson collapsed in Pueblo, Colorado, on September 25, 1919. A week later, in Washington, he suffered a massive stroke.[24]

On November 19, the Senate refused to ratify the treaty, but that was not the end of the battle. "I think a majority of the people of the country desire a League," Henry Cabot Lodge had written to Henry White in April, "but . . . will insist on some very vital amendments." During the months of the president's slow and only partial recovery, the Senate debated changes that would allow the United States to join the League on its own terms. But factions in the Senate could not agree with one another, and the president would not agree to any changes at all. On March 19, 1920, the Senate finally rejected the Versailles Treaty. The United States remained technically at war with Germany until August 25, 1921, when the two nations signed a separate peace.[25]

By that time, the people of the United States, shaken by nineteen months of war and more than two years of domestic upheaval, had chosen a new Republican president, Warren G. Harding, who promised them a "return to normalcy." That was, to many, a comforting phrase, but it was also misleading. The Great War had changed the world and America's place in it. No longer a military power (facing no appreciable outside threat, by 1923 the government slashed the regular army to 137,000 men), the United States was unquestionably the world's greatest economic power, and as business-government cooperation continued after the war, it employed that power to increase its influence around the world. The United States assisted in the reconstruction of Europe, helped to negotiate war debt disputes, promoted stability in the Far East—and even began cooperating on an unofficial level with committees of the new League of Nations in efforts to assure the continuing peace and stability that was so vital to the nation's own interests. Although at the end of the Great War it possessed the world's largest navy, America took the lead in naval disarmament, bringing representatives of the European powers and Japan to Washington in 1921 and securing, early in 1922, agreements on limiting the number of each country's capital ships. Americans were still leery of entangling alliances and distrustful of manipulative foreign powers. Their

increasing reluctance to admit immigrants from troubled foreign lands led to the Emergency Quota Law of 1921 and the Immigration Act of 1924, which limited the number of immigrants to be admitted each year and established national quotas. Yet by the rainy night of February 19, 1923, when General Henry T. Allen became the last member of the U.S. occupation force to leave Germany, Americans were starting to understand their country's new influence in the world—and to grasp the implications of the nation's increasing power. "I suppose that the people of the United States have learned more about international relations within the past eight years than they had learned in the preceding eighty years," venerable statesman Elihu Root observed a few months before General Allen boarded the train in Coblenz. "They are, however, only at the beginning of the task."[26]

ACKNOWLEDGMENTS

Creating *America and the Great War* has been an epic adventure, one reflecting the importance, complexity, and excitement of the World War I era. I am profoundly grateful for all the help and guidance I have received along the way.

David M. Kennedy has made this a richer and wiser book with his graceful introduction and his cogent comments on the draft text. His own hallmark work on America during the Great War, *Over Here*, remains an incomparable resource and an inspiration. Chrisopher Capozzola's thought-provoking questions and suggestions helped shape the early chapters, and I learned much from his own work on World War I, *Uncle Sam Wants You*.

I have become a great admirer of picture editor Athena Angelos's many talents during our work together on a number of projects, and I salute her again now for her tenacious research within the huge and varied Library of Congress collections on the World War I era, her exceedingly perceptive eye, and her wise counsel.

It has been a great pleasure to work with our colleagues at Bloomsbury USA: publishing director George Gibson, managing editor Laura Phillips, assistant editor Callie Garnett, and copyeditor Kate Scott. This book is a tribute to their great patience, close attention to detail, and sage advice.

The Library of Congress is fortunate to have such a talented and dedicated staff, several of whom were especially helpful on this book. Helena Zinkham, director of Collections and Services and chief of the Prints and Photographs Division, has done much to support and facilitate development of *America and the Great War*. In the Prints and Photographs Division, Reference Assistant Jon Eaker, whose knowledge of the war and the division's World War I collections is encyclopedic, provided much welcome guidance and many excellent suggestions. Reference Section Head Barbara Orbach Natanson, Photography Curator Beverly Brannan, Fine Prints Curator Katherine Blood, Popular and Applied Graphic Arts Curators Sara Duke and Martha Kennedy, and Reference Librarian Jan Grenci introduced Athena and me to a stunning array of materials and the stories behind them. Sahr Conway-Lanz and Ryan Reft, twentieth-century historians in the Manuscript Division, provided valuable guidance through that division's immense trove of World War I materials and also read and commented on the book's draft text. Robert Patrick, who recently retired as director of the Veterans History Project, and VHP specialist Megan Harris acquainted us with some of the American soldiers of the Great War whose artifacts and memories the VHP preserves. My lively discussions with the multitalented Cheryl Regan of the Interpretive Programs Office, exhibition director of the library's major World War I presentation (spring 2017 to January 2019), helped sharpen my approach to the book. Thanks also go to Reference Librarian Will Elsbury for revealing the existence of the four-hundred-volume collection of newspaper clippings that is a unique window into the day-by-day American wartime experience.

Over the past five years, many gifted interns from universities across the country (as well as Belgium and Gibraltar) have helped conduct the research for this book. I wish I could mention them all by name. Each one seized upon his or her assignment with zeal, tracking down answers to questions, exploring and reporting on the contents of various library collections. They were boons to this book and to the Library of Congress, and I thank them all.

Finally, very special thanks to my dauntless colleagues in the library's Publishing Office. Former Director of Publishing Ralph Eubanks was instrumental in launching the book. Interim director William "Jake" Jacobs supported the project with grace and good humor as has the current Director of Publishing, Becky Clark. The office was extremely fortunate to have the assistance of two excellent editorial assistants while the book was being developed: Beth Kerr and Keith Shovlin. I monopolized much of Keith's time with World War I research assignments, and I thank him for his detailed reports. Senior Editors Susan Reyburn, Aimee Hess, and Peter Devereaux took time from their own projects to read and comment on draft text, and Susan created the "battle boxes" that enhance chapters 1 and 2. It is a joy to be a part of this small (but mighty!) Publishing Office staff. My colleagues' love of books, appreciation for history, and devotion to producing work of the highest quality are a constant inspiration.

Any flaws and infelicities that remain in the text are entirely my own.

—Margaret E. Wagner

APPENDIX

WORLD WAR I COLLECTIONS AT THE LIBRARY OF CONGRESS

The largest library in the world and an institution known as both America's Library and the Nation's Memory, the Library of Congress is located in three large buildings on Capitol Hill in Washington, D.C., and on the Packard Campus for Audio-Visual Conservation in Culpeper, Virginia. As of 2017, the centennial of U.S. involvement in World War I, the Library's collections number more than 162 million items, on all subjects and in almost all media. Reflecting America's membership in the community of nations and the diverse origins of its people, the Library's collections are international in scope, including material in more than 470 languages. Yet the heart of the Library is found in its vast collections of written, visual, recorded, and electronic materials that chronicle the origins and development of the United States of America. It holds especially rich collections on World War I, some of which are accessible online.

For the Library of Congress Web Guide to World War I Materials, visit **www.loc.gov/rr/program/bib/wwi/wwi.html.** This site provides links to online digital collections, webcasts, newspaper articles, exhibits, bibliographies, finding aids, image collections, and more from around the Library.

World War I collection highlights from the various Library divisions:

GENERAL COLLECTIONS (HUMANITIES AND SOCIAL SCIENCES DIVISION, HSS)

www.loc.gov/rr/main

The General Collections include thousands of volumes pertaining to the war, from memoirs, diaries, and letters published during the conflict to present-day histories. These collections include accounts and analyses of individual battles, treatments of various aspects of the war (e.g., naval warfare, weaponry, intelligence gathering, politics, government, and diplomacy); books on war-related fiction and poetry; regimental histories and bound volumes of material from veterans' organizations; and almanacs, chronologies, and encyclopedias. To browse items in the General Collections, use the online catalog at **catalog.loc.gov/**. For an annotated bibliography on general World War I histories, see **www.loc.gov/**

rr/main/ww1/books.html; for an annotated bibliography of military newspapers, see www.loc.gov/rr/main/ww1/news-general.html.

GEOGRAPHY AND MAP DIVISION (G&M)

www.loc.gov/rr/geogmap/

The Geography and Map Division holds a large collection of World War I maps that are both primary and secondary sources. The division has published two guides to these materials: A *List of Atlases and Maps Applicable to the World War; comp. under the direction of Philip Lee Phillips, chief, Division of Maps* (1918), and *Maps of the First World War: An Illustrated Essay and List of Select Maps in the Library of Congress* (2014), by Ryan J. Moore.

The division's special collections include material from Tasker Howard Bliss, chief military adviser to Woodrow Wilson during the Paris Peace conference of 1919; Charles Pelot Summerall, commander of the Fifth Division in France; Willard B. Prince, a noncommissioned officer and mapmaker; and a number of smaller collections from officers and enlisted men. The bulk of the military maps are so-called "trench maps" that depict military situations in France, the Alps, the Balkans, the Middle East and elsewhere. These are complemented by intelligence maps, training maps, supply line maps, airfield maps, and other maps necessary to execute military operations. Maps illustrating the war at sea primarily consist of British intelligence maps of German commerce raiding, U-boats, and minefields. These maps are located in atlases and cataloged collections, as well as the Titled Collection under the categories of Europe, World War I, and United States Military. The Titled Collection is not represented in the online catalog. Commercial maps and propaganda maps that were created to illustrate wartime issues to the public are generally part of the Titled Collection.

There are a large number of maps related to postwar negotiations; these include proposals for territorial changes, boundary lines, and demographic studies. Some of the maps were created by Wilson's advisers, such as Isaiah Bowman, and others were published by numerous mapmakers from around the world.

MANUSCRIPT DIVISION (MSS)

www.loc.gov/rr/mss

The Manuscript Division maintains the richest and most extensive holdings anywhere of personal papers and other manuscript collections documenting the American experience regarding World War I. The division holds the papers of Woodrow Wilson, which include his White House files, and the papers of most of his wartime cabinet, including Secretary of State William Jennings Bryan, Secretary of State Robert Lansing, Secretary of War Newton D. Baker, Secretary of the Navy Josephus Daniels, Secretary of the Treasury William G. McAdoo, and Postmaster General Albert S. Burleson. The papers of Theodore Roosevelt and William H. Taft can be found in this division as well as those of prominent wartime congressional figures such as Robert M. La Follette (in the La Follette Family Papers), Elihu Root, George W. Norris, and William E. Borah. Also noteworthy among the collections of government officials are the papers of George Creel, propagandist and chairman of the Committee on Public Information.

In addition to many lower-rank soldiers and sailors, most of the top military leaders of the American war effort have collections in the Manuscript Division, including generals John J. Pershing, Peyton C. March, Tasker H. Bliss, and Leonard Wood. Experience of the war in Europe is documented through collections such as those of the tank commander George Patton and the Red Cross relief worker Rebekah Crawford (in the Rebekah Crawford and Linda Clarke-Smith Papers). Other collections provide perspectives on the political and social impact of the war at home, such as the papers of the National Association for the Advancement of Colored People (NAACP), the peace activist and leading suffragist Carrie Chapman Catt, and Professor Robert M. McElroy, educational director of the National Security League. In all, the Manuscript Division possesses more than two hundred collections that relate to virtually every aspect of the American experience of World War I.

To examine all Manuscript Division online finding aids, see **www.loc.gov/rr/mss/f-aids/mssfa.html**.

MOTION PICTURE, BROAD-CASTING & RECORDED SOUND DIVISION (M/BRS)

www.loc.gov/rr/mopic/

The rich collections of the Motion Picture, Broadcasting & Recorded Sound Division include thousands of films and sound recordings related to the war. Among the moving image holdings are official films made by the U.S. Army Signal Corps for training purposes; propaganda films distributed by the Committee on Public Information's Division of Films for presentation to the public; official war films produced in England, France, and Germany; *On the Firing Line with the Germans*, a 1915 film documenting the German Army drive against Russian forces along the Eastern front (once thought to be lost, the film was reconstructed by conservation specialists at the Library's National Audio-Visual Conservation Center in 2015); war-related films from the Theodore Roosevelt Collection of the ex-president and his son Quentin; excerpts from contemporary newsreels; actuality films documenting battles, parades, Liberty Bond drives, military and political leaders, women in the workforce, and industrial expansion; film and television documentaries from later periods that use archival footage; and a wealth of fiction films from the war years and later, including two from the Mary Pickford Collection, *The Little American* (1917) and *Johanna Enlists* (1918), and two versions, silent and sound, of *All Quiet on the Western Front* (1930), painstakingly restored at the center. The recorded sound collections include "American Leaders Speak," talks by prominent figures recorded between 1918 and 1920, many on war-related topics; popular songs of the time included in the Library's "National Jukebox"; and an interview with a Long Island man who recorded broadcasts for the Secret Service of encoded messages on American shipping intended to be picked up by German submarines.

MUSIC DIVISION (MUS)/ PERFORMING ARTS READING ROOM

www.loc.gov/rr/perform/

Accessed through the Performing Arts Reading Room, the 20.5 million items in the custody of the Music Division include a variety of materials pertaining to World War I. These include a rich store of wartime sheet music, grouped under the call number M1646. The sheet music has been digitized and may be found among the Library's digitized collections at **www. loc.gov/collections/world-war-i-sheet-music/ about-this-collection/.**

Some collections devoted to individual artists also contain World War I materials, particularly the large Irving Berlin Collection, **hdl.loc.gov/loc.music/eadmus. mu012008**. Berlin was in the army during the Great War and produced a Broadway musical performed by his fellow soldiers at Camp Upton in Yaphank, New York. The division also holds a collection devoted to Austrian-American violinist Fritz Kreisler, who spent a year in the *Austrian* army during the period of American neutrality, before mustering out because of wounds and emigrating to the United States.

Great-War-related individual items in the Music collections include a manuscript sketch of George M. Cohan's classic song, "Over There." **lccn.loc.gov/2013562143**.

PRINTS AND PHOTOGRAPHS (P&P)

www.loc.gov/rr/print

With more than seventy-five thousand pictures relating to World War I, P&P collections are a valuable resource for learn-ing about many aspects of the Great War. The most common types of photography are images created for publication in newspapers, including home-front activities and images created by soldiers to chronicle their military service. Most of the visual material was created during the war (1914–1918), but a portion deals with such postwar topics as injured veterans, pension distribution, and the aftermath of war in European cities.

American involvement in the war is well represented. In addition, the collection has many items, primarily of German origin, expressing the point of view of the Central Powers. Aviation is a particular strength of the photo documentation, collected in large part by the former Library of Congress Division of Aeronautics. The photographs show airplanes from nearly every country involved and some examples of dirigibles. Some photographs show aircraft construction, including women working in aircraft factories. A large portion of the pictures exist in lots grouped by subject, provenance, or format. The wide array of formats includes photographic prints and negatives, panoramic photographs, stereograph cards, posters, cartoons, artist prints, and drawings.

Thousands of items are available online as digital images. For more information, see the research guide "World War I in Pictures: An Overview of Prints & Photographs Division Collections," at **www.loc. gov/rr/print/coll/wwicoll.html**.

RARE BOOK AND SPECIAL COLLECTIONS (RBSCD)

www.loc.gov/rr/rarebook/

The Rare Book and Special Collections of the Library contain nearly 1 million items, including thousands of items relating to World War I. Included are published memoirs, correspondence, and diaries as well as poetry and political and historical accounts. Among the highlights are the library and memorabilia of President Woodrow Wilson, including the gold medal, sash, and certificate from his receipt of the Nobel Peace Prize in 1920. Other collections show the war from many different perspectives. The North American Woman Suffrage Association collection includes materials describing the work of American women to aid the war effort; the Radical Pamphlet and Anarchist Pamphlet Collections describe antiwar efforts; and a variety of published works show the experiences of American soldiers and relief workers participating on the front lines. To browse items in the Rare Book and Special Collections Division, visit the Library's online catalog at **catalog.loc.gov** and type in, as a subject, United States-History-World War I.

SCIENCE, TECHNOLOGY & BUSINESS (ST&B)

www.loc.gov/rr/scitech/

The major repository of technical reports at the Library of Congress is the Technical Reports and Standards (TRS) unit in this division. Along with the millions of government-issued documents, TRS also houses a large number of technical reports distributed by foreign governments, universities, and research institutes, as well as a number of major international organizations. TRS also has historical U.S. Federal and Military Specifications on microfilm.

The L'Aerophile Collection in the technical reports unit of ST&B contains primary source material covering the U.S. effort during World War I. In the collection are newspapers, photographs, blueprints, and typed manuscripts focusing on many aspects of aeronautics, including issues of *Plane News*, a newspaper printed in France during the war by the American Expeditionary Forces; a manuscript of the history of the Ninety-sixth Bomb Squadron; photographs of naval aviation along with reports about aviator activities; blueprints of planes and diagrams for air tactics; and a variety of items about air force pioneer Henry H. ("Hap") Arnold. See **www.loc.gov/rr/scitech/trs/trslaerophile.html**.

SERIAL AND GOVERNMENT PUBLICATIONS DIVISION (S&GP)

www.loc.gov/rr/news/

The division's newspaper collection, one of the largest and most comprehensive in the world, includes thousands of World War I era newspapers from the United States and other nations. Issues may be available on microfilm or original paper either in bound volumes or as loose issues. The division also provides free electronic access to tens of thousands of other U.S. newspaper pages, 1914–1922. Highlights of the division's collection are newspaper rotogravure sections from both the *New York Times* (1914–1919) and the *New York Tribune* (1916–1919); *The War of the Nations: Portfolio in Rotogravure Etchings* (1919); the *Stars and Stripes* military newspaper (1918–1919); and the *Chronicling America: Historic American Newspapers* website, all accessible digitally at **www. loc.gov/newspapers/collections/?st=gallery& sb=title_s**. For researchers with particular needs, the rotogravures are held in original paper, and the *Stars and Stripes* is in microfilm and bound facsimile editions.

An additional valuable resource is four hundred volumes (eighty thousand pages) of newspaper clippings in *World War History: Daily Records and Comments as Appeared in American and Foreign Newspapers, 1914–1926*. Compiled after the war under the direction of Otto Spengler, owner of a clipping service, for the New-York Historical Society, the set provides chronological access to an unparalleled breadth and depth of newspaper coverage of the war.

VETERANS HISTORY PROJECT (VHP)

www.loc.gov/vets

The Veterans History Project holdings include nearly four hundred collections documenting the firsthand experiences of individual World War I veterans. Their stories are conveyed through personal correspondence, diaries, memoirs, and photographs donated by veterans and their families, and by oral history interviews conducted by volunteer interviewers. VHP collections offer a glimpse into the day-to-day lives of enlisted men and officers, and document a wide variety of experiences, from vivid accounts of frontline combat to the reflections of rear echelon troops. The World War I holdings are continuously expanding as individuals across the country donate treasured pieces of their family history to the Library of Congress, so that future generations may hear directly from veterans and better understand the realities of war.

More than one hundred collections have been fully digitized and are available via the VHP's online database at **memory. loc.gov/diglib/vhp/html/search/search.html**. Selected collections have been featured in installments of VHP's *Experiencing War* series: "World War I: The Great War" **www.loc.gov/vets/stories/ex-war-wwi.html**, and "World War I Remembered: 100 Years Later" **www.loc.gov/vets/stories/ex-war-wwi-100.html**.

NOTES

PROLOGUE

Epigraphs: Woodrow Wilson, *A Crossroads of Freedom: The 1912 Campaign Speeches of Woodrow Wilson.* John Wills Davidson, ed. (New Haven: Yale University Press, 1956), 16–18. Thomas Edison quoted in David Traxel, *Crusader Nation: The United States in Peace and the Great War, 1898–1920* (New York: Vintage Books, 2007), 3.

1 Frederick Jackson Turner, "The Significance of the Frontier in American History," available online at www.learner.org/workshops/primarysources/corporations/docs/turner2.html.

2 Nell Irvin Painter, *Standing at Armageddon: The United States, 1877–1919* (New York: W. W. Norton & Company, 2008), 263.

3 Ibid.

4 Edward Robb Ellis, *Echoes of Distant Thunder: Life in the United States, 1914–1918* (New York: Kodansha International, 1996), 40. Ellis states that in 1914, "Nearly one-third of the population [of 98,646,491] was foreign-born, and of this third 15,000,000 were *European*-born immigrants, including 3,000,000 adults unable to speak English and 9,000,000 who read foreign-language papers exclusively" (emphasis in original).

5 Gorton Carruth, *Encyclopedia of American Facts and Dates*, 8th ed. (New York: Harper & Row, 1987), 425. See also Washington Irving Chambers Papers, Manuscript Division, Library of Congress.

6 Tony Jannus, "An Enduring Legacy of Aviation," www.tonyjannusaward.com/history/. Russell Naughton, "The Pioneers: Katherine (1891–1977) and Marjorie (1896–1975) Stinson," www.ctie.monash.edu.au/hargrave/stinson_bio.html (accessed Aug. 9, 2014).

7 "1912 Cadillac Model 30 News, Pictures, Specifications, and Information," at www.conceptcarz.com/vehicle/z13393/Cadillac-Model-30.aspx. "1910–1919," at American Cultural History—The Twentieth Century website, http://kclibrary.lonestar.edu/decade10.html (median income for the decade) (accessed June 29, 2014).

8 Reduction of Model T price noted at Eyewitness to History website, www.eyewitnesstohistory.com/ford.htm. Traxel, *Crusader Nation*, 198–200. "Model T Ford—the Freedom Machine," online at www.thenewamerican.com/culture/history/item/12226-model-t-ford-%E2%80%94-the-freedom-machine (accessories for the Model T) (accessed June 29, 2014).

9 PBS, *American Experience*, "The Workers," www.pbs.org/wgbh/americanexperience/features/general-article/panama-workers/; PBS, *American Experience*, "Timeline: Creating the Canal," www.pbs.org/wgbh/americanexperience/features/timeline/panama/2/ (both accessed Aug. 2, 2014).

10 Quoted in Charles Emmerson, *1913: In Search of the World Before the Great War* (New York: PublicAffairs, 2013), ix. Francis Wrigley Hirst, *The Six Panics and Other Essays* (London: Methuen & Co., Ltd., 1913), 232.

11 "Titanic and Other White Star Line Ships: The Owner, the Chairman, the Captain, and the Officers," www.titanic-whitestarships.com/Owners2.htm (accessed Aug. 9, 2012). Nancy C. Unger, *Fighting Bob La Follette, the Righteous Reformer* (Madison: Wisconsin State Historical Press, 2008), 221. The shipping trust Morgan headed was the International Mercantile Marine Company.

12 On the U.S. investigation, see "Senate Committee Taking Testimony on Causes of Titanic Disaster" (picture showing senators with Ismay and other White Star officials), the *Day Book* (Chicago), April 26, 1912; "Titanic Investigation Resumed at Washington," *Bryan (TX) Daily Eagle and Pilot*, April 22, 1912; U.S. Capitol Visitor Center, "The Power of Investigation: the Titanic Disaster 1912," www.visitthecapitol.gov/exhibition-hall/timeline?c=74&y=69 (accessed Aug. 16, 2014); Titanic

Inquiry Project, www.titanicinquiry.org/ (accessed Aug. 16, 2014).

13 Kristen Iversen, *Molly Brown: Unraveling the Myth* (Boulder, CO: Johnson Books, 1999), 173 (statement to reporter), 174. "Mrs. Margaret Brown (Molly Brown) (née Tobin), *Encyclopedia Titanica*, www.encyclopedia-titanica.org/titanic-survivor/molly-brown.html (accessed Sept. 18, 2014).

14 United States Senate, "Titanic Disaster Hearings: The Official Transcript of the 1912 Senate Investigation," www.senate.gov/reference/reference_item/titanic.htm (accessed October 2014).

15 "Liner Sinks in 14 Minutes," *New York Times*, May 30, 1912. For more information on the demise of the *Empress of Ireland* see Robert D. Ballard and Rick Archbold, *Lost Liners* (New York and Toronto: Hyperion/Madison Press, 1997), 106–15.

16 Steven Biel, "Heroism of Men on Titanic Used as Barb Against the Women's Suffrage Movement," *Denver Post* blog, April 13, 2012, http://blogs.denverpost.com/titanic/2012/04/13/heroism-men-board-titanic-barb-womens-suffrage-movement/ (accessed October 2013). Biel quotes a letter written by W. C. Rickster and published by the *St. Louis Post-Dispatch*: "When a woman talks woman's rights, she [should] be answered with the word Titanic—just Titanic." See also Unger, *Fighting Bob La Follette*, 221–22 (concern over steerage victims).

17 "Lax Inspection of Meat Worse Than Loss of a Titanic," *Washington Times*, May 11, 1912, final edition, 1.

18 For a comprehensive preview of the NAACP meeting, see "The Meeting of the National Association for the Advancement of Colored People," *Broad Ax* (Chicago), April 27, 1912.

19 Noble Lee Sissle, "Memoirs of 'Jim' Europe," carbon copy of a typescript, Manuscript Division, Library of Congress, 21. See also Dan Morgenstern, "Music: The Night Ragtime Came to Carnegie Hall," *New York Times*, July 9, 1989.

20 Carruth, *Encyclopedia of American Facts and Dates*, 423–25.

21 On Europe's May 2, 1912, concert and his later recording contract see Sissle, "Memoirs of 'Jim' Europe"; "History of the Hall—1912, James Reese Europe and His Clef Club Orchestra Perform," www.carnegiehall.org/History/Timeline/Timeline.aspx?id=4294968751; Christopher Tremewan Martin, "Castles and Europe: Race Relations in Ragtime," master's thesis, Florida State University, 2005, available at http://diginole.lib.fsu.edu/islandora/object/fsu:180970/datastream/PDF/view; Greg Miner, "James Reese Europe and the Clef Club Orchestra," at Harpguitars website, www.harpguitars.net/players/europe,public.htm.

22 Library of Congress, "Emile Berliner," at American Memory website, http://memory.loc.gov/ammem/berlhtml/berlgramo.html.

23 According to Irving L. Allen, *City in Slang: New York Life and Popular Speech* (New York: Oxford University Press, 1993), "Another slang term in use by 1910 was *flickers*. The projected images of the silents were said to flicker on the screen; the variant *flicks* was used briefly in the camp speech of the 1950s and 1960s" (109). Emmerson, 1913, 201. Museum of the Moving Image, "Making Movies in New York: 1912," www.movingimage.us/films/2012/11/10/detail/making-movies-in-new-york-1912/.

24 Wendi A. Maloney, "1912 Amendment Adds Movies to Copyright Law," *Copyright Notices*, March 2012, 16.

25 Carruth, *Encyclopedia of American Facts and Dates*, 424.

26 Ellis, *Echoes of Distant Thunder*, 124–25.

27 See relevant portions in "History of Publishing," *Encyclopedia Britannica* online, www.britannica.com/EBchecked/topic/482597/history-of-publishing/28597/Book-publishing.

28 George Perkins, Barbara Perkins, and Phillip Leininger, eds., *Benét's Reader's Encyclopedia of American Literature* (New York: HarperCollins Publishers, 1991), 433, 653–54, 664–72, 678–75, 798. John Whiteclay Chambers II, *The Tyranny of Change: America in the Progressive Era 1890–1920* (New Brunswick, NJ: Rutgers University Press, 2000), 114.

29 The name derives from Chautauqua County, New York, the location of the first, nontraveling program. See Charlotte M. Canning, *The Most American Thing in America: Circuit Chautauqua as Performance* (Iowa City: University of Iowa Press, 2005).

30 Roosevelt quoted in "Traveling Culture: Circuit Chautauqua in the Twentieth Century; What Was Chautauqua?" at University of Iowa Libraries website, www.lib.uiowa.edu/sc/tc/.

31 Canning, *The Most American Thing in America*, 158.

32 William Jennings Bryan, *The Value of an Ideal* (New York: Funk & Wagnalls Company, 1914), 30–31.

33 Canning, *The Most American Thing in America*, 165–66; full text of "Acres of Diamonds" at the Temple University website, www.temple.edu/about/history/acres-diamonds.

34 Jyotsna Sreenivasan, ed., *Poverty and the Government in America: A Historical Encyclopedia* (Santa Barbara, CA: ABC-CLIO, 2009), 1: 210. James L. Huston, *Securing the Fruits of Labor: The American Concept of Wealth Distribution, 1765–1900* (Baton Rouge: Louisiana State University Press, 1998), 84.

35 The provenance of this widely quoted Brandeis statement is discussed in depth by Peter Scott Campbell, "Democracy v. Concentrated Wealth: In Search of a Louis D. Brandeis Quote," online at www.greenbag.org/v16n3/v16n3_articles_campbell.pdf (accessed Aug. 21, 2014). The statement is also quoted on the Brandeis University website, http://www.brandeis.edu/legacyfund/bio.html, and in Irving Dilliard, ed., *Mr. Justice Brandeis, Great American* (St. Louis, MO: The Modern View Press, 1941), 42.

36 "The 17th Amendment to the U.S. Constitution: Direct Election of U.S. Senators (1913)," at Our Documents website, www.ourdocuments.gov/doc.php?flash=true&doc=58 (accessed Aug. 17, 2014).

37 For a brief description of one of the United States' worst industrial accidents, see Alan Brinkley, *The Unfinished Nation: A Concise History of the American People*, 2nd ed. (New York: Alfred A Knopf, 1997), who notes that the workers "had been trapped inside the burning building because management had locked the emergency exits to prevent malingering" (600–601).

38 Quoted in Dee Garrison, *Mary Heaton Vorse: The Life of an American Insurgent* (Philadelphia: Temple University Press, 1989), 53.

39 Carruth, *Encyclopedia of American Facts and Dates*, 427. Steve Golin, "The Silk Strike of 1913," http://patersongreatfalls.org/silkstrike.html (accessed Oct. 7, 2014). John Luskin, *Lippmann, Liberty, and the Press* (Tuscaloosa: University of Alabama Press, 1972), 21.

40 For information on the Colorado strike and the Ludlow massacre and its aftermath, see Ellis, *Echoes of a Distant Thunder*, 62–90. Alan Dawley, *Changing the World: American Progressives in War and Revolution* (Princeton, NJ: Princeton University Press, 2003), 27–28. PBS, *The American Experience*, "Primary Resources: The Ludlow Massacre," www.pbs.org/wgbh/americanexperience/features/primary-resources/rockefellers-ludlow/ (accessed October 2013).

41 "Report of the Commission on Industrial Relations," *Monthly Review of the U.S. Bureau of Labor Statistics* 1, no. 5 (November 1915): 48–49. Mrs. J. Borden [Florence] Harriman, *From Pinafores to Politics* (New York: Henry Holt & Company, 1923), 133.

42 Harriman, *From Pinafores to Politics*, 95.

43 On the New Jersey reforms, see "American President—A Reference Resource: Woodrow Wilson, Front Page," at University of Virginia, Miller Center website, http://millercenter.org/president/wilson/essays/biography/1 (accessed Aug. 21, 2014); H. W. Brands, *Woodrow Wilson* (New York: Times Books/Henry Holt & Company, 2003), 17 (New Jersey speech), 19.

44 A number of excellent sources deal with the campaign to secure Wilson's nomination. See John Milton Cooper, Jr., *Woodrow Wilson: A Biography* (New York: Alfred A. Knopf, 2009), chapter 7 (quote by Ellen Wilson, 142), and Robert Carl Scott, "William McCombs and the 1912 Democratic Presidential Nomination of Woodrow Wilson, *Arkansas Historical Quarterly* 44, no. 3 (Autumn 1985): 246–59.

45 Nick Salvatore, *Eugene V. Debs: Citizen and Socialist*, 2nd ed. (Urbana: University of Illinois Press, 2007), 242, 254–56.

46 Theodore Roosevelt, "Case Against the Reactionaries," www.theodore-roosevelt.com/images/research/speeches/trreactionairies.pdf (accessed Sept. 14, 2014). See also Painter, *Standing at Armageddon*, 267–68.

47 Traxel, *Crusader Nation*, 29.

48 Ibid. Harriman, *From Pinafores to Politics*, 99–101.

49 "Hail New Party in Fervent Song," *New York Times*, August 6, 1912. For descriptions of the Progressive convention, see James Chace, *1912* (New York: Simon & Schuster, 2004), 161–68; Traxel, *Crusader Nation*, 33–35; Painter, *Standing at Armageddon*, 268–69.

50 Cooper, *Woodrow Wilson: A Biography*, 156–57.

51 Harriman, *From Pinafores to Politics*, 110.

52 Woodrow Wilson, *A Crossroads of Freedom*, 16–18.

53 Theodore Roosevelt, "Confession of Faith," at TeachingAmericanHistory.org, http://teachingamericanhistory.org/library/document/confession-of-faith/ (accessed Sept. 23, 2014).

54 Information provided in a personal communication from Dr. Dennis M. Conrad, historian, Naval History and Heritage Command, June 30, 2014.

55 Jack McCallum, *Leonard Wood: Rough Rider, Surgeon, Architect of American Imperialism* (New York: New York University Press, 2006), 236, 278.

56 Ibid., 243–45, 278; Jack C. Lane, *Armed Progressive: General Leonard Wood* (Lincoln: University of Nebraska Press, 2009), 169–70. As noted at "Monroe Doctrine (1823), Our Documents," www.ourdocuments.gov/doc.php?flash=true&doc=23, "The Monroe Doctrine was articulated in President James Monroe's seventh annual message to Congress on December 2, 1823. The European powers, according to Monroe, were obligated to respect the Western Hemisphere as the United States' sphere of interest."

57 On German and Japanese ambitions in Mexico, see Barbara W. Tuchman, *The Zimmermann Telegram* (New York: The Macmillan Company, 1966), 27–38, and McCallum, *Leonard Wood*, 243. On Japanese-American tensions, see "Japan War Scare of 1906–1907," at GlobalSecurity.org, www.globalsecurity.org/military/ops/japan1906.htm (accessed Sept. 29, 1914).

58 McCallum, *Leonard Wood*, 256.

59 Cooper, *Woodrow Wilson*, 163.

60 Chace, *1912*, 230–31; Traxel, *Crusader Nation*, 37; "Would-be Assassin Is John Schrank, Once Saloon-Keeper Here," *New York Times*, October 15, 1912.

61 Chace, *1912*, 234–35; Traxel, *Crusader Nation*, 38.

62 See, e.g., "The Balkan Powers Opposed to Turkey," *Commoner* (Lincoln, NE), November 8, 1912, 6 (the *Commoner* was published by William Jennings Bryan). "Men and Nations in the Balkan Mixup," *Evening Times* (Grand Fords, ND), October 21, 1912. "The Balkan War Cloud Looms up Once More," Willmar (MN) *Tribune*, October 16, 1912. "The Balkan Trouble," *Yorkville (SC) Enquirer*, October 18, 1912. "Balkan Strife Battle of Two Civilizations, Historian Says," *Washington (D.C.) Herald*, October 20, 1912. "Defenses of Islam's Bulwark on Plains of Thrace Crumble: Fighting Bulgarians Take More Outposts of Adrianople," *San Francisco Call*, October 27, 1912.

63 Margaret MacMillan, *The War That Ended Peace: The Road to 1914* (New York: Random House, 2013), notes the *Times*'s (London) November 22, 1912, opinion that "the conflict in the Near East is approaching the stage when European Governments will need perspicacity and prudence if it is to be prevented from becoming a European conflict" (488–89) and writes, "The great powers . . . were both shocked and worried by the dramatic changes in the Balkans" (476–77).

64 On voting results, see *Presidential Campaign Posters from the Library of Congress* (Philadelphia: Quirk Books), 1912; "Election of 1912," The American Presidency Project, www.presidency.ucsb.edu/showelection.php?year=1912; Eric Foner, *Give Me Liberty! An American History*, 2nd ed. (New York: W. W. Norton & Company, 2008), 712-713; Candice Millard, *The River of Doubt: Theodore Roosevelt's Darkest Journey* (New York: Doubleday, 2005), notes the enmity of many Republicans toward Roosevelt,

as expressed in a *Philadelphia Inquirer* editorial: "By giving vent to his insatiate ambition, he [Roosevelt] has elevated the democratic party to the control of the nation" (13).

65 United States Congress, House Committee on Banking and Currency, *Report of the Committee Appointed Pursuant to House Resolutions 429 and 504 to Investigate the Concentration of Control of Money and Credit* (Washington, D.C.: Government Printing Office, 1913), 129, 161. Ellis, *Echoes of Distant Thunder*, 45–46. Painter, *Standing at Armageddon*, 273–74.

66 "Constitution of the United States, Amendments 11–17," National Archives and Records Administration, www.archives.gov/exhibits/charters/constitution_amendments_11-27.html.

67 McCallum, *Leonard Wood*, 257–58; "Orozco, Pascual, Jr.," at Texas Historical Association website, www.tshaonline.org/handbook/online/articles/for08 (accessed Oct. 6, 2014).

68 Ellis, *Echoes of Distant Thunder*, 15–16. Sheridan Harvey, Janice E. Ruth, Barbara Orbach Natanson, Sara Day, and Evelyn Sinclair, eds., *American Women: A Library of Congress Guide for the Study of Women's History and Culture in the United States* (Washington, D.C.: Library of Congress, 2001), 33–34.

69 "Official Program: Woman Suffrage Procession, Washington, D.C., March 3, 1913," page 2, Rare Book and Special Collections Division, Library of Congress. The Library's Manuscript Division also holds a copy of the official program. The program cover can be viewed at http://cdn.loc.gov/service/pnp/ppmsca/12500/12512r.jpg.

70 Harvey et al., *American Women*, 32–33. Estimates of the number of marchers range, in various sources, from five thousand to ten thousand.

71 January 20 became the official date for Inauguration Day with ratification of the Twentieth Amendment to the U.S. Constitution in 1933.

72 Woodrow Wilson, "First Inaugural Address, Tuesday, March 4, 1913," at Yale Law School, Avalon Project website, http://avalon.law.yale.edu/20th_century/wilson1.asp.

73 Brinkley, *The Unfinished Nation*, 621.

74 Woodrow Wilson, "Address to a Joint Session of Congress on Trusts and Monopolies, January 20, 1914," American Presidency Project, www.presidency.ucsb.edu/ws/index.php?pid=65374 (accessed October 2014).

75 Cooper, *Woodrow Wilson*, 229. Ellis, *Echoes of a Distant Thunder*, 52–53 (Lodge quote).

76 Wilson made this specific assurance in his letter of October 21, 1912, to Bishop Alexander Walters of the African Methodist Episcopal Zion Church, who in 1912 headed the National Colored Democratic League: "I want to assure them [African Americans] through you that should I become President of the United States they may count upon me for absolute fair dealing and for everything by which I could assist in advancing the interest of their race in the United States." Quoted in Cooper, *Woodrow Wilson*, 170–71 (citing Arthur S. Link, ed., *Papers of Woodrow Wilson*, 69 vols. [Princeton, NJ: Princeton University Press, 1966–1983], 25: 449).

77 Eric S. Yellin, *Racism in the Nation's Service: Government Workers and the Color Line in Woodrow Wilson's America* (Chapel Hill: University of North Carolina Press, 2013), 143–45. Cooper, *Woodrow Wilson*, 170–71. Regarding the November 1914 meeting between Wilson and a delegation for which Trotter also served as spokesman, see, "President Resents Negro's Criticism," *New York Times*, November 13, 1914.

78 Carruth, *Encyclopedia of American Facts and Dates*, 426–29. "Lincoln Memorial Building Statistics," at National Park Service website, http://www.nps.gov/linc/historyculture/lincoln-memorial-building-statistics.htm.

79 John Garry Clifford, *The Citizen Soldiers: The Plattsburg Training Camp Movement, 1913–1920* (Lexington: University Press of Kentucky, 1972), 11–13.

80 Jack C. Lane, *Armed Progressive*, 181.

81 Cooper, *Woodrow Wilson*, notes that the waters were most deeply troubled in Japan, where "public indignation exploded . . . ultimately causing the cabinet there to

fall" (211–12; quote on 212). Carruth, *Encyclopedia of American Facts and Dates*, 426.

82 George C. Herring, *From Colony to Superpower: U.S. Foreign Relations Since 1776* (New York: Oxford University Press, 2008), 391.

83 Cooper, *Woodrow Wilson*, 242.

84 Herring, *From Colony to Superpower*, 394. Martin Donell Kohout, "Victoriano Huerta," at Texas State Historical Association website, www.tshaonline.org/handbook/online/articles/fhu81 (accessed October 2014). Tuchman, *Zimmermann Telegram*, 47. McCallum, *Leonard Wood*, 260.

85 Alan Dawley, *Changing the World: American Progressives in War and Revolution* (Princeton, NJ: Princeton University Press, 2003), 19–20. John Keegan, *The First World War* (New York: Vintage Books, 2000), 10–12. Norman Angell, *The Great Illusion: A Study of the Relation of Military Power in Nations to Their Economic and Social Advantage* (New York and London: G. P. Putnam's Sons, 1910). There were many subsequent editions of the book, which was translated into more than twenty languages.

86 Michael Kazin, *A Godly Hero: The Life of William Jennings Bryan* (New York: Anchor Books/Random House, 2006), 218.

87 Traxel, *Crusader Nation*, 84.

88 The Peace Palace, and the Carnegie Library therein, still exists. In addition to the Permanent Court of Arbitration, the Peace Palace now houses the International Court of Justice (known before World War II as the Permanent Court of International Justice) and the Hague Academy of International Law. See "A Brief History of the Peace Palace," at www.peacepalacelibrary.nl/100years/peacepalace/ (accessed May 26, 2014).

89 On the buildup to war, see MacMillan, *The War That Ended Peace*, especially chapter 17, "Preparing for War or Peace," where the author notes, "War increasingly came to be seen as a way out of Russia's dilemma, a way to bring Russian society together" (508), and "What was dangerous was that the [German] military were increasingly accepting war as inevitable, even desirable" (510).

90 Edward Mandell House, *The Intimate Papers of Colonel House*, ed. Charles Seymour, 4 volumes (Boston: Houghton Mifflin Company, 1926), 1: 249.

91 Mildred Aldrich, *A Hilltop on the Marne* (Boston: Houghton Mifflin Company, 1915), 37–38.

92 Harriman, *From Pinafores to Politics*, 150. Walter Millis, *Road to War: America 1914–1917* (Boston: Houghton Mifflin Company, 1935), 31.

93 Mira Wilkins, *The History of Foreign Investment in the United States, 1914–1945* (Cambridge, MA: Harvard University Press, 2004), 2–3, 9–10.

94 MacMillan, *The War That Ended Peace*, 594, 596. Arthur S. Link, *Wilson: The Struggle for Neutrality*, [vol. 3 of a 5-volume biography] (Princeton: Princeton University Press), 3: (citing the *New York Times*, July 28, 1914).

95 Clifford, *The Citizen Soldiers*, 31 (citing Walter Lord, *The Good Years: From 1900 to the First World War* [New York: Harper & Brothers, 1960], 315).

96 MacMillan. *The War That Ended Peace*, 604. Harriman, *From Pinafores to Politics*, 157.

97 Wilkins, *The History of Foreign Investment in the United States, 1914–1945*, 2–3, 9–10. MacMillan, *The War That Ended Peace*, 614–15.

98 Harriman, *From Pinafores to Politics*, 157.

CHAPTER 1

Epigraphs: Woodrow Wilson, "Second Annual Message, December 8, 1914," American Presidency Project, www.presidency.ucsb.edu/ws/?pid=29555 (accessed December 2014). General Leonard Wood quoted in John Patrick Finnegan, *Against the Specter of a Dragon: The Campaign for American Military Preparedness, 1914–1917* (Westport, CT: Greenwood Press, 1974), 72 (citing General Leonard Wood, letter to Theodore Roosevelt, September 17, 1915, Theodore Roosevelt Papers, Incoming Correspondence, Box 289, Manuscript Division, Library of Congress).

1 "And the war came" is a phrase used most notably by Abraham Lincoln in his Second Inaugural Address, March 4, 1865; see "Second Inaugural Address of

Abraham Lincoln," at Yale Law School website, http://avalon.law.yale.edu/19th_century/lincoln2.asp.

2   Quoted in Barbara Tuchman, *August 1914* (1962; repr., London: Macmillan, 1980), 123 (citing Princess Evelyn Blücher, *An English Wife in Berlin* [London: Constable, 1920], 137).

3   Frank P. Chambers, *The War Behind the War: A History of the Political and Civilian Fronts* (New York: Arno Press, 1972), 7.

4   Margaret MacMillan, *The War That Ended Peace: The Road to 1914* (New York: Random House, 2013), 619 (Poincaré's assurances). Mildred Aldrich, *A Hilltop on the Marne* (Boston: Houghton Mifflin Company, 1915), 49.

5   Edith Wharton, *Fighting France: From Dunkerque to Belfort* (New York: Charles Scribner's Sons, 1915), 14–15.

6   Quoted in Naomi W. Cohen, *A Dual Heritage: The Public Career of Oscar S. Straus* (Philadelphia: The Jewish Publication Society of America, 1969), 235 (citing Straus letter to Walter Hines Page, August 2, 1914, the Walter Hines Page Papers, Houghton Library, Harvard College Library, Harvard University).

7   "Treaty of Alliance between Germany and Turkey, 2 August, 1914," at Yale Law School, Avalon Project website, http://avalon.law.yale.edu/20th_century/turkgerm.asp (accessed April 2015).

8   MacMillan, *The War That Ended Peace*, 625.

9   The unification of the various German states into the nation of Germany took place in 1871.

10 The Schlieffen Plan was named for its principal developer, Field Marshal Alfred von Schlieffen (1833–1913). The military historian John Keegan, in *The First World War* (New York: Vintage Books/Random House, 2000), called it "the most important government document written in any country in the first decade of the twentieth century" (28). For a detailed discussion of the plan, see Keegan, 28-37.

11 "Statement by Sir Edward Grey" (to the House of Commons), August 3, 1914, full text at http://hansard.millbanksystems.com/commons/1914/aug/03/

statement-by-sir-edward-grey (accessed December 2014).

12 Ibid.

13 Quoted in MacMillan, *The War That Ended Peace*, 625 (citing Edward Grey, *Twenty-five Years, 1892–1916* [London: Hodder and Stoughton, 1925] 2:20).

14 Allan Nevins, ed., *The Letters and Journal of Brand Whitlock*, 2 vols. (New York: Appleton-Century Company, 1936), 2: 3. MacMillan, *The War That Ended Peace*, 630 (citing Ross Gregory, *Walter Hines Page: Ambassador to the Court of St. James's* [Lexington: University Press of Kentucky, 1970], 51–52).

15 George H. Nash, *The Life of Herbert Hoover: The Humanitarian, 1914–1917* [vol. 2 of 3-vol. biography] (New York: W. W. Norton & Company, 1988), 4–10. *New York Evening Telegram*, August 5, 1914, Otto Spengler (compiler), *World War History: Daily Records and Comments as Appeared in American and Foreign Newspapers, 1914–1926*, 400 vols. (New York: Argus Press Clipping Bureau, 1928[?]), 3: 5 (held at the Library of Congress). Mrs. J. Borden [Florence] Harriman, *From Pinafores to Politics* (New York: Henry Holt & Company, 1923), 162–63.

16 Robert D. Ward, "The Origin and Activities of the National Security League, 1914–1919," *The Mississippi Valley Historical Review* 47, no. 1 (June 1960): 51–52. John C. Edwards, *Patriots in Pinstripe: Men of the National Security League* (Washington, D.C.: University Press of America, 1982), 3.

17 MacMillan, *The War That Ended Peace*, 627.

18 "Multitudes Cheer at Bulletin Boards," *New York Times*, August 5, 1914.

19 Walter Millis, *The Road to War: America 1914–1917* (1935; repr., New York: Howard Fertig, 1970), 41.

20 Marie Louise Degen, *The History of the Woman's Peace Party* (New York: Burt Franklin Reprints, 1974), 22 (citing Jane Addams, *The Second Twenty Years at Hull House* [New York: The Macmillan Company, 1930], 117–19). "Kronprinzessin Cecilie," at www.greatships.net/kronprinzessincecilie.html (accessed March 2015). Jeffrey J. Safford, *Wilsonian Maritime Diplomacy*,

1913–1921 (New Brunswick, NJ: Rutgers University Press, 1978), 43.

21 John Milton Cooper, *Woodrow Wilson: A Biography* (New York: Alfred A. Knopf, 2009), 260–63.

22 Chambers, *The War Behind the War*, 191. David Traxel, *Crusader Nation: The United States in Peace and the Great War, 1898–1920* (New York: Alfred A Knopf, 2006), 123–24. Barbara Tuchman, *The Guns of August* (Toronto: Bantam Books, 1976), 201, 204.

23 United States Relief Commission in Europe, *Report on Operations of United States Relief Commission in Europe* (Washington, D.C.: U.S. Government Printing Office, 1914), 2–3.

24 Ibid., 4–7, 36–37. Nash, *Life of Herbert Hoover: The Humanitarian*, 15.

25 Harriman, *From Pinafores to Politics*, 163.

26 Sean Dennis Cashman, *America in the Age of the Titans: The Progressive Era and World War I* (New York: New York University Press, 1988), 10–11.

27 Millis, *The Road to War*, 53.

28 Mira Wilkins, *The History of Foreign Investment in the United States, 1914–1945* (Cambridge, MA: Harvard University Press, 2004), 15–16 (Herman Metz). M. Ryan Floyd, *Abandoning American Neutrality: Woodrow Wilson and the Beginning of the Great War, August 1914–December 1915* (London: Palgrave Macmillan, 2013), 57–58 (Goodyear).

29 Ethel C. Phillips, "American Participation in Belligerent Commercial Controls 1914–1917," *American Journal of International Law* 27, no. 4 (October 1933): 675–93.

30 Spengler, *World War History*, 3: 97 (*Philadelphia North American*), 3:97 (*New York American*). Also see Justus D. Doenecke, *Nothing Less Than War: A New History of America's Entry into World War I* (Lexington: University Press of Kentucky, 2011), 66–67.

31 Quoted in Safford, *Wilsonian Maritime Diplomacy*, 38 (citing *Literary Digest*, August 15, 1914, 256, and *New York American*, August 8, 1914).

32 Ibid., 39–40.

33 Ibid., 41. Wilkins, *History of Foreign Investment in the United States*, 15.

34 Samuel McCune Lindsay, "Purpose and Scope of War Risk Insurance," *Annals of the American Academy of Political and Social Sciences* 79 (September 1918): 52–68.

35 Wilkins, *History of Foreign Investment in the United States*, 14, 643n.68. McAdoo to Wilson, August 16, 1914, William Gibbs McAdoo Papers, Library of Congress. Also see Safford, *Wilsonian Maritime Diplomacy*, 44–45, 47.

36 Safford, *Wilsonian Maritime Diplomacy*, 45–46. Woodrow Wilson, "Proclamation of Neutrality by the President of the United States of America," *American Journal of International Law* 9, no. 1, Supplement: Official Documents (January 1915): 110–14. The article notes that, in addition to the initial proclamation, issued August 4, 1914, regarding the declarations of war "between Austria-Hungary and Servia [sic] and between Germany and Russia and between Germany and France," the administration issued "identical proclamations . . . for the following belligerents: Germany and Great Britain, signed August 5, 1914; Austria-Hungary and Russia, signed August 7, 1914; Great Britain and Austria-Hungary, signed August 13, 1914; France and Austria-Hungary, signed August 14, 1914, Belgium and Germany, signed August 18, 1914; Japan and Germany, signed August 24, 1914; Japan and Austria-Hungary, signed August 27, 1914; Belgium and Austria-Hungary, signed September 1, 1914." David M. Kennedy, *Over Here: The First World War and American Society* (Oxford: Oxford University Press, 1980), 303–4 (Jusserand quote, citing *Foreign Relations of the United States*, Supplement, 1914, 492). Arthur S. Link, *Wilson: The Struggle for Neutrality, 1914–1915* [vol. 3 of 5-vol. biography] (Princeton, NJ: Princeton University Press, 1960), 90n.54 (on Jusserand), 87 (*Chicago Evening Post*).

37 Woodrow Wilson, "Address to a Joint Session of Congress: 'Appeal for Additional revenue,' September 4, 1914," American Presidency Project, www.presidency.ucsb.edu/ws/?pid=65383 (accessed March 2015). Edwin R. A. Seligman, "The War Revenue Act," *Political Science Quarterly* 33, no. 1 (March 1918), 2. See also, *Bender's War Revenue Law 1914: An Act to Increase the internal*

revenue, and for other purposes, Approved October 22, 1914, Annotated . . . (Albany, NY: Matthew Bender & Co, 1914).

38 For immigrant and first-generation population statistics, see M. Ryan Floyd, *Abandoning American Neutrality*, 12; and Traxel, *Crusader Nation*, 139–40. Link, *Wilson: The Struggle for Neutrality*, 62–64, 132–36.

39 Traxel, *Crusader Nation*, 147 (Lansing quote). John Douglas Forbes, *J. P. Morgan, Jr., 1867–1943* (Charlottesville: University Press of Virginia, 1981), 88–89 (commercial agreement).

40 Mary Boyle O'Reilly, "Woman Writer Sees Horrors of Battle," *Seattle Star*, September 23, 1914.

41 Richard Harding Davis, *With the Allies* (New York: Charles Scribner's Sons, 1917), 84–91.

42 Emmet Crozier, *American Reporters on the Western Front, 1914–1918* (New York: Oxford University Press, 1959), 41–42.

43 Link, *Wilson: The Struggle for Neutrality*, 31–32. M. L. Sanders, "Wellington House and British Propaganda During the First World War, *Historical Journal* 18, no. 1 (March 1975): 119–20.

44 *The Case of Belgium in the Present War: An Account of the Violation of the Neutrality of Belgium and of the Laws of War on Belgian Territory* (New York: The Macmillan Company, 1914), vi–vii.

45 Theodore Roosevelt, "The World War: Its Tragedies and Its Lessons," *Outlook*, September 23, 1914, 169–78 (quotes on 169 and 172). Wilson's response was reported in the *Day Book* (Chicago), September 17, 1914. See also Link, *Wilson: The Struggle for Neutrality*, 70–72.

46 Nash, *The Life of Herbert Hoover: The Humanitarian*, 17–18. Brand Whitlock, *Belgium Under the German Occupation: A Personal Narrative*, 2 vols. (London: William Heinemann, 1919), 1: 222.

47 Nash, *The Life of Herbert Hoover: The Humanitarian*, 19–33.

48 Ibid., 36–38. Edward T. Devine, "Belgian Relief Measures," *American Review of Reviews* 50 (July–December 1914): 689–94.

49 Devine, "Belgian Relief Measures," 689–94. William Crowell Edgar, *The Millers' Belgian Relief Movement 1914–15, Conducted by the Northwestern Miller: Final Report of Its Director* (Minneapolis: The Northwestern Miller, 1915), 5–18. *The War from This Side: Editorials from the North American, Philadelphia*, 2 vols. (Philadelphia: J. B. Lippincott Company, 1915), 1: 233–38. J. St. George Joyce, ed., *Story of Philadelphia* (Philadelphia: Rex Printing House, 1919), 311. Rockefeller Foundation Annual Report 1913–1914, online at www.rockefellerfoundation.org/app/uploads/Annual-Report-1913-1914.pdf (accessed February 2015).

50 *The American Women's War Relief Fund: A Record of Its Work, Christmas, 1914* (London: Vacher & Sons, Ltd., 1914), pamphlet, Prints and Photographs Division, Library of Congress. Arlen J. Hansen, *Gentlemen Volunteers: The Story of the American Ambulance Drivers in the Great War, August 1914–September 1918* (New York: Arcade Publishing, 1996), xvii, 21–26.

51 Merle Curti, *American Philanthropy Abroad* (New Brunswick, NJ: Transaction Books, 1988), 228–31. Lindsay Sarah Krasnoff, "The Role of the U.S. Diplomatic Community in France, 1914," Preview Edition, September 15, 2014 (Washington, D.C.: U.S. Department of State: Office of the Historian), online at http://s3.amazonaws.com/static.history.state.gov/wwi/views-from-embassy-paris/Views%20from%20Embassy%20Paris%20WWI.pdf (accessed July 28, 2016). Hansen, *Gentlemen Volunteers*, 4–5. "Ski Ambulance for French," *New York Times*, December 25, 1915. Alan Price, *The End of the Age of Innocence: Edith Wharton and the First World War* (New York: St. Martin's Press, 1996), 28–29, 196n (ski sleighs).

52 Curti, *American Philanthropy Abroad*, 226–27. Edwin W. Morse, *The Vanguard of American Volunteers in the Fighting Lines and in Humanitarian Service, August 1914–April 1917* (New York: Charles Scribner's Sons, 1919), 95–112. Foster Rhea Dulles, *American Red Cross, a History* (New York: Harper & Brothers Publishers, 1950), 132–34.

53 Dwight R. Messimer, *The Baltimore Sabotage Cell: German Agents, American Traitors, and the U-Boat Deutschland*

During World War I (Annapolis, MD: Naval Institute Press, 2015), 16. William Twining, *Karl Llewellyn and the Realist Movement*, 2nd ed. (New York: Cambridge University Press, 2012), 91, 535–43 (quote on 540). Advertisement for a lecture by Karl Nickerson Llewellyn, Yale, 1915, *Oklahoma City Times*, July 19, 1915, 3.

54 Woodrow Wilson, "Message on Neutrality," August 20, 1914, website of University of Virginia, Miller Center, http://millercenter.org/president/wilson/speeches/speech-3791. Morse, *Vanguard of American Volunteers*, 15 (Thaw), 54–55 (Seeger), 83–84 (Starr). "Corporal Eugene Jacques Bullard, First Black American Fighter Pilot," *Air and Space Power Journal*, online at www.airpower. maxwell.af.mil/apjinternational/apj-s/2005/3tri05/chivaletteeng.html (accessed April 2015).

55 Alan Seeger, *Letters and Diary of Alan Seeger* (New York: Charles Scribner's Sons, 1917), 49. Seeger himself did not take part in the Christmas Truce. He had rotated behind the lines. He "spent a unique and agreeable kind of Christmas in Cuiry." "Saturday, January 30, 1915" (news roundup), *Bellman*, January 30, 1915, 135.

56 *The War from This Side*, 1: 233–36. John Callan O'Laughlin to The Honorable Lemuel P. Padgett, draft letter, October 3, 1914, Box 6, "Christmas Ship," John Callan O'Laughlin Papers, Manuscript Division, Library of Congress.

57 John Callan O'Laughlin to President Woodrow Wilson, draft letter, Feb. 1, 1915, Box 6, "Christmas Ship," John Callan O'Laughlin Papers, Manuscript Division, Library of Congress.

58 Ibid.

59 Ibid.

60 Ibid.

61 Finnegan, *Against the Specter of a Dragon*, 22 (Murray quote). Traxel, *Crusader Nation*, 141 (Fifth Avenue march).

62 Degen, *The History of the Woman's Peace Party*, 29–33, 38–42. Thomas J. Knock, *To End All Wars: Woodrow Wilson and the Quest for a New World Order* (New York: Oxford University Press, 1992), 50–51.

63 Finnegan, *Against the Specter of a Dragon*, 24. Mrs. Constance (Lodge) Gardner, *Augustus Peabody Gardner* (Cambridge, MA: privately printed, 1919), 16–17. Link, *Wilson: The Struggle for Neutrality*, 140.

64 Roosevelt was not the only one concerned about a possible German invasion. In 1914, Americans could read a new English translation of a report originally prepared in 1901 for the German General Staff, which included this passage in a section titled "Consideration of Landing Operations against Powers That Can Be Reached Only by Sea": "It must be deemed a possibility that the battle fleet of the United States would not risk an engagement at sea except to avoid a disaster, but would await, in its fortified harbors, a favorable opportunity to strike. It is evident, then, that a naval war against the United States cannot be carried on with success without at the same time inaugurating action on land. Because of the great extensions of the United States it would not be satisfactory for the operation of an invading army to be directed toward conquering the interior of the land. It is almost a certainty, however, that a victorious assault on the Atlantic coast, tying up the importing and exporting business of the whole country, would bring about such an annoying situation that the government would be willing to treat for peace." Freiherr von Edelsheim, *Operations upon the Sea: A Study, Translated from the German* (New York: The Outdoor Press, 1914), 87–88.

65 Finnegan, *Against the Specter of a Dragon*, 24–26. "Japs at the Open Door," *Day Book* (Chicago), February 23, 1915. Bruce A. Elleman, *International Competition in China, 1899–1991: The Rise, Fall, and Eventual Success of the Open Door Policy* (New York: Routledge, 2015), 28. Nigel Hawkins, *The Starvation Blockades* (Barnsley, UK: Leo Cooper, 2002), 34.

66 Finnegan, *Against the Specter of a Dragon*, 25–26. Woodrow Wilson, "Second Annual Message, December 8, 1914," American Presidency Project www.presidency. ucsb.edu/ws/?pid=29555 (accessed April 2015).

67 Finnegan, *Against the Specter of a Dragon*, 58–60. Jack C. Lane, *Armed Progressive: General Leonard Wood* (Lincoln: University of Nebraska Press, 2009), 190. The 1914 American Legion is not to be confused with the veterans

organization established after World War I, which was founded by, among others, Theodore Roosevelt, Jr. See "A Moment in Time" at the American Legion website, www.legion.org/moment-in-time/160099/why-wasnt-teddy-roosevelt-jr-first-national-commander-american-legion.

68   John Carver Edwards, *Patriots in Pinstripe: Men of the National Security League* (Washington, D.C.: University Press of America, 1982), 6–8.

69   Wilson to Hon. Oscar Underwood, House of Representatives, October 17, 1914, Arthur S. Link, ed. *Papers of Woodrow Wilson*, 69 vols. (Princeton: Princeton University Press, 1979), 31: 168-174 (quote, 170-71).

70   Quoted in Vincent P. De Santis, *The Shaping of Modern America: 1877–1920*, 3rd ed. (Wheeling, IL: Harlan Davidson, Inc., 2000), 220.

71   Nancy C. Unger, *Fighting Bob La Follette: The Righteous Reformer* (Madison: Wisconsin Historical Society Press, 2008), 231.

72   Ibid.

73   De Santis, *The Shaping of Modern America*, 220. Daniel Amsterdam, "Down and Out (Again): America's Long Struggle with Mass Unemployment," *Origins: Current Events in Historical Perspective* 5, no. 3 (December 2011), online at http://origins.osu.edu/article/down-and-out-again-america-s-long-struggle-mass-unemployment (accessed March 2015).

74   Harriman, *From Pinafores to Politics*, 165.

75   Ibid., 169–70. "Unit 9: World War I and the Great Migration, 1915–1920," at New Jersey State Library website, www.njstatelib.org/research_library/new_jersey_resources/digital_collection/unit_9_world_war_i/. James N. Gregory, *The Southern Diaspora: How the Great Migrations of Black and White Southerners Transformed America* (Chapel Hill: University of North Carolina Press, 2005), 24.

76   "The Birth of a Nation and Black Protest," at the George Mason University, Roy Rosenzweig Center for History and New Media website, http://chnm.gmu.edu/episodes/the-birth-of-a-nation-and-black-protest/. "NAACP: A Century in the Fight for Freedom, 1909–2009," online

exhibition at Library of Congress website, www.loc.gov/exhibits/naacp/founding-and-early-years.html. "N. Y. Stage Letter," *Day Book* (Chicago), April 26, 1915, praises "that marvelous photo spectacle, 'The Birth of a Nation,'" while noting, "Racial antagonism stirred up by the handling of the south's negro problem in this film has caused a tremendous amount of discussion of the production, and culminated in the throwing of eggs at the screen and a small-sized riot in the theater the other day." Advertisement for *Birth of a Nation* at the Oliver Theater in the *South Bend* (IN) *News-Times*, November 25, 1915, calling the film "D. W. Griffith's Mighty Spectacle . . . Men and women journey Hundreds of miles to see It. Nothing like it ever seen since the dawn of civilization." Advertisement in the *Omaha Sunday Bee*, November 14, 1915, 6-b, declares, in a line of large boldface type, that "The Birth of a Nation" is the "Eighth Wonder of the World." Carruth, *Encyclopedia of American Facts and Dates*, 433. Southern Poverty Law Center, *Ku Klux Klan: A History of Racism and Violence*, 6th ed. (Montgomery, AL: Southern Poverty Law Center, 2011), 17, available online at www.splcenter.org/sites/default/files/downloads/publication/Ku-Klux-Klan-A-History-of-Racism.pdf.

77   Harriman, *From Pinafores to Politics*, 176–85.

78   Keegan, *First World War*, 234–49.

79   Rouben Paul Adalian, "American Diplomatic Correspondence in the Age of Mass Murder: The Armenian Genocide in the U.S. Archives," in Jay Winter, ed., *America and the Armenian Genocide of 1915* (Cambridge, UK: Cambridge University Press, 2003), 150, 155.

80   Suzanne E. Moranian, "The Armenian Genocide and American Missionary Relief Efforts," in Winter, *America and the Armenian Genocide*, 185-213 (see especially 192, 194).

81   Ibid., 185–213 (see especially 192, 194–96). Samantha Power, *"A Problem from Hell": America and the Age of Genocide* (New York: Basic Books, 2013), chapter 1 (especially 6–12). Susan B. Harper, "American Humanitarianism and the Armenian Crucible, 1915–1923," Nineteenth Annual Vardanants Day Armenian Lecture, Library of Congress, May 7, 2015.

82 Jane Addams, Emily G. Balch, and Alice Hamilton, *Women at the Hague: The International Peace Congress of 1915*, with an introduction by Mary Jo Deegan (Amherst, NY: Humanity Books, 2003), especially 40–42, 123–30. Jane Addams, *Peace and Bread in Time of War* (New York: The Macmillan Company, 1922), 12–18.

83 Addams, *Peace and Bread*, 19.

84 Gerard J. Fitzgerald, "Chemical Warfare and Medical Response During World War I," *American Journal of Public Health* 98, no. 4 (April 2008): 611–25, online at www.ncbi.nlm.nih.gov/pmc/articles/PMC2376985/ (accessed May 2015). M. Geoffrey Miller, ed., "Gas-Poisoning," online article excerpted from the first edition of Arthur F. Hurst, *Medical Diseases of the War* (London: 1917), at www.vlib.us/medical/gaswar/chlorine.htm.

85 Hawkins, *The Starvation Blockades*, 59–79 ("Mines!"). For U.S. press coverage of the British declaration, see e.g., "All North Sea Made War Zone," *Chicago Tribune*, November 3, 1914, page 2.

86 Robert W. Tucker, *The Law of War and Neutrality at Sea* (Clark, NJ: Lawbook Exchange, 2006), 285, notes, "The customary law in force at the outbreak of World War I was at once the product of, and designed to regulate, 'in-shore' or 'close' blockades—i.e., blockades maintained by a line of vessels stationed in the immediate vicinity of the blockaded coasts." The introduction of submarines and the increased power and reach of both land-based and naval artillery made such blockades untenable. See also Hawkins, *Starvation Blockades*, 15, 80–83.

87 Link, *Wilson: The Struggle for Neutrality*, 173–74 (U.S. December 26, 1914, protest), 189 (German distribution of food and Grey quote). On German government food action, see also Hawkins, *Starvation Blockades*, 89.

88 Link, *Wilson: The Struggle for Neutrality*, 200–18. Edward Mandell House, *The Intimate Papers of Colonel House*, ed. Charles Seymour, 4 vols (Boston: Houghton Mifflin Company, 1926), 1: 361.

89 Link, *Wilson: The Struggle for Neutrality*, 320 (German declaration), 322–23 (protest to Germany). "Text of American Notes to Germany and England on the Safety of Our Ships and Use of Our Flag," *New York Times*, February 12, 1915.

90 Link, *Wilson: The Struggle for Neutrality*, 331, 336–39, 350. Letter to John C. O'Laughlin from A. von Bruening [?], March 25, 1915, John Callan O'Laughlin Papers, Box 5, Manuscript Division, Library of Congress.

91 Link, *Wilson: Struggle for Neutrality*, 350–53.

92 Ibid., 356–59. Hawkins, *Starvation Blockades*, 105.

93 A brief description of the *Carib* and its demise can be found online at www.wrecksite.eu/wreck.aspx?17350. See also Link, *Wilson: The Struggle for Neutrality*, 356n.26. Link refers to another cargo vessel sunk by mines in February 1915, the *Evelyn*, as American, though it seems to have been of British registry.

94 Link, *Wilson: The Struggle for Neutrality*, 358–59. "The Week in Review," *Journal of Education* 18, no. 14 (April 8, 1915): 379.

95 Letter from A. von Bruening [?] to John C. O'Laughlin, March 25, 1915.

96 Link, *Wilson: The Struggle for Neutrality*, 356–57, 366–67. Hawkins, *Starvation Blockades*, 105. "German Embassy Issues Warning," *New York Times*, May 1, 1915. Erik Larson, *Dead Wake: The Last Crossing of the Lusitania* (New York: Crown Publishers, 2015), 93 (Vanderbilt quote), 300 (number of passengers).

97 Figures for U.S. casualties in various sources range from 123 to 128. This book uses the lower figure, as does Erik Larson's extensively researched 2015 volume, *Dead Wake* (300).

98 Link, *Wilson: The Struggle for Neutrality*, 377 (the *Nation* quote). Edmund Morris, *Colonel Roosevelt* (New York: Random House, 2010), 419.

99 Link, *Wilson: The Struggle for Neutrality*, 377–79. Morris, *Colonel Roosevelt*, 421.

100 House, *Intimate Papers*, 1: 434. Link, *Wilson: The Struggle for Neutrality*, 304–7 (Japan), 379–82 (*Lusitania* reaction), 470 (Mexico). Kendrick A. Clements, *The Presidency of Woodrow Wilson* (Lawrence: University Press of Kansas, 1992), 125 (Wilson to Edith Galt).

101 Woodrow Wilson, "Address to Naturalized Citizens at Convention Hall, Philadelphia, May 10, 1915," *American Presidency Project*, www.presidency.ucsb.edu/ws/?pid=65388.

102 "No Need to Fight, If Right: President Makes Appeal to New Citizens in Philadelphia," *New York Times*, May 11, 1915. Morris, *Colonel Roosevelt*, 420–21.

103 See, e.g., "Atrocities Planned by German Commanders to Inspire Terror: Germans' Belgian Outrages Proved, Says Bryce Report," *New York Tribune*, May 13, 1915; "Bryce Report of German Outrage," *Ogden Standard* (UT), May 12, 1915, and "Bryce Committee's Report on Deliberate Slaughter of Belgian Non-combatants," a three-page summary published in the *New York Times*, May 13, 1915. In subsequent decades, the report was proved to be a mélange of verifiable fact and exaggerated statistics, with an occasional dip into fantasy. See John Horne and Alan Kramer, *German Atrocities, 1914: A History of Denial* (New Haven, CT: Yale University Press, 2001), 232–37, and James Morgan Read, *Atrocity Propaganda, 1914–1919* (New York: Arno Press, 1972), 200–209.

104 See, e.g., "President Wilson's Note to Germany," *New York Times*, May 15, 1915, which reprinted the full text of the lengthy note, and "Note Dignified but Forceful, Wilson Uses No Threats in Representations to Berlin," *Mt. Vernon Democratic Banner* (OH), May 14, 1915. Link, *Wilson: The Struggle for Neutrality*, 410, quotes the *New York World* ("an outlaw who assumes no obligation toward society") as an example of U.S. press reaction.

105 Link, *Wilson: The Struggle for Neutrality*, 389, 417, 421–25, 427–28. Clements, *Presidency of Woodrow Wilson*, 126. Justus D. Doenecke, *Nothing Less Than War: A New History of America's Entry into World War I* (Lexington: University Press of Kentucky, 2011), 82.

106 Finnegan, *Against the Specter of a Dragon*, 64–70. Finnegan notes (65) that the Plattsburg businessmen's camp inspired three others around the nation in the summer of 1915, at Fort Sheridan, Illinois, the Presidio, California, and America Lake, Washington. "Juniors Wire the President," subtitle of "All Look to Wilson, Promising Support," *New York Times*, May 11, 1915.

107 Link, *Wilson: The Struggle for Neutrality*, 590–91. Robert D. Ward, "The Origin and Activities of the National Security League," *Mississippi Valley Historical Review* 47, no. 1 (June 1960): 55. J. Stuart Blackton, *Battle Cry of Peace* (Brooklyn, NY: The M. P. Publishing Co., 1915), "Publisher's Note."

108 A. Lawrence Lowell, *A League to Enforce Peace* (Boston: World Peace Foundation, 1915), World Peace Foundation Pamphlet Series, V, no. 5 (October 1915), first page of text (pages unnumbered). "League to Enforce Peace is Launched," *New York Times*, June 18, 1915. *Guide to the Microfilm Edition of the Records of the American Union Against Militarism, 1915–1922* (Woodbridge, CT: Scholarly Resources Inc., 2005), v, online at http://microformguides.gale.com/Data/Download/8392000C.pdf (accessed May 2015).

109 U.S. Senate Historical Minute Essay, "July 2, 1915, Bomb Rocks Capitol," www.senate.gov/artandhistory/history/minute/Bomb_Rocks_Capitol.htm. "The SS Armenian Sailed Between UK and N. America, Sunk in 1915," www.panarmenian.net/eng/news/151022/. Link, *Wilson: The Struggle for Neutrality*, 431–41s.

110 Link, *Wilson: The Struggle for Neutrality*, 565–87. Robert H. Zieger, *America's Great War: World War I and the American Experience* (Lanham, MD: Rowman & Littlefield, 2000), 24–25.

111 Link, *Wilson: The Struggle for Neutrality*, 554–58, 645–50. Barbara W. Tuchman, *The Zimmermann Telegram* (New York: The Macmillan Company, 1966), 85–87.

112 Tuchman, *Zimmermann Telegram*, 67–85. Link, *Wilson: The Struggle for Neutrality*, 561–64, 636, 650–51. Edward Robb Ellis, *Echoes of Distant Thunder: Life in the United States, 1914-1918* (New York: Kodansha International, 1996), 172–79, 187. Messimer, *Baltimore Sabotage Cell*, 6–12. Martin Donell Kohout, "Huerta, Victoriano," in *The Handbook of Texas Online*, https://tshaonline.org/handbook/online/articles/fhu81. Martin Donell Kohout, "Orozco, Pascual, Jr.," in *The Handbook of Texas Online*, https://tshaonline.org/handbook/online/articles/for08 (both accessed May 2015).

113 Tuchman, *Zimmermann Telegram*, 89 [emphasis in original].

114 Link, *Wilson: The Struggle for Neutrality*, 682–91 (*Spectator* quote on 691).

115 Cable to rulers of belligerent nations, Papers Relating to the Ford Peace Plan, Manuscript Division, Library of Congress.

116 Woodrow Wilson, "Third Annual Message, December 7, 1915," American Presidency Project, www.presidency. ucsb.edu/ws/?pid=29556.

FIRST BATTLE OF THE MARNE (PAGE 48)

1 Martin Gilbert, *The First World War: A Complete History* (London: Weidenfeld & Nicolson, 1994), 77.

2 "The War in the Air—Observation and Reconnaissance," firstworldwar.com, www.firstworldwar.com/airwar/ observation.htm. "First Battle of Marne," *History* website, www.history.com/topics/world-war-i/first-battle-of-marne. Alfred J. Andrea, ed., *World History Encyclopedia*, 21 vols. (Santa Barbara, CA: ABC-CLIO, 211), 3: 747.

3 Gilbert, *First World War*, 72.

4 John Keegan, *An Illustrated History of the First World War* (New York: Alfred A. Knopf, 2001), 100.

5 "Following the Victors," dispatch to the *London Daily News*, special cable to the *New York Times*, Sept 12, 1914, 2.

6 Andrea, *World History Encyclopedia*, 3: 749.

7 Ibid., 747.

8 Ibid., 749.

9 Harry Carr, "The Checkerboard of the War," *Los Angeles Times*, September 13, 1914, 15.

10 "Editorial Points," *Boston Daily Globe*, September 15, 1914, 10.

GALLIPOLI CAMPAIGN (PAGE 68)

1 Andrea, *World History Encyclopedia*, 2: 461.

2 Ibid., 462.

3 Keegan, *An Illustrated History of the First World War*, 232.

4 Ibid., 234. Gilbert, *First World War* (Weidenfeld & Nicolson), 226.

5 Andrea, *World History Encyclopedia* 2: 464 and 3: 1021.

6 Grant, *World War I*, 113, 140.

7 "WWI Gallipoli," at Army (website of Australian army), www.army.gov.au/Our-history/History-in-Focus/WWI-Gallipoli.

8 "Heroism Slaughtered by Unpreparedness," editorial, *Washington Post*, January 8, 1916, 6.

9 "Collegians on War," editorial, *New York Times*, January 12, 1916, 12.

SECOND BATTLE OF YPRES (PAGE 72)

1 Alfred J. Andrea, ed., *World History Encyclopedia*, 21 vols. (ABC-CLIO), 4: 1279.

2 Keegan, *An Illustrated History of the First World War*, 176. Earlier, the Germans had used nonlethal tear gas on the Eastern front.

3 Andrea, *World History Encyclopedia*, 4: 1281.

4 R. G. Grant, *World War I: The Definitive Visual History* (Washington, D.C.: Smithsonian/DK, 2014), xx.

5 "British in White-Hot Rage as German Savagery Grows," *New York Tribune*, June 9, 1915, 1.

6 "A German-American Thinks 'All the Howl,'. . ." *Baltimore Sun*, May 17, 1915, 6.

CHAPTER 2

Epigraph: *Addresses of President Wilson, January 27–February 3, 1916* (Washington, D.C.: Government Printing Office, 1916), 16.

1 J. George Frederick, "America's Business Boom," *The American Review of Reviews* 53, no. 1 (January 1916), 42–55 (quote, 43; Russian orders, 44). Robert H. Zieger, *America's Great War: World War I and the American Experience* (Lanham, MD: Rowman & Littlefield, 2000), 29–30 (Morgan contracts and Allied experts). Martin Horn, "A Private Bank at War: J. P. Morgan & Co. and France, 1914–1918," *Business History Review* 74, no. 1

(Spring 2000): 85–112 (on 86, the author notes that Morgan became the agent for France in May 1915).

2 Arthur S. Link, *Wilson: Campaigns for Progressivism and Peace, 1916–1917* [vol. 5 of 5-vol. biography] (Princeton, NJ: Princeton University Press, 1965), 10 (interference with mails). Thomas A. Bailey, "The United States and the Blacklist During the Great War," *Journal of Modern History* 6, no. 1 (March 1934), 15 (Trading with the Enemy Act), 18 (Lansing protest). "American Liner Is Held Up at Sea: British Remove Teutons Aboard Steamer China," *Rock Island Argus*, February 19, 1916. "American Liner China Is Held Up on the High Sea," *Omaha Daily Bee*, February 24, 1916. Arthur S. Link, *Wilson: Confusions and Crises, 1915–1916* [vol. 4 of 5-vol. biography] (Princeton, NJ: Princeton University Press, 1964), 91 (quoting C. Spring-Rice to Grey, January 13, 1916). Zieger, *America's Great War*, 16 (increase in exports). Harry N. Scheiber, "World War I as Entrepreneurial Opportunity: Willard Straight and the American International Corporation," *Political Science Quarterly* 84, no. 3 (September 1969), 486–511 (statistics on increase in American exports, 497).

3 Burton I. Kaufman, *Efficiency and Expansion: Foreign Trade Organization in the Wilson Administration, 1913–1921* (Westport, CT: Greenwood Press, 1974), 117–24 (banks' foreign branches), 124–28 (shipping bill). Frederick, "America's Business Boom," 42–55 (quote, page 55). Scheiber, "World War I as Entrepreneurial Opportunity," 486–511 (Vanderlip, 500; Straight trip, 501). For more information about Willard Straight's overseas experience and views on the value of international commerce, see Herbert Croly, *Willard Straight* (New York: The Macmillan Company, 1924), available online at the Hathi Trust website, http://catalog.hathitrust.org/Record/010074627.

4 For more detailed information on the military situation at the end of 1915, see John Keegan, *The First World War* (New York: Vintage Books, 2000), 256, 265, 274–77, and G. J. Meyer, *A World Undone: The Story of the Great War 1914 to 1918* (New York: Delta Trade Paperbacks, 2007), 363–68.

5 Keegan, *First World War*, 256, 274–77. Meyer, *A World Undone*, 363–68. William Van Der Kloot, *World War I Fact Book: The Great War in Graphs and Numbers* (Stroud, UK: Amberley Publishing, 2010), 36, 39. "Conscription: the First World War; Your Country Needs You," at www.parliament.uk/about/living-heritage/transformingsociety/private-lives/yourcountry/overview/conscription/ (accessed June 2015).

6 Meyer, *A World Undone*, 368–69 (Falkenhayn on "end of military effort," 368). Keegan, *First World War*, 274–75, 277 (Haig-Joffre debate and author's statement re: plans), 278 (Falkenhayn, "forces of France will bleed").

7 "Henry Ford Back, Admits an Error, Denies Deserting," *New York Times*, January 3, 1916. Barbara S. Kraft, *The Peace Ship: Henry Ford's Pacifist Adventure in the First World War* (New York: Macmillan Publishing Co., 1978), 151–81, 207. Keegan, *First World War*, 280. Louis Lochner, "The Neutral Conference for Continuous Mediation at Stockholm," *Advocate of Peace (1894–1920)* 78, no. 8 (August 1916): 238–41 (date of first conference session, 238). Martin Gilbert, *The First World War: A Complete History* (New York: Henry Holt & Company, 1996), 231 (nine-hour barrage at Verdun).

8 "Henry Ford Back, Admits an Error, Denies Deserting." Judith Bloom Fradin and Dennis Brindell Fradin, *Jane Addams, Champion of Democracy* (New York: Clarion Books, 2006), 138–39.

9 John S. D. Eisenhower, *Intervention! The United States and the Mexican Revolution, 1913–1917* (New York: W. W. Norton & Company, 1993), 214–16. Barbara W. Tuchman, *The Zimmermann Telegram* (New York: The Macmillan Company, 1958), 92–94. Miguel A. Levario, "The El Paso Race Riot of 1916," in *War Along the Border: The Mexican Revolution and Tejano Communities*, ed. Arnoldo De León (College Station: Texas A&M University Press, 2012), 140–43.

10 "H. L. Wilson for War," *New York Times*, January 13, 1916. Link, *Wilson: Confusions and Crises*, 202–3. "Armed Intervention Demanded in Senate," *New York Times*, January 13, 1916 (Borah quote). Ben Procter, *William Randolph Hearst: Final Edition, 1911–1951* (New York: Oxford University Press, 2007), 49. "Send Our Army, Says Roosevelt," *New York Times*, January 14, 1916.

11 Levario, "El Paso Race Riot of 1916," 143–44.

12 Link, *Wilson: Confusions and Crises*, 202–5. "Carranza Orders Death of Bandits," *New York Times*, January 17, 1916. "Carranza's Revenge! Villistas Shot for Murder of Americans," *Day Book* (Chicago), January 27, 1916.

13 Tuchman, *Zimmermann Telegram*, 93. Link, *Wilson: Confusions and Crises*, 14, notes that the newly married Wilsons "returned to Washington—and reality—on January 3, 1916." Arthur S. Link, ed., *The Papers of Woodrow Wilson*, 69 vols. (Princeton, NJ: Princeton University Press, 1966–1983), 35: 399 (Wilson letter to Lucy Marshall Smith and Mary Randolph Smith, Dec. 27, 1915). John Gardner Coolidge, *A War Diary in Paris, 1914–1917* (Cambridge, MA: Privately printed, 1931), 101.

14 Link, *Wilson: Confusions and Crises*, 134–35 (text of House-Grey Memorandum), 138 (Wilson's insertion of "probably"). David Stevenson, *Cataclysm: The First World War as Political Tragedy* (New York: Basic Books, 2005), 120 (no cabinet or congressional input).

15 For more background on the House-Grey Memorandum, see Link, *Wilson: Confusions and Crises*, chapter 4 (101–41). On 138, Link notes that the French "would of course welcome American military support, but they were not interested in a negotiated peace, and could not, on account of French public opinion, afford to be interested so long as there was any hope of an Allied military victory." Stevenson, *Cataclysm*, 110 (German declaration), 119 (Sainte-Adresse). Regarding the rising pressure in Germany to institute unrestricted submarine warfare, see Link, *Wilson: Confusions and Crises*, 86–88, 165–66, 179–86. See also "Grey Wins Fight Against Making Blockade Tighter: Tells Commons to Injure Neutrals Would Turn the World Against England," *New York Times*, January 27, 1916.

16 Link, *Wilson: Confusions and Crises*, 98–100. Robert Lansing, *War Memoirs of Robert Lansing* (Westport, CT: Greenwood Press, 1970), 102. "Secretary Lansing's Official Explanation of New Delay in Lusitania Settlement," *New York Times*, February 17, 1916. Coolidge, *War Diary in Paris*, 105.

17 "Secretary Lansing's Official Explanation of New Delay in Lusitania Settlement," *New York Times*, February 17, 1916. Link, *Wilson: Confusions and Crises*, 142–45. Regarding the American public's not yet being psychologically prepared to enter the war, see Charles Callan Tansill, *America Goes to War* (Boston: Little, Brown & Company, 1938), 418, and Lansing, *War Memoirs*, 102–4. The January 1916 memorandum included in the Lansing reveals both the secretary of state's determination that Americans were still too divided in opinions about the belligerents to be ready for war and his strong anti-German views.

18 Daniel M. Smith, *Robert Lansing and American Neutrality, 1914–1917* (New York: Da Capo Press, 1972), 114–23, 125. "America May Put Armed Steamships in Warship Class, Citizens of United States Probably Will Be Warned to Shun Such Vessels, Result of Berlin Order," *New York Times*, February 12, 1916. Link, *Wilson: Confusions and Crises*, 162 (House plea to president), 151 (Grey to British ambassador to the United State re: "wholesale sinking"), 160–62 (Grey to cabinet re: "unfriendly" or "unneutral").

19 Smith, *Robert Lansing and American Neutrality*, 125. John Callan O'Laughlin to Theodore Roosevelt, February 23, 1916, John Callan O'Laughlin Papers, Manuscript Division, Library of Congress. Link, *Wilson: Confusions and Crises*, 167–78 (Wilson quote, 172–73).

20 Link, *Wilson: Confusions and Crises*, 46–48. Charles Chatfield, *For Peace and Justice: Pacifism in America 1914–1941* (Knoxville: University of Tennessee Press, 1971), 23.

21 *Addresses of President Wilson, January 27–February 3, 1916*, 65 (danger), 68 (challenge to opponents).

22 Chatfield, *For Peace and Justice*, 23. "Swing Around the Circle Against Militarism," *Survey* 36 (April–September 1916): 95–96. Link, *Wilson: Campaigns for Progressivism and Peace*, 3 (Ford in two state primaries).

23 *Addresses of President Wilson, January 27–February 3, 1916*, 37 (Chicago), 17 (Pittsburgh).

24 Helen Keller, "Strike Against War," in *Voices of a People's History of the United States*, ed. Howard Zinn and Anthony Arnove, 284–88 (quote, 285), online at the Gifts of Speech website, http://gos.sbc.edu/k/keller.html.

25 *Addresses of President Wilson, January 27–February 3, 1916*, 28 (fire), 32 (money).

26 Woodrow Wilson, "Third Annual Message, December 7, 1915," American Presidency Project, www.presidency. ucsb.edu/ws/?pid=29556 (accessed July 2015). Commander, Navy Reserve Force Public Affairs, "Navy Reserve Celebrates 98 Years of Service," March 1, 2013, at America's Navy website, www.navy.mil/submit/ display.asp?story_id=72449 (accessed August 2015). "Timeline of the Navy Reserve," at the Navy Reserve Centennial website, http://navyreservecentennial. com/history/ (accessed August 2015). Frank Freidel, *Franklin D. Roosevelt: The Apprenticeship* (Boston: Little, Brown & Company, 1952), 256–58. Ralph Barton Perry, *The Plattsburg Movement* (New York: E. P. Dutton & Company, 1921), 139–40. John Garry Clifford, *The Citizen Soldiers: The Plattsburg Training Camp Movement, 1913–1920* (Lexington: University Press of Kentucky, 1972), 182–84.

27 Clifford, *Citizen Soldiers*, 184. Edward Marshall, "Edison's Plan for Preparedness," *New York Times*, May 30, 1915. Zieger, *America's Great War*, 66–67. Lloyd N. Scott, *Naval Consulting Board of the United States* (Washington, D.C.: Government Printing Office, 1920), 31 (Daniels quote), 34 (length of survey). Freidel, *Franklin D. Roosevelt*, 259. Roosevelt's initial skepticism about the Naval Consulting Board led him to write to a friend, with edgy humor, that most proposed members were "like Henry Ford, who until he saw a chance for publicity free of charge, thought a submarine was something to eat!" Nevertheless, he did also see in the board the promise of technical progress.

28 Link, *Wilson: Confusions and Crises*, 50, notes the concern of Senator Benjamin R. Tillman, chairman of the Senate Naval Affairs Committee, that an American naval buildup would result "in what could only be a disastrous naval race with Britain." On the other hand, naval expansion undoubtedly received a boost from a report by the Naval General Board that stated, among other things, "Our present Navy is not sufficient to give due weight to the diplomatic remonstrances of the United States in peace or to enforce its policies in war." The report is quoted in George W. Baer, *One Hundred Years of Sea Power: The U.S. Navy, 1890–1990*

(Stanford, CA: Stanford University Press, 1994), 59–60. United States War Department General Staff, *Statement of a Proper Military Policy for the United States* (Washington, D.C.: Government Printing Office, 1915), 9 (chart, "Preparedness of the Great Powers for Oversea Expedition" showing strength of other armies), 21–22 (outlining recommendations for regular army strength totaling 281,000, including such support units as quartermaster and ordnance).

29 Russell F. Weigley, *Towards an American Army: Military Thought from Washington to Marshall* (New York: Columbia University Press, 1962), 217–19. Link, *Wilson: Confusions and Crises*, 17–18 (War Department plan), 39–40 (Garrison resignation threat; Wilson to James Hay). George C. Herring Jr., "James Hay and the Preparedness Controversy, 1915–1916," *Journal of Southern History* 30, no. 4 (November 1964): 383–404 (392–94, congressional opposition to the Continental Army).

30 Herring, "James Hay and the Preparedness Controversy," 383–404, 386 (Hay quote). Richard Drake, *The Education of an Anti-Imperialist: Robert La Follette and U.S. Expansion* (Madison: University of Wisconsin Press, 2013), 164. "Lodge Opens Fire on Wilson Policies," *New York Times*, March 17, 1916. Weigley, *Towards an American Army*, 219.

31 David M. Kennedy, *Over Here: The First World War and American Society* (New York: Oxford University Press, 1980), 114–16.

32 Link, *Wilson: Confusions and Crises*, 50–53 (resignation; Link notes here that Assistant Secretary of War Henry Breckinridge, who led the mission to rescue Americans stranded in Europe, also resigned), 54 (Baker appointment). C. H. Cramer, *Newton D. Baker: A Biography* (Cleveland: The World Publishing Company, 1961), 8 ("reliable radical"). "Villa vs. Baker," *Survey* 36 (April–September 1916), 33 (Baker quote).

33 W. Elliot Brownlee, "Wilson and Financing the Modern State: The Revenue Act of 1916," *Proceedings of the American Philosophical Society* 129, no. 2 (June, 1985): 173–210 (175, 17 percent of taxes). Scott Hollenbeck and Maureen Keenan Kahr, "Ninety Years of Individual Income and Tax Statistics, 1916–2005," *Statistics of*

Income Bulletin, Winter 2008, article online at the Internal Revenue Service website, www.irs.gov/pub/irs-soi/16-05intax.pdf (see especially tables 1 and 1a).

34 Jyotsna Sreenivasan, ed., *Poverty and the Government in America: A Historical Encyclopedia* (Santa Barbara, CA: ABC-CLIO, 2009), 1: 210; James L. Huston, *Securing the Fruits of Labor: The American Concept of Wealth Distribution, 1765–1900* (Baton Rouge: Louisiana State University Press, 1998), 84. Brownlee, "Wilson and Financing the Modern State," 173–210 (182–83, Kitchin quote; 185, Stephens quote; 196, *New York World*).

35 Brownlee, "Wilson and Financing the Modern State," 173–210 (189, Hull; 202, munitions tax; 203, Ford quote).

36 Ibid., 173–210 (183–84, 186, labor organizations' recommendations re: taxes). Ronald L. Filippelli, ed., *Labor Conflict in the United States: An Encyclopedia* (New York: Garland Publishing, 1990), 26–27 (Arizona), 120–21 (garment workers), 368–70 (transit workers), 172–73 (Washington State), 330–32 (Minnesota), 495–96 (Standard Oil). Elizabeth Williams, *Pittsburgh in World War I: Arsenal of the Allies* (Charleston, SC: The History Press, 2013), 47–52 (Pittsburgh strike).

37 Filippelli, *Labor Conflict in the United States*, 461–63. "Bomb Kills Six [*sic*], Injures Scores in Defense Parade," *New York Times*, July 23, 1916. "An End to the Mooney Case?" *Milwaukee Journal*, August 27, 1952. "San Francisco's Future," description of propagandistic film clip prepared after the explosion, at the Library of Congress website, www.sfmuseum.org/loc/prepday.html. Zachary Crockett, "The Worst Act of Terrorism in San Francisco History," online article posted October 27, 2014, at http://priceonomics.com/the-worst-act-of-terrorism-in-san-francisco/. Mooney and Billings were finally released from prison in 1939. Mooney was officially pardoned that year; Billings was pardoned in 1961.

38 Eisenhower, *Intervention!*, 217–27. It should be noted that estimates of the strength of both the U.S. garrison at Columbus and the Villa force that raided the town vary widely. It seems likely, however, that the garrison on the night of the raid included about three hundred men and that Villa's force was somewhere between four hundred and five hundred, though some estimates, especially those based on early reports, set Villa's force at more than a thousand.

39 Eisenhower, *Intervention!*, 226. Clarence C. Clendenen, *The United States and Pancho Villa: A Study in Unconventional Diplomacy* (Ithaca, NY: Cornell University Press, 1961), 241–42. Initial pursuit of Villa on the morning of March 10 was undertaken by Major Frank Tompkins leading thirty-two troopers. He was soon reinforced by twenty-four additional men led by Lieutenant James Castleman. Link, *Wilson: Confusions and Crises*, 206, 211–14. Joseph P. Tumulty, *Woodrow Wilson As I Know Him* (Garden City, NY: Doubleday, Page & Company, 1921), 157–60.

40 Eisenhower, *Intervention!*, 237. Link, *Wilson: Confusions and Crises*, 208, 210, 214. Tuchman, *Zimmermann Telegram*, 95–96. Meirion Harries and Susie Harries, *The Last Days of Innocence: America at War, 1917–1918* (New York: Random House, 1997), 31. Clendenen, *United States and Pancho Villa*, 297–99.

41 Eisenhower, *Intervention!*, 234–35, 238.

42 Benjamin D. Foulois, with C. B. Glines, *From the Wright Brothers to the Astronauts: The Memoirs of Major General Benjamin D. Foulois* (New York: McGraw-Hill Book Company, 1968), 126–29 (quote, 129). Eisenhower, *Intervention!*, 253 (truck purchase), 255 (U.S. vs. German aircraft expenditures). Edmund Morris, *Colonel Roosevelt* (New York: Random House, 2010), 465–66. Rebecca Robbins Raines, *Getting the Message Through: A Branch History of the U.S. Army Signal Corps* (Washington, D.C.: Center of Military History, 2011), 151.

43 Link, *Wilson: Confusions and Crises*, 228.

44 Ibid., 229–234. Coolidge, *A War Diary in Paris*, 114.

45 Coolidge, *A War Diary in Paris*, 113–14. Clendenen, *United States and Pancho Villa*, 266–69. Eisenhower, *Intervention!*, 270–80. Link, *Wilson: Confusions and Crises*, 285.

46 Link, *Wilson: Confusions and Crises*, 285–86. Clendenen, *United States and Pancho Villa*, 268–69.

47 Link, *Wilson: Confusions and Crises*, 250–52. Woodrow Wilson, "Address to a Joint Session of Congress on German Violations of International Law, April 19, 1916," American Presidency Project, www.presidency. ucsb.edu/ws/?pid=65390.

48 Link, *Wilson: Confusions and Crises*, 256–61. Keegan, *First World War*, 283 (Verdun), 300–301 (Kut and Austro-Hungarian Italian offensive). Dwight R. Messimer, *The Baltimore Sabotage Cell: German Agents, American Traitors, and the U-Boat Deutschland During World War I* (Annapolis, MD: Naval Institute Press, 2015), 12–16. 31–40.

49 Naresh Fernandes, "American Roots of the Indian Independence Movement," *New York Times*, August 14, 2012. Ruth Price, *The Lives of Agnes Smedley* (New York: Oxford University Press, 2005), 54, notes, "On the advice of the BIC [Berlin India Committee], a veritable stream of silver had flowed from the German Consulate in San Francisco into Ghadr Party [independence movement] coffers since the beginning of the European war." Already of revolutionary bent at age twenty-four in 1916, the Missouri-born Smedley was a firm supporter of Indian independence. Dennis Bryant, "Annie Larsen Affair," at Maritime Professional website, www.maritimeprofessional.com/blogs/post/annie-larsen-affair-14761 (accessed September 2015). Francis M. Carroll, "America and the 1916 Rising," in *1916, the Long Revolution*, ed. Gabriel Doherty and Dermot Keogh (Cork, Ireland: Mercier Press, 2007), 121–40 (123, Taft and Roosevelt support).

50 Carroll, "America and the 1916 Rising," 121–40 (132–33, support for Casement; 136, coded message to Devoy, German transport). BBC History, "Sir Roger Casement and the German Connection," at BBC website www. bbc.co.uk/history/british/easterrising/insurrection/in02. shtml (accessed September 2015). Robert Schmuhl, "'All Changed, Changed Utterly': Easter 1916 and America," UCD/Notre Dame Lectures, Series 6, Spring 2012, at UCDscholarcast website, www.ucd.ie/scholarcast/transcripts/1916_and_america.pdf. Keegan, *First World War*, 268. Keegan notes that the new commander of the German High Seas Fleet, Reinhard Scheer, "made four [sorties] in April and May; in the April sortie he succeeded in reaching the English east coast and . . .

bombarding Lowestoft. The demonstration, timed to coincide with the Irish nationalist Easter Rising, of which Germany had foreknowledge, caused dismay in Britain but emphasized once again that . . . [German] High Seas Fleet operations must be limited to tip-and-run against targets close enough to home for it to beat a retreat before the Royal Navy's heavy units could steam south and intervene."

51 Link, *Wilson: Campaigns for Progressivism and Peace*, 15–16 (Howells quote). Carroll, "America and the 1916 Rising," 121–40 (see especially 137–38 for U.S. reactions to executions). For succinct details regarding Roger Casement's humanitarianism, see the *Encyclopedia Britannica* online, http://academic.eb.com/EBchecked/topic/97875/Sir-Roger-Casement.

52 Link, *Wilson: Confusions and Crises*, 270–79.

53 Ibid., 275–79. Link, *Wilson: Campaigns for Progressivism and Peace*, 16–20.

54 Link, *Wilson: Campaigns for Progressivism and Peace*, 10–16, 20–23, 32–33.

55 Ibid., 19, 23–26. Woodrow Wilson, "Address delivered at the First Annual Assemblage of the League to Enforce Peace: American Principles, May 27, 1916," American Presidency Project, www.presidency.ucsb.edu/ws/?pid=65391 (accessed September 2015).

56 Link, *Wilson: Campaigns for Progressivism and Peace*, 26–27, 30–31, 33. A. J. L. Waskey and Spencer C. Tucker, "Portugal," in *World War I Encyclopedia*, ed. Spencer C. Tucker, 5 vols. (Santa Barbara, CA: ABC-CLIO, 2005), 3: 931–32.

57 "Dominican Republic, 1916–1924," at U.S. Department of State Archive http://2001-2009.state.gov/r/pa/ho/time/wwi/108649.htm (accessed September 2015). Link, *Wilson: Campaigns for Progressivism and Peace*, 80–83 (Denmark).

58 Martin Donell Kohout, "Glenn Springs Raid," *Handbook of Texas Online*, at Texas State Historical Association website, www.tshaonline.org/handbook/online/articles/jcgdu (accessed September 2015). Tuchman, *Zimmermann Telegram*, 97–100. Tuchman cites reports from U.S. consul William Canada as a major source of information

about German activities in Mexico, along with reports from Special Agent Rodgers (probably James Linn Rodgers, special representative of the State Department to the de facto Government of Mexico at that time; see United States Department of State, *Register of the Department of State* [Washington, D.C.: U.S. Government Printing Office, 1918], 133). Link, *Wilson: Confusions and Crises*, 297–98.

59 "The National Conventions," editor's review, *North American Review* 204, no. 728 (July 1916): 1–28 (2, "reconsecration"). Morris, *Colonel Roosevelt*, 452–54 (support for his nomination and comment to Hiram Johnson), 457–59. Link, *Wilson: Campaigns for Progressivism and Peace*, 1–6.

60 Morris, *Colonel Roosevelt*, 459. Link, *Wilson: Campaigns for Progressivism and Peace*, 6–7 ("bearded iceberg"). "The National Conventions," 1–28 (5–7, Hughes acceptance letter). John Fox, "Charles Evans Hughes," www.pbs.org/wnet/supremecourt/democracy/robes_hughes.html (accessed September 2015).

61 Link, *Wilson: Confusions and Crises*, 299–301 (Scott quote, 301). "Mexican Raiders Kill 3 in Texas," *New York Times* June 16, 1916 (the *Times* headline does not reflect the fact that one soldier died of his wounds later). Dick D. Heller, Jr., "San Ygnacio, Tx," *Handbook of Texas Online*, at Texas State Historical Association website, https://tshaonline.org/handbook/online/articles/hls15 (accessed September 2015).

62 Link, *Wilson: Campaigns for Progressivism and Peace*, 42–46.

63 Ibid., 38–42, 48. "Democratic Party Platform of 1916," American Presidency Project www.presidency.ucsb.edu/ws/?pid=29591 (accessed September 2015).

64 Eisenhower, *Intervention!*, 294–303. Link, *Wilson: Confusions and Crises*, 303–18. Link, *Wilson: Campaigns for Progressivism and Peace*, 51–55, 120–23. H. B. (Dave) Wharfield, *10th Cavalry & Border Fights* (El Cajon, CA: Privately printed, 1965), 27–46. "U.S. Cavalry in Bloody Battle," *Ogden Standard* (Ogden City, Utah), June 22, 1916. "Twelve American Negro Soldiers Massacred in Mexican Ambush," *Daily Gate City and Constitution-Democrat* (Keokuk, IA), June 22, 1916. "The Country

Hovering on the Brink of War," *Bryan (TX) Daily Eagle and Pilot*, June 22, 1916. "Clash Stirs Washington," *New York Times*, June 22, 1916.

65 Link, *Wilson: Confusions and Crises*, 310–18. Theodore Roosevelt, *Letters and Speeches* (New York: The Library of America, 2004), 707–8 (letter to Newton Diehl Baker, July 6, 1916).

66 "What Verdun Means," *North American*, June 27, 1916, in *The War from This Side: Editorials from the North American* (Philadelphia), 4 vols. (Philadelphia: J. B. Lippincott Company, 1916), 2: 439–43. Ed Klekowski and Libby Klekowski, *Eyewitnesses to the Great War: American Writers, Reporters, Volunteers and Soldiers in France, 1914–1918* (Jefferson, NC: McFarland & Company, 2012), 112 (Musgrave), 113 (King), 118–20 (Bullard).

67 Klekowski and Klekowski, *Eyewitnesses to the Great War*, 56–75, 89–92.

68 Ibid., 58–62, 88–92. Coleman Tileston Clark and Salter Storrs Clark, Jr., *Soldier Letters* (privately printed, 1919), 26. "Verdun Americans in Baseball Game: Ambulance Section Nines Play Within Range of the German Guns," *New York Times*, October 22, 1916.

69 Klekowski and Klekowski, *Eyewitnesses to the Great War*, 126–33. See also James R. McConnell, *Flying for France: With the American Escadrille at Verdun* (New York: Doubleday, Page & Company, 1917). McConnell was killed in action in March 1917.

70 Meyer, *A World Undone*, 438–41. Keegan, *First World War*, 286–95, 298.

71 Kennedy, *Over Here*, 183 (Empey). Don Hutchison, *The Great Pulp Heroes* (Buffalo, NY: Mosaic Press, 1996), 202. Alan Seeger, *Letters and Diary of Alan Seeger* (New York: Charles Scribner's Sons, 1917), 205, 211–15. Irving Werstein, *Sound No Trumpet: The Life and Death of Alan Seeger* (New York: Thomas Y. Crowell Company, 1967), 127–29.

72 Werstein, *Sound No Trumpet*, 129–30. "Mrs. Wharton's Charity," letter to the editor, *New York Times*, March 18, 1916. Edith Wharton, ed., *The Book of the Homeless* (New York: Charles Scribner's Sons, 1916), see especially

the introduction by Theodore Roosevelt, ix–x, and the preface by Edith Wharton, xix–xxv.

73 Klekowski and Klekowski, *Eyewitnesses to the Great War*, 38-39, 98. "Ambulance Corps in France Filmed," *New York Times*, July 6, 1916.

74 Merle Curti, *American Philanthropy Abroad* (New Brunswick, NJ: Transaction Books, 1988), 231–45. "The 20,000 Battle-Blinded: Ways in Which They Can Be Helped to Become Self-Supporting," letter to the editor, *New York Times*, June 14, 1916. "The French American Hall of Fame: Mrs. Nina Larrey Duryea," *La France: An American Magazine* 4, no. 7 (April 1920): 346. Julius Goldzier, "German and Austro-Hungarian Relief in Chicago," *American Red Cross Magazine* 11, no. 2 (February 1916): 47–49. "Famous Polish Pianist to Play for War Relief," *Bridgeport (CT) Evening Farmer*, April 10, 1916. See also an item on page 6 of the *Washington (D.C.) Herald*, February 24, 1916: "The Secretary of the Navy gave Paderewski and his Polish Relief Committee an hour's interview yesterday, during which every officer and clerk on duty in that part of the Navy Department made an excuse to pass through the secretary's office." "Says Thousands Starve in Syria: Neutral Traveler Says 60,000 to 80,000 Died of Hunger," *Grand Forks (ND) Herald*, August 14, 1916. "80,000 Have Died from Starvation in Syria," *Harrisburg (PA) Telegraph*, August 12, 1916. "The Allied Bazaar," advertisement, *New York Sun*, May 31, 1916. "Spirit of Belgium Thrills the Bazaar," *New York Times*, June 11, 1916.

75 Kennedy, *Over Here*, 308–11. Thomas A. Bailey, "The United States and the Blacklist During the Great War," *Journal of Modern History* 6, no. 1 (March 1934), 15–16, 22. Link, *Wilson: Campaigns for Progressivism and Peace*, 65–69. "When Britain Stoops to Folly," *New York Times*, July 20, 1916.

76 Messimer, *The Baltimore Sabotage Cell*, 54–80. Link, *Wilson: Campaigns for Progressivism and Peace*, 69. "The German Supersubmarine's Sensational Arrival at Baltimore Chronicled in Pictures," *Philadelphia Evening Public Ledger*, July 10, 1916.

77 Edward Robb Ellis, *Echoes of Distant Thunder: Life in the United States, 1914–1918* (New York: Kodansha International, 1996), 191–92. Messimer, *The Baltimore Sabotage Cell*, 79–80, 124–39. "Hail of Shrapnel as Explosion Rocks New York City," *New York Sun*, July 31, 1916. Morris, *Colonel Roosevelt*, 468–69. Link, *Wilson: Campaigns for Progressivism and Peace*, 113–16. "Submarine Disappears: Navy Searchers Find 216 Survivors from Wrecks and End Hunt," *New York Times*, October 10, 1916.

78 "Hughes Accepts, Attacks Record of His Opponent," *New York Times*, August 1, 1916. "Full Text of Mr. Hughes's Speech of Acceptance," *New York Times*, August 1, 1916. Morris, *Colonel Roosevelt*, 466, 470–72.

79 Link, *Wilson: Campaigns for Progressivism and Peace*, 93, 121–23, 165–75, 184–86. Keegan, *First World War*, 308, 352. Gilbert, *First World War* (Holt, 1996), 282–83.

80 Link, *Wilson: Campaigns for Progressivism and Peace*, 173–75, 178–84.

81 Ibid., 83–102 (Wilson quote, 84). "Cabinet Considers Railway Crisis," *Day Book* (Chicago), August 4, 1916. "Army Fearing Railroad Strike . . . War Department Officials Fear That Strike . . . Would Seriously Hamper the Food Supply at Mexican Border," *Daily Ardmoreite* (Ardmore, OK), August 15, 1916. "Preparing for the Strike—Both Sides Firm and President Urges Postponement," *Tonopah (NV) Daily Bonanza*, August 30, 1916. "8-Hour Bill Agreed Upon, Senators Hear Men's Side," *Washington (D.C.) Times*, August 31, 1916. Kennedy, *Over Here*, 304–5.

82 Link, *Wilson: Campaigns for Progressivism and Peace*, 94, 99, 103–12, 116–20, 140–45, 148–58. Harriman, *From Pinafores to Politics*, 202–4.

83 Tuchman, *Zimmermann Telegram*, 114–16, 122. Link, *Wilson: Campaigns for Progressivism and Peace*, 176, 206, 208.

84 Link, *Wilson: Campaigns for Progressivism and Peace*, 212–19, 227–32, 233–39.

85 Woodrow Wilson, "Address to the Senate of the United States: 'A World League for Peace,'" January 22, 1917, American Presidency Project, www.presidency.ucsb.edu/ws/?pid=65396 (accessed October 1916). Link, *Wilson: Campaigns for Progressivism and Peace*, 264–68.

86 Link, *Wilson: Campaigns for Progressivism and Peace,* 269–77. Tuchman, *Zimmermann Telegram,* 137–41.

87 Tuchman, *Zimmermann Telegram,* 138. Link, *Wilson: Campaigns for Progressivism and Peace,* 289.

88 Tuchman, *Zimmermann Telegram,* 142–47.

89 Link, *Wilson: Campaigns for Progressivism and Peace,* 290. Tuchman, *Zimmermann Telegram,* 7, 149. Lansing, *War Memoirs,* 209–11.

BATTLE OF JUTLAND (PAGE 123)

1 Alfred J. Andrea, ed., *World History Encyclopedia,* 21 vols. (Santa Barbara, CA: ABC-CLIO), 2: 619.

2 Andrea, *World History Encyclopedia,* 2: 619.

3 Imperial War Museum, "Battle of Jutland," www.iwm. org.uk/history/battle-of-jutland.

4 Ibid.

5 Ibid.

6 "Views Expressed on Jutland Battle," *Christian Science Monitor,* July 11, 1916, 2.

7 Andrea, *World History Encyclopedia,* 2: 624 and 3: 841.

8 "Reuterdahl Sees Lesson for U.S. in Jutland Fight," *St. Louis Post-Dispatch,* June 6, 1916, 20.

BATTLE OF THE SOMME (PAGE 134)

1 Andrea, *World History Encyclopedia,* 4: 1103; death figures from Martin Gilbert, *The First World War: A Complete History* (London: Weidenfeld & Nicolson, 1994), 299. John Keegan, *The First World War* (New York: Vintage Books, 2000), 286–99 (casualty figures, 298–99).

2 "Hideous Juggernaut Is Called 'Tank' by British Soldiers on Somme," *Detroit Free Press,* Sept. 17, 1916, 4.

3 "Revising the Scriptures," *Current Opinion* 61, no. 6 (December 1916): 374 (armadillos); "British Use New Traveling Fort in Somme Drive," *Christian Science Monitor,* September 18, 1916, 1; "Hideous Juggernaut Is Called 'Tank' by British Soldiers on Somme," 4 (quotation).

4 Keegan, *First World War,* 299.

5 Gilbert, *First World War* (Weidenfeld & Nicolson), 200, says six miles. Keegan, *First World War,* 280, says seven miles. R. G. Grant, *World War I: The Definitive Visual History* (Washington, D.C.: Smithsonian/DK, 2014), says "no more than 7.5 miles" (185).

6 "Famous 'Tanks' of Somme Battle Had Their Origin at Peoria, Ill.," *St. Louis Post-Dispatch,* September 19, 1916.

CHAPTER 3

Epigraphs: Woodrow Wilson, "Address to a Joint Session of Congress Requesting a Declaration of War Against Germany, April 2, 1917," American Presidency Project, www.presidency.ucsb.edu/ws/index.php?pid=65366 (accessed December 2015). George Norris quoted in Geoffrey R. Stone, *Perilous Times: Free Speech in Wartime, from the Sedition Act of 1798 to the War on Terrorism* (New York: W. W. Norton & Company, 2004), 137.

1 John Gardner Coolidge, *A War Diary in Paris, 1914–1917* (Cambridge, MA: Privately printed, 1931), 188–89. Arthur S. Link, *Wilson: Campaigns for Progressivism and Peace, 1916–1917* [vol. 5 of 5-vol. biography] (Princeton, NJ: Princeton University Press, 1965), 291–94 (citing *New York World,* February 1, 1917). Theodore Roosevelt to G. E. Roosevelt, February 1, 1917, Roosevelt Papers, Manuscript Division, Library of Congress.

2 "German-American Editorial Comments on Developments," *Daily Missoulian* (Missoula, MT), February 4, 1917. "'Fight,' Says Bryan, 'To Last, If Invaded,'" *New York Times,* February 3, 1917. "U.S. Crisis Theme of William H. Taft," *Evening Star* (Washington, D.C.), February 3, 1917.

3 Link, *Wilson: Campaigns for Progressivism and Peace,* 293–97 (the passage in quotes [296] is from a letter Secretary of the Interior Franklin Lane wrote to his brother on February 9, 1917, reporting on the cabinet meeting).

4 Wilson's concern over the dominance of the white race is revealed in Robert Lansing, *War Memoirs of Robert Lansing* (Westport, CT: Greenwood Press, 1935/1970), 212, in which Lansing reports a conversation with Wilson on the evening of January 31, 1917, just after receipt of the

German declaration of unrestricted submarine warfare: "The President, though deeply incensed at Germany's insolent notice, said that he was not yet sure what course we must pursue and must think it over; that he had been more and more impressed with the idea that 'white civilization' and its domination over the world rested largely on our ability to keep the country intact, as we would have to build up the nations ravaged by the war." See also David F. Houston, *Eight Years with Wilson's Cabinet: 1913–1920*, 2 vols. (Garden City, NY: Doubleday, Page & Company, 1926), 1: 229, regarding the February 2 cabinet meeting: "The President asked what we thought should be done. 'Shall I break off diplomatic relations with Germany?' He immediately followed this question with a somewhat startling statement. He would say frankly that, if he felt that, in order to keep the white race or part of it strong to meet the yellow race—Japan, for instance, in alliance with Russia, dominating China—it was wise to do nothing, he would do nothing, and would submit to anything and any imputation of weakness or cowardice."

5 Link, *Wilson: Campaigns for Progressivism and Peace*, 293, 297. Houston, *Eight Years with Wilson's Cabinet*, 1: 230.

6 Woodrow Wilson, "Address to a Joint Session of Congress on the Severance of Diplomatic Relations with Germany, February 3, 1917," American Presidency Project, www.presidency.ucsb.edu/ws/index.php?pid=65366.

7 Link, *Wilson: Campaigns for Progressivism and Peace*, 301–9, 328–36. David M. Kennedy, *Over Here: The First World War and American Society* (New York: Oxford University Press, 1980), 11. Martin Blumenson, *The Patton Papers, 1885–1940* (New York: Da Capo Press, 1998), 370–71.

8 "Mobilizing the American Red Cross," *Red Cross Magazine* 12, no. 3 (April 1917); 83–85, notes that the cost of each base hospital was about $25,000, exclusive of bandages and hospital gowns. See also Edward Eyre Hunt, "What Happened When the Break Came: How Our Red Cross was Mobilized," in the same issue, 85–88. "Organization of Columns Begins: Col. Jefferson R. Kean, Medical Corps, U.S.A., Is Authorized by the War Department to Aid Red Cross Preparedness," *American Red Cross Magazine* 11, no. 3 (March 1916): 83.

9 Edward M. Coffman, *The War To End All Wars: The American Military Experience in World War I* (Madison: University of Wisconsin Press), 18 ("On April 1, 1917, there were only 5791 officers and 121,797 enlisted men in the regulars, supplemented by 80,446 National Guard officers and men on federal service. The bulk of this force still remained on the Mexican border. As a second line, the army looked to another 101,174 guardsmen who were under state control. The active force of regulars and guardsmen were prepared neither in organization nor in equipment for service in Europe"). Peyton C. March, *The Nation at War* (New York: Doubleday, Doran & Company, 1932), 1, states that the total strength of the regular army in 1917 (officers and men) was 127,588.

10 John Garry Clifford, *The Citizen Soldiers: The Plattsburg Training Camp Movement, 1913–1920* (Lexington: University Press of Kentucky, 1972), 239, 259. "The Organization of the National Research Council," at National Academy of Sciences website, www.nasonline.org/about-nas/history/archives/milestones-in-NAS-history/organization-of-the-nrc.html (accessed December 2015).

11 Christopher Capozzola, *Uncle Sam Wants You: World War I and the Making of the Modern American Citizen* (New York: Oxford University Press, 2008), 88–90. Carrie Brown, *Rosie's Mom: Forgotten Women Workers of the First World War* (Boston: Northeastern University Press, 2002), 80. Dorothy Salem, *To Better Our World: Black Women in Organized Reform, 1890–1920* (Brooklyn, NY: Carlson Publishing, 1990), 202–3.

12 National Security League, *Proceedings of the Congress of Constructive Patriotism* (New York: National Security League, 1917), 4, 126–35. Barbara J. Steinson, *American Women's Activism in World War I* (New York: Garland Publishing, 1982), 300–304.

13 Tom G. Hall, "Wilson and the Food Crisis: Agricultural Price Control during World War I," *Agricultural History* 47, no. 1 (January 1973): 25–46 (food riots, 38; 25, Hall notes that that food prices rose 46 percent between July 1916 and April 1917 and would rise another 45 percent by December 1917). "One Killed, Several Injured: Food Riot," *Bemidji (MN) Daily Pioneer*, February 22, 1917.

"Brownsville Women Attack Patrolman, Wrecking Carts," *New York Tribune*, February 22, 1917. "Mitchel Orders City-Wide Survey of Food Situation," *New York Times*, February 22, 1917. "Killed in Food Riots," *Dakota County Herald* (Dakota City, NE), March 1, 1917. George H. Nash, *The Life of Herbert Hoover: The Humanitarian* [vol. 2 of 3-vol. biography] (New York: W. W. Norton & Company, 1988), 312–14.

14 Nash, *Life of Herbert Hoover: The Humanitarian*, 314. CRB shipments resumed on February 24, after a guarantee to the Allies that the cargoes would be inspected in Halifax, Nova Scotia, or some other friendly port outside the war zone, and after acquiescing to Germany's demand that they only travel the northern route. "Capital Again Sees a Crisis: Wilson Considers Asking Congress for Authority to Arm Ships," *New York Times*, February 15, 1917.

15 Link, *Wilson: Campaigns for Progressivism and Peace*, 305–7. "Urge Peace in Chicago: Coliseum Meeting Wants a Referendum Vote of the Nation," *New York Times*, February 19, 1917. Meirion Harries and Susie Harries, *The Last Days of Innocence: America at War, 1917–1918* (New York: Random House, 1997), 67 (Addams quote).

16 Link, *Wilson: Campaigns for Progressivism and Peace*, 314–22, 385–86.

17 Kennedy, *Over Here*, 8. Mrs. J. Borden [Florence] Harriman, *From Pinafores to Politics* (New York: Henry Holt & Company, 1923), 215–16. Link, *Wilson: Campaigns for Progressivism and Peace*, 317–18, 340–41, 344–46 (Link states [346]: "The Zimmermann telegram did not convert Wilson to war or even prompt him to decide to ask Congress for authority to arm American ships. He had already made that decision. It simply caused him to lose all faith in the German government.").

18 Barbara W. Tuchman, *The Zimmermann Telegram* (New York: The Macmillan Company, 1958), 145–46. Woodrow Wilson, "Address to a Joint Session of Congress: Request for Authority, February 26, 1917," American Presidency Project, www.presidency.ucsb.edu/ws/?pid=65398. Link, *Wilson: Campaigns for Progressivism and Peace*, 346–50.

19 Link, *Wilson: Campaigns for Progressivism and Peace*, 349–52.

20 Tuchman, *Zimmermann Telegram*, 175–87 (Round Table Dining Club, 181). Link, *Wilson: Campaigns for Progressivism and Peace*, 354–57. "City Germans Doubt Note Is Authentic," *New York Times*, March 2, 1917. "Plot Awakens Congress," *New York Times*, March 2, 1917. "Comment of Today's Newspapers on the German Attempted Intrigue Against the United States," *New York Times*, March 2, 1917.

21 Link, *Wilson: Campaigns for Progressivism and Peace*, 354, 359–62. Richard Drake, *The Education of an Anti-Imperialist: Robert La Follette and U.S. Expansion* (Madison: University of Wisconsin Press, 2013), 168–71. La Follette was not alone in his opinion. On February 27, members of the Emergency Peace Federation sent congressmen the following plea regarding the armed-ships bill: "The Emergency Peace Federation protests against the proposal that Congress should abdicate any of its Constitutional functions. To center in one man the tremendous power of virtually waging war is not that 'new freedom' or 'wider democracy' which, we were told a few years ago, was the goal of the American nation. We believe the precedent to be a dangerous one." See "Peace Advocates Protest," *New York Times*, February 28, 1917. Drake also provides the full roster of senators who joined La Follette and Norris in opposing the armed-ships bill: Republicans Albert B. Cummings of Iowa, Moses F. Clapp of Minnesota, William S. Kenyon of Iowa, Asle J. Gronna of North Dakota, and John D. Works of California, as well as Democrats William J. Stone of Missouri, James K. Vardaman of Mississippi, James A. O'Gorman of New York, William F. Kirby of Arkansas, and Harry Lane of Oregon. Richard Lowitt, *George W. Norris: The Persistence of a Progressive, 1913–1933* (Urbana: University of Illinois Press, 1971), 63. John Callan O'Laughlin to Theodore Roosevelt, March 7, 1917, O'Laughlin Papers, Manuscript Division, Library of Congress. In his reply the following day, Roosevelt (who called the armed-ships bill "almost worthless" and armed neutrality "timid war") also called the senators treasonous—but went further: "I feel infinitely more keenly that the President is a thousand times more to blame than all the senators combined. They

did badly, but they did badly only because of all the shameful things he has done, and the good things he has shamefully left undone, during the past four years."

22 Link, *Wilson: Campaigns for Progressivism and Peace*, 361, 367–69. Woodrow Wilson, "Inaugural Address, March 5, 1917," American Presidency Project, www.presidency.ucsb.edu/ws/?pid=25832 (accessed February 2016).

23 Capozzola, *Uncle Sam Wants You*, 106, 112. "Historical Overview of the National Woman's Party," in *Women of Protest: Photographs from the Records of the National Woman's Party*, at Library of Congress website, www.loc.gov/collections/women-of-protest/articles-and-essays/historical-overview-of-the-national-womans-party/ (accessed March 2016).

24 Harries and Harries, *Last Days of Innocence*, 68 (citing Arthur S. Link, ed., *Papers of Woodrow Wilson*, 69 vols. [Princeton, NJ: Princeton University Press, 1966–1983], 41: 412). Mark Ellis, *Race, War, and Surveillance: African Americans and the United States Government During World War I* (Bloomington: Indiana University Press, 2001), 2–4.

25 "Debs Urges Strike If Nation Fights," *New York Times*, March 8, 1917. Kennedy, *Over Here*, 11–12, 26–28. "Labor to Discuss National Crisis: Gompers Calls Great Council in Washington to Determine Role of Wage Earners," *New York Times*, March 5, 1917. "Wilson Appeals to Patriotism to Avert Strike: Sends Lane, Wilson, Willard, and Gompers of Defense Council Here to Mediate," *New York Times*, March 17, 1917.

26 Marcus H. Holcomb, "Connecticut in the Van," *American Review of Reviews* 57, no. 5 (May 1918): 520–21. Link, *Wilson: Campaigns for Progressivism and Peace*, 418, 396–97. Harries and Harries, *Last Days of Innocence*, 69.

27 Martin Gilbert, *The First World War: A Complete History* (New York: Henry Holt & Company, 1996), 315. "Russia in the Hands of Revolutionary Party . . . Ministry Imprisoned, Army Sides with the People and Duma," *Tonopah (NV) Daily Bonanza*, March 15, 1917. "Ray of Sparkling Light Pierces Russian Darkness . . . Right at Last Overpowers Might," *Daily Gate City and Constitution-Democrat* (Keokuk, IA), March 16, 1917.

"Kaiser Must Abdicate, Too," *Tacoma (WA) Times*, March 16, 1917. "Russia Now a Republic," *East Oregonian* (Pendleton, OR), March 17, 1917. Link, *Wilson: Campaigns for Progressivism and Peace*, 375, 393–96.

28 Lansing, *War Memoirs*, 237. Kennedy, *Over Here*, 10. Link, *Wilson: Campaigns for Progressivism and Peace*, 401–4.

29 Link, *Wilson: Campaigns for Progressivism and Peace*, 408, 416–17. Elting E. Morison, *Admiral Sims and the Modern American Navy* (New York: Russell & Russell, 1968), 337–40. Coffman, *War to End All Wars*, 92–93. Admiral William S. Sims, letter to his wife, March 31, 1917, Sims Papers, Manuscript Division, Library of Congress. See also Ed Klekowski and Libby Klekowski, *Americans in Occupied Belgium, 1914–1918: Accounts of the War from Journalists, Tourists, Troops and Medical Staff* (Jefferson, NC: McFarland & Company, 2014), chapter 11, which notes that Ambassador Whitlock and various other Americans, particularly those associated with the Committee for Relief in Belgium, remained in the country until April 2. The Germans allowed some American businessmen to remain a bit longer.

30 "Destroyed in 'Safe Zone.' Tanker Healdton Torpedoed without Warning in North Sea," *New York Times*, March 23, 1917. Link, *Wilson: Campaigns for Progressivism and Peace*, 416-417. Norman E. Saul, *War and Revolution: The United States and Russia, 1914–1921* (Lawrence: University Press of Kansas, 2001), 91–93. "Pacifists Pester Till Mayor Calls Them Traitors," *New York Times*, March 24, 1917.

31 Link, *Wilson: Campaigns for Progressivism and Peace*, 417–18. Robert D. Ward, "The Origin and Activities of the National Security League, *Mississippi Valley Historical Review* 47, no. 1 (June 1960): 58. "Off to Rouse West in Nation's Defense: Henry L. Stimson and Frederic R. Coudert Open Tour in Detroit Today," *New York Times*, April 2, 1917. Kennedy, *Over Here*, 14–15.

32 Link, *Wilson: Campaigns for Progressivism and Peace*, 421–23. Kennedy, *Over Here*, 15. Capozzola, *Uncle Sam Wants You*, 26. "Lodge Knocks Down Pacifist Assailant," *New York Times*, April 3, 1917. Harriman, *From Pinafores to Politics*, 212–14.

33 Link, *Wilson: Campaigns for Progressivism and Peace*, 423–27. Kennedy, *Over Here*, 13-14. Drake, *Education of an Anti-Imperialist*, 176. Woodrow Wilson, "Address to a Joint Session of Congress Requesting a Declaration of War Against Germany, April 2, 1917," American Presidency Project, www.presidency.ucsb.edu/ws/?pid=65366.

34 Link, *Wilson: Campaigns for Progressivism and Peace*, 429–30. Kennedy, *Over Here*, 20–24. Drake, *Education of an Anti-Imperialist*, 177–83. "28 of American Ship Aztec Are Believed Lost," *Grand Fords (ND) Herald*, April 3, 1917. "U.S. Armed Steamer Aztec Sunk off France by German U-Boat. Many American Sailors Missing," *Bisbee (AZ) Daily Review*, April 3, 1917. "American Steamer Missourian Sunk," *Norwich (CT) Bulletin*, April 6, 1917. "American Ship Sunk; Crew Saved; Unarmed Missourian . . . Is Destroyed in Mediterranean," *New York Times*, April 6, 1917.

35 "The City's Streets Aglow with Flags," *New York Times*, April 17, 1917 (Geraldine Farrar and street-corner speech). Kennedy, *Over Here*, 26. "New Song 'America Here's My Boy,'" *South Bend (IN) News-Times*, April 11, 1917. "High School Athletes Leave Sport for Army," *Daily Missoulian* (Missoula, MT), April 11, 1917. "Take Sons to Stations—Record Day for Enlisting" (dateline Chicago), *Daily Missoulian* (Missoula, MT), April 11, 1917.

36 Jack C. Lane, *Armed Progressive: General Leonard Wood* (Lincoln: University of Nebraska Press), 200–201. Clifford, *Citizen Soldiers*, 198–200. John Whiteclay Chambers II, *Draftees or Volunteers: A Documentary History of the Debate over Military Conscription in the United States, 1787–1973* (New York: Garland Publishing, 1975), 220. Kennedy, *Over Here*, 145–47. Frederic L. Paxson, *America at War, 1917–1918* (Boston: Houghton Mifflin Company, 1939), 4–5. BBC "Viewpoint: 10 Big Myths about World War One Debunked," *BBC News Magazine*, www.bbc.com/news/magazine-25776836, includes, as one myth, "The upper class got off lightly" and states that "the social and political elite were hit disproportionately hard by WW1. Their sons provided the junior officers whose job it was to lead the way over the top and expose themselves to the greatest danger as an example to their men. Some 12% of the British army's ordinary soldiers were killed during the war, compared with 17% of its officers. Eton alone lost more than 1,000 former pupils—20% of those who served. UK wartime Prime Minister Herbert Asquith lost a son, while future Prime Minister Andrew Bonar Law lost two. Anthony Eden [another future prime minister] lost two brothers, another brother of his was terribly wounded, and an uncle was captured." John Whiteclay Chambers II, *To Raise an Army: The Draft Comes to Modern America* (New York: The Free Press, 1987), 126 (citing Wilson to Mrs. George Bass, May 4, 1917, Wilson Papers, Library of Congress).

37 Chambers, *Draftees or Volunteers*, 233–66 (Bryant, 263; Eastwood, 265). Kennedy, *Over Here*, 145–49. Edmund Morris, *Colonel Roosevelt* (New York: Random House, 2010), 486–87. "Clark in Debate Opposes Draft," *New York Times*, April 26, 1917. "Draft Advocates Lead Opening Day of House Debate," *New York Times*, April 24, 1917. Chambers, *To Raise an Army*, 164.

38 John W. Hillje, "New York Progressives and the War Revenue Act of 1917," *New York History* 53, no. 4 (October 1972): 437–59 (Pinchot and Scripps quotes, 446). Kennedy, *Over Here*, 107–8.

39 Paxson, *America at War*, 10–14. Kennedy, *Over Here*, 107, 109. Ranajoy Ray Chaudhuri, *The Changing Face of American Banking* (New York: Palgrave Macmillan, 2014), 74.

40 Kennedy, *Over Here*, 109. Robert B. Bruce, "America Embraces France: Marshal Joseph Joffre and the French Mission to the United States, April–May 1917," *Journal of Military History* 66, no. 2 (April 2002): 407–41. Bruce notes U.S. suspicions of the British: "The British Empire's powerful navy and dominion over Canada made it the only Great Power that could realistically project its military might into the Western Hemisphere . . . The British alliance with Japan, a nation that the United States increasingly viewed as a major threat to its interests in Asia, caused many nightmarish scenarios to evolve in the minds of America's senior leaders during the years of American neutrality. In fact, as recently as December 1916 . . . General [Hugh] Scott had testified before the Senate Military Affairs Committee that the U.S. Army had to be built up in order to defend against

a possible Anglo-Japanese invasion from Canada" (427). Regarding the importance of Irish independence to Americans, see 427–28. See also "Home Rule Outside Balfour's Mission," *New York Times*, May 7, 1917, which states, "There was a revival of reports today that the Irish home rule question was forming an important part of Mr. Balfour's reports to his home Government, and that he was emphasizing the necessity of a settlement in order to secure the whole-hearted cooperation from the United States for carrying on the war."

41 Harriman, *From Pinafores to Politics*, 220. Bruce, "America Embraces France," 407–41 (on the ecstatic reception that Joffre received in early May on a tour of American cities, 430–35). David F. Trask, *The United States in the Supreme War Council: American War Aims and Inter-Allied Strategy, 1917–1918* (Middletown, CT: Wesleyan University Press, 1961), 20, addresses the lack of perfect harmony between the two major Allies: "Long before the United States entered World War I, the Allied Powers had become aware of the weakness resulting from the failure to coordinate their efforts on the Western Front. Unfortunately for the Allies, several early attempts to improve inter-Allied cooperation had come to naught."

42 Paxson, *America at War*, 10–14. Kennedy, *Over Here*, 319–24. "Hunger Is Greatest Enemy Now; Want Bread and Meat, Not Men and Guns," *Daily Gate City and Constitution-Democrat* (Keokuk, IA), April 23, 1917 (see subhead "What the Allies Want from United States More Than Anything Else Just Now is Plenty of Food, Must Have It or They Perish"). Morison, *Admiral Sims*, 343–46. George H. Nash, *The Life of Herbert Hoover: Master of Emergencies, 1917–1918* [vol. 3 of 3-vol. biography] (New York: W. W. Norton & Company, 1996), 36, 11.

43 Gilbert, *First World War* (Holt, 1996), 320–23. John Keegan, *The First World War* (New York: Vintage Books, 2000), 324–30. Bruce, "America Embraces France," 407–41 (see especially 417–18).

44 Bruce, "America Embraces France," 407–41 (see especially 417, 421–22, 429). Kennedy, *Over Here*, 170. David F. Trask, *The AEF and Coalition Warmaking, 1917–1918* (Lawrence: University Press of Kansas, 1993), 5–6.

45 Chambers, *To Raise an Army*, 166, cites the British and French missions as one of the elements that helped move Wilson's plan for conscription through Congress: "Marvin Jones, a rural Texas Democrat . . . later recalled that the Allied Missions had helped bring home to many in Congress that the United States was being catapulted into an active international role: 'The whole picture of this country was changing all at once.'" Bruce, "America Embraces France," 421, states, "As late as 3 April, [U.S. Army Chief of Staff Hugh] Scott had opposed sending American forces to fight in Europe and was especially wary of 'entangling alliances' with European powers. Yet after the arrival of Joffre in Washington, the two men had quickly established a good personal relationship . . . Perhaps sensing that the Wilson administration was leaning toward the idea of sending an American force overseas, Scott had begun to warm to the idea of Franco-American military cooperation."

46 Harriman, *From Pinafores to Politics*, 222. Chambers, *To Raise an Army*, 167. Capozzola, *Uncle Sam Wants You*, 26 (aliens to register), 58 (conscientious objectors). Trask, *The AEF and Coalition Warmaking*, 14. Morris, *Colonel Roosevelt*, 494.

47 Link, *Wilson: Campaigns for Progressivism and Peace*, 398–99. According to John L. Heaton, *Cobb of "The World": A Leader in Liberalism* (New York: E. P. Dutton & Company, 1924), 268–70, Cobb recalls the conversation taking place on April 2. Link, *Wilson*, states that there is no record of Cobb visiting the White House that day of Wilson's request for a declaration of war; but Cobb did visit on March 19, while Wilson was still deliberating, making that the more logical date. There seems little doubt that the conversation *did* take place.

48 "Woman Finds Scrap o' Paper Saying Plan 'All Ready' for Destruction of Eddystone," *Philadelphia Evening Ledger*, April 11, 1917. "Eddystone Disaster Victims Monument," www.findagrave.com/cgi-bin/fg.cgi?page=gr&GRid=8040557 (accessed September 2012; March 2016). Woodrow Wilson, "Address to a Joint Session of Congress Requesting a Declaration of War Against Germany, April 2, 1917," American Presidency Project, www.presidency.ucsb.edu/ws/?pid=65366 (accessed March 2016). Ellis, *Race, War, and Surveillance*, 5–6. "Germans to Incite Revolt of

Negroes?" *Lancaster (SC) News*, April 6, 1917. "Trying to Incite Negroes to War," *Barre (VT) Daily Times*, April 6, 1917. Fannie Fern [Phillips] Andrews, *A Call to Patriotic Service: To the Teachers of the United States* (Boston: 1917), 1–2.

49 Kennedy, *Over Here*, 24–25. Capozzola, *Uncle Sam Wants You*, 151. Woodrow Wilson, "Third Annual Message, December 7, 1915," American Presidency Project, www.presidency.ucsb.edu/ws/index.php?pid=29556 (accessed March 2016). Geoffrey Stone, *Perilous Times: Free Speech in Wartime, from the Sedition Act of 1798 to the War on Terrorism* (New York: W. W. Norton & Company, 2004), 151.

50 Frances H. Early, *A World Without War: How U.S. Feminists and Pacifists Resisted World War I* (Syracuse, NY: Syracuse University Press), 19–21. Stone, *Perilous Times*, 148–49. Kennedy, *Over Here*, 25–26.

51 John Reed, "Whose War," *Masses* 9, no. 6 (April 1917): 11–12. On page 8 of this same issue of the magazine, a one-paragraph article titled "Wilson or the Truth?" seemed to reflect the Espionage Bill debate then in progress: "In the name of loyalty to President Wilson, a censorship and suppression of free speech, incompatible with the elementary principles of democratic liberty for which President Wilson stands, is threatening the press and platforms of this country. It will be a fine test of his devotion to these principles, if this threat is fulfilled. We hope that he may find time in the engrossments of his task, to remind these zealous Prussians of the military arm, that we are not yet an empire, even though we go to war." Stone, *Perilous Times*, 149–50. Alan Axelrod, *Selling the Great War: The Making of American Propaganda* (New York: Palgrave Macmillan, 2009), 98.

52 Stone, *Perilous Times*, 150–51.

53 The Sedition Act of 1798, signed into law by President John Adams, severely restricted criticism of the government and was chiefly designed to silence and weaken the president's political opposition. Stone, a legal historian, in *Perilous Times*, 33–44, writes, "In this act the Federalists [Adams's party] (and the U.S. government) declared war on dissent." The act caused a furor and was allowed to expire in 1801. A short background and the text of the act are available through the Library of Congress website at www.loc.gov/rr/program/bib/ourdocs/Alien.html. The Espionage Act of 1917 remains in force.

54 Woodrow Wilson, "Speech in Washington Monument Grounds: 'The German Plot,' June 14, 1917," American Presidency Project, www.presidency.ucsb.edu/ws/index.php?pid=65400 (accessed March 2016). Kennedy, *Over Here*, 26. Stone, *Perilous Times*, 151–53. Capozzola, *Uncle Sam Wants You*, 151.

55 Capozzola, *Uncle Sam Wants You*, 41–42. Theodore Kornweibel, Jr., *"Investigate Everything": Federal Efforts to Compel Black Loyalty During World War I* (Bloomington: Indiana University Press, 2002), 10–11. Ellis, *Race, War, and Surveillance*, vii (four hundred BI agents). Paul L. Murphy, *World War I and the Origin of Civil Liberties in the United States* (New York: W. W. Norton & Company, 1979), 89–90, 94–95. Kennedy, *Over Here*, 81–83. Kennedy notes that on June 4, 1917, President Wilson wrote to the attorney general questioning the wisdom of "such an organization [as APL] operating in the United States," but beyond that the president made little real effort to curb the APL's activities. Stone, *Perilous Times*, 156–57. Terry Teachout, *The Skeptic: A Life of H. L. Mencken* (New York: HarperCollins, 2002), 144–45.

56 Arlen J. Hansen, *Gentlemen Volunteers: The Story of American Ambulance Drivers in the Great War, August 1914–September 1918* (New York: Arcade Publishing, 1996), 161–64. Richard S. Kennedy, *Dreams in the Mirror: A Biography of e. e. cummings* (New York: Liveright Publishing Corporation, 1980), 137–58. Virginia Spencer Carr, *Dos Passos: A Life* (Evanston, IL: Northwestern University Press, 2004), 121–26. Townsend Ludington, ed., *The Fourteenth Chronicle: Letters and Diaries of John Dos Passos* (Boston: Gambit, 1973), 79, 85. Morris, *Colonel Roosevelt*, 498.

57 Will Irwin, "First Aid to America," *Saturday Evening Post*, March 24, 1917, 6–7, 109–14. For understandable reasons, Hoover was not actually named in this lengthy article. Irwin identified him only as "Jones."

58 "Suggests War Honors for Army of Farmers," *New York Times*, April 6, 1917. Charles Lathrop Pack, *The War Garden Victorious* (Philadelphia: J. B. Lippincott Company, 1919), 2, 9–10. Elaine F. Weiss, *Fruits of*

Victory: The Woman's Land Army of America in the Great War (Washington, D.C.: Potomac Books, Inc.), 21–22, 25. Nash, *Life of Herbert Hoover: Master of Emergencies*, 7–26. "President's Outline of Food Control Program for Conserving and Stimulating Our War Supply," *New York Times*, May 20, 1917.

59 Lawrence E. Gelfand, *The Inquiry: American Preparations for Peace, 1917–1919* (New Haven, CT: Yale University Press, 1963), 44–45. Arthur P. Young, *Books for Sammies: The American Library Association and World War I* (Pittsburgh: Beta Phi Mu, 1981), xi, 10.

60 Clifford, *Citizen Soldiers*, 229–32, notes, on page 231, that "even with the quick start, the obstacles were such that the opening of the camps had to be pushed back a week to May 15." The author also notes that of the 43,000 men twenty-one to forty-five years of age that attended the first training session, ending in mid-August, 27,341 successfully earned commissions. The camps continued training officers, though for a period civilian trainees were replaced by army and National Guard noncoms.

61 Blumenson, *Patton Papers*, 384, 387–92. Trask, *The AEF and Coalition Warmaking*, 6. John J. Pershing, *My Experiences in the First World War*, 2 vols. (1931; repr., New York: Da Capo Press, 1995), 1: 34, 43.

62 "The Vanguard," *Red Cross Magazine* 12, no. 6 (July 1917), 228–29.

63 Saul, *War and Revolution*, 106 (House quote), 109, 112–13. "Peace Mission Aided by Berlin: Russian Radicals Allowed to Cross from Berne on Way to Petrograd," *New York Times*, April 16, 1917. "Russian Socialists Assail England: Peace Agitators, Reaching Stockholm, Aided in Travels by Germany," *Evening Star* (Washington, D.C.), April 15, 1917. "Talk of Dictatorship to Save Russia; Kerensky Gives Warning of Disaster; War Minister Resigned in Despair," *New York Times*, May 15, 1917. "Kerensky as Russia's Leader of the Hour," *New York Times*, May 19, 1917. Gilbert, *First World War* (Holt, 1996), 332–33.

64 Saul, *War and Revolution*, 153–54. Harriman, *From Pinafores to Politics*, 220–22. Herbert Croly, *Willard*

Straight (New York: The Macmillan Company, 1924), 479.

65 Harriman, *From Pinafores to Politics*, 217. Mary Chamberlain, "Women and War Work," *Survey* 38, no. 7 (May 19, 1917): 153–54. Kennedy, *Over Here*, 262. Brown, *Rosie's Mom*, 109–10.

66 Axelrod, *Selling the Great War*, 67, 230. Wilson's Executive Order 2594 specified that the CPI was "to be composed of the Secretary of State, the Secretary of War, the Secretary of the Navy, and a civilian who shall be charged with the executive direction of the Committee. As Civilian Chairman of this Committee, I appoint Mr. George Creel. The Secretary of State, the Secretary of War, and the Secretary of the Navy are authorized each to detail an officer or officers to the work of the Committee." Executive Order 2594, American Presidency Project, http://www.presidency.ucsb.edu/ws/?pid=75409. See also Kennedy, *Over Here*, 60.

67 Kennedy, *Over Here*, 59–60. Stone, *Perilous Times*, 153. George Creel, *How We Advertised America* (New York: Arno Press, 1972), 16–23. George Creel, *Rebel at Large: Recollections of Fifty Crowded Years* (New York: G. P. Putnam's Sons, 1947), 156–61. Axelrod, *Selling the Great War*, 86–90.

68 Creel, *Rebel at Large*, 160–65. Creel, *How We Advertised America*, 3. Axelrod, *Selling the Great War*, 84, 91, 113–15, 136–38, 159–61, 189–91. Kennedy, *Over Here*, 61.

69 Nancy K. Bristow, *Making Men Moral: Social Engineering During the Great War* (New York: New York University Press, 1996), 5. Fosdick's border investigations and subsequent report did not include the Punitive Expedition itself, although Fosdick did visit the expedition's U.S. supply base at Columbus, New Mexico. There he saw evidence of General Pershing's own program for fighting the ravages of venereal disease, a bane that sapped troops' morale and fighting strength. Pershing's program included rigorous drills and sports and controlled prostitution, with both soldiers and prostitutes regularly examined by medical staff. Though frowned upon by most reformers, who favored eradication of prostitution rather than control, the Pershing experiment resulted in a much lower rate of "noneffective men per thousand" for troops in his

expedition than throughout the army as a whole. See James A. Sandos, "Prostitution and Drugs: The United States Army on the Mexican-American Border, 1916–1917," *Pacific Historical Review* 49, no. 4 (November 1980): 621–45.

70 Bristow, *Making Men Moral*, 1–8, 13 (invisible armor), 18 (Wilson), 36 (affiliates), 98 (moral zones), 138–39 (African American troops). Capozzola, *Uncle Sam Wants You*, 132–34. Kennedy, *Over Here*, 186.

71 Trask, *The AEF and Coalition Warmaking*, 15. Chambers, *To Raise an Army*, 180–81, 210–11. Kennedy, *Over Here*, 150–55. Capozzola, *Uncle Sam Wants You*, 26–28. "Ten Million Men Ready to Obey Draft Law; No Disturbances Expected," and "Officers to Arrest All Who Interfere with Registration," both in the *Bisbee (AZ) Daily Review*, June 5, 1917. "Jail Awaits Man Who Is Delinquent Registration Day," *Bemidji (MN) Daily Pioneer*, May 24, 1917. "Patriotic Meetings Mark Registration," *New York Times*, June 6, 1917. "Registration Day Features," *Daily Gate City and Constitution-Democrat* (Keokuk, IA), June 5, 1917. "All Philadelphia Stirred by Patriotic Response of Its Many Young Men on Registration Day," *Philadelphia Evening Ledger*, June 5, 1917.

72 Richard W. Stewart, ed., *American Military History, Volume 2, The United States Army in a Global Era, 1917–2008*, 2nd ed. (Washington, D.C.: Center of Military History, United States Army, 2010), 9. The author notes that although the Sixteenth, Eighteenth, Twenty-sixth, and Twenty-eighth infantry regiments were among the army's most battlefield ready, they were so severely understrength that when the First Division sailed, about two thirds of each regiment were raw recruits.

73 Forrest C. Pogue, *George C. Marshall: Education of a General* (New York: Viking Press, 1963), 143–44. Pershing, *My Experiences in the First World War*, 1: 58–59. Blumenson, *Patton Papers*, 395–96. Albert Gleaves, *A History of the Transport Service: Adventures and Experiences of United States Transports and Cruisers in the World War* (New York: George H. Doran Company, 1921), 33–35, 41. Commander of convoy operations in the Atlantic during the war, Gleaves noted in this account that the first three convoys transporting the First Division left New York on June 14 at two-hour intervals; the fourth

was delayed twenty-four hours because of "belated dispatches and stores."

74 George W. Baer, *One Hundred Years of Sea Power: The U.S. Navy, 1890–1990* (Stanford, CA: Stanford University Press, 1994), 65 (War Plan Black), 73. Jean Ebbert and Marie-Beth Hall, *The First, the Few, the Forgotten: Navy and Marine Corps Women in World War I* (Annapolis, MD: Naval Institute Press, 2002), ix, 4–5; the authors note that both the army and the navy had accepted women nurses since 1901 and 1908, respectively, but "those women were not enlisted, nor were they commissioned, although they were generally treated as officers." "Philadelphia Woman Enlists in the Navy: Miss Loretta Walsh, Chief Yeoman, Said to Have Set Precedent for the World," *New York Times*, March 22, 1917. "First Woman Recruit in U.S. Navy, *Day Book* (Chicago), March 26, 1917. "Philadelphia Girl Is First Woman to Enlist in United States Navy," *Topeka (KS) State Journal*, March 27, 1917. Frank Freidel, *Franklin D. Roosevelt: The Apprenticeship* (Boston: Little, Brown & Company, 1952), 326 (J. P. Morgan).

75 Gleaves, *A History of the Transport Service*, 25–26 (statistics), 29. Edmund E. Day, "The American Merchant Fleet: A War Achievement, a Peace Problem," *Quarterly Journal of Economics* 34, no. 4 (August 1920): 567–606. Kennedy, *Over Here*, 305, 329. Kennedy notes, 329, that the extensive use of Allied ships for transportation resulted in part from President Wilson's reluctance to divert U.S. merchantmen that were engaged in trade with Brazil and Japan. Freidel, *Roosevelt: The Apprenticeship*, 326–27.

76 Judy Rumerman, "The U.S. Aircraft Industry During World War I," at U.S. Centennial of Flight Commission website www.centennialofflight.net/essay/Aerospace/WWi/Aero5.htm (accessed April 2016). "American Officer on a Mission to France," *Butte (MT) Daily Post*, July 6, 1917. Greenwich (CT) Historical Society, "Col. Raynal Cawthorne Bolling," www.greenwichfacesthegreatwar.org/colonel-raynal-cawthorne-bolling.php (accessed April 2016). National Air and Space Museum, "De Havilland DH-4," http://airandspace.si.edu/collections/artifact.cfm?object=nasm_A19190051000 (accessed April 2016). Pershing, *My Experiences in the First World War*, 1: 160–61. Fred

Howard, *Wilbur and Orville: A Biography of the Wright Brothers* (Mineola, NY: Dover Publications, 1998), 410–15. "Plan to Build 3,500 War Airplanes and Train 5,000 Aviators in a Year," *New York Times*, May 21, 1917. "Air Bill Is Signed; Need 110,000 Fliers," *New York Times*, July 25, 1917.

77 Stewart, *American Military History*, 18–19. Saul, *War and Revolution*, 108, states, "General Scott was an appointment of convenience, since he was considered too old-fashioned to retain his post in a wartime administration." Bullitt Lowry, "Bliss, Tasker Howard (1853–1930)," in *The United States in the First World War: An Encyclopedia*, ed. Anne Cipriano Venzon (New York: Garland Publishing, 1995), 94–95. Robert H. Ferrell, *Woodrow Wilson and World War I, 1917–1921* (New York: Harper & Row, 1985), 25. Kennedy, *Over Here*, 126–29. Trask, *The AEF and Coalition Warmaking*, 14.

78 Chambers, *To Raise an Army*, 182–86, 212. Chambers notes, 186, "An additional 109,000 men joined the navy" by the end of June as well. D. M. Giangreco, *The Soldier from Independence: A Military Biography of Harry Truman* (Minneapolis: Zenith Press, 2009), 22–29. Stewart, *American Military History*, 21. Blumenson, *Patton Papers*, 407–9. Clemens P. Work, *Darkest Before Dawn: Sedition and Free Speech in the American West* (Albuquerque: University of New Mexico Press, 2005), 70 (first draft number). Gilbert, *First World War* (Holt, 1996), 350.

79 Chambers, *To Raise an Army*, 212–13. Capozzola, *Uncle Sam Wants You*, 30. Oklahoma Historical Society, "Green Corn Rebellion," at Oklahoma Historical Society website, www.okhistory.org/publications/enc/entry.php?entry=GR022 (accessed November 2015). Kennedy, *Over Here*, 155n.

80 Ronald L. Filippelli, ed., *Labor Conflict in the United States: An Encyclopedia* (New York: Garland Publishing, 1990), 75–76, 376–78. Work, *Darkest Before Dawn*, 60–69, 80. Harries and Harries, *Last Days of Innocence*, 186.

81 Filippelli, *Labor Conflict in the United States*, 44–45, 76. Work, *Darkest Before Dawn*, 71–73, 90–94. Capozzola, *Uncle Sam Wants You*, 126–31. Kennedy, *Over Here*, 263–64.

82 Work, *Darkest Before Dawn*, 95–96, 113–14.

83 Stone, *Perilous Times*, 172–73. Work, *Darkest Before Dawn*, 109–10. "30 Germans Are Arrested in South Dakota for Opposing the War and the Draft Law," *New York Times*, August 28, 1917. Anthony Slide, ed., *Robert Goldstein and "The Spirit of '76"* (Metuchen, NJ: The Scarecrow Press, 1993), xviii–xix, 115–31, 207–11, 216–21.

84 Work, *Darkest Before Dawn*, 100–102, 106, 110–29; 260–61 (the full text of the Montana Sedition Act).

85 Filippelli, *Labor Conflict in the United States*, 162–63. Elliott Rudwick, *Race Riot at East St. Louis*, July 2, 1917 (Urbana: University of Illinois Press, 1982), 41–67. Kennedy, *Over Here*, 281–82. Robert Asher, "Documents of the Race Riot at East St. Louis," *Journal of the Illinois State Historical Society (1908–1984)* 65, no. 3 (Autumn, 1972), 327–36. Kelly Miller, "America on Trial: Race Riots and the Fight for World Democracy," letter to the editor, *Evening Star* (Washington, D.C.), July 7, 1917. "Big Race Riot in East St. Louis; Mobs in Streets," *Morgan City (LA) Daily Review*, July 3, 1917. "Between 20 and 250 Die in Race War," *Rock Island (IL) Argus*, July 3, 1917. "Army Begins Inquiry into Race Rioting," *New York Times*, July 5, 1917. "Labor Denies Riot Blame," *New York Times*, July 6, 1917. "Fiends Incarnate! Cowardly Police and Militia Search Negroe's [sic] Homes . . . Then Turn Them over to the Bloodthirsty Demons Clamoring for Their Lives," *Kansas City Sun*, July 7, 1917.

86 Jonathan Rosenberg, *How Far the Promised Land? World Affairs and the American Civil Rights Movement from the First World War to Vietnam* (Princeton, NJ: Princeton University Press, 2006), 34. The four black army regiments were the Twenty-fourth and Twenty-fifth Infantry and the Ninth and Tenth Cavalry. When the war began there were also eight black National Guard units in northern states. See Chambers, *To Raise an Army*, 222.

87 Gail Buckley, *American Patriots: The Story of Blacks in the Military from the Revolution to Desert Storm* (New York: Random House, 2001), 178. Hal S. Chase, "Struggle for Equality: Fort Des Moines Training Camp for Colored Officers, 1917," *Phylon* 39 no. 4 (Fourth Quarter, 1978):

297–310. Kornweibel, *"Investigate Everything,"* 133–34. Chambers, *To Raise an Army,* 222–23. Adriane Lentz-Smith, *Freedom Struggles: African Americans and World War I* (Cambridge, MA: Harvard University Press, 2009), 59–69. Robert V. Haynes, *A Night of Violence: The Houston Riot of 1917* (Baton Rouge: Louisiana State University Press, 1976), 116–84, 296. Kennedy, *Over Here,* 159–60.

88 Chambers, *To Raise an Army,* 223–25. Chase, "Struggle for Equality," 297–310. Arthur E. Barbeau and Florette Henri, *The Unknown Soldiers: African-American Troops in World War I* (New York: Da Capo Press, 1996), 74. Arthur W. Little, *From Harlem to the Rhine: The Story of New York's Colored Volunteers* (New York: Covici Friede, 1936), 67–69. Kennedy, *Over Here,* 160–61.

89 John F. Callahan to Clara Morehouse, n.d., probably early December 1917, Callahan Papers, Miscellaneous Manuscript Collection, Manuscript Division, Library of Congress. Nancy Gentile Ford, *Americans All! Foreign-Born Soldiers in World War I* (College Station: Texas A&M University Press, 2001) 3, 30–31, 67–87 (Gutowski quote, 70). Ford notes that many Czechs, Slovaks, and other immigrants who were still technically citizens of the Austro-Hungarian Empire but who had "long called for the defeat of the Central Powers" were greatly distressed at their ineligibility for U.S. service after the December declaration of war and "worked to have the 'technical enemy alien' status removed" (30–31). James Brown Scott, "War between Austria-Hungary and the United States," *American Journal of International Law* 12, no. 1 (January 1918): 165–72.

90 "Teaching with Documents: Sow the Seeds of Victory! Posters from the Food Administration During World War I," at National Archives website, www.archives. gov/education/lessons/sow-seeds/ (accessed April 2016). Ronald Schaffer, *America in the Great War: The Rise of the War Welfare State* (New York: Oxford University Press, 1991), 34–39. Kennedy, *Over Here,* 123, 127, 253–56. Paxson, *America at War,* 80–87, 213–16. "Records of the U.S. Sugar Equalization Board, Inc.," Guide to Federal Records, National Archives website, www.archives.gov/ research/guide-fed-records/groups/006.html (accessed April 2016). Woodrow Wilson, "Proclamation 1419 – Government Assumption of Control of Transportation Systems, December 26, 1917," American Presidency Project, www.presidency.ucsb.edu/ws/?pid=24412 (accessed April 2016).

91 Paxson, *America at War,* 127–31. Kennedy, *Over Here,* 312–14. Thomas A. Bailey, "The United States and the Blacklist During the Great War," *Journal of Modern History* 6, no. 1 (March 1934): 14–35 (U.S. blacklist material, 32–33).

92 "Act Oct. 6, 1917 . . . Section 19, Print, Newspaper or Publication in Foreign Languages," at Cornell University Law School, Legal Information Institute website, www.law.cornell.edu/uscode/html/uscode50a/ usc_sec_50a_00000019----000-.html (accessed April 2016). Laura M. Calkins, "Censorship," Spencer C. Tucker, ed., *World War I: The Definitive Encyclopedia and Document Collection,* 5 vols. (Santa Barbara, CA: ABC-CLIO, 2014), 1: 368.

93 Gilbert, *First World War* (Holt, 1996), 342–43, 349–50, 374. Keegan, *First World War,* 338–39. Saul, *War and Revolution,* 184. Michael S. Neiberg, *Fighting the Great War: A Global History* (Cambridge, MA: Harvard University Press, 2005), 218–25.

94 Rod Paschall, *The Defeat of Imperial Germany, 1917–1918* (Chapel Hill, NC: Algonquin Books of Chapel Hill, 1989), 67–77, 90-102, Keegan, *First World War,* 347–50, 360–68. Neiberg, *Fighting the Great War,* 263–69, 272–75, 285–88. Gilbert, *First World War* (Holt, 1996), 353–55, 361–65, 369, 376. Ray Stannard Baker, *Woodrow Wilson: Life and Letters,* 7 vols. (New York: Greenwood Press, 1968), 7: 354. Trask, *The AEF and Coalition Warmaking,* 31–33 (Bliss quote, 32–33). Harries and Harries, *Last Days of Innocence,* 209–10.

95 Trask, *The AEF and Coalition Warmaking,* 15, 24. William Manchester, *American Caesar: Douglas MacArthur, 1880–1964* (Boston: Little, Brown & Company, 1978), 79. Pogue, *George C. Marshall,* 151–53. Gilbert, *First World War* (Holt, 1996), 358–59, 365. Pershing, *My Experiences in the First World War,* 1: 120–21, 148–49, 161.

96 Pogue, *George C. Marshall,* 155. Gilbert, *First World War* (Holt, 1996), 372–73. Harries and Harries, *Last Days*

of Innocence, 211–12. Pershing, *My Experiences in the First World War*, 1: 249–50.

97 Harries and Harries, *Last Days of Innocence*, 202–3. "Treasury Department Issues Form for Second Liberty Loan Subscribers," *New York Times*, October 2, 1917. "President's Proclamation Calling on Citizens for Meatless, Porkless and Wheatless Periods," *New York Times*, January 18, 1918. Chambers, *To Raise an Army*, 167, 175, 185. Croly, *Willard Straight*, 479–80. Samuel McCune Lindsay, "Purpose and Scope of War Risk Insurance," *Annals of the American Academy of Political and Social Science* 79, War Relief Work (Sept. 1918): 52–68.

98 Harriman, *From Pinafores to Politics*, 232–35.

99 Trask, *The AEF and Coalition Warmaking*, 25. Howard, *Wilbur and Orville*, 413–15. Harries and Harries, *Last Days of Innocence*, 194–96, 213. "Senate Inquires into Failure to Equip and Clothe Our Soldiers in the Camps; Sugar and Coal Shortage Also Taken Up," *New York Times*, December 12, 1917.

100 Harries and Harries, *Last Days of Innocence*, 194–95. Paschall, *Defeat of Imperial Germany*, 131–32.

CHAPTER 4

Epigraphs: Brand Whitlock quoted in Allan Nevins, ed. *The Letters and Journal of Brand Whitlock*, 2 vols. (New York: D. Appleton-Century Company, 1936), 2: 471. Captain Lloyd Williams quoted in Rod Paschall, *The Defeat of Imperial Germany, 1917–1918* (Chapel Hill, NC: Algonquin Books of Chapel Hill, 1989), 156. Robert A. Ferrebee, "Retreat Hell! We Just Got Here," at American Legion website, www.legion.org/stories/other/retreat-hell-we-just-got-here (accessed May 2016).

1 Frank H. Simonds, "The Fifth Campaign," *American Review of Reviews* 57, no. 1 (January 1918): 37. "Great Snow Storm Hits Middle West," *New York Sun*, January 2, 1918. "Measures to Relieve Coal Scarcity in East Started," *Bisbee (AZ) Daily Review*, January 1, 1918. "Open Tunnels of Pennsylvania R.R. for Coal Trains: McAdoo Orders That Preference Be Given to Fuel Shipments in the Tubes," *New York Times*, January 2, 1918. "Rush Coal and Food Here, Is [Regional] Director Smith's First Order to Railways of East," *New York*

Evening World, January 2, 1918. "Cut Passenger Trains a Fifth: McAdoo Orders Drastic Curtailment into Effect Today to Help Move Traffic," *New York Times*, January 6, 1918. "New England to Get Coal from Naval Stores," *Weekly Journal-Miner* (Prescott, AZ), January 2, 1918. Marshall H. Saville, "The Guatemala Earthquake of December 1917 and January 1918," *Geographical Review* 5, no. 6 (June 1918): 459–69 (quote, 469). "Guatemala's Misfortune," *New York Times*, January 1, 1918, notes, "Our naval vessels in the vicinity have been directed to give aid." "Relief Being Hurried for Earthquake Ridden City," *Bisbee (AZ) Daily Review*, January 1, 1918. "Earthquake Destroys City of Guatemala," *Hopkinsville Kentuckian*, January 1, 1918. "Guatemala Near Total Wreck from Quake," *Weekly Journal-Miner* (Prescott, AZ), January 2, 1918. In "See It as Our Duty to Help Guatemala," *New York Times*, April 21, 1918, the reporter notes Dr. Saville's statement about Guatemala's early severing of relations with Germany and his related assertion that the Guatemalan ruler, Manuel Estrada Cabrera, "has dealt with the enemy with a strong hand, keeping the 7,000 Germans, who are engaged in coffee raising, under stern control."

2 Arthur S. Link, ed., *The Papers of Woodrow Wilson*, 69 vols. (Princeton: Princeton University Press, 1984) 46: 19–21 (quoted text, 20).

3 "Writes Poem for Hoover," *Bemidji (MN) Daily Pioneer*, January 2, 1917.

4 "Fuel Administrator Issues Drastic Order," *St. Mary Banner* (Franklin, Parish of St. Mary, LA), January 19, 1918. "Congress Is in Uproar over Fuel Order Which Would Paralyze States," *El Paso (TX) Herald*, January 17, 1918. "White House Is Flooded with Protests Against Orders Closing Industrial Plants for Period of Five Days, Starting on Friday," *Democratic Banner* (Mt. Vernon, OH), January 18, 1918. "Congress in Great Furore [*sic*]," and "Senate in an Uproar," *Ogden (UT) Standard*, January 17, 1917. "City's Business Protests: Head of Commerce Chamber Calls Order 'Aid to the Enemy,'" *New York Times*, January 17, 1918. "Gompers Doubts Wisdom of Order," *New York Times*, January 18, 1918. David M. Kennedy, *Over Here: The First World War and American Society* (New York: Oxford University Press, 1980), 124. Seward W. Livermore, *Politics Is*

Adjourned: Woodrow Wilson and the War Congress, 1916–1918 (Middletown, CT: Wesleyan University Press, 1966), 86, notes, "In New York alone, eighteen British liners loaded with war material and in need of thirty thousand tons of coal were unable to depart, while eighty American or other vessels were in a similar plight."

5 Livermore, *Politics Is Adjourned*, 67–76. Kennedy, *Over Here*, 123–25. "Camp Epidemics Laid to Want of Winter Equipment," *New York Times*, December 29, 1917.

6 Livermore, *Politics Is Adjourned*, 81–82. "Munitions Dep't: New Cabinet Bureau Proposed by Bill in U.S. Senate," *Topeka (KS) State Journal*, January 4, 1918. "New Cabinet Post: Senator Chamberlain Introduces Measure Providing Secretary of Munitions," *Red Cloud (NE) Chief*, January 10, 1918. "Secretary of Munitions and Supplies May Come as Result [of] Investigation," *Arizona Republican* (Phoenix, AZ), January 4, 1918. "Here's Job Teddy Would Fit Nicely," *Evening Times-Republican* (Marshalltown, IA), January 4, 1918. "Declares America Has Fallen Down in Its War Work," *New York Times*, January 20, 1918 (Chamberlain red tape quote).

7 "Text of President Wilson's Statement Defending the Administration's War Work," *New York Times*, January 22, 1918. Livermore, *Politics Is Adjourned*, 88–94. Kennedy, *Over Here*, 125. David F. Trask, *The AEF and Coalition Warmaking, 1917–1918* (Lawrence: University Press of Kansas, 1993), 26–27. "War Problems Shifting," *New York Times*, January 29, 1918. "Baker Denies Inefficiency; Secretary of War Refutes Charges of Chamberlain," *Ogden (UT) Standard*, January 28, 1918.

8 Ray Stannard Baker, *Woodrow Wilson, Life and Letters*, 7 vols. (New York: Greenwood Press, 1968), 7: 504. Livermore, *Politics Is Adjourned*, 98–99. Kennedy, *Over Here*, 125. Frederic L. Paxson, "The American War Government, 1917–1918," *American Historical Review* 26, no. 1 (October 1920): 54–76 (characterization of Overman Bill, 70).

9 Livermore, *Politics Is Adjourned*, 106–15. Kennedy, *Over Here*, 233–35.

10 Trask, *The AEF and Coalition Warmaking*, 42. American Battle Monuments Commission, *93d Division, Summary of Operations in the World War* (Washington, D.C.: U.S. Government Printing Office, 1944), 1–4. Arthur W. Little, *From Harlem to the Rhine: The Story of New York's Colored Volunteers* (New York: Covici Friede, 1936), 99, 126–44. According to the *Jazz in America* website, "Timeline," www.jazzinamerica.org/JazzResources/Timeline/1910/1919, the term "jazz" first appeared in print in 1913.

11 Trask, *The AEF and Coalition Warmaking*, 42. John J. Pershing, *My Experiences in the First World War*, 2 vols. (1931; repr., New York: Da Capo Press, 1995), 1: 338n (February AEF strength). Norman E. Saul, *War and Revolution: The United States and Russia, 1914–1921* (Lawrence: University Press of Kansas, 2001), 230–31, 239–48, 264.

12 Trask, *The AEF and Coalition Warmaking*, 38–42. Frederick Palmer, *Bliss, Peacemaker: The Life and Letters of General Tasker Howard Bliss* (New York: Dodd, Mead & Company, 1934), 216. Pershing, *My Experiences in the First World War*, 1: 271–76. Forrest C. Pogue, *George C. Marshall: Education of a General* (New York: Viking Press, 1963), 161–62. For a discussion of American army doctrine in 1917–1918, and the marked differences between it and Allied doctrine that had evolved from bitter experience over more than two years, see Mark Ethan Grotelueschen, *The AEF Way of War: The American Army and Combat in World War I* (New York: Cambridge University Press, 2007), particularly chapter 1, "Doctrine, Dogma, and Development in the AEF." The author notes, "Shortly after arriving in Europe, Pershing recognized that Allied combat methods not only differed from American doctrine, they often directly contradicted it. In no way was their deviance more egregious to Pershing than in their reliance on firepower [artillery, machine guns, automatic rifles, etc.] and their diminished emphasis on the rifle-and-bayonet armed infantryman. Significantly, he despised those Allied attacks that he said were 'based upon the cautious advance of infantry with prescribed objectives, where obstacles had been destroyed and resistance largely broken by artillery'" (31, quoting Pershing, *My Experiences in the First World War*, 2: 237, where Pershing also states, "Our mission required an aggressive offensive based on self-reliant infantry").

13 John Maxwell Hamilton and Robert Mann, eds., *A Journalist's Diplomatic Mission: Ray Stannard Baker's World War I Diary* (Baton Rouge: Louisiana State University Press, 2012), 14, 38. "Fears Worldwide Ruin: Lansdowne Wants Allies to Restate Aims as Step Toward Ending Conflict," *New York Times*, November 30, 1917. Kennedy, *Over Here*, 354. Adam Tooze, *The Deluge: The Great War and the Remaking of Global Order, 1916–1931* (New York: Viking, 2014), 71. David Lloyd George, *British War Aims: Statement by the Right Honorable David Lloyd George, January Fifth, Nineteen Hundred and Eighteen* (New York: George H. Doran Company, 1918), 1–4, 7–8, 10, 13–15. Charles Seymour, *The Intimate Papers of Colonel House*, 4 vols. (Boston: Houghton Mifflin Company, 1926-1928) 3: 340, reprints the text of a January 5, 1918, cable from British Foreign Minister Balfour to Colonel House explaining that a successful outcome of the government's negotiations with labor leaders, then at a critical juncture, was "absolutely indispensable from the military point of view for the development of man-power on the Western Front" and the outcome "depended mainly on the immediate publication" of a declaration of war aims. Balfour also noted that, while there had been no opportunity to consult the other Allies, the British statement was "in accordance with the declarations hitherto made by the President on this subject."

14 Seymour, *Intimate Papers of Colonel House*, 3: 341. Saul, *War and Revolution*, 202–11, 215–19, 247, 253 (Reed quote, 211).

15 Woodrow Wilson, "Address to a Joint Session of Congress on the Conditions of Peace, January 8, 1918," American Presidency Project, www.presidency.ucsb. edu/ws/index.php?pid=65405 (accessed May 2016). Lawrence E. Gelfand, *The Inquiry: American Preparations for Peace, 1917–1919* (New Haven, CT: Yale University Press, 1963), x–xi, 30–31 (Lippmann quote, 48).

16 Kennedy, *Over Here*, 352–54. Saul, *War and Revolution*, 218, 241–44.

17 Meirion Harries and Susie Harries, *The Last Days of Innocence: America at War, 1917–1918* (New York: Random House, 1997), 220 (Clemenceau). "Appeals to German People," *New York Times*, January 9,

1918, notes, "The only real outspoken criticism [in Congress] came from Republicans who saw in one of the war aims specified by the president a declaration that would commit the Allies and their enemies to the establishment of free trade for all the world for a basis of peace. If this . . . would permit Germany as well as other nations to dump their products in American ports and bring them into competition with American production, the Republicans, it was asserted, would enter a vigorous protest." Seymour, *Intimate Papers of Colonel House*, 3: 341, 345–49. "Are Allies Depending on Verbal Artillery?" *Evening Capital News* (Boise, ID), January 9, 1918. See also Woodrow Wilson, "Address to Congress on International Order, February 11, 1918," American Presidency Project, www.presidency.ucsb. edu/ws/?pid=110448. In this speech, Wilson finds unsatisfactory German Chancellor Georg von Hertling's response to the Fourteen Points. Reiterating the content and spirit of the Fourteen Points, Wilson specifies four principles to be used as foundations for peace. Quickly dubbed the "Four Points," these, too, were widely circulated and served to boost Wilson's popularity among Allied civilians.

18 "American Socialists for Immediate Peace," *New York Times*, February 10, 1918.

19 "Bigelow Tells of Beating," *New York Times*, January 14, 1918. "Pacifist Whipped in Kuklux Style," *New York Times*, October 30, 1917. Kennedy, *Over Here*, 73. National Civil Liberties Bureau, *War-Time Prosecutions and Mob Violence* (New York: National Civil Liberties Bureau, July 1918), 6. Geoffrey R. Stone, *Perilous Times: Free Speech in Wartime, from the Sedition Act of 1798 to the War on Terrorism* (New York: W. W. Norton & Company, 2004), 171–72, notes that, after a successful appeal, the government finally dismissed the charges against Mrs. Stokes in November 1921. Christopher Capozzola, *Uncle Sam Wants You: World War I and the Making of the Modern American Citizen* (New York: Oxford University Press, 2008), 158.

20 Scott A. Merriman, "'An Intensive School of Disloyalty': The C. B. Schoberg Case Under the Espionage and Sedition Acts in Kentucky During World War I," *Register of the Kentucky Historical Society* 98, no. 2 (Spring 2000): 179–204, notes that the detectives had to

reinstall the dictograph twice (each time removing and replacing with matching swatches the wallpaper under which they had tucked its wires), once when the shop was being painted and once for undetermined reasons. Bothered by the constant ticking, "they tried to wind the clock down so that it would stop working, but someone wound it again, and the detectives had to become accustomed to the sound" (187). All three men appealed their convictions, unsuccessfully, for years. In late June 1921, after the men had served six months in prison, President Harding commuted their sentences—though Feltman still had to pay a reduced fine of $10,000.

21 "Roosevelt Attacks Objectors to War," *New York Times*, January 31, 1918. "Charge of Sedition Stirs Clubwomen," *New York Times*, February 2, 1918. Capozzola, *Uncle Sam Wants You*, 59–60, 114–16. See also, Mrs. J. Hungerford Milbank, "Now for an Army of Women Soldiers," *Washington Post*, February 22, 1914. "New York Women Are Drilling for Possible War," *Tomahawk* (White Earth, Becker County, MN), May 4, 1916.

22 Martin Gilbert, *The First World War: A Complete History* (New York: Henry Holt & Company, 1996), 329. David R. Woodward, *The American Army and the First World War* (New York: Cambridge University Press, 2014), 162. "Loss of the Troopship Tuscania," at Welcome to Islay Info website, www.islayinfo.com/loss-troopship-tuscania-islay.html (accessed May 2016). Some *Tuscania* victims were buried on Isle of Islay, off the coast of Scotland, and islanders helped many of the survivors. Harold L. Dunne, [Descriptive Account of the Sinking of the Ship Tuscania, 1918], typescript, Miscellaneous Manuscript Collection, Manuscript Division, Library of Congress. "American Troop Ship Sunk: Tuscania Submarined off the Northern Coast of Ireland," *Tonopah (NV) Daily Bonanza*, February 7, 1918. "American Soldiers Faced Death Heroically as the Transport Tuscania Sank," *Harrisburg (PA) Telegraph*, February 8, 1918. "Troop Ship Sunk . . . Disaster Stirs American People," *Ogden (UT) Standard*, February 7, 1918. In a supplementary article, "Women Laugh in Great Disaster," also on page 1, the *Ogden Standard* reported, "The survivors are proud of the behavior of the only two

women on the Tuscania. They went down a rope in fine style, laughing." According to a 1966 reminiscence by Arnold Joerns, "The Night the Tuscania Went Down" *Chicago Tribune*, April 17, 1966, the women were British stewardesses traveling as passengers: "When the Tuscania was torpedoed they came on deck," Joerns remembered, "and one of our boys hollered, 'Step aside, boys, the ladies are coming.' The women went down the ropes as fancy as any sailor and later distinguished themselves by rescuing four men from the water." Clemens P. Work, *Darkest Before Dawn: Sedition and Free Speech in the American West* (Albuquerque: University of New Mexico Press, 2005), 124, notes the shock with which the people in Montana greeted the news of the *Tuscania*'s sinking with five soldiers from the state among the dead. The news gave a boost to the state legislature's deliberations that resulted in passage of the nation's most restrictive sedition act on February 22, one speaker warning that "German's spy system, which 'reaches its poisoned tentacles into every part of the world,' would surely carry 'every disloyal utterance and every treasonable act . . . in exaggerated form' back to German soldiers, thereby causing 'some certain company or unit to make just one more stand for the Kaiser and autocracy.'"

23 Rod Paschall, *The Defeat of Imperial Germany, 1917–1918* (Chapel Hill, NC: Algonquin Books of Chapel Hill, 1989), 132, 135–46. Harries and Harries, *Last Days of Innocence*, 227–28. John J. Pershing, *My Experiences in the First World War*, 1: 353–56 (Sixth Engineers, 355). John Keegan, *The First World War* (New York: Vintage Books, 2000), 396–400. Trask, *The AEF and Coalition Warmaking*, 42. American Battle Monuments Commission, *3d Division, Summary of Operations in the World War* (Washington, D.C.: U.S. Government Printing Office, 1944), 1–9. "Great German Offensive Begun upon Fifty Mile Front of Cambrai Sector," *Arizona Republican* (Phoenix, AZ), March 22, 1918. "Big Drive Is On," *Albuquerque (NM) Morning Journal*, March 22, 1918. "Paris Bombarded; British Are Falling Back," *Ogden (UT) Standard*, March 23, 1918. "Great German Drive Is Furious Attack," *Daily Gate City and Constitution-Democrat* (Keokuk, IA), March 25, 1918.

24 E. S. Gorrell and Phil Carroll, "Colonel Raynal Cawthorne Bolling: Lawyer-Cavalryman-Flyer," *U.S. Air*

Service 3, no. 2 (March 1920), 18–20, notes that Bolling's driver was taken prisoner and reported the circumstances of Bolling's death after his release. Bolling Air Force Base, outside Washington, D.C., is named for Colonel Bolling. Major Paul H. Clark to Commander in Chief [AEF], "Subj. Military Situation," March 26, 1918, Paul Hedrick Clark Papers, Manuscript Division, Library of Congress.

25 Mildred Aldrich, *The Peak of the Load: The Waiting Months on the Hilltop from the Entrance of the Stars and Stripes to the Second Victory on the Marne* (Boston: Mall, Maynard & Company, 1918), 157–63.

26 AEF divisions were more than twice the size of typical Allied or German divisions. See Grotelueschen, *AEF Way of War*, 27n.41: "During 1918, typical British divisions averaged 11,800 men, French divisions just 11,400, and German divisions about 12,300. For each nation, the official authorized strength of the division was about fifteen thousand men. Certain British divisions, such as the Canadian and Australian, were larger—with a total strength of about twenty-one thousand men; some French divisions, such as the 1st Moroccan, were close to that size."

27 Pershing, *My Experiences in the First World War*, 1: 369 (map with location of U.S. divisions). American Battle Monuments Commission, *3d Division, Summary of Operations in the World War* (Washington, D.C.: U.S. Government Printing Office, 1944), 1. The 32D "Red Arrow" Veteran Association, "The 32D 'Red Arrow' Division in World War I: From the 'Iron Jaw Division' to 'Les Terribles,'" www.32nd-division.org/history/ww1/32-ww1.html (accessed June 2016). Transporting a full division was a time-consuming process requiring several ships. The leading elements of the Thirty-second left the United States in mid-January. Some units were on the *Tuscania* when it went down in February—thirteen of the division's soldiers among the dead. All elements of the division were not in France until the end of March, at which point the Thirty-second still required training in techniques of Western Front combat.

28 Pershing, *My Experiences in the First World War*, 1: 356–67 (refugees, 359; statement to Foch, 365). Keegan, *First World War*, 402–3. Harries and Harries, *Last Days of Innocence*, 229. "Allied Crisis Causes English Cabinet to Abandon Objection to One Leader . . . Foch Is Supreme General," *Arizona Republican* (Phoenix, AZ), March 30, 1918. "Pershing Offers Troops for Battle," *Evening Star* (Washington, D.C.), March 29, 1918. "Pershing Offers Army for Great Battle," *New York Times*, March 30, 1918. "Pershing's Offer of American Army to Foch Delights French," *Daily Ardmoreite* (Ardmore, OK), March 30, 1918. "Offer of U.S. Army Thrills French Nation," *Evening Times-Republican* (Marshalltown, IA), March 30, 1918.

29 Grotelueschen, *AEF Way of War*, 70. American Battle Monuments Commission, *26th Division, Summary of Operations in the World War* (Washington, D.C.: U.S. Government Printing Office, 1944), 5. John S. D. Eisenhower, *Yanks: The Epic Story of the American Army in World War I* (New York: The Free Press, 2001), 87–88. Harries and Harries, *Last Days of Innocence*, 238–39. Steven Casey, *When Soldiers Fall: How Americans Have Confronted Combat Losses from World War I to Afghanistan* (New York: Oxford University Press, 2014), 19. Corporal John F. Callahan, undated letter (probably early 1919) to Clara Morehouse, Miscellaneous Manuscripts Collection, Manuscript Division, Library of Congress.

30 Peyton C. March, *The Nation at War* (Garden City, New York: Doubleday, Doran & Company, 1932), 38–41, 187. Jill Frahm, "The Hello Girls: Women Telephone Operators with the American Expeditionary Forces During World War I," *Journal of the Gilded Age and Progressive Era* 3, no. 3 (July 2004): 271–93, notes, "Between March and October 1918, the AEF sent 233 women to France to operate the switchboards of its military telephone system" (274). Carol R. Byerly, "The U.S. Military and the Influenza Pandemic of 1918–1919," *Public Health Reports* 125, Supplement 3: The 1918–1919 Influenza Pandemic in the United States (April 2010): 82–91, states that "military medical officers soon understood that the wave of influenza that had run through many U.S. training camps during the spring of 1918 constituted a first wave of the [Spanish flu] pandemic. Fourteen of the largest training camps had reported influenza outbreaks in March, April, or May, and some of the infected troops carried the virus with them aboard ships to France" (85). Edward M.

Coffman, *The War to End All Wars* (Madison: University of Wisconsin Press, 1986), 162–63. Pershing, *My Experiences in the First World War*, 1: 388.

31 Woodrow Wilson, "Speech at the Opening of the Third Liberty Loan Campaign, delivered in the Fifth Regiment Armory, Baltimore: 'Force to the Utmost,' April 6, 1918," American Presidency Project, www.presidency.ucsb.edu/ws/?pid=65406 (accessed June 2016).

32 Chambers, *To Raise an Army*, 213. Elizabeth William, *Pittsburgh in World War I: Arsenal of the Allies* (Charleston, SC: The History Press, 2013), 66. Kennedy, *Over Here*, 165–66. Joan M. Jensen, *The Price of Vigilance* (Chicago: Rand McNally & Company, 1968), 191–92. Capozzola, *Uncle Sam Wants You*, 44.

33 "Court-Martial for Spies: Chamberlain Bill Would Take Sedition Cases from Criminal Courts," *New York Times*, April 17, 1918 (includes the text of the proposed bill). "Urges Bill to Court Martial for Espionage," *Grand Forks (ND) Herald*, April 17, 1918. "President Opposes Chamberlain Bill," *Evening Star* (Washington, D.C.), April 22, 1918. "Court Martial of Spies Opposed," *Evening Current* (Carlsbad, NM). "The Kaiser 'The Beast of Berlin,' A Picture Every American Should See!" advertisement in the *Topeka (KS) State Journal*, April 6, 1918. "A Sensational Expose of the Private Life of the Kaiser, the Mad Dog of Europe: The Kaiser 'The Beast of Berlin,'" advertisement, *South Bend (IN) News-Times*, May 13, 1918. Geoffrey R. Stone, *Perilous Times: Free Speech in Wartime, from the Sedition Act of 1798 to the War on Terrorism* (New York: W. W. Norton & Company, 2004), 184–85. Kennedy, *Over Here*, 79–81.

34 E. A. Schwartz, "The Lynching of Robert Prager, the United Mine Workers, and the Problems of Patriotism in 1918," *Journal of the Illinois State Historical Society* 95, no. 4 (Winter 2002–2003): 414–37. H. C. Peterson and Gilbert C. Fite, *Opponents of War, 1917–1918* (Madison: University of Wisconsin Press, 1957), 202–4. Kennedy, *Over Here*, 68. Stone, *Perilous Times*, 188. Ann Hagedorn, *Savage Peace: Hope and Fear in America*, 1919 (New York: Simon & Schuster, 2007), 42 (1918 lynching of African Americans).

35 Stone, *Perilous Times*, 186, 190–91.

36 Paschall, *The Defeat of Imperial Germany*, 146–49. Harries and Harries, *Last Days of Innocence*, 231. Gilbert, *First World War* (Holt, 1996), 412–13. Keegan, *First World War*, 405. Hamilton and Mann, *A Journalist's Diplomatic Mission*, 55, note that Ray Stannard Baker wrote in his diary on April 7, 1918: "Mr. Wilson's Baltimore speech is published this morning and receives wide comment and varied approval." "Hold Fast and Fight It Out to the Last Man, Our Backs Are to the Wall, Haig Tells His Army," *New York Times*, April 13, 1918. "'Our Backs to the Wall,' Says Haig," *New York Tribune*, April 13, 1918. "'Fight to Death,' Haig Tells Men," *Daily Missoulian* (Missoula, MT), April 13, 1918. "British Ordered to Die in Their Tracks to Stop Huns from Taking Big War Bases," *Harrisburg (PA) Telegraph*, April 13, 1918. "Haig's 'Back to Wall!'" *Tacoma (WA) Times*, April 13, 1918. "Haig Orders English Troops to Hold Ground at Any Cost," *Bisbee (AZ) Daily Review*, April 13, 1918.

37 Philip Gibbs, "Tired Army Stirred by Haig; British Exhausted by Weeks of Fighting Stagger Up to Face Attacks," *New York Times*, April 15, 1918. Pershing, *My Experiences in the First World War*, 1: 360–67, reports, regarding the attitude of some Allied leaders toward the AEF, an April 3, 1918, exchange with General Pétain over the omission of the AEF from a joint resolution. Pétain retorted, "There is no American army as such, as its units are either in training or are amalgamated with the British and French," to which Pershing replied, "There may not be an American army in the force functioning now, but there soon will be, and I want this resolution to apply to it when it becomes a fact" (1: 375–76). Pershing prevailed. March, *Nation at War*, 76–77. Harries and Harries, *Last Days of Innocence: America at War*, 233–34.

38 "American Soldier Has Made Good as Fighter," *Bridgeport (CT) Times and Evening Farmer*, April 17, 1918. "America Ready to Strike Says Baker," *Abbeville (SC) Press and Banner*, April 19, 1918. "America's Right Arm Is in France, Bared to Strike a Gigantic Blow, Says Baker; Body at Home Must Support It," *Grand Forks (ND) Herald*, April 17, 1918. "Return of Baker to Make Changes in Army Measure," *Washington (D.C.) Herald*, April 17, 1918. Francis William O'Brien, ed. *The Hoover-Wilson Wartime Correspondence* (Ames: Iowa State

University Press), 164. Anne Wintermute Lane and Louise Herrick Wall, eds. *The Letters of Franklin K. Lane* (Boston: Houghton Mifflin Company, 1922), 267.

39 Saul, *War and Revolution*, 262–66. "Japanese in Vladivostok" (quoted passage), *New York Times*, April 6, 1918. "Russians Charge Japan Is Invading," *New York Times*, April 8, 1918. "British Forces Land with Japs at Vladivostok," *Daily Capital Journal* (Salem, OR). The British had sent 50 marines to protect their consulate. April 8, 1918. "Kato Landed Force on Own Initiative," *Evening Star* (Washington, D.C.), April 8, 1918.

40 Saul, *War and Revolution*, 266. Harries and Harries, *Last Days of Innocence*, 239–40. John S. D. Eisenhower, *Yanks: The Epic Story of the American Army in World War I* (New York: The Free Press, 2001), 89–90. Gilbert, *First World War* (Holt, 1996), 416 (Lloyd George and Haig). H. W. Crocker III, *The Yanks Are Coming! A Military History of the United States in World War I* (Washington, D.C.: Regnery History, 2014), 76–77.

41 Eisenhower, *Yanks*, 121–22. Robert Lee Bullard, *Personalities and Reminiscences of the War* (Garden City, New York: Doubleday, Page & Company, 1925), 181–82, 196–97. Harries and Harries, *Last Days of Innocence*, 240. Pershing, *My Experiences in the First World War*, 2: 54–55.

42 Pershing, *My Experiences in the First World* War, 2: 20–29.

43 Kennedy, *Over Here*, 125–26. Trask, *The AEF and Coalition Warmaking*, 27. Chambers, *To Raise an Army*, 198–99.

44 Chambers, *To Raise an Army*, 194–96, 201–2. "Drastic Amendment to Select Service Law Puts Man Power at Work to Offset Hun Power," *Daily Ardmoreite* (Ardmore, OK), May 23, 1918 (Crowder quote). "Men at Non-Essential Labor Must Join Army," *Tonopah (NV) Daily Bonanza*, May 23, 1918. "'Work or Fight,' Crowder Orders," *Oklahoma City Times*, May 23, 1918 (includes list of no longer exempt occupations).

45 Chambers, *To Raise an Army*, 195. Harries and Harries, *Last Days of Innocence*, 285–88. "Daniels Starts Fight on Navy Profiteers," *New York Times*, April 29, 1918. "Board Reports Profiteering on Enormous Scale," *New York Times*, June 30, 1918. "Looting the Nation at War Still Goes On; Financial Reports of the Great Corporations Show Unparalleled Profits," *Nonpartisan Leader* (Fargo, ND), May 6, 1918. "'Real War Profits Tax' in $8,000,000,000 Revenue," *Philadelphia Evening Public Ledger*, June 7, 1918. "Records of the National War Labor Board," www.archives.gov/research/guide-fed-records/groups/002.html (accessed June 2016). Kennedy, *Over Here*, 79–81, 267–68. Ronald Schaffer, *America in the Great War: The Rise of the War Welfare State* (New York: Oxford University Press, 1991), 36. Peterson and Fite, *Opponents of War*, 235–36. Stone, *Perilous Times*, 186. Andrew Glass, "Congress Passes the Sedition Act, May 16, 1918," *Politico*, May 16, 2016, www.politico.com/story/2012/05/congress-passes-the-sedition-act-may-16-1918-076336 (Meyer London) (accessed July 2016).

46 Little, *From Harlem to the Rhine*, 192–201. Hagedorn, *Savage Peace*, 93–97. Arthur E. Barbeau and Florette Henri, *The Unknown Soldiers: African-American Troops in World War I* (New York: Da Capo Press, 1996), 116–17. "Privates Johnson and Roberts, Colored," *New York Evening World*, May 22, 1918. "Negro Soldiers Heroes, Fight Off 20 Enemy Attackers," *Tacoma (WA) Times*, May 20, 1918. "Colored Soldiers Win War Cross," *Evening Star* (Washington, D.C.), May 20, 1918. Johnson and Roberts were awarded the French Croix de Guerre, and the encounter placed the entire 369th Regiment in the spotlight—their commanding officer, Arthur Little, wrote in his memoirs, "Our colored volunteers from Harlem had become, in a day, one of the famous fighting regiments of the World War." Ernest Allen, Jr. "'Close Ranks': Major Joel E. Spingarn and the Two Souls of Dr. W. E. B. Du Bois," *Contributions in Black Studies* 3 (1979), article 4, available at http://scholarworks.umass.edu/cibs/vol3/iss1/4 (accessed June 2016). For President Wilson's proclamation against mob violence, "President Woodrow Wilson's Proclamation of July 26, 1918, Denouncing Lynching," see www.amistadresource.org/documents/document_07_06_030_wilson.pdf.

47 Woodrow Wilson, "Proclamation 1444—Red Cross Week, May 4, 1918," American Presidency Project, www.presidency.ucsb.edu/ws/?pid=24407 (accessed June 2016). "President Leads Red Cross Parade," *New York Times*, May 19, 1918. "5,000,000 in Day's Parade,"

New York Times, May 19, 1918 (describing other parades in Washington, D.C., Boston, and Cleveland). Carlos Baker, *Ernest Hemingway: A Life Story* (New York: Collier Books/Macmillan, 1969), 39–40. "House Bill Takes Limit Off Army," *New York Times*, May 26, 1918. Chambers, *To Raise an Army*, 196. Woodrow Wilson, "Address to Congress on the Need for Increased Taxation for War Purposes, May 27, 1918," American Presidency Project, www.presidency.ucsb.edu/ws/?pid=110492 (accessed June 2016).

48 Roy G. and Gladys C. Blakely, "The Revenue Act of 1918," *American Economic Review* 9, no. 2 (June 1919): 213–43, report that the bill was not approved until February 24, 1919 (214n.1). Livermore, *Politics Is Adjourned*, 115–21. Kennedy, *Over Here*, 237–38. Stone, *Perilous Times*, 211n. Stone writes that Berger was indicted after his nomination but before the vote, in which he "received more than 100,000 votes, despite the criminal charges pending against him." Seward W. Livermore, "The Sectional Issue in the 1918 Congressional Elections," *Mississippi Valley Historical Review* 35, no. 1 (June 1948): 29–60 (Republican platform, 32).

49 Paschall, *Defeat of Imperial Germany*, 151–53. Harries and Harries, *Last Days of Innocence*, 246–47. Gilbert, *First World War* (Holt, 1996), 425–26. Keegan, *First World War*, 406–7.

50 Harries and Harries, *Last Days of Innocence*, 240–45. Gilbert, *First World War* (Holt, 1996), 426–27. Hunter Liggett, *A.E.F.: Ten Years Ago in France* (New York: Dodd, Mead and Company, 1928), 68–70.

51 "U-Boats Raid U.S. Coast!" *Tacoma (WA) Times*, June 3, 1918. "15 Craft off Atlantic Coast Sunk by German Subs," *Bismarck (ND) Tribune*, June 3, 1918. "U-Boats Sink Ships off the U.S. Coast," *Evening Star* (Washington, D.C.), June 3, 1918. Josephus Daniels, *Our Navy at War* (Washington, D.C.: Pictorial Bureau, 1922), 187–205 (quote, 189).

52 Elting E. Morison, *Admiral Sims and the Modern American Navy* (New York: Russell & Russell, 1968), 413–17. C. Paul Vincent, *The Politics of Hunger: The Allied Blockade of Germany, 1915–1919* (Athens: Ohio University Press, 1985), 48–49, 57n.68. "America to Get 12 Japanese Ships," *New York Times*, March 29, 1918. "44 Ships Delivered by Our Yards in May," *New York Times*, June 5, 1918.

53 Alfred W. Crosby, *America's Forgotten Pandemic: The Influenza of 1918* (New York: Cambridge University Press, 1989), 17–26. Major Paul H. Clark to Commander-in-Chief, May 27, 1918. Paul Hedrick Clark Papers, Manuscript Division, Library of Congress.

54 Harries and Harries, *Last Days of Innocence*, 247–72. Paschall, *Defeat of Imperial Germany*, 155–59. Michael S. Neiberg, *Fighting the Great War: A Global History* (Cambridge, MA: Harvard University Press, 2005), 328–29.

55 H. Geraldine Lester, "British Emergency Legislation," *California Law Review* 7, no. 5 (July 1919): 323–39, notes, "April 18, 1918, Military Service (no. 2) Act . . . raised the age of compulsory enlistment to 51 for every male British subject who had been in Great Britain at any time since August 14, 1915 . . . The age was further extended to 56 for qualified medical practitioners, and the King by an order in council could extend the age to 56 for men generally or any class of men" (324). Pershing, *My Experiences in the First World War*, 2: 82. Richard W. Stewart, ed., *American Military History, Volume II, The United States Army in a Global Era, 1917–2008* (Washington, D.C.: Center of Military History, 2010), 21. Harries and Harries, *Last Days of Innocence*, 275. Chambers, *To Raise an Army*, 198. "Crowder Greets 1918 Draft Class," *New York Times*, June 5, 1918.

56 Eugene V. Debs, "'The Canton, Ohio, Speech' (June 16, 1918)," in *Voices of a People's History of the United States*, ed. Howard Zinn and Anthony Arnove (New York: Seven Stories Press, 2004), 295–97. Joan M. Jensen, *The Price of Vigilance* (Chicago: Rand McNally & Company, 1968), 173. Harries and Harries, *Last Days of Innocence*, 305. Capozzola, *Uncle Sam Wants You*, 64.

57 "Third-Term Boom for Wilson Wins Cheers in Indiana," *New York Times*, June 20, 1918. "Let 1920 Take Care of Itself," *New York Times*, June 21, 1918 (criticism of convention). Livermore, *Politics Is Adjourned*, 169–84. Kennedy, *Over Here*, 238–39. "Blames President Wilson: Townsend Calls His Intervention in Michigan 'Unjust Meddling,'" *New York Times*, June 30, 1918. "Couples

Wilson in Attack on Ford: President Called 'Greatest Political Autocrat' by Osborn," *New York Times*, June 16, 1918. Guy Cramer, "Ford's Entry May Mean New Ethical Code for Business," *Washington (D.C.) Times*, June 23, 1918, observes, with some glee, that "Henry Ford's entry into politics at President Wilson's urgent request has kicked up more dust in Michigan than could the swarm of flivvers his great factories roll out."

58 Seward W. Livermore, "The Sectional Issue in the 1918 Congressional Elections," *Mississippi Valley Historical Review* 35, no. 1 (June 1948): 29–60. Livermore, *Politics Is Adjourned*, 169–84. Jensen, *Price of Vigilance*, 195.

59 Saul, *War and Revolution*, 289, 301–2. Encyclopædia Britannica online, s.v. "Tomas Masaryk," www.britannica.com/biography/Tomas-Masaryk (accessed July 4, 2016). Anna M. Cienciala, "The Birth of Czechoslovakia, 1914–1920," lecture notes, http://acienciala.faculty.ku.edu/hist557/lect12.htm (accessed July 2016).

60 "Women Who Have Played Their Part on Battlefields," *Bridgeport (CT) Times and Evening Farmer*, June 29, 1918. Mrs. J. Borden [Florence] Harriman, *From Pinafores to Politics* (New York: Henry Holt & Company, 1923), 279–81.

61 Saul, *War and Revolution*, 293–94. Harries and Harries, *Last Days of Innocence*, 311–14 (German quote 314). Paschall, *Defeat of Imperial Germany*, 159–60. Gilbert, *First World War* (Holt, 1996), 440–42. Keegan, *First World War*, 409.

62 Harries and Harries, *Last Days of Innocence*, 314–21. Gilbert, *First World War* (Holt, 1996), 443, 446 (Ludendorff). Keegan, *First World War*, 409. Paschall, *Defeat of Imperial Germany*, 160.

63 Keegan, *First World War*, 409. C. Paul Vincent, *The Politics of Hunger: The Allied Blockade of Germany, 1915–1919* (Athens: Ohio University Press, 1985), 49–50. Nigel Hawkins, *The Starvation Blockades* (Barnsley, UK: Leo Cooper, 2002), 234–37.

64 Pershing, *My Experiences in the First World War*, 2: 171–75. Paschall, *Defeat of Imperial Germany*, 164–69. Harries and Harries, *Last Days of Innocence*, 322.

65 Pershing, *My Experiences in the First World War*, 2: 192n. Paschall, *Defeat of Imperial Germany* 167–69. Grotelueschen, *AEF Way of War*, 45 (Pershing to McAndrew).

66 Woodrow Wilson, *Address of President Wilson Delivered at Mount Vernon, July 4, 1918* (Washington, D.C.: Government Printing Office, 1918), 4–5. Vincent P. Franklin, "The Philadelphia Race Riot of 1918," *Pennsylvania Magazine of History and Biography* 99, no. 3 (July 1975): 336–50 (Williams statement, 338–39).

67 Allen, "'Close Ranks.'" W. E. B. Du Bois, editorial, "Close Ranks," *Crisis* 16, no. 3 (July 1918): 111, full text available at http://americainclass.org/wp-content/uploads/2012/02/crisis-closeranks.pdf. Mark Ellis, *Race, War, and Surveillance: African Americans and the United States Government during World War I* (Bloomington: Indiana University Press, 2001), 170. Franklin, "The Philadelphia Race Riot of 1918," 336–50.

68 "Bitter Race Riot in Philadelphia," *Greeneville (TN) Daily Sun*, July 29, 1918. "One Killed, 61 Injured in Philadelphia Riot," *El Paso (TX) Herald*, June 29, 1918. "Marines on Duty in Philadelphia Because of Riots," *Bridgeport (CT) Times and Evening Farmer*, July 29, 1918. "Philadelphia Race Riots Cost Three Lives; 60 Hurt," *Evening World* (NYC), July 29. "Breeding Patriotism in Hog Island Mud!" *Daily Ardmoreite* (Ardmore, OK), July 19, 1918. "Wilson Leads Cheering of 100,000 as Hog Island Launches Its First Ship," *New York Tribune*, August 6, 1918. "Women in War Work," *Evening Star* (Washington, D.C.), July 28, 1918. "Lutheran Pastor Joins Y War Work," and "Thanks Given for Aiding Red Cross," *Arizona Republican* (Phoenix, AZ), July 7, 1918. "American Woman Furthest Front," *Camden (TN) Chronicle*, August 2, 1918 (Clara Simmons). "Patriotic Societies Stand for Practical Patriotism," *Bridgeport (CT) Times and Evening Farmer*, July 1, 1918. "Salvation Army Drive!" *Estancia (NM) News-Herald*, July 18, 1918. "Hundred Thousand Camp Fire Girls in War Work," *Evening Star* (Washington, D.C.), July 21, 1918.

69 "Roll of Honor: Heroes of Nearby States Who Gave Their Lives in Defense of Liberty," *Potosi (MO) Journal*, July 3, 1918. "America's Roll of Honor: War Casualty List . . . ," *Chattanooga (TN) News*, July 12, 1918.

"Today's Casualty List Contains Sixty Names," *Daily Gate City and Constitution-Democrat* (Keokuk, IA), July 15, 1918. "The Nation's Honor Roll," *New York Sun*, August 4, 1918. "Casualty List, American Army in Europe," *Keowee Courier* (Pickens Court House, SC), August 7, 1918. Jensen, *Price of Vigilance*, 194–96, notes that government regarded the $50 bounty as "reimbursement for expenses." "Slackers Quoted $50 on Hoof Now: Policeman Claiming Bounty Must Bring in His Quarry Whole and Breathing," *New York Sun*, July 11, 1918. "Nearly 5,000 Men Were Rounded Up in Dragnet of Chicago Police to Get Slackers and Unregistered Aliens—One Man Was Shot," *Barre (VT) Daily Times*, July 12, 1918. "Slacker Raid in Chicago," *Grand Forks (ND) Herald*, July 12, 1918.

70   Saul, *War and Revolution*, 304, 328. "German Ambassador Murdered at Moscow," *New York Tribune*, July 7, 1918. "Russian Peasants in Revolt Against Bolshevik Rule," *New York Sun*, July 8, 1918. "Russia May Play New Part in World Conflict," *Grand Forks (ND) Herald*, July 8, 1918. "Counter-Revolution Started in Moscow," *New York Evening World*, July 8, 1918. "Former Czar Shot by Order Bolsheviki," *Tonopah (NV) Daily Bonanza*, July 20, 1918. "Bolsheviki See Defeat in Siberia," and "Czecho-Slovaks Continue Advance," both in *Oklahoma City (OK) Times*, July 17, 1918. "The New Masters of Siberia: Masaryk, Leader of the Czecho-Slovaks, Tells the Aims of His Followers," *New York Sun*, Magazine Section, July 14, 1918. "Bolshevik Regime Passing in Siberia: 40,000 Czechs Hold Trans-Siberian Road at Several Points," *Evening Star* (Washington, D.C.), July 21, 1918. "Execution of Czar Approved," *Daily Gate City and Constitution-Democrat* (Keokuk, IA), July 26, 1918. "Ex-Czar Shot by Bolsheviki Without Trial," *New York Tribune*, July 21, 1918.

71   Saul, *War and Revolution*, 297–98, 312–13, 315–18, 322, 337 (Chicherin). Konrad H. Jarausch, "Cooperation or Intervention? Kurt Riezler and the Failure of German Ostpolitik, 1918," *Slavic Review* 31, no. 2 (June 1972): 381–98 (supplemental treaties, 395). Gilbert, *First World War*, 452–53. J. Adam Tooze, *The Deluge: The Great War, America, and the Remaking of the Global Order 1916–1931* (New York: Viking, 2014), 353–54.

72   Crosby, *America's Forgotten Pandemic*, 30, 37–40. Saul, *War and Revolution*, 315. "1,000 Workmen Are Ill of Spanish Influenza," *Evening Star* (Washington, D.C.), August 11, 1918 (the workmen in the headline were German). "Influenza . . . ," *Abbeville (SC) Press and Banner*, August 13, 1918 (London deaths, Austria-Hungary). "Spanish Influenza," *Daily Gate City and Constitution-Democrat* (Keokuk, IA), August 14, 1918 (report of sick ship passengers in New York City). "8 Spanish Grip Suspects Here; One Victim Dead," *New York Tribune*, August 14, 1918. "No Quarantine Here Against Influenza; Patients from Norwegian Vessel Had Disease on Shipboard, and Now Have Pneumonia," *New York Times*, August 15, 1918. "Epidemic Guard for Port," *New York Times*, August 19, 1918. Francesco Aimone, "The 1918 Influenza Epidemic in New York City: A Review of the Public Health Response," *Public Health Reports* 125, Supplement 3 (2010): 71–79.

73   "No Quarantine Here Against Influenza." "Spanish Influenza," *New York Times*, August 16, 1918. Keegan, *First World War*, 410–12 (black day, 412). American Battle Monuments Commission, *33d Division: Summary of Operations in the World War* (Washington, D.C.: U.S. Government Printing Office, 1944), 6–17. Gilbert, *First World War* (Holt, 1996), 450–52 (Rupprecht, 451–52).

74   Paschall, *Defeat of Imperial Germany*, 172–81. Kennedy, *Over Here*, 193–95. Gilbert, *First World War* (Holt, 1996), 457 (Ludendorff evacuation order). Keegan, *First World War*, 413.

75   Capozzola, *Uncle Sam Wants You*, 45–49. Chambers, *To Raise an Army*, 213–14. "Draft Raids Here Anger Senators," *New York Times*, September 6, 1918. "Halt Senate Action upon Slacker Raids," *New York Times*, September 7, 1918.

76   "Eighteen to Forty-Five," *New York Times*, September 15, 1918. Capozzola, *Uncle Sam Wants You*, 21. Chambers, *To Raise an Army*, 198. Edmund Morris, *Colonel Roosevelt* (New York: Random House 2010), 540 (U.S. vs. British and French manpower).

77   Livermore, *Politics Is Adjourned*, 185–86, 209–14.

78   Woodrow Wilson, "Address delivered at the First Annual Assemblage of the League to Enforce Peace:

American Principles, May 27, 1916," *American Presidency Project*, www.presidency.ucsb.edu/ws/?pid=65391. Livermore, *Politics Is Adjourned*, 212. "Wilson Stirs Audience: Calls It 'a People's War' That Must End in a League of Peace," *New York Times*, September 28, 1917. "Bay State Asks Aid in Influenza Fight," *New York Times*, September 27, 1918. "Stop Gatherings in Pennsylvania: All Saloons and Amusement Places Closed in Fight on Influenza," *Evening Star* (Washington, D.C.), October 4, 1918. "Alarm Felt Here over 1,695 New Influenza Cases," *New York Evening World*, October 4, 1918.

79 Paschall, *Defeat of Imperial Germany*, 184–88. Harries and Harries, *Last Days of Innocence*, 349–69. Kennedy, *Over Here*, 195–98. Neiberg, *Fighting the Great War*, 350–52. Gilbert, *First World War* (Holt, 1996), 465–66.

80 Neiberg, *Fighting the Great War*, 349. Gilbert, *First World War* (Holt, 1996), 466–68, 470. Paschall, *Defeat of Imperial Germany*, 187–91. Harries and Harries, *Last Days of Innocence*, 380–402. Kennedy, *Over Here*, 198–200.

81 Gilbert, *First World War* (Holt, 1996), 468, 483, 488, 491, 494. René Albrecht-Carrié, "Italian Foreign Policy, 1914–22," *Journal of Modern History* 20, no. 4 (December 1948): 326–39 (Austrian armistice, 335). Neiberg, *Fighting the Great War*, 352–56. "Wilson's Note to Germany and Hun's Reply," *Bismarck (ND) Tribune*, October 14, 1918. Livermore, *Politics Is Adjourned*, 214–17.

82 Paschall, *Defeat of Imperial Germany*, 213–17. Gilbert, *First World War* (Holt, 1996), 493–94. Pershing, *My Experiences in the First World War* 2: 359–367.

83 Livermore, *Politics Is Adjourned*, 224–26. Gilbert, *First World War* (Holt, 1996), 494–95, 498, 500. Woodrow Wilson, "Address to a Joint Session of Congress Concerning the Terms of Armistice Signed by Germany, November 11, 1918," *American Presidency Project*, www.presidency.ucsb.edu/ws/?pid=117697.

84 Margaret MacMillan, *Paris 1919: Six Months That Changed the World* (New York: Random House, 2003), 58–59, 225–26.

EPILOGUE

Epigraphs: Ray Stannard Baker quoted in Burl Noggle, *Into the Twenties: The United States from Armistice to Normalcy* (Urbana: University of Illinois Press, 1974), 134. Warren G. Harding, "Inaugural Address, March 4, 1921," *American Presidency Project*, www.presidency.ucsb.edu/ws/?pid=25833.

1 Mildred Aldrich, *When Johnny Comes Marching Home* (Boston: Small, Maynard & Company, 1919), 125–25. For a description of some armistice day celebrations, see Ann Hagedorn, *Savage Peace: Hope and Fear in America, 1919* (New York: Simon & Schuster, 2007), 5–7.

2 Though it was the most important document ending WWI, the treaty between the Allied Powers and Germany (Versailles Treaty) was one of several instruments that had to be signed before the war was officially over. The others were the Treaty of Saint Germain (with Austria, signed September 10, 1919), Treaty of Neuilly (with Bulgaria, signed November 27, 1919), Treaty of Trianon (with Hungary, signed June 4, 1920), and the Treaty of Sèvres (with Turkey, signed August 10, 1920). See "Treaties of Paris," *Encyclopedia Britannica* online, https://www.britannica.com/topic/Treaties-of-Paris-1919-1920.

3 Although the United States declared its independence in 1776, it took some time to settle on the present form of government. From 1781 to 1789, the country operated under the Articles of Confederation, which did not provide for an executive branch of government and in other ways also proved unworkable. The Constitution of the United States of America was formally adopted by the states in 1789, and Washington was inaugurated for the first of two terms as president of the United States in April of that year.

4 Hagedorn, *Savage Peace*, 21–23. "President Wilson's Projected Trip to Europe Argued before the Supreme Court of Public Opinion," *New York Times*, November 26, 1918. "Would Vacate Wilson's Office," *New York Times*, December 3, 1918. "Senators Clash Over Trip," *New York Times*, December 4, 1918. John Milton Cooper, Jr., *Woodrow Wilson: A Biography* (New York: Alfred A. Knopf, 2009), 456–58 (Wilson quote, 455–56).

5 Cooper, *Woodrow Wilson*, 456–58 (Lodge quote, 457).

6 Margaret MacMillan, *Paris 1919: Six Months That Changed the World* (New York: Random House, 2003), 3, 15–16, 20, 22. Hagedorn, *Savage Peace*, 19–20. George C. Herring, *From Colony to Superpower: U.S. Foreign Relations since 1776* (Oxford: Oxford University Press, 2008), 420 (Keynes quote).

7 Woodrow Wilson, "Address to the Senate of the United States: 'A World League for Peace,'" American Presidency Project, http://www.presidency.ucsb.edu/ws/index.php?pid=65396; both quoted phases are from this speech. MacMillan, *Paris 1919*, notes that "Wilson had said much about general principles but had mentioned few specifics" (8) and "throughout the Peace Conference he clung to the belief that he spoke for the masses and that, if only he could reach them . . . they would rally to his views." Cooper, *Woodrow Wilson*, 461–62 (statement to Creel, 462).

8 David M. Kennedy, *Over Here: The First World War and American Society* (New York: Oxford University Press, 1980), 247–49. Burl Noggle, *Into the Twenties: The United States from Armistice to Normalcy* (Urbana: University of Illinois Press, 1974), 21–32 (Adler), 36–37. Noggle observes that Congress seemed more preoccupied with partisan politics than U.S. reconstruction: "Between May 16, 1918, and January 31, 1919, eleven resolutions and bills introduced in the two houses of Congress proposed formation of committees on reconstruction. Not one resolution or bill passed . . . partisanship . . . permeated reconstruction" (46–47). State governments and the Council for National Defense were more active, though to little lasting effect (52–55).

9 Kennedy, *Over Here*, 247 (Eliot).

10 Peyton C. March, *The Nation At War* (New York: Doubleday, Doran & Company, 1932), 310–12. United States Department of the Army, Historical Division, *United States Army in the World War, 1917–1919*, 17 vols. (Washington, D.C.: U.S. Government Printing Office, 1948), 11: 1, 19, 23.

11 Noggle, *Into the Twenties*, 10–11 ($50,000,000 a day), 18 (embarkation centers).

12 Ibid., 13–17. Benedict Crowell and Robert Forrest Wilson, *Demobilization: Our Industrial and Military Demobilization after the Armistice, 1918–1920* (New Haven: Yale University Press, 1921), 21 (description of Le Mans).

13 Arthur W. Little, *From Harlem to the Rhine* (New York: Covici Friede, 1936), 361. March, *The Nation at War*, 325 (number of parades by June 30). Frederic L. Paxson, *American Democracy and the World War*, Vol. 3, *Postwar Years, Normalcy, 1918–1923* (Berkeley, CA: University of California Press, 1948), 7–8 (Pershing and the First Division).

14 Noggle, *Into the Twenties* notes that "by the end of August, 1919, only 40,000 American troops remained in Europe, all of them either logistical units or remnants of the American occupying forces in the German Rhineland" (14–15). Hagedorn, *Savage Peace*, 84–86 (Michigan lobbying). March, *The Nation at War*, 150 (Archangel casualties). Norman E. Saul, *War and Revolution: The United States and Russia, 1914–1921* (Lawrence: University of Kansas Press, 2001), 370–75.

15 "Scores of Strikes throughout Country Paralyze Industry," *Lake County Times* (Hammond, IN), August 29, 1919. "Butte Miners Walk off Job," and "8,000 Shipbuilders Strike on Delaware River," both in the *Butte (MT) Daily Bulletin*, February 07, 1919. "Telegraphers' Strike Growing," *Butte (MT) Daily Bulletin*, June 13, 1919. "Phone Service Badly Paralized! [*sic*]," *Evening Caledonian* (St. Johnsbury, VT). "Firemen Strike; Want Own Union," *South Bend (IN) News-Times*, April 12, 1919. Kennedy, *Over Here*, 272 (one in five workers).

16 Kennedy, *Over Here*, 270–74, 288 (Hanson quote). Geoffrey R. Stone, *Perilous Times: Free Speech in Wartime, from the Sedition Act of 1798 to the War on Terrorism* (New York: W. W. Norton & Company, 2004), 221. "First General Strike in United States Halts Seattle Industry Prompty [*sic*] at 10," *East Oregonian* (Umatilla County, OR), February 6, 1919. Edgar B. Herwick III, "The Boston Police Strike That Impacted Labor for Generations," WGBH http://news.wgbh.org/post/boston-police-strike-impacted-labor-generations (accessed August 2016). Regin Schmidt, *Red Scare: FBI*

and the Origins of Anticommunisim in the United States, 1919–1943 (Copenhagen: Museum Tusculanum Press, 2000), 26–27. Ronald L. Filippelli, ed., *Labor Conflict in the United States: An Encyclopedia* (New York: Garland Publishing, 1990), 498–509.

17 Stone, *Perilous Times*, 221–22. Kennedy, *Over Here*, 288–89. Schmidt, *Red Scare*, 26. "Bomb Injures Ex-Senator's Wife, Maims a Servant," *New York Times*, April 30, 1918. "Terrorists Send Out Bombs," *Tonopah (NV) Daily Bonanza*, April 30, 1919. "Search for Bomb Senders," *Democratic Banner* (Mount Vernon, OH), May 2, 1919. "Bomb Plot against 22 [*sic*] Leading Men of Nation Is Foiled by Mere Chance," *Great Falls (MT) Tribune*, May 1, 1919. "36 Were Marked as Victims by Bomb Conspirers," *New York Times*, May 1, 1919. Christopher Capozzola, *Uncle Sam Wants You: World War I and the Making of the Modern American Citizen* (New York: Oxford University Press, 2008), 211.

18 Schmidt, *Red Scare*, 200. Stone, *Perilous Times*, 222–30. Capozzola, *Uncle Same Wants You*, 202. Kennedy, *Over Here*, 289, 292. Kenneth D. Ackerman, *Young J. Edgar: Hoover and the Red Scare*, 1919–1920 (Falls Church, VA: Viral History Press, 2011), 36.

19 Noggle, *Into the Twenties*, 157. Cameron McWhirter, *Red Summer: The Summer of 1919 and the Awakening of Black America* (New York: Henry Holt & Company, 2011), 112 (Toomer quote).

20 Herring, *From Colony to Superpower*, 418 (Masaryk quote). Kendrick A. Clements, *The Life of Herbert Hoover: Imperfect Visionary, 1918–1928* (Palgrave Macmillan, 2010), 1–11.

21 Woodrow Wilson, "Address to Congress on International Order," February 11, 1918. American Presidency Project http://www.presidency.ucsb.edu/ws/index.php?pid=110448 (accessed August 2016). Robert Lansing, *The Peace Negotiations: A Personal Narrative* (Boston: Houghton Mifflin Company, 1921), 97. See also MacMillan, *Paris 1919*, 11–13.

22 Herring, *From Colony to Superpower*, 418 (Ho Chi Minh), 437 (area under imperial control). For information on the Pan-African Congress of 1919, see Adriane Lentz-Smith, *Freedom Struggles: African Americans and World War I* (Cambridge: Harvard University Press, 2009), 161–68; and Clarence G. Contee, "Du Bois, the NAACP, and the Pan-African Congress of 1919," *Journal of Negro History* 57, no. 1 (Jan, 1972), 13–28 (especially 23–25).

23 MacMillan, *Paris 1919*, 193 (reparations and war guilt), 474–78 (House quote, 477). For the full text of the Versailles Treaty, see Yale Law School, the Avalon Project, http://avalon.law.yale.edu/subject_menus/versailles_menu.asp.

24 Herring, *From Colony to Superpower*, 428–32. Kennedy, *Over Here*, 359–361.

25 Kennedy, *Over Here*, 362. Herring, *From Colony to Superpower*, 432–35. Letter from Henry Cabot Lodge to Henry Wilson, April 8, 1919, Henry Wilson Papers, Manuscript Division, Library of Congress. "US Peace Treaty with Germany," WWI Document Archive, https://wwi.lib.byu.edu/index.php/US_Peace_Treaty_with_Germany. See also Cooper, *Woodrow Wilson*, 506–59. Because the League of Nations Covenant was incorporated into the other treaties between the Allies and the Central Powers, the United States also signed separate treaties with Austria and Hungary in 1921. (The country had not declared war on the other Central Powers.)

26 Noggle, *Into the Twenties*, 29 (reduced army strength). Herring, *From Colony to Superpower*, 434–56. Selig Adler, *The Isolationist Impulse: Its Twentieth-Century Reaction* (London: Abelard-Schuman, 1957), 118 (Root quote).

BIBLIOGRAPHY

LIBRARY OF CONGRESS MANUSCRIPT COLLECTIONS

(See also Appendix, World War I Collections in the Library of Congress). Papers of:

Henry T. Allen

Newton Diehl Baker

Belgian Children's Letters to President Woodrow Wilson

Albert Jeremiah Beveridge

Albert Burleson

James M. Cain

Paul Hedrick Clark

Cosby Family (Spencer Cosby)

Rebekah Crawford and Linda Clarke-Smith

George Creel

Josephus Daniels

Elmer Holmes Davis (Carolyn A. Wilson letters)

Benjamin Delahauf Foulois

Hermann Hagedorn

Florence Jaffray Harriman

La Follette Family (Robert La Follette, Sr.)

William G. McAdoo

Peyton C. March

Miscellaneous Manuscript Collection

    Ralph M. Brown

    John F. Callahan

    Arthur Chelton Chandler

    John W. Colbert

    Harold L. Dunne (account of *Tuscania* sinking)

    Emma L. George

    Charlotte Everett Hopkins

    Dorothy Kitchen O'Neill

NAACP Records

John Callan O'Laughlin

Papers Relating to the Ford Peace Plan

George Patton

John Pershing

Leighton W. Rogers

Theodore Roosevelt

Charles Edward Russell

Hugh Lenox Scott

William Snowden Sims

Stanley Washburn

Henry White

Brand Whitlock

Woodrow Wilson

LIBRARY OF CONGRESS VETERANS HISTORY PROJECT COLLECTIONS

(See also Appendix, World War I Collections in the Library of Congress)

Jesse A. Anderson

Leo Joseph Bailey

Clarence Bauer

Denver Easton Bratcher

Robert A. Burns

Andrew Gbur

Harold L. Hard

Benjamin Kaufman

John C. Laing

Robert Pearson Lawrence

Robert Leib

David R. Ollendorf

Clyde Wilbur Russell

Elmer Holmes Van Schoick

Philip E. Scholz

Eugene F. Sharkoff

Frederick Albert Tyas

James Richard Waggener

BOOKS

Ackerman, Kenneth D. *Young J. Edgar: Hoover and the Red Scare, 1919–1920*. Falls Church, VA: Viral History Press, 2011.

Adler, Selig. *The Isolationist Impulse: Its Twentieth-Century Reaction*. London: Abelard-Schuman, 1957.

Addams, Jane. *Peace and Bread in Time of War*. New York: Macmillan Company, 1922.

Addams, Jane, Emily G. Balch, and Alice Hamilton. *Women at The Hague: The International Peace Congress of 1915.* With introduction by Mary Jo Deegan. Amherst, NY: Humanity Books, 2003.

Aldrich, Mildred. *A Hilltop on the Marne.* Boston: Houghton Mifflin Company, 1915.

———. *The Peak of the Load: The Waiting Months on the Hilltop from the Entrance of the Stars and Stripes to the Second Victory on the Marne.* Boston, MA: Small, Maynard and Company, 1918.

———. *When Johnny Comes Marching Home.* Boston, MA: Small, Maynard and Company, 1919.

Allen, Irving. *City in Slang: New York Life and Popular Speech.* New York: Oxford University Press, 1993.

American Battle Monuments Commission. *1st Division, Summary of Operations in the World War.* Washington, D.C.: U.S. Government Printing Office, 1944.

———. *2nd Division, Summary of Operations in the World War.* Washington, D.C.: U.S. Government Printing Office, 1944.

———. *3rd Division, Summary of Operations in the World War.* Washington, D.C.: U.S. Government Printing Office, 1944.

———. *26th Division, Summary of Operations in the World War.* Washington, D.C.: U.S. Government Printing Office, 1944.

———. *33rd Division, Summary of Operations in the World War.* Washington, D.C.: U.S. Government Printing Office, 1944.

———. *42nd Division, Summary of Operations in the World War.* Washington, D.C.: U.S. Government Printing Office, 1944.

———. *93rd Division, Summary of Operations in the World War.* Washington, D.C.: U.S. Government Printing Office, 1944.

American Women's War Relief Fund. *The American Women's War Relief Fund: A Record of Its Work, Christmas, 1914.* London: Vacher and Sons, Ltd., 1914.

Andrews, Fannie Fern [Phillips]. *A Call to Patriotic Service: To the Teachers of the United States.* Boston, MA: 1917.

Angell, Norman. *The Great Illusion: A Study of the Relation of Military Power in Nations to Their Economic and Social Advantage.* New York and London: G.P. Putnam's Sons, 1910.

Axelrod, Alan. *Selling the Great War: The Making of American Propaganda.* New York: Palgrave Macmillan, 2009.

Baer, George W. *One Hundred Years of Sea Power: The U. S. Navy, 1890–1990.* Stanford, CA: Stanford University Press, 1994.

Baker, Carlos. *Ernest Hemingway: A Life Story.* New York: Collier Books/Macmillan, 1969.

Baker, Ray Stannard. *Woodrow Wilson: Life and Letters.* New York: Greenwood Press, 1968.

Ballard, Robert D. and Rick Archbold. *Lost Liners.* New York and Toronto: Hyperion/Madison Press, 1997.

Barbeau, Arthur E., and Florette Henri. *The Unknown Soldiers: African-American Troops in World War I.*

Blackton, J. Stuart. *Battle Cry of Peace.* Brooklyn, NY: The M. P. Publishing Co., 1915.

Blucher von Wahlstatt, Evelyn Mary. *An English Wife in Berlin: A Private Memoir of Events, Politics, and Daily Life in Germany throughout the War and the Social Revolution of 1918.* London: Constable and Company, Ltd., 1920.

Blumenson, Martin. *The Patton Papers, 1885–1940.* New York: Da Capo Press, 1998.

Brands, H. W. *Woodrow Wilson.* New York: Times Books/ Henry Holt & Company, 2003.

Brinkley, Alan. *The Unfinished Nation: A Concise History of the American People.* 2nd ed. New York: Alfred A Knopf, 1997.

Bristow, Nancy K. *Making Men Moral: Social Engineering during the Great War.* New York: New York University Press, 1996.

Brown, Carrie. *Rosie's Mom: Forgotten Women Workers of the First World War.* Boston, MA: Northeastern University Press, 2002.

Bryan, William Jennings. *The Value of an Ideal.* New York: Funk & Wagnalls Company, 1914.

Buckley, Gail. *American Patriots: The Story of Blacks in the Military from the Revolution to Desert Storm.* New York: Random House, 2001.

Bullard, Robert Lee. *Personalities and Reminiscences of the War.* Garden City, NY: Doubleday, Page & Company, 1925.

Canning, Charlotte M. *The Most American Thing in America: Circuit Chautauqua as Performance.* Iowa City: University of Iowa Press, 2005.

Capozzola, Christopher. *Uncle Sam Wants You: World War I and the Making of the Modern American Citizen*. New York: Oxford University Press, 2008.

Carr, Virginia Spencer. *Dos Passos: A Life*. Evanston, IL: Northwestern University Press, 2004: 121–26.

Carroll, Francis M. "America and the 1916 Rising." In *1916, the Long Revolution*. Edited by Gabriel Doherty and Dermot Keogh, 121–140. Cork, Ireland: Mercier Press, 2007.

Carruth, Gorton. *Encyclopedia of American Facts and Dates*, 8th ed. New York: Harper & Row, 1987.

Casey, Steven. *When Soldiers Fall: How Americans Have Confronted Combat Losses from World War I to Afghanistan*. New York: Oxford University Press, 2014.

The Case of Belgium in the Present War: An Account of the Violation of the Neutrality of Belgium and of the Laws of War on Belgian Territory. New York: Macmillan Company, 1914.

Cashman, Sean Dennis. *America in the Age of the Titans: The Progressive Era and World War I*. New York: New York University Press, 1988.

Chace, James. *1912*. New York: Simon & Schuster, 2004.

Chambers, Frank P. *The War behind the War: A History of the Political and Civilian Fronts*. New York: Arno Press, 1972.

Chambers, John Whiteclay II. *To Raise an Army: The Draft Comes to Modern America*. New York: The Free Press, 1987.

———. *Draftees or Volunteers: A Documentary History of the Debate over Military Conscription in the United States, 1787–1973*. New York: Garland Publishing, 1975.

———. *The Tyranny of Change: America in the Progressive Era 1890–1920*. New Brunswick, NJ: Rutgers University Press, 2000.

Chatfield, Charles. *For Peace and Justice: Pacifism in America 1914–1941*. Knoxville: The University of Tennessee Press, 1971.

Chaudhuri, Ranajoy Ray. *The Changing Face of American Banking*. New York: Palgrave Macmillan, 2014.

Clements, Kendrick A. *The Presidency of Woodrow Wilson*. Lawrence: University Press of Kansas, 1992.

———. *The Life of Herbert Hoover: Imperfect Visionary, 1918–1928*. New York: Palgrave Macmillan, 2010.

Clendenen, Clarence C. *The United States and Pancho Villa: A Study in Unconventional Diplomacy*. Ithaca, NY: Cornell University Press, 1961.

Clifford, John Garry. *The Citizen Soldiers: The Plattsburg Training Camp Movement, 1913–1920*. Lexington: The University Press of Kentucky, 1972.

Coffman, Edward M. *The War to End All Wars: The American Military Experience in World War I*. Madison, WI: University of Wisconsin Press.

Cohen, Naomi W. *A Dual Heritage: The Public Career of Oscar S. Straus*. Philadelphia, PA: The Jewish Publication Society of America, 1969.

Coolidge, John Gardner. *A War Diary in Paris, 1914–1917*. Cambridge, MA: Privately printed at Riverside Press, 1931.

Cooper, John Milton, Jr. *Woodrow Wilson: A Biography*. New York: Alfred A. Knopf, 2009. Kindle edition.

Cramer, C. H. *Newton D. Baker: A Biography*. Cleveland, OH: The World Publishing Company, 1961.

Creel, George. *How We Advertised America*. New York: Arno Press, 1972.

———. *Rebel at Large: Recollections of Fifty Crowded Years*. New York: G. P. Putnam's Sons, 1947.

Croly, Herbert. *Willard Straight*. New York: Macmillan Company, 1924.

Crosby, Alfred W. *America's Forgotten Pandemic: The Influenza of 1918*. New York: Cambridge University Press, 1989.

Crowell, Benedict and Robert Forrest Wilson, *Demobilization: Our Industrial and Military Demobilization after the Armistice, 1918–1920*. New Haven: Yale University Press, 1921.

Crozier, Emmet. *American Reporters on the Western Front, 1914–1918*. New York: Oxford University Press, 1959.

Curti, Merle. *American Philanthropy Abroad*. New Brunswick, NJ: Transaction Books, 1988.

Daniels, Josephus. *Our Navy at War*. Washington, D.C.: Pictorial Bureau, 1922.

Davis, Richard Harding. *With the Allies*. New York: Charles Scribner's Sons, 1917.

Dawley, Alan. *Changing the World: American Progressives in War and Revolution*. Princeton, NJ: Princeton University Press, 2003.

Degen, Marie Louise. *The History of the Women's Peace Party*. New York: Burt Franklin Reprints, 1974. Originally published by the Johns Hopkins Press, 1939.

De Santis, Vincent P. *The Shaping of Modern America: 1877–1920*. 3rd ed. Wheeling, IL: Harland Davidson, Inc., 2000.

Dillard, Irving, ed. *Mr. Justice Brandeis, Great American*. St. Louis, MO: Modern View Press, 1941.

Doenecke, Justus D. *Nothing Less Than War: A New History of America's Entry into World War I*. Lexington: University Press of Kentucky, 2011.

Drake, Richard. *The Education of an Anti-Imperialist: Robert La Follette and U.S. Expansion*. Madison, WI: The University of Wisconsin Press, 2013.

Dulles, Foster Rhea. *American Red Cross: A History*. New York: Harper & Brothers Publishers, 1950.

Ebbert, Jean and Marie-Beth Hall. *The First, the Few, the Forgotten: Navy and Marine Corps Women in World War I*. Annapolis, MD: Naval Institute Press, 2002.

Edgar, William Crowell. *The Millers' Belgian Relief Movement 1914–15, conducted by the Northwestern Miller: Final Report of its Director*. Minneapolis, MN: Northwestern Miller, 1915.

Edwards, John C. *Patriots in Pinstripes: Men of the National Security League*. Washington, D.C.: University Press of America, 1982.

Eisenhower, John S. D. *Intervention! The United States and the Mexican Revolution, 1913–1917*. New York: W. W. Norton & Company, 1993.

———. *Yanks: The Epic Story of the American Army in World War I*. New York: The Free Press, 2001.

Elleman, Bruce A. *International Competition in China, 1899–1991: The Rise, Fall, and Eventual Success of the Open Door Policy*. New York: Routledge, 2015.

Ellis, Edward Robb. *Echoes of Distant Thunder: Life in the United States, 1914–1918*. New York: Kodansha International, 1996.

Ellis, Mark. *Race, War, and Surveillance: African Americans and the United States Government during World War I*. Bloomington, IN: Indiana University Press, 2001.

Emmerson, Charles. *1913: In Search of the World before the Great War*. New York: PublicAffairs, 2013. Kindle edition.

Ferrell, Robert H. *Woodrow Wilson and World War I, 1917–1921*. New York: Harper & Row, 1985.

Filippelli, Ronald L., ed. *Labor Conflict in the United States: An Encyclopedia*. New York: Garland Publishing, 1990.

Finnegan, John Patrick. *Against the Specter of a Dragon: The Campaign for American Military Preparedness, 1914–1917*. Westport, CT: Greenwood Press, 1974.

Fite, Gilbert C., and H.C. Peterson. *Opponents of War, 1917–1918*. Madison, WI: The University of Wisconsin Press, 1957.

Floyd, M. Ryan. *Abandoning American Neutrality: Woodrow Wilson and the Beginning of the Great War, August 1914–December 1915*. New York: Palgrave Macmillan, 2013.

Forbes, John Douglas. *J.P. Morgan, Jr., 1867–1943*. Charlottesville: University Press of Virginia, 1981.

Ford, Nancy Gentile. *Americans All! Foreign-born Soldiers in World War I*. College Station, TX: Texas A&M University Press, 2001.

———. *The Great War and America: Civil-Military Relations During World War I*. Westport, CT: Praeger Security International, 2008.

Foulois, Benjamin D. *From the Wright Brothers to the Astronauts: The Memoirs of Major General Benjamin D. Foulois*. With C. B. Glines. New York: McGraw-Hill Book Company, 1968.

Fradin, Judith Bloom, and Dennis Brindell Fadin. *Jane Addams: Champion of Democracy*. New York: Clarion Books, 2006.

Freidel, Frank. *Franklin D. Roosevelt: The Apprenticeship*. Boston: Little, Brown and Company, 1952.

Gardner, Constance. *Augustus Peabody Gardner, Major, United States National Guard, 1865–1918*. Cambridge, MA: Privately printed at Riverside Press, 1919.

Garrison, Dee. *Mary Heaton Vorse: The Life of an American Insurgent*. Philadelphia: Temple University Press, 1989.

Gelfand, Lawrence E. *The Inquiry: American Preparations for Peace, 1917–1919*. New Haven, CT: Yale University Press, 1963.

George, David Lloyd. *British War Aims: Statement by the Right Honorable David Lloyd George, January Fifth, Nineteen Hundred and Eighteen*. New York: George H. Doran Company, 1918.

Giangreco, D. M. *The Soldier from Independence: A Military Biography of Harry Truman*. Minneapolis, MN: Zenith Press, 2009.

Gilbert, Martin. *The First World War: A Complete History*. New York: Henry Holt & Company, 1994.

Gleaves, Albert. *A History of the Transport Service: Adventures and Experiences of United States Transports and Cruisers in the World War*. New York: George H. Doran Company, 1921.

Gregory, James N. *The Southern Diaspora: How the Great Migrations of Black and White Southerners Transformed America*. Chapel Hill: The University of North Carolina Press, 2005.

Gregory, Ross. *Walter Hines Page: Ambassador to the Court of St. James's*. Lexington: University Press of Kentucky, 1970.

Grotelueschen, Mark Ethan. *The AEF Way of War: The American Army and Combat in World War I*. New York: Cambridge University Press, 2007.

Hagedorn, Ann. *Savage Peace: Hope and Fear in America, 1919*. New York: Simon & Schuster, 2007.

Hamilton, John Maxwell, and Robert Mann, eds. *A Journalist's Diplomatic Mission: Ray Stannard Baker's World War I Diary*. Baton Rouge, LA: Louisiana State University Press, 2012.

Hansen, Arlen J. *Gentlemen Volunteers: The Story of the American Ambulance Drivers in the Great War, August 1914–September 1918*. New York: Arcade Publishing, 1996.

Harries, Merion and Susan Harries. *The Last Days of Innocence: America at War, 1917–1918*. New York: Random House, 1997.

Harriman, Florence Jaffray. *From Pinafores to Politics*. New York: Henry Holt & Company, 1923.

Harvey, Sheriden, Janice E. Ruth, Barbara Orbach Natanson, Sarah Day, and Evelyn Sinclair, eds. *American Women: A Library of Congress Guide for the Study of Women's History and Culture in the United States*. Washington, D.C.: Library of Congress, 2001.

Haynes, Robert V. *A Night of Violence: The Houston Riot of 1917*. Baton Rouge, LA: Louisiana State University Press, 1976.

Hawkins, Nigel. *The Starvation Blockades*. Barnsley, South Yorkshire, UK: Leo Cooper, 2002.

Heaton, John L. *Cobb of "The World": A Leader in Liberalism*. New York: E. P. Dutton & Company, 1924: 268–270.

Herring, George C. *From Colony to Superpower: U.S. Foreign Relations since 1776*. New York: Oxford University Press, 2008.

Hirst, Francis Wrigley. *The Six Panics and Other Essays*. London: Methuen & Co., Ltd., 1913.

Horne, John and Alan Kramer. *German Atrocities, 1914: A History of Denial*. New Haven, CT: Yale University Press, 2001.

House, Edward Mandell. *The Intimate Papers of Colonel House*. Edited by Charles Seymour. Boston: Houghton Mifflin Company, 1926.

Houston, David F. *Eight Years with Wilson's Cabinet: 1913–1920*. Garden City, NY: Doubleday, Page & Company, 1926.

Howard, Fred. *Wilbur and Orville: A Biography of the Wright Brothers*. Mineola, NY: Dover Publications, 1998.

Huston, James L. *Securing the Fruits of Labor: The American Concept of Wealth Distribution, 1765–1900*. Baton Rouge, LA: Louisiana State University Press, 1998.

Iversen, Kristen. *Molly Brown: Unraveling the Myth*. Boulder, CO: Johnson Books, 1993.

Jensen, Joan M. *The Price of Vigilance*. Chicago, IL: Rand McNally & Company, 1968.

Joyce, George, ed. *Story of Philadelphia*. Philadelphia: Rex Printing House, 1919.

Kaufman, Burton I. *Efficiency and Expansion: Foreign Trade Organization in the Wilson Administration, 1913–1921.* Westport, CT: Greenwood Press, 1974.

Kazin, Michael. *A Godly Hero: The Life of William Jennings Bryan.* New York: Anchor Books/Random House, 2006. Kindle edition.

Keegan, John. *The First World War.* New York: Vintage Books, 2000. Originally published by Hutchinson in 1998.

Kennedy, David M. *Over Here: The First World War and American Society.* Oxford/New York: Oxford University Press, 1980.

Kennedy, Richard S. *Dreams in the Mirror: A Biography of e. e. cummings.* New York: Liveright Publishing Corporation, 1980: 137–58.

Klekowski, Ed and Libby Klekowski. *Eyewitness to the Great War: American Writers, Reporters, Volunteers, and Soldiers in France, 1914–1918.* Jefferson, NC: McFarland & Company, 2012.

Knock, Thomas J. *To End All Wars: Woodrow Wilson and the Quest for a New World Order.* New York: Oxford University Press, 1992.

Kornweibel, Theodore Jr. *"Investigate Everything": Federal Efforts to Compel Black Loyalty during World War I.* Bloomington, IN: Indiana University Press, 2002: 10–11.

Kraft, Barbara S. *The Peace Ship: Henry Ford's Pacifist Adventure in the First World War.* New York: Macmillan Company, 1978.

Lane, Anne Wintermute and Louise Herrick Wall, eds. *The Letters of Franklin K. Lane.* Boston, MA: Houghton Mifflin Company, 1922.

Lane, Jack C. *Armed Progressive: General Leonard Wood.* Lincoln: University of Nebraska Press, 2009. Originally published by Presidio Press in 1978.

Lansing, Robert. *The Peace Negotiations: A Personal Narrative.* Boston: Houghton Mifflin Company, 1921).

———. *War Memoirs of Robert Lansing.* Westport, CT: Greenwood Press, 1970.

Larson, Erik. *Dead Wake: The Last Crossing of the Lusitania.* New York: Crown Publishers, 2015.

Lentz-Smith, Adriane. *Freedom Struggles: African Americans and World War I.* Cambridge, MA: Harvard University Press, 2009.

Levario, Miguel A. "The El Paso Race Riot of 1916." In *War Along the Border: The Mexican Revolution and Tejano Communities.* Edited by Arnoldo De León, 140-143. College Station, TX: Texas A&M University Press, 2012.

Library of Congress. *Presidential Campaign Posters from the Library of Congress.* Philadelphia: Quirk Books, 2012.

Liggett, Hunter. *A.E.F.: Ten Years Ago in France.* New York: Dodd, Mead and Company, 1928.

Link, Arthur S. *Wilson: Campaigns for Progressivism and Peace, 1916–1917.* Princeton, NJ: Princeton University Press, 1965.

———. *Confusions and Crises, 1915–1916.* Princeton, NJ: Princeton University Press, 1964.

———. *The Struggle for Neutrality 1914–1915.* Princeton, NJ: Princeton University Press, 1960.

Little, Arthur W. *From Harlem to the Rhine: The Story of New York's Colored Volunteers.* New York: Covici Friede, 1936.

Livermore, Seward W. *Politics Is Adjourned: Woodrow Wilson and the War Congress, 1916–1918.* Middletown, CT: Wesleyan University Press, 1966.

Lord, Walter. *The Good Years: From 1900 to the First World War.* New York: Harper, 1960.

Lowell, A. Lawrence. *A League to Enforce Peace.* Boston: World Peace Foundation, 1915.

Lowitt, Richard. *George W. Norris: The Persistence of a Progressive, 1913–1933.* Urbana, IL: University of Illinois Press, 1971.

Ludington, Townsend, ed. *The Fourteenth Chronicle: Letters and Diaries of John Dos Passos.* Boston, MA: Gambit, 1973.

Luskin, John. *Lippman, Liberty, and the Press.* Tuscaloosa: University of Alabama Press, 1972.

Macmillan, Margaret. *The War That Ended Peace: The Road to 1914.* New York: Random House, 2013.

———. *Paris 1919: Six Months That Changed the World.* New York: Random House, 2003.

Manchester, William. *American Caesar: Douglas MacArthur, 1880–1964*. Boston, MA: Little, Brown and Company, 1978.

March, Peyton C. *The Nation at War*. Garden City, NY: Doubleday, Doran & Company, 1932.

McCallum, Jack. *Leonard Wood: Rough Rider, Surgeon, Architect of American Imperialism*. New York: New York University Press, 2006.

McConnell, James R. *Flying for France: With the American Escadrille at Verdun*. New York: Doubleday, Page & Company, 1917.

McWhirter, Cameron. *Red Summer: The Summer of 1919 and the Awakening of Black America*. New York: Henry Holt & Company, 2011.

Messimer, Dwight R. *The Baltimore Sabotage Cell: German Agents, American Traitors, and the U-Boat Deutschland during World War I*. Annapolis, MD: Naval Institute Press, 2015.

Meyer, G. J. *A World Undone: The Story of the Great War 1914 to 1918*. New York: Delta Trade Paperbacks, 2007.

Millard, Candace. *The River of Doubt: Theodore Roosevelt's Darkest Journey*. New York: Doubleday, 2005.

Millis, Walter. *The Road to War: America, 1914–1917*. New York: Howard Fertig, 1970. Originally published by Houghton Mifflin Company in 1935.

Moranian, Suzanne E. "The Armenian Genocide and American Missionary Relief Efforts." In *America and the Armenian Genocide of 1915*. 185–213. Cambridge: Cambridge University Press, 2003.

Morison, Elting E. *Admiral Sims and the Modern American Navy*. New York: Russell & Russell, 1968.

Morris, Edmund. *Colonel Roosevelt*. New York: Random House, 2010.

Morse, Edwin W. *The Vanguard of American Volunteers in the Fighting Lines and in Humanitarian Service, August 1914–April 1917*. New York: Charles Scribner's Sons, 1919.

Murphy, Paul J. *World War I and the Origin of Civil Liberties in the United States*. New York: W. W. Norton, 1979: 89–90, 94–95.

Murray, Robert K. *Red Scare: A Study in National Hysteria, 1919-1920*. Westport, CT: Greenwood Press, 1980.

Nash, George H. *The Life of Herbert Hoover: Vol. 2: The Humanitarian, 1914–1917*. New York: W. W. Norton & Company, 1988.

National Civil Liberties Bureau. *War-Time Prosecutions and Mob Violence*. New York: NCLB, July 1918.

National Security League. *Proceedings of the Congress of Constructive Patriotism*. New York: National Security League, 1917.

Neiberg, Michael S. *Fighting the Great War: A Global History*. Cambridge, MA: Harvard University Press, 2005.

Noggle, Burl. *Into the Twenties: The United States from Armistice to Normalcy*. Urbana: University of Illinois Press, 1974.

O'Brien, Francis William, ed. *The Hoover-Wilson Wartime Correspondence*. Ames, IA: Iowa State University Press.

Pack, Charles Lathrop. *The War Garden Victorious*. Philadelphia, PA: J. B. Lippincott Company, 1919.

Painter, Neil Irvin. *Standing at Armageddon: The United States, 1877–1919*. New York: W. W. Norton, 2008.

Palmer, Frederick. *Bliss, Peacemaker: The Life and Letters of General Tasker Howard Bliss*. New York: Dodd, Mead & Company, 1934.

Paschall, Rod. *The Defeat of Imperial Germany, 1917–1918*. Chapel Hill, NC: Algonquin Books of Chapel Hill, 1989.

Paxson, Frederic L. *America at War, 1917–1918*. Boston: Houghton Mifflin Company, 1939.

———. *Postwar Years, Normalcy, 1918–1923*. Berkeley: University of California Press, 1948.

Perkins, George, Barbara Perkins, and Phillip Leininger, eds. *Benet's Reader's Encyclopedia of American Literature*. New York: HarperCollinsPublishers, 1991.

Perry, Barton. *The Plattsburgh Movement*. New York: E. P. Dutton & Company, 1921.

Pershing, John J. *My Experiences in the First World War*, New York: Da Capo Press, 1995.

Pogue, Forrest C. *George C. Marshall: Education of a General*. New York: Viking Press, 1963.

Price, Alan. *The End of the Age of Innocence: Edith Wharton and the First World War*. New York: St. Martin's Press, 1996.

Price, Ruth. *The Lives of Agnes Smedley*. New York: Oxford University Press, 2005.

Procter, Ben. *William Randolph Hearst: Final Edition, 1911–1951*. New York: Oxford University Press, 2007.

Raines, Rebecca Robbins. *Getting the Message Through: A Branch History of the U.S. Army Signal Corps*. Washington, D.C.: Center of Military History, 2011.

Read, James Morgan. *Atrocity Propaganda, 1914–1919*. New York: Arno Press, 1972.

Roosevelt, Theodore. *Letters and Speeches*. New York: The Library of America, 2004.

Rosenberg, Jonathan. *How Far the Promised Land? World Affairs and the American Civil Rights Movement from the First World War to Vietnam*. Princeton, NJ: Princeton University Press, 2006.

Rudwick, Elliot. *Race Riot at East St. Louis, July 2, 1917*. Urbana, IL: University of Illinois Press, 1982.

Safford, Jeffrey J. *Wilsonian Maritime Diplomacy, 1913–1921*. New Brunswick, NJ: Rutgers University Press, 1978.

Saul, Norman E. *War and Revolution: The United States and Russia, 1914–1921*. Lawrence, KS: University Press of Kansas, 2001.

Salem, Dorothy. *To Better Our World: Black Women in Organized Reform, 1890–1920*. Brooklyn, NY: Carlson Publishing, 1990.

Salvatore, Nick. *Eugene V. Debs: Citizen and Socialist*. Urbana: University of Illinois Press, 2007.

Schmidt, Regin. *Red Scare: FBI and the Origins of Anticommunism in the United States, 1919–1943*. Copenhagen: Museum Tusculanum Press, 2000.

Scott, Lloyd N. *Naval Consulting Board of the United States*. Washington, D.C.: U.S. Government Printing Office, 1920.

Seeger, Alan. *Letters and Diary of Alan Seeger*. New York: Charles Scribner's Sons, 1917.

Seymour, Charles. *The Intimate Papers of Colonel House*. Boston, MA: Houghton Mifflin Company, 1928.

Southern Poverty Law Center. *Ku Klux Klan: A History of Racism and Violence*. 6th Ed. Montgomery, AL: Southern Poverty Law Center, 2011.

Smith, Daniel M. *Robert Lansing and American Neutrality, 1914–1917*. New York: Da Capo Press, 1972.

Spengler, Otto, comp. *World War History: Daily Records and Comments as Appeared in American and Foreign Newspapers, 1914–1926*. New York: Argus Press Clipping Bureau, c. 1928.

Sreenivasan, Jyotsna, ed. *Poverty and the Government in America: A Historical Encyclopedia*. Santa Barbara, CA: ABC-CLIO, 2009.

Steinson, Barbara J. *American Women's Activism in World War I*. NY: Garland Publishing, 1982.

Stevenson, David. *Cataclysm: The First World War as Political Tragedy*. New York: Basic Books, 2005.

Stewart, Richard W., ed. *American Military History*, 2nd ed. Washington, D.C.: Center of Military History, United States Army, 2005.

Stone, Geoffrey R. *Perilous Times: Free Speech in Wartime, from the Sedition Act of 1798 to the War on Terrorism*. New York: W. W. Norton & Company, 2004.

Tansill, Charles Callan. *America Goes to War*. Boston: Little, Brown and Company, 1938.

Teachout, Terry. *The Skeptic: A Life of H. L. Mencken*. New York: HarperCollins, 2002: 144–45.

Tooze, Adam. *The Deluge: The Great War and the Remaking of Global Order, 1916–1931*. New York: Viking, 2014.

Trask, David F. *The AEF and Coalition Warmaking, 1917–1918*. Lawrence, KS: University Press of Kansas, 1993.

———. *The United States in the Supreme War Council: American War Aims and Inter-Allied Strategy, 1917–1918*. Middletown, CT: Wesleyan University Press, 1961.

Traxel, David. *Crusader Nation: The United States in Peace and the Great War, 1898–1920*. New York: Vintage Books, 2007. Kindle edition.

Tuchman, Barbara W. *The Guns of August*. New York: Macmillan, 1980. Originally published by Constable in 1962.

————. *The Zimmermann Telegram*. New York: Macmillan Company, 1966. First published 1958 by Viking Press.

Tucker, Robert W. *The Law of War and Neutrality at Sea*. Clark, NJ: Lawbook Exchange, 2006.

Spencer C. Tucker, ed. *World War I Encyclopedia*. Santa Barbara, CA: ABC-CLIO, 2005.

Tumulty, Joseph P. *Woodrow Wilson As I Know Him*. Garden City, NY: Doubleday, Page & Company, 1921.

Twining, William. *Karl Llewellyn and the Realist Movement*. Second Edition. New York: Cambridge University Press, 2012.

Unger, Nancy C. *Fighting Bob La Follette, the Righteous Reformer*. Madison: Wisconsin State Historic Press, 2008.

United States Congress, House Committee on Banking and Currency. *Report of the Committee Appointed Pursuant to House Resolutions 429 and 504 to Investigate the Concentration of Control of Money and Credit*. Washington, D.C.: Government Printing Office, 1913.

United States Department of State. *Register of the Department of State*. Washington, D.C.: U.S. Government Printing Office, 1918.

United States Presidents. *A Compilation of the Messages and Papers of the Presidents*. New York: Bureau of National Literature, 1918.

United States. Relief Commission in Europe. *Report on Operations of United States Relief Commission in Europe*. Washington, D.C.: U.S. Government Printing Office, 1914.

United States War Department General Staff. *Statement of a Proper Military Policy for the United States*. Washington, D.C.: U.S. Government Printing Office, 1915.

Van der Kloot, William. *World War I Fact Book: The Great War in Graphs and Numbers*. Gloucestershire, UK: Amberley Publishing, 2010.

Venzon, Anne Cipriano, ed. *The United States in the First World War: An Encyclopedia*. New York: Garland Publishing, 1995.

Vincent, Paul. *The Politics of Hunger: The Allied Blockade of Germany, 1915–1919*. Athens, OH: Ohio University Press, 1985.

The War from This Side: Editorials from the North American, Philadelphia. Philadelphia: J. B. Lippincott Company, 1915.

Weigley, Russell F. *Towards an American Army: Military Thought from Washington to Marshall*. New York: Columbia University Press, 1962.

Weiss, Elaine F. *Fruits of Victory: The Woman's Land Army of America in the Great War*. Washington, D.C: Potomac Books, Inc.

Werstein, Irving. *Sound No Trumpet: The Life and Death of Alan Seeger*. New York: Thomas Y. Crowell Company, 1967.

Wharfield, H. B. (Dave). *10th Cavalry & Border Fights*. El Cajon, CA: Printed by author, 1965.

Wharton, Edith ed. *The Book of the Homeless*. New York: Charles Scribner's Sons, 1916.

————. *Fighting France: From Dunkerque to Belfort*. New York: Charles Scribner's Sons, 1915.

Whitlock, Brand. *Belgium under the German Occupation: A Personal Narrative*. London: William Heinemann, 1919.

Whitlock, Brand. *The Letters and Journal of Brand Whitlock: The Journal*. Edited by Allan Nevins. New York: Appleton-Century Company, 1936.

Wilkins, Mira. *The History of Foreign Investment in the United States, 1914–1945*. Cambridge, MA: Harvard University Press, 2004.

Williams, Elizabeth. *Pittsburgh in World War I: Arsenal of the Allies*. Charleston, SC: History Press, 2013.

Wilson, Woodrow. *A Crossroads of Freedom: The 1912 Campaign Speeches of Woodrow Wilson*. Edited by John Wells Davidson. New Haven, CT: Yale University Press, 1956.

————. *Addresses of President Wilson, January 27–February 3, 1916*. Washington, D.C.: U.S. Government Printing Office, 1916.

————. *The Papers of Woodrow Wilson*. Edited by Arthur S. Link. Princeton, NJ: Princeton University Press, 1980.

Winter, Jay ed. *America and Armenian Genocide of 1915*. Cambridge: Cambridge University Press, 2003.

Woodward, David R. *The American Army and the First World War*. New York: Cambridge University Press, 2014.

Work, Clemens P. *Darkest before Dawn: Sedition and Free Speech in the American West*. Albuquerque, NM: University of New Mexico Press, 2005.

Yellin, Eric S. *Racism in the Nation's Service: Government Workers and the Color Line in Woodrow Wilson's America*. Chapel Hill: University of North Carolina Press, 2013.

Young, Arthur P. *Books for Sammies: The American Library Association and World War I*. Pittsburgh, PA: Beta Phi Mu, 1981.

Zieger, Robert H. *America's Great War: World War I and the American Experience*. Lanham, MD: Rowman & Littlefield, 2000.

MAGAZINE ARTICLES

Asher, Robert. "Documents of the Race Riot at East St. Louis." *Journal of the Illinois State Historical Society (1908-1984)* 65, no. 3 (Autumn 1972): 327–336.

Bailey, Thomas A. "The United States and the Blacklist during the Great War." *Journal of Modern History* 6, no. 1 (March 1934): 15–18.

Blakely, Roy G. and Gladys C. "The Revenue Act of 1918." *American Economic Review* 9, no. 2 (June 1919): 213–243.

Brownlee, W. Elliot. "Wilson and Financing the Modern State: The Revenue Act of 1916." *Proceedings of the American Philosophical Society* 129, no. 2 (June 1985): 173–210.

Byerly, Carol R. "The U.S. Military and the Influenza Pandemic of 1918-1919." *Public Health Reports* 125, Supplement 3: The 1918–1919 Influenza Pandemic in the United States (April 2010): 82–91.

Carroll, Phil and E. S. Gorrell. "Colonel Raynal Cawthorne Boiling: Lawyer-Cavalryman-Flyer." *U.S. Air Service* 3, no. 2 (March 1920): 18–20.

Chase, Hal S. "Struggle for Equality: Fort Des Moines Training Camp for Colored Officers, 1917," *Phylon* 39, no. 4 (1978) 297–310.

Contee, Clarence G. "Du Bois, the NAACP, and the Pan-African Congress of 1919," *Journal of Negro History* 57, no. 1 (January 1972), 13–28.

Day, Edmund E. "The American Merchant Fleet: A War Achievement, a Peace Problem." *Quarterly Journal of Economics* 34, no. 4 (August 1920): 567–606.

Devine, Edward T. "Belgian Relief Measures." *American Review of Reviews* 50 (July–December 1914): 689–694.

Frahm, Jill. "The Hello Girls: Women Telephone Operators with the American Expeditionary Forces during World War I." *Journal of the Gilded Age and Progressive Era* 3, no. 3 (July 2004): 271–93.

Frederick, J. George. "America's Business Boom." *American Review of Reviews* 53, no. 1 (January 1916): 42–55.

"French American Hall of Fame: Mrs. Nina Larrey Duryea." *La France: An American Magazine* IV, no. 7 (April 1920): 346.

Goldzier, Julius. "German and Austro-Hungarian Relief in Chicago." *American Red Cross Magazine* XI, no. 2 (February 1916): 47–49.

Hall, Tom G. "Wilson and the Food Crisis: Agricultural Price Control during World War I." *Agricultural History* 47, no. 1 (January 1973): 25–46.

Harvey, George. "The National Conventions." Review of the 1916 Democratic and Republican Nominating Conventions. *North American Review* 204, no. 728 (July 1916): 1–28.

Herring, George C. Jr. "James Hay and the Preparedness Controversy, 1915–1916." *Journal of Southern History* 30, no. 4 (November 1964): 383–404.

"High School Athletes Leave Sport for Army." *Daily Missoulian* [Missoula, MT], April 11, 1917.

Holcomb, Marcus H. "Connecticut in the Van," *American Review of Reviews* 57, no. 5 (May 1918): 520–21.

Hillje, John W. "New York Progressives and the War Revenue Act of 1917." *New York History* 53, no. 4 (October 1972): 437–59.

Hollenbeck, Scott and Maureen Keenan Kahr. "Nine Years of Individual Income and Tax Statistics, 1916–2005." *Statistics of Income Bulletin*, Winter 2008. www.irs.gov/pub/irs-soi/16-05intax.pdf

Horn, Martin. "A Private Bank at War: J. P. Morgan & Co. and France, 1914–1918." *Business History Review* 74, no. 1 (Spring 2000): 85–112.

Lester, H. Geraldine. "British Emergency Legislation." *California Law Review* 7, no. 5 (July 1919): 323–39.

Lindsay, Samuel McCune. "Purpose and Scope of War Risk Insurance." *Annals of the American Academy of Political and Social Science* 79 (September 1918): 52–68.

Livermore, Seward W. "The Sectional Issue in the 1918 Congressional Elections." *Mississippi Valley Historical Review* 35, no. 1 (June, 1948): 29–60.

Lochner, Louis. "The Neutral Conference for Continuous Mediation at Stockholm." *Advocate of Peace (1894–1920)* 78, no. 8 (August 1916): 238–41.

Maloney, Wendi A. "1912 Amendment Adds Movies to Copyright Law." *Copyright Notices*, March 2012, 16.

Martin, Christopher Tremewan. "Castles and Europe: Race Relations in Ragtime." *Electronic Theses, Treatises and Dissertations Paper* 2721 (2005), Florida State University DigiNole Commons.

Merriman, Scott A. "'An Intensive School of Disloyalty': The C.B. Schoberg Case under the Espionage and Sedition Acts in Kentucky during World War I." *Register of the Kentucky Historical Society* 98, no. 2 (Spring 2000): 179–204.

"Organization of Columns begins: Col. Jefferson R. Kean, Medical Corps, U.S.A., Is Authorized by the War Department to Aid Red Cross Preparedness." *American Red Cross Magazine* 11, no. 3 (March 1916): 83.

Paxson, Frederic L. "The American War Government, 1917-1918." *American Historical Review* 26, no. 1 (October 1920): 54–76.

Phillips, Ethel C. "American Participation in Belligerent Commercial Controls." *American Journal of International Law* 27, no. 4 (October 1933): 675–93.

"Officers to Arrest All Who Interfere with Registration." *Bisbee [AZ] Daily Review*, June 5, 1917.

"Report of the Commission on Industrial Relations." *Monthly Review of the U.S. Bureau of Labor Statistics* 1, no. 5 (November 1915): 48–49.

Sanders, M. L. "Wellington House and British Propaganda during the First World War." *Historical Journal* 18, no. 1 (March 1975): 119–20.

Sandos, James A. "Prostitution and Drugs: The United States Army on the Mexican-American Border, 1916–1917." *Pacific Historical Review* 49, no. 4 (Nov. 1980): 621–45.

Schreiber, Harry N. "World War I as Entrepreneurial Opportunity: Willard Straight and the American International Corporation." *Political Science Quarterly* 84, no. 3 (September 1969): 486–511.

Schwartz, E. A. "The Lynching of Robert Prager, the United Mine Workers, and the Problems of Patriotism in 1918." *Journal of the Illinois State Historical Society* 95, no. 4 (Winter 2002/2003): 413–37.

Scott, James Brown. "War between Austria-Hungary and the United States." *American Journal of International Law* 12, no. 1 (Jan 1918): 165–72.

Scott, Robert Carl. "William McCombs and the 1912 Democratic Presidential Nomination of Woodrow Wilson." *Arkansas Historical Quarterly* 44, no. 3 (Autumn 1985): 246–59.

Seligman, Edwin R. A. "The War Revenue Act." *Political Science Quarterly* 33, no. 1 (March 1918): 2.

Simonds, Frank H. "The Fifth Campaign." *American Review of Reviews* LVII, no. 1 (January 1918): 37.

"Swing Around the Circle Against Militarism." *Survey* 36 (April–September 1916): 95–96.

"The Vanguard." *Red Cross Magazine* 12, no. 6 (July 1917): 228–29.

Ward, Robert D. "The Origin and Activities of the National Security League, 1914–1919." *Mississippi Valley Historical Review* 47, no. 1 (June 1960): 51–52.

"Week in Review." *Journal of Education* 18, no. 14 (April 8 1915): 379.

"What Happened When the Break Came: How our Red Cross was Mobilized." *Red Cross Magazine* 12, no. 3 (April 1917), 83–88.

Wilson, Woodrow. "Proclamation of Neutrality by the President of the United States of America." In "Official Documents," supplement, *American Journal of International Law* 9, no. 1 (January 1915): 110–14.

IMAGE INFORMATION

Many images in this book are from the Library's Prints & Photographs Division and can be viewed or downloaded at http://www.loc.gov/pictures/. Items from other divisions are noted using the abbreviations listed below or by a condensed URL. Contact the appropriate custodial division or Duplication Services of the Library of Congress http://www.loc.gov/duplicationservices/, (202) 707-5640 for additional assistance. Images that were cropped or restored for use in this book are noted with asterisks.

Abbreviations for custodial divisions

CA   Chroniclingamerica.loc.gov

GC   General Collections

G&M   Geography and Map Division

MSS   Manuscript Division

MUS   Music Division

SER   Serial and Government Publications Division

PROLOGUE: 1912–JULY 1914: A NEW AGE AND A NEW PRESIDENT

2: LC-DIG-ppmsca-25656. *3:* left LC-USZ62-45022, right GC. *4:* left LC-DIG-ds-09929, right CA. *5:* left GC, right LC-USZ62-121013. *6:* GC. *7:* left MUS loc.gov/item/ihas.100004621/, right LC-USZ62-8646. *8:* left GC, right LC-DIG-ppmsca-26094. *9:* LC-USZ62-50736. *10:* left LC-USZ62-110605, lower LC-DIG-ppmsca-36728. *11:* LC-DIG-nclc-02730. *12:* LC-DIG-ds-10032. *13:* top LC-DIG-hec-03371, bottom LC-USZ62-7633. *14:* LC-USZ62-116075. *15:* left LC-DIG-ppmsca-27850 right MSS Republican Campaign Collection. *16:* MSS Woodrow Wilson Papers. *17–18:* GC. *19:* LC-DIG-ggbain-10878. *20:* LC-DIG-ggbain-11695. *21:* LC-DIG-ggbain-14712. *22:* LC-DIG-ppmsca-12512. *23:* LC-USZ62-67446. *24:* LC-DIG-hec-20467*. *25:* LC-DIG-hec-02890. *26:* LC-DIG-ggbain-15834. *27:* LC-DIG-ppmsca-27893. *30:* LC-DIG-ggbain-15555.

CHAPTER 1: AUGUST 1914– DECEMBER 1915: AMERICA, EXEMPLAR OF PEACE

34: LC-DIG-ds-09947. *35:* LC-DIG-ggbain-16893. *36:* left LC-USZC2-3931, right LC-USZC4-5031. *37:* LC-USZ62-77293. *38:* GC. *39:* SER. *41:* G&M lccn.loc.gov/2013593057*. *43:* LC-USZ62-33041. *44:* LC-DIG-hec-05364. *46:* G&M lccn.loc.gov/2011588648. *47:* LC-DIG-ds-09965. *49:* LC-DIG-ggbain-18562. *50:* GC. *51:* LC-USZ62-96198. *52–53:* GC. *54:* top LC-DIG-ds-09950, center LC-DIG-ggbain-20850, bottom LC-DIG-ds-09951. *55:* LC-DIG-ggbain-17571. *56:* left LC-USZC4-9854, right CA. *57:* GC. *58:* LC-DIG-ggbain-17746*. *59:* LC-DIG-ggbain-17770. *60:* LC-DIG-ggbain-17020. *70:* LC-USZC4-11179. *73:* LC-DIG-ds-09935. *74:* LC-USZC4-3600. *75:* LC-DIG-hec-05419. *76:* GC. *77:* LC-DIG-ds-09955. *78:* LC-USZC4-1129. *79:* LC-DIG-ds-09762. *80:* LC-USZ62-72967. *81:* LC-DIG-hec-02574. *82:* LC-USZC4-9034. *83:* GC. *84–85:* MSS Belgian Children's Letters.

CHAPTER 2: JANUARY 1916– JANUARY 1917: "HE KEPT US OUT OF WAR"

88: LC-DIG-ds-09949. *89:* GC. *90:* top LC-DIG-ds-09943*, center & bottom MSS Leighton W. Rogers Papers. *91:* LC-DIG-ds-09959 to -09964. *92:* LC-USZ62-16391. *93:* LC-DIG-ds-09936. *94:* CA. *96:* LC-USZ62-21328. *97:* left LC-USZ62-54062, right LC-DIG-hec-04761. *99:* LC-DIG-ds-09934. *100:* LC-DIG-ds-09925. *101:* LC-DIG-ds-09761. *102:* GC. *104:* top LC-DIG-hec-07121, bottom LC-USZ62-96837. *105:* LC-DIG-hec-06949. *107:* LC-USZ62-96837. *108:* LC-USZ62-47911. *109:* LC-DIG-ggbain-21569. *110:* LC-DIG-ds-09942. *111:* LC-DIG-ppmsca-35149. *113:* LC-USZ62-77350. *114:* LC-DIG-ggbain-21862. *115:* LC-DIG-ds-09933. *116:* LC-USZ62-114561. *117:* MSS John J. Pershing Papers. *118:* LC-DIG-ds-09954. *119:* LC-DIG-hec-30348. *121:* LC-DIG-ds-09928. *123:* left LC-DIG-npcc-19557, right LC-DIG-agc-7a15119. *126:* LC-DIG-ggbain-22965. *127:* LC-DIG-ds-03468. *128:* top LC-DIG-ggbain-22021,

bottom LC-DIG-ggbain-22037. *129:* LC-USZ62- 26810.
130: LC-DIG-ds-09958. *132:* LC-USZC4-6260. *133:* LC-
DIG-ggbain-21982. *135:* GC. *136:* LC-DIG-ds-09927.
137: LC-DIG-ds-09953. *138:* LC-DIG-ds-09952. *140:*
LC-USZ62-130625. *141:* LC-USZC2-4075. *143:* LC-
DIG-ds-09926. *144:* top GC, bottom LC-DIG-hec-08039*.
145: LC-DIG-ggbain-23342. *147:* MSS loc.gov/resource/
mnwp.276016.

CHAPTER 3: FEBRUARY–DECEMBER 1917: "THE YANKS ARE COMING"

151: LC-USZC4-5150. *152:* CA. *154:* LC-USZC4-5762.
157: top National Archives ID 302025, bottom LC-
USZC4-13594. *159:* LC-USZ62-97510. *160:* LC-
DIG-hec-11589. *161:* left LC-USZ62-97538, right
LC-DIG-ggbain-25191. *163:* GC. *164:* LC-DIG-
ggbain-23837. *165:* MUS lccn.loc.gov/2013568887. *167:*
LC-DIG-ds-09930. *169:* LC-DIG-ggbain-24399. *170:* left
LC-DIG-ggbain-24372, right LC-DIG-ds-09940. *171:*
top LC-DIG-hec-08400, bottom MSS William S. Sims
Papers. *172:* LC-DIG-ds-09966. *174:* LC-DIG-ds-09967.
175: LC-USZC4-7753. *176:* LC-DIG-ds-09937. *179:*
LC-DIG-hec-08918. *180:* top LC-USZC4-2793, bottom
MSS Hermann Hagedorn Papers. *Inset:* GC lccn.loc.
gov/19019695. *181:* LC-DIG-ds-09968. *182:* top LC-
DIG-ds-09948*, bottom LC-DIG-ggbain-24467. *183:*
top LC-DIG-ppmsca-40926, bottom LC-USZC4-3179.
184: LC-DIG-ppmsca-09897. *186:* LC-USZC4-2921.
187: LC-USZ62-129000. *188:* LC-DIG-npcc-18612.
189: LC-DIG-hec-08285. *191:* left GC, right Courtesy of
Jonathan Eaker. *192:* top LC-DIG-npcc-30796, bottom LC-
DIG-ds-09941. *193:* LC-USZC4-8368. *194:* VHP Clarence
C. Bauer (AFC/2001/001/53910). *195:* top LC-USZC4-2010,
bottom LC-USZ62-51591. *196:* LC-DIG-hec-07644. *197:*
LC-DIG-ds-09938. *198:* LC-USZC4-2977. *199:* LC-
DIG-hec-09268*. *200:* GC. *201:* LC-DIG-npcc-32967.
203: LC-USZ62-59236. *204:* LC-DIG-ds-00894. *205:*
LC-USZ62-62353. *206:* LC-USZC4-10228. *207:* LC-
DIG-ds-09939. *208:* LC-DIG-ggbain-24971. *209:* LC-
USZ62-22543. *211:* LC-DIG-acd-2a10054.

CHAPTER 4: 1918: FOR VICTORY AND LASTING PEACE

214: LC-DIG-ds-09932. *215:* top LC-DIG-ds-09797 &
09796, bottom LC-DIG-npcc-00568. *216:* LC-USZC4-1126.
217: LC-USZC4-9942. *218:* LC-DIG-ggbain-28059. *220:*
LC-DIG-ds-09800. *221:* LC-DIG-hec-31070. *223:* LC-
USZ62-78094. *224:* GC. *225:* LC-DIG-ggbain-28373.
226: LC-DIG-ggbain-07113. *228:* LC-DIG-ppmsca-39793.
229: LC-DIG-ggbain-15493. *230:* LC-USZC4-6419. *231:*
VHP John C. Laing (AFC200/001/5228). *232:* MSS Paul
Hedrick Clark Papers. *233:* LC-DIG-npcc-20340. *234:*
VHP Earle C. Smith (AFC/2001/001/12817). *235:* LC-DIG-
hec-10485. *236:* LC-USZC4-2950. *237:* LC-DIG-ds-09798.
238: LC-DIG-ds-09799. *239:* LC-USZC4-9013. *240:* GC
lccn.loc.gov/19025995. *241:* LC-DIG-ppmsca-08204. *242:*
LC-USZ62-96469. *243:* LC-DIG-bbc-1389f. *244:* LC-
USZ62-107709. *245:* GC. *246:* LC-DIG-ggbain-26838. *247:*
LC-DIG-ds-09802. *248:* CA. *249:* top LC-USZ62-39224,
bottom lccn.loc.gov/19025995. *250:* LC-DIG-pga-03875.
251: LC-USZC4-10224. *252:* LC-DIG-hec-01584. *254:*
LC-DIG-hec-06897. *255:* LC-USZ62-62917. *256:* LC-
DIG-ggbain-26866. *258:* MSS John Callan O'Laughlin
Papers. *260:* LC-DIG-ds-09804. *261:* LC-DIG-hec-11140.
262: LC-DIG-ds-09969. *263:* LC-DIG-ds-09737*. *264:*
LC-USZC4-7564*. *265:* LC-DIG-ds-09795. *266:* LC-
USZ62-137180. *267:* loc.gov/pictures/item/2007663173/.
268: LC-USZ62-32617. *270:* lccn.loc.gov/2009440621.
271: LC-DIG-hec-11401. *272:* LC-DIG-ds-09803. *273:*
LC-DIG-ds-09801. *274:* LC-USZ62-86993. *275:* LC-
USZ62-39139. *277:* LC-DIG-ppmsca-09634. *278:* LC-DIG-
stereo-1s04264.

EPILOGUE

280: LC-DIG-ppmsca-08124. *281:* LC-DIG-hec-32155.
282: LC-DIG-ppmsca-11440. *283:* GC & American Legion
Digital Archive. *284:* LC-DIG-hec-12889. *285:* left LC-
DIG-npcc-18495, right GC lccn.loc.gov/20026587. *286:*
LC-USZ62-77540. *287:* LC-USZ62-38919. *288:* G&M. *289:*
LC-DIG-ds-10034. *290:* left LC-USZ62-136027, right LC-
USZ62-132969. *291:* LC-DIG-npcc-01931. *292:* LC-DIG-
hec-31562. *293:* Courtesy of Margaret E. Wagner.

INDEX

A NOTE ON
THE AUTHORS

Margaret E. Wagner is the author of *The Library of Congress Illustrated Timeline of the Civil War*, *The American Civil War: 365 Days*, and *World War II: 365 Days* and coauthor of *The Library of Congress Civil War Desk Reference* and *The Library of Congress World War II Companion*. A senior writer and editor in the Library of Congress Publishing Office, she lives in Arlington, Virginia.

David M. Kennedy is Donald J. McLachlan Professor of History Emeritus at Stanford University. He is the author of *Freedom from Fear: The American People in Depression and War, 1929–1945*, which won the Pulitzer Prize in History, *Over Here: The First World War and American Society*, which was a Pulitzer Prize finalist, and *Birth Control in America: The Career of Margaret Sanger*, which won a Bancroft Prize. He lives in Palo Alto, California.